THE STORY OF
EDINBURGH
JOHN PEACOCK

First published 2017

Phillimore, an imprint of The History Press
The Mill, Brimscombe Port
Stroud, Gloucestershire, GL5 2QG
www.thehistorypress.co.uk

British Library Cataloguing in Publication Data.
A catalogue record for this book is available from the British Library.

ISBN 978 0 7509 8252 8

Typesetting and origination by The History Press
Printed and bound by CPI Group (UK) Ltd

CONTENTS

City and castle of Edinburgh, William Edgar, 1765

One

EDINBURGH DURING THE PREHISTORIC ERA

The Palaeolithic Period

Palaeolithic man lived during the Ice Age. There is no evidence of people inhabiting Scotland at this time, but they may have moved north during the warmer interglacial periods. Subsequent ice sheets would have removed any fragile evidence of their presence, but the most northerly remains of Palaeolithic man are the skull and bones of a woman found in Upper Teasdale. The last major ice sheets began their retreat before 8,000 BC and temperatures rose. The land around Edinburgh would have resembled the tundra; freezing cold with permafrost restricting any settlement, few trees and a short growing season.

The Mesolithic Age

From about 8,000 BC temperatures began to rise and Britain entered the period called the Mesolithic (or Old Stone Age). The people inhabiting the country at this time were hunter-gatherers with no permanent homes, although work done at Star Carr in East Yorkshire suggests that this area might have contained a settlement occupied over a long period of time.

Edinburgh contained large bodies of fresh water as well as easy access to the sea, so fish, shellfish and wildfowl offered a varied diet. Hunters used small stone tools called microliths which would be attached to wood to make spears and arrows. Elk and aurochs (large wild cattle) shared the land with red deer, while bears and wolves were not just dangers to these animals but also to the Mesolithic hunters.

Mesolithic Visitors to Edinburgh

A group of Mesolithic people began to work their way north along the edge of the northern sea until their progress was halted by a wide saltwater estuary. They worked their way along its southern shore until they found a stream of fresh water at what is today Cramond. This is the earliest encampment known from this era in Scotland. Burnt hazelnuts and a few microliths indicated that a settlement, however brief, had existed by the shore at the mouth of the Almond as long ago as 8,000 BC. At this time, sea levels were much lower and the wide Firth of Forth may have been little more than a large river.

Trees were slowly beginning to colonise Scotland, but the melted ice may have provided large areas of marsh. A land bridge still stretched from south-east England to the Continent. This disappeared around 5,800 BC and the North Sea was a gulf open only to the north and sheltered from the prevailing west winds by northern Britain. Early man would have used this coastal highway to enter the north and exploit the resources they found here.

A few clipped microliths have been found in excavations at Kaimes Hill near Balerno, but such stone tools can only be dated to the period by their shape. Most of the tools used by Mesolithic man would have been made of more perishable materials, leaving no evidence of their presence.

Tsunami

About 8,000 years ago, an undersea landslip off the Norwegian coast triggered a tsunami. A huge wave (or waves) spread south, striking the east coast of northern Britain. At this time, the sea only extended south as far as Lincolnshire. The land bridge to Europe, which we call Doggerland, still linked Britain with the continental mainland. Those living by the coast faced losing everything as no warning could have alerted them to the coming disaster. However, those on the high ground, now at the heart of modern Edinburgh, would have been beyond the reach of the tsunami.

The Neolithic Revolution

During the Neolithic period man began to take control of his environment. Trees were cut down and the land turned over to the growing of crops such as wheat and barley, and animals – cattle, sheep and pigs – were starting to be domesticated. Wood, bone and antlers provided tools for these early farmers, and stone axes, some of which have survived, were probably their most prized possessions.

This cultivation led to the development of small permanent settlements. However, it appears that Neolithic people did not live in isolated pockets of the country. The monumental circles built during this era would have required more manpower than could be provided by a few small villages, and axes mined from rock in various parts of the land have been found far from their points of origin. In Scotland, Neolithic people built the tomb chamber of Maes Howe and raised the Ring of Brodger and the Stones of Callainish. Stonehenge, the Avebury Ring and Sudbury Hill all date from this era, suggesting that Neolithic communities had some kind of central authority who could organise large work parties.

Edinburgh in the Neolithic Age

The low land in the west of Edinburgh was covered by two large freshwater lochs, known later as Corstorphine and Gogar Lochs. John Laurie's map of 1766 still shows the remains of one of these lochs to the west of Corstorphine. Fish and waterfowl would have supplemented the diet of our early ancestors.

To the east of the city lie Duddingston and Dunsapie Lochs, which may have covered a greater area than they do today. Close by, terraces designed to cultivate the higher (drier) ground can still be seen on the slopes of Arthur's Seat. However, a date cannot be placed on their origins. They may have been constructed by later Iron Age farmers who built settlements on the high ground in the area.

Neolithic people had few personal possessions and most of the remains of their settlements are found in the more remote parts of the country. The distribution of these artefacts may relate more to later disturbances by ploughing and construction than the density of their population. Orkney possesses many fine archaeological sites dating from this period of history.

The Bronze Age

Bronze, an alloy consisting of approximately 90 per cent copper and 10 per cent tin, proved superior to stone and during the second millennium BC, bronze technology was used to produce axes, swords and spearheads. Although both copper and tin were found in Britain and Ireland, the sources of these metal ores were considerable distances apart, and this must have stimulated trade. The Great Orme in Llandudno, North Wales, has the largest known prehistoric copper mine and the tin resources of Cornwall have been exploited from these times right up to the twentieth century.

Stone, bones and antlers still provided Bronze Age man with many of his tools, and the extraction of copper from the Great Orme was carried out using stone tools. Bronze, judging from the remains of artefacts found all over Britain, was chiefly used to make weapons and objects of high status. Often the remains of these bronze objects are found in close proximity, leading them to be designated as 'hoards'.

The Duddingston Hoard

In 1778 a large hoard of Bronze Age metal objects was discovered in the bed of Duddingston Loch. The bulk of this consisted of the remains of thirty-two swords and fourteen spearheads. Other objects removed from the site were a rapier (a narrow sword), a dagger and a ring from a cauldron. J. Graham Callander, director of the National Museum of Antiquities, wrote in his article in *Proceedings of the Society of Antiquarians of Scotland* 1921–22, 'I think the hoard is rather a founder's stock of weapons collected and broken up for the purposes of recasting'. A later theory suggests that these deposits were religious offerings deliberately placed by their owners as gifts to the gods. Some of this hoard can be seen in the National Museum of Scotland.

Other Bronze Age Remains

Another hoard was discovered in 1869, during the excavation of a house in Grosvenor Crescent. Although not as large as the Duddingston discovery, it consisted of fourteen swords, a socket axe and part of a bronze pin. Five socket axes were also found at Bells Mills in the Dean Village, by the Water of Leith. The remains of Bronze Age swords, socket axes and spearheads have also been found on Arthur's Seat, in Murrayfield, at Gogar House and in other parts of the city.

Evidence of settlement is harder to find. Excavations in Edinburgh Castle from 1988–91 revealed the remains of hearths and the charcoal from these was radiocarbon dated to between 972 and 830 BC. This would place the settlement at the very end of the Bronze Age in Scotland.

The Iron Age

The development of iron tools began in Britain towards the end of the second millennium BC, although dates can never be precise at such distance times. Iron had major advantages over bronze; it was a harder substance and was plentiful in Britain. Unlike bronze, which was a mixture of copper and tin, iron could be sourced from a single site.

The people of the Iron Age continued to farm the land using the same methods as their predecessors. They lived in large roundhouses which could accommodate extended families and possibly even some livestock.

The Hill Fort

These high fortified sites are common in the north and west of Britain. This should not be surprising, since this part of Britain contains most of the upland areas on the island. The presence of such fortifications has led some historians to conclude that the Iron Age was a time of increased warfare; others have argued that the

forts offered more than a protected site and may have been symbolic – 'Look at us, we are here!' Could they have been centres of trade or religious worship?

Despite two millennia of destruction, there are still plenty of Iron Age sites in and around Edinburgh. A chain of hill forts from the late Iron Age stretched across the Lothians. The chief of these was Traprain Law. Excavations here during the early 1920s unearthed many pieces of Roman silver which are now displayed in the National Museum of Scotland in Chambers Street.

One of the largest forts in the Lothians stood on Kaimes Hill, just to the west of Balerno, with an outlying fort on neighbouring Dalmahoy Hill. Excavations on these two sites have discovered hut circles (the remains of prehistoric roundhouses) and ramparts dating from the last millennium BC. Kaimes had a well-defended entrance which included *chevaux de frise* – stones placed close to the entrance to obstruct an attack made by chariots or cavalry.

Work at Edinburgh Castle has uncovered evidence of settlement there during the Iron Age, but the limited area available for excavation and the succession of later buildings has restricted our knowledge of the inhabitants of the rock. Across the valley, on Arthur's Seat, the remains of four forts or defended farmsteads have been found. Much of the low land in central Edinburgh may have suffered from flooding and thus Iron Age farmers would have preferred to live on the higher, drier ground.

The hill forts suggest that the people here were ruled by an elite, possibly based on military power. They spoke a form of Old Welsh rather than the Gaelic of the inhabitants of Ireland.

Homes

The roundhouses, with their low walls which were constructed from various materials, and their high conical roofs, provided homes large enough for extended families. Some of them could be 8–12m in diameter. These homes can be found within the hill forts, or as independent settlements probably guarded by a ditch and a fence.

Local cattle rustlers were not the only problem facing these early farmers. Wolves and bears still shared the land with Iron Age people, although little is known of their numbers or the threat they might have presented to the inhabitants living in the first millennium BC.

Dry summers and aerial photography have enabled archaeologists to locate many more Iron Age homesteads (roundhouses) in Britain. Over thirty such sites have been found close to Traprain Law. However, this cannot be taken as showing a high density of settlement as not all of them would have been occupied at the same time.

The Scottish Iron Age stretched from around 900 BC until the fifth century AD.

Two

THE FIRST MILLENNIUM

The First Century

The Roman occupation of southern Britain began in AD 43 with the arrival of a large invasion force. When Vespasian became emperor, he appointed one of his supporters, Julius Agricola, to the post of governor. Agricola had served in Britain before, so the problems facing the Romans were not new to him.

Agricola launched an attack into Scotland. The *Votadini*, the Roman name for the people who lived around Edinburgh and in the Lothians, appear to have offered no resistance as Agricola led his troops through central Scotland to the Tay around AD 81.

The army, we are told by Tacitus, was supported by a fleet which searched for suitable harbours to land marines in support of the army. So, Roman ships might have been operating in the Firth of Forth at this time. However, there is no evidence in either Edinburgh or the surrounding territory of any military settlement.

Eventually, problems on the Danube forced the Romans to reduce their military commitment in Britain.

The Fort at Cramond

In AD 142 the Roman Army, under the orders of the Emperor Antonius Pius, established a new frontier between the Forth and the Clyde. To support this new project, the Romans built forts close to the mouths of the Almond and the Esk. However, no fort was built at the mouth of the larger Water of Leith; sandbanks may have made the estuary difficult to navigate even for the small vessels of the time.

The fort at Cramond stood on the high ground near the mouth of the river. Today, most of its foundations lie beneath the church and its cemetery. Much of the fort has been destroyed by later developments over many centuries.

Cramond was garrisoned by auxiliary soldiers who would have been responsible for the route along the south of the Forth, linking the fort with Carriden at the eastern end of the Antoine Wall. Cramond appears to have been a supply depot for troops based on the wall.

The Romans abandoned both the fort at Cramond and the wall around AD 164, but Emperor Septimus Severus reoccupied it at the beginning of the third century. His expedition against the tribes of the north ended with his death. The Romans then withdrew behind Hadrian's Wall.

The Independent British Kingdoms

The lands between the two walls were inhabited by Britons who were linguistically (speaking a type of Welsh) and culturally related to those tribes living in Roman Britain. The western lands formed the Kingdom of Strathclyde, with its capital on Dumbarton Rock. In the east, the land was ruled by the Gododdin (known to the Romans as the *Votadini*) whose first capital stood on Traprain Law. Later they established their centre of power at the fortress of Din Edin which is generally interpreted as Castle Rock in Edinburgh.

The poet Aneirin, mourning the last days of the Gododdin, proclaims:

O woe to us from
grief, from unending sadness,
for the good men who
came from Dunedin,
the chosen men who came from
every wise land.

The Gododdin occupied a series of hill forts on the high ground looking across the Forth. Kaimes Hill (near Balerno) was a large Iron Age fort which was still occupied during these years.

Nothing is known about life in Edinburgh during the third and fourth centuries. Across the broad estuary of the Forth lay the Pictish kingdoms, while to the south was the military power of Rome. It is likely that traders from both north and south would visit the settlements around Edinburgh.

Piracy in the Fourth Century

However, times were changing. Internal battles for control and pressures from the tribes along the Danube were sucking dry the resources of the Roman Empire. Lacking an adequate navy to retaliate against raiders the Romans were reduced to building a series of coastal forts. The Scots from Ireland, the Picts from the north and various tribes from Europe took the opportunity to loot the rich coastal lands of southern Britain. What part the Gododdin played in these ventures we do not know.

Religious Beliefs in the Fourth and Fifth Centuries

Celtic religious beliefs lingered on in Roman Britain. The Romans generally tolerated the religious beliefs of conquered people, providing they did not oppose their control of the province. North of Hadrian's Wall, Roman gods had no influence. Little is known about the religious practices of the Britons, but much of it was based on the earth, sky and seasons. Some of their festivals, like Beltane (1 May), Samhain (Halloween) and Yule are still remembered today. Plants such as oak, yew and mistletoe were sacred to their worshippers. The religious elite of the Britons during the conquest had represented a real threat to the Romans.

The fourth century saw massive changes in the Roman Empire. The wife of Constantius, the new governor, was a Christian convert who would have encouraged her fellow Christians. Her son, Constantine, became Roman Emperor and made Christianity the official religion of the Empire. A cemetery, discovered at Edinburgh's airport, contained some fifty burials. The report, in the *Proceedings of the Society of Antiquarians of Scotland 1977*, on the excavations pointed out:

> The cemetery consisted of long stone cists assumed to have contained skeletons laid on their backs and, with only a few exceptions, oriented east to west with the heads at the west end.

Pagan burials were placed on a north–south alignment, so these must have been Christians. Radiocarbon tests dated the remains to the early fifth century. Christianity, therefore, may have arrived in Edinburgh from the south as early as the fourth century.

Aneirin, in his poem, lamented the last days of the Gododdin at the end of the sixth century:

> The beloved prince Caredig
> He'd keep his battle-station like a man
> Despite pain, despite the grief of earth,
> Purposefully he defended his post –
> May he be welcomed in Communion
> To perfect union with the Trinity.

However, most of the poem shows the Gododdin and their allies as fierce warlords high on drink as they launched a suicidal attack on the Angles. Binge drinking, it seems, is not a modern invention!

Political Divisions in the Fifth Century

To gain any understanding of the political divisions in the fifth century we must forget the modern borders which separate Scotland and England. The British kingdoms stretched from the Channel all the way to central Scotland. The southern shore of the Firth of Forth and, in the west, the north bank of the Clyde, formed the northern frontier. Beyond this, the land was ruled by the Picts. Thus Edinburgh, instead of being at the heart of the country, was part of the northern frontier.

During this century, the British people who lived in the south were being pressed by invaders (settlers) from the Continent. However, none of these tribes (Angles, Saxons and Jutes) are recorded as entering northern waters. It was a slow process. The Anglo-Saxon Chronicle records an attack on Portsmouth at the beginning of the sixth century, but by this time much of the south-east was ruled by Angle or Saxon chieftains.

In the north, the main enemy were the Scots, who had sailed across the sea from Ireland. Around AD 430, Cunedda and an army from Gododdin marched from central Scotland into North Wales to prevent the Scots from gaining a foothold on the coast. Such a move suggests that the Britons still possessed some central power which was organising the free movement of troops. This was also the time when the old Iron Age hillforts like Traprain and Kaimes were abandoned. The capital then moved to Edin or, as we know it today, Edinburgh.

Life in the Fifth Century

The land was ruled by a chieftain, or king, who was supported by a warrior elite. According to Aneirin:

It was usual
for powerful men to defend Gododdin in battle riding
Quick horses

The farmers, however, used oxen to plough the fields, although much of this work may still have been done by hand. For the ordinary people, life would have been hard. They would have been at the mercy of the well-armed men who provided the king's bodyguard. Their diet was based on grain (barley and oats) which would be converted into soup, bread and beer, while hunting and gathering still supplemented their food stock.

To the west of Edinburgh lay the two large lochs of Corstorphine and Gogar. No doubt much of the land next to these bodies of water was covered in marsh. The area may have been rich in fish and wildfowl. Shellfish would have been picked up at low tide on the shores of the Forth and even in the middle of the nineteenth century, oyster beds could still be found in the Firth. To the east, around Arthur's Seat, the lochs would have been more extensive than they are today.

Slavery had been common in prehistoric and Roman times, but the Christian Church had set about abolishing it. By the end of the century, Christianity had penetrated the northern British kingdoms and, no doubt, led to conflict between the Pagans and the Christians.

The Sixth Century

Plague

By the beginning of the sixth century, any central authority among the Britons had disappeared. Most of the south-east of the island was now occupied by migrants (mainly Angles, Saxons and Jutes), although the British kingdoms appear to have controlled much of the north and west. In fact, under strong leadership they were able to launch a counter-attack. This is the age in which the legendary hero, Arthur, may have lived. Nennius claims that the king defeated the Saxons in many battles, 'The eleventh [battle] was at the mountain which is called Agned'. However, it is difficult to understand how he could have fought the Saxons around Edinburgh, since there are no records of any Saxons living in these northern lands.

The plague appeared in the East during the early 540s and spread slowly across the Mediterranean lands of the old Roman Empire. After that, the infection entered Gaul (France) before reaching the shores of Britain around AD 550. It struck the Britons severely, even killing the King of Gwynedd. Edinburgh was at this point populated by Britons and they too may have suffered severe losses.

The English invaders, however, appear to have been immune to the plague. This could have been because there was little social contact between the two groups. Bede criticises the British Christians for their failure to send missionaries to the Saxons. Not until the seventh century are there any records of alliances made between the Britons and the Angles. Then, Penda of Mercia allied himself with the kings of Gwynedd to destroy Northumbria.

The End of British Rule

Throughout the sixth century, the fortress on the Castle Rock was still ruled by the kings of the Gododdin, but events began to change rapidly. The Angles had already established themselves in York and in AD 547 a group of warriors led by Ida occupied the great crag at Bamburgh. These new invaders threatened the British kingdoms of the Gododdin, Strathclyde and Rheged (Cumbria).

Two attacks were launched by the Britons against the Angles, but it is impossible to connect them. Urien of Rheged, Rhydderch of Strathclyde and their allies besieged Bamburgh, but disaster struck when Urien was killed by one of his British allies.

The Gododdin and their British allies met in Edinburgh and prepared (by drinking large quantities of mead) to attack, not the Bernician Angles in Bamburgh, but the Deirans based in York. It is possible that they marched south through Cumbria (Rheged) and crossed the Pennines over Stainmore hoping to surprise the Angles. This surprise attack did not succeed, for they were trapped at Catterick and massacred.

The loss of the king and his chieftains left Edinburgh and the surrounding country undefended. The potential beneficiaries were the Scots and the Angles (English). Around AD 603, Ethelfrid of Northumbria defeated the Scots at Degsastan, leaving Edinburgh facing an attack from the Northumbrians. However, the attack never came. A civil war between the Bernician and Deiran Angles may have delayed matters, but sometime after AD 630 the Angles occupied the city and established their headquarters on Castle Rock.

The Angles in Edinburgh

King Edwin was converted by Roman missionaries. A bishopric was established for a few years at Abercorn, to the west of Edinburgh. The growing power of the Northumbrians finally led to an alliance between Cadwalla, the British King of Gwenedd (probably North Wales, Cheshire and southern Lancashire), and Penda, the Anglian Prince of Mercia (the English Midlands). Edwin and most of his leading chieftains were killed at the Battle of Heathfield in October 633, according to Bede.

The death of Edwin led to the return of the sons of Ethelfrid. They had been living in exile with the Scots and the Picts, where they were converted to Christianity. The Christians of the north owed their allegiance to Iona (founded by St Columba), and St Aiden arrived from that abbey at the invitation of St Oswald, King of Northumbria. The new Celtic Church set up its headquarters on the island of Lindisfarne, near Oswald's stronghold of Bamburgh.

The Christians in Edinburgh would have had to follow the traditions of the Celtic Church. However, King Oswy, Oswald's brother and successor, found it impossible to live with two Christian Churches in his kingdom and, after a conference, decided to recognise the authority of Rome. Thus the Church in Edinburgh also came under the authority of the papacy and this would continue for the next 900 years.

The Angles (and their Saxon contemporaries) built in wood, so there are few remains of their villages. Two small trenches opened in the Grassmarket revealed some evidence of an Anglian settlement beneath the Castle Rock. At Ratho, on the western edge of the city, a *grubenhaus* (sunken house) was found. It contained a clay loom weight, suggesting it might have been used for weaving.

The End of the Kingdom of Northumbria

The Anglian Kingdom fell into a rapid decline during the second half of the eighth century. According to the Scottish historian John of Forden, six Northumbrian kings were murdered in these times while three others were forced to abdicate. Two more chose a safer route by retiring into a monastery.

The Anglo-Saxon Chronicle reported for the year 793:

> In this year terrible portents appeared over Northumbria and miserably frightened the inhabitants: there were exceptional flashes of lightning and fiery dragons were seen flying in the air. A great famine soon followed these signs; and a little later after that in the same year ... the harrying of the heathen miserably destroyed God's church in Lindisfarne by rapine and slaughter.

The Vikings had arrived.

The Vikings

Various names are given to these invaders from Scandinavia – Norse, Northmen, Danes and Vikings. The first assaults on these islands were probably motivated by a search for loot, and soon the Danes created a military force which destroyed the Angle and Saxon kingdoms in the south. Only Wessex (land of the West Saxons) offered sufficient resistance to survive. In the north, the Scots and the Picts united under the Scottish king, Fergus McAlpine. The new kingdom fought the Viking invaders, but large territories in the north and the Western Isles fell to the Northmen.

As the ninth century drew on, the raiders became more organised. Finally, a large army, known as 'the Host', took York in March 867, killing many of Northumbria's leaders. However, Bernicia and its northern stronghold of Edinburgh remained under the control of the Angles. Seven years later, Halfdan led an army of Viking warriors across the Tyne and launched attacks on the Picts and Britons of Strathclyde. Edinburgh may well have been captured by the Vikings at this time, but no evidence is available to prove this.

In the early years of the tenth century, three Viking brothers, Ragnall, Sitric and Godred, took control of Bernicia. In AD 915 Ealdred, called the 'son of

Eadulf of Bamburgh', fled to the court of the Scottish king, Constantine. The Northumbrian Angles were defeated in battle with the Vikings the following year. Constantine had launched raids deep into the Viking-controlled lands (Dunbar and Melrose were even attacked), but in 918 he was defeated in a battle with Ragnall. The Battle of the Tyne Hills must have secured Viking power in Edinburgh and the Lothians.

The English in the North

In 934 Athelstan brought his army north supported by a fleet of ships. It is possible that Edinburgh might have been occupied by the forces of the English king. The land of the Scots (north of the Forth) was attacked. The power of the English king now reached the central belt of modern Scotland. Finally, in 937, Athelstan won a stunning victory at Brunanburh (site unknown) over the Scots and their allies.

Despite their victories, Edinburgh remained the northern fortress of the kingdom, although further pressure from the Danes led to the town being abandoned. Thus, during the reign of Idulb (954–962), the Scots occupied Edinburgh.

The Church in Edinburgh

By AD 854, according to Simon of Durham, Edinburgh had its own parish church. We cannot be sure of its dedication (to St Giles) or its position in the Anglian settlement.

An excavation in the early years of the twentieth century revealed the foundations of a small building below the medieval choir of the abbey church at Holyrood. These walls were aligned on a slightly different orientation than the later church, leading the archaeologists to conclude that this appeared 'to indicate the prior existence of a still earlier church'. David I's twelfth-century abbey may have been constructed on a site which already had religious connections.

Three

THE HOUSE OF CANMORE

Malcolm and Margaret

Malcolm Canmore, the son of Duncan I, became King of Scots with the military support of Siward, the Earl of Northumbria. His father had been defeated and killed by Macbeth whose wife, Grouch, was a member of the Scottish royal family. Until 1100 it was the custom in Scotland for the throne to pass to a brother rather than the eldest son. After Duncan's death Malcolm lived in exile in northern England.

Following the Norman Conquest, a small group of refugees arrived in the Forth and among them were Edgar Atheling and his sister, Margaret. They were the grandchildren of Edmund Ironside, the last Saxon King of England. Malcolm, who was then a widower, married Margaret, and she spent much of her time trying to bring the Church in Scotland into line with the mainstream western Church.

The queen was a supporter of the revived monastic movement which was sweeping across Europe and she wished to develop the abbeys at Dunfermline and St Andrew's. A ferry, later known as the Queen's Ferry, was set up to help pilgrims to cross the Forth and visit these religious sites.

Scotland was faced with the growing influence of people and ideas from the south. Many Scots resented this and looked back to their Celtic roots.

In 1093, Malcolm and his eldest son, Edward, died fighting in Northumberland. A few days later, Margaret Atheling, Queen of Scots, died in the Castle of the Maidens (Edinburgh).

The Civil War

The first to claim the throne was Malcolm's brother, Donald Ban. This was not unusual as many early Scottish kings were succeeded by their brothers. It was a return to the old Celtic ways.

Margaret died on 16 November 1093 in the castle, which was besieged by Donald Ban and his army. His main force was placed at the eastern gate of the castle. Margaret's servants took her body out by a secret gate on the west side.

However, it seems likely that the castle was surrendered to the new king in return for allowing the priest to remove Margaret's body.

The English followers of Malcolm and Margaret were driven out of the country. Duncan, Malcolm's son by his first wife, invaded Scotland with the support of William Rufus. His reign proved short and after he was killed Donald returned to the throne. Having lost one Scottish king, William Rufus then turned to Edgar, one of the sons of Malcolm and Margaret. Edgar then invaded Scotland and defeated Donald.

Although Edgar was now King of Scots, large parts of the country, particularly in the north and west, were only nominally under his authority. Edinburgh Castle was the centre of his power in the Lothians, with much of the land that is now part of the city providing food for the royal court when it visited the castle.

The Sons of Malcolm and Margaret

Edgar was the first of the three sons who were to reign over Scotland. Little is known of the reign of Edgar, but Edinburgh remained an important royal fortress. At that time, there was no particular royal centre. The king moved round the country with his court; the royal presence was the only way to ensure his control over the various districts. The royal court could not be supported by one place, so they would have to move on when supplies were exhausted. Edinburgh Castle was probably a great storehouse of food and timber (for fuel) acquired from the surrounding royal lands.

Alexander succeeded his brother as king. He founded the Abbey of Inchcolm on the island in the Forth. There are no records to show what lands were given to support the new abbey on this rocky island.

Alexander was in turn succeeded by his brother, David, who became one of the most influential Scottish kings. He had spent much time in England, where he was Earl of Huntingdon. David grew up with the Norman aristocracy of England and would have seen at first hand the growing influence of the new monasteries.

The Founding of the Royal Burgh

When did Edinburgh become a royal burgh? We do not know. We do not even know who granted the charter, but it must have been one of the sons of Malcolm and Margaret, sometime in the first quarter of the century. Certainly, by the time David I founded the Abbey of Holyrood (generally credited with being around 1128), it had royal burgh status. In fact, by this time it must have been a prosperous burgh with a slaughter business producing fat, tallow and hides. The abbey received a portion of the profits.

The original burgh was situated on the narrow ridge of land sloping down from Castle Rock. There can be no doubt that the proximity to the entrance of the castle enabled it to grow. The royal court frequently stayed here and that would have created a demand for goods and services. The burgh was in the heart of the prosperous agricultural land of the Lothians, and Edinburgh became the chief market centre.

The main difficulty facing the merchants of Edinburgh was the lack of a harbour. Goods could be transported by cart in a dry summer – otherwise everything went by packhorse. Wine would have had to be imported for the king and his court. Water was the only way to carry large quantities of goods over long distances, but the only available harbour was at the mouth of the Water of Leith.

The land round the estuary was probably divided between the Abbey of Holyrood, the estate of Restalrig and the king. As the kings' tenants, the burgesses may have had the right to tie up ships along the Shore (the east bank of the river).

David I

David I was brought up in England among the Norman rulers. He was Earl of Huntingdon and brother to the English queen. He had many tenants who would look to him for support and rewards. When David returned to Scotland as king many of these followers came with him. Robert de Brus and Walter Fitz Alan (the Steward) were to produce descendants who would rule Scotland for over 400 years. The new king also owned Cumbria and the silver mines found there. This added to the country's prosperity, and the king minted silver coins in Edinburgh.

The Abbey of Holyrood

The founding of the Abbey of Cluny in France at the beginning of the tenth century began the growth of a monastic movement in Western Europe. It became the custom for kings and wealthy noblemen to give land to the monasteries.

New orders, like the Cistercians and Carthusians, drew up strict rules, while other orders became more open and served at large in the community. The Augustine Canons of Holyrood were one of these.

The abbeys swallowed up large amounts of money and property in Scotland during the twelfth century and they also acquired churches. Holyrood was given St Cuthbert's and its chapels of Corstorphine and Liberton. The parishioners were expected to contribute a tenth (called *tiends*) of their income to maintain their church and its priest. Much of the wealth was being transferred from the parishes to the monasteries, leading to the weakening of the Church's work among the laity. For the king, it offered a supply of educated men who could attend to the business of government.

According to legend, David I set out on a hunting trip from the castle but in the confusion of the chase he became separated from his followers. Suddenly, a large stag with huge antlers appeared in his path. His horse reared up and the king was thrown to the ground. He naturally feared the worst as he stared up at those antlers. Then a bright light in the form of a cross shone between them. In a moment, the stag and the Holy Cross (*Rood* is another name for the Cross) had vanished. The king returned safely to Edinburgh and decided to found an abbey to give thanks for his rescue from the stag by the appearance of the Cross. Alwin, his chaplain, became the first abbot.

The Canongate

The charter which led to the foundation of the Abbey of Holyrood allowed the canons to establish a burgh. Soon afterwards, they set up a burgh between the abbey and the royal burgh of Edinburgh. The canons would have to pass through it on their way to the castle. The church of the castle, St Mary's, belonged to the abbey and the inhabitants of this new burgh worshipped at the abbey church (the Canongate did not receive its own church until the late 1680s). They would also have had to have their grain ground in the canons' mills. The burgesses of the Canongate were allowed to trade in the markets of Edinburgh as if they were burgesses of the royal burgh.

St Cuthbert's

King David granted land to the Church of St Cuthbert, beneath the castle. From the description given in the charter, this appears to have covered the Grassmarket and the King's Stables. The land bordered the King's Garden, suggesting that David had a private garden on the north side of the rock. The church and its revenues had been given by the king to the Abbey of Holyrood.

The Forest of Drumsheugh

'Royal Forest' was a legal term and not a botanical one. The Norman kings of England had set aside large tracts of land as hunting preserves. The inhabitants of the forests were prohibited from taking any animals, but this could be hard when the odd rabbit might mean the difference between a good meal and starvation. Royal forests were not totally covered with trees and probably most of Drumsheugh consisted of scrubland. The Forest of Drumsheugh consisted of a large area of land stretching west from Arthur's Seat through the Grange and Morningside.

Tofts and the King's Officers

The burgh was divided into plots of land called 'tofts'. In Edinburgh, these probably consisted of a piece of land bordering the High Street. A house would be constructed with a wooden frame and infilled with wattle and daub, and roofed with straw or even heather. The plot of land behind the house would be cultivated to provide a few vegetables and to keep animals. Some craftsmen might also have had workshops in the gardens. Bakers, for example, would need to keep their ovens away from the house in case sparks set off a fire.

In the royal burgh, the tofts were the property of the king. His official, called the sheriff, would be responsible for the collection of the rents. Much of this may have been paid in kind, rather than cash; the Sheriff of Edinburgh needed to ensure a plentiful store of goods to supply the royal court when it visited the burgh.

During the early years of his reign, David gave tofts to Dunfermline Priory and Holyrood Abbey. The founding charter for Holyrood was witnessed by 'Norman the Sheriff' – it seems probable that he was Sheriff of Edinburgh. Another royal official was the constable, who was responsible for the upkeep and defence of the castle – two charters issued by the king in Edinburgh were witnessed by 'Edward the Constable'.

Arthur's Seat and Dunedin

The origins of the name 'Arthur's Seat' are unknown. Three charters, all issued in the reign of David I, refer to the area of Arthur's Seat as 'the Crag'. It is very unlikely that any British warlord of the early sixth century would have been fighting Angles in the Lothians, so the popular theory that it was named after the King Arthur of legend is improbable. The first recorded Anglian settlement did not occur in the north until the middle of the century and that was in Bamburgh. Mr Macnamara, a librarian at the King's Inns in Dublin, translated Arthur's Seat as:

ART	ADHAIR	SIGH	AIT
Great, noble	fire	hill	charming

(or the 'Fire Tabernacle of the Charming Hill')

He also suggested 'Dunedin' as *Dun* (fort) and *Eaden* (cliff) – 'fort on the cliff'. During the twelfth and thirteenth centuries, the castle was often referred to as the 'Castle of the Maidens'.

One suggestion is that the summit of the crag was:

The spot most probably on which St Monenna in 7th or 8th centuries built one of her rock perched churches in honour of St Michael the Archangel and reared the walls of the primitive convent which may have given the place it's most ancient name 'the Castle of the Maidens'.

These are all interesting and, possibly informed, suggestions but are suppositions and not facts. It is unlikely we will ever know how Arthur's Seat or the Castle of the Maidens acquired their names.

The Lands Bordering Edinburgh

In the twelfth century, Duddingston was known as 'Treverlen' and the land belonged to Uviet. He bequeathed the estate to Kelso Abbey. Now, two great abbeys – Holyrood and Kelso – held adjoining lands, and a dispute occurred between them over the boundary in the area of Arthur's Seat. Henry, son of King David, drew up a document to settle the matter.

Such disputes were probably quite common. Holyrood was also in conflict with Newbattle Abbey over land close to Dalkeith and Malcolm IV (Henry's son) confirmed Kelso Abbey's right to the lands of Dodin, from which Duddingston appears to have acquired its name.

The countryside around Edinburgh was probably sparsely populated, with the people living in small hamlets called 'tuns'. The Holyrood Charter gave property and rights to the abbey in Saughton, Broughton and Inverleith (North Leith). Mills using the power of the Water of Leith would have formed small settlements at the Dean Village and Canonmills. Corstorphine and Liberton had their own chapels and presumably large enough congregations to help finance them.

William the Lion, 1165–1214

Malcolm IV died in 1165 and was succeeded by his brother, William. He was to reign over Scotland longer than any other medieval king.

Edinburgh remained one of a number of places where the king would stay and carry out his royal government. The new king became embroiled in the struggles against Henry II of England which were led by the King of France and Henry's own sons. William was captured by the English while on an expedition in Northumberland.

In 1174 the king was forced to hand over a group of castles, which included Edinburgh, to Henry II. An English garrison took over the castle and the Scots were removed. The main party to suffer, apart from the king himself, was Holyrood Abbey, as it would have had its revenues from the castle church (not St Margaret's Chapel) curtailed. The king compensated them with money from the rents of mills in Cramond and Liberton and lands in Merchiston and Clermiston.

The English appointed 'Alan from Richmond' as constable of the castle. Money (£26 13s 4d) was spent on repairing the fortifications, and the constable was paid 50 marks for half a year. How much of this went into his own pocket and how much was spent on the garrison is not recorded. The castle was returned to the Scots in 1186.

Council of Holyrood

Shortly after the handing over of the castle to the English, the papal legate, Cardinal Vivian, arrived in Scotland with full authority from the Pope. During the twelfth and thirteenth centuries, papal power was at its height and even distant lands like Scotland were not immune to its influence. John of Fordun, writing 200 years later, must have based his facts on contemporary evidence for he even names the date – 1 August – when the council opened in Holyrood Abbey. The cardinal was described as 'Crushing and trampling upon everything he came across, ready to clutch and not slow to snatch' by John of Fordun in his *Chronicle of the Scottish Nation*.

The Burgh at the Time of William the Lion

Edinburgh was a royal burgh and the rents for the properties, known as tofts, were paid to the king. Responsibility for the collection of these dues belonged to the Sheriff of Edinburgh. The burgh had the right to hold a market, and goods sold in this market were subject to a tax payable to the king.

At this time, most of the buildings (called 'lands') would face the market place, which we know as the High Street today. Behind them would be long strips of enclosed land sloping down from the ridge into the valleys on the north and south sides of the burgh. Many of the inhabitants would keep livestock – cows for milk and cheese, hens for eggs, and pigs for meat. They would also grow vegetables such as kale (a type of cabbage), beans and peas. The land might also have been used by baxters (bakers) and brewers, who would want to keep ovens away from their homes. In one corner of the market place stood the burgh church, dedicated to St Giles. It would not have been such an imposing structure as the present-day St Giles.

The inhabitants of the burgh formed three distinctive groups. The most powerful of these were the merchants. They were wealthy men who ran their businesses but took no part in manual labour. Wool and hides (for leather) were medieval Scotland's main exports. Some of this wool was spun and then woven into a cheap, coarse cloth. Spinners, weavers, waulkers (washers of the newly woven cloth) and dyers all played their part in the wool merchants' trade. So, too, did the chapmen whose packhorses would transport the goods to distant outworkers. We do not know whether they had any formal part in the governing of the burgh at this time. A charter granted in Edinburgh was witnessed by two men, Richardo de Deuel and Godrido, who are described as 'magistro'.

The second group of people were the craftsmen who had learnt the necessary skills to master the trade from their elders. They produced the goods for sale in the burgh and kept their trade secrets within a small group. The arrival of the king and the court at the castle would have been good for business. The only craftsman we know who worked in Edinburgh at this time was a goldsmith called Pagan. He obtained land on the north side of the Church of St Giles.

The third group, the unskilled workers and apprentices who were learning a trade, formed the bulk of the population of the burgh. They had no status in the burgh and could be a source of disorder, especially during festivals when they received time off from their work. Most of them would be tied to their employer and expected to live on his premises.

Beyond the Burgh

The lands beyond the burgh were owned by the three great powers of medieval Scotland – the king, the Church and the barons. Most of this last group had migrated via England from northern France.

Much of Duddingston had become the property of Kelso Abbey. The land was probably rented to tenant farmers, as they do not appear to have constructed any monastic buildings.

The high land at Lochend, dropping down into South Leith, formed the manor of the Lestalrig. Thomas de Lestalrig served as Sheriff of Edinburgh in the last years of William the Lion. The coast, in these times, followed the line of Commercial and St Bernard's Streets and boats would either be pulled up upon or moored to the south bank of the Water of Leith, now known as 'the Shore'. This may have been the property of the king.

North Leith, Newhaven, Broughton and the Canongate formed the large estate of Holyrood Abbey. They had their mills at Canonmills, while those of the burgh were further upstream in the Dean Gorge.

The lands around Granton had been granted by charter to the de Melville family.

The land at the western edge of the modern city was probably royal domain. William granted rents from his mill at Cramond and lands in Clermiston to Holyrood in compensation for the loss of the chapel in the castle.

The west of the city was dominated by two large bodies of water – Gogar Loch and Corstorphine Loch. Gogar was one of the manors held by Ralph of Graham, while Saughton had been granted to Holyrood in the founding charter.

Much of the area to the south of the burgh was covered by the Royal Hunting Forest of Drumsheugh. Some of it must have been given to the burgh as grazing land for their cattle, thus forming the district of Boroughmuir. The king also retained land in Merchiston.

The lands of Braid appear to have acquired their name from Henry de Brade, who was Sheriff of Edinburgh around the year 1200. Further south, the king's brother (David, Earl of Lennox) held Morton (probably Mortonhall), while the Melvilles of Granton, together with Holyrood Abbey, were the main landowners at Liberton. Randolf de Soulis possessed land in Gilmerton, some of which he gave to Kelso Abbey, while the estates of Cousland and Pentland belonged to the Graham family, who also held land in Gogar.

The Thirteenth Century

The thirteenth century was a time of rapid growth in some parts of Europe. The climate appears to have been very favourable to agriculture and the opening of silver mines in central Europe led to an increase in silver coinage. By the middle of the century, Edinburgh merchants would have possessed silver pennies minted in Scotland.

Italy and Flanders became great manufacturing and trading centres, and during this century Berwick was Scotland's most important port, no doubt exporting wool clipped from Border sheep. Cross-border relations were generally peaceable, in contrast to those in the following century.

It is probable that this century saw the development of three new suburbs. The Lawnmarket (Land Mercat) lay close to the west gate, which turned south down the Bow, and the gate leading to the castle also lay close by. To the south, the Cowgate and the Grassmarket provided extra space for the inhabitants between the burgh and the Burgh Loch situated in the Meadows.

King Alexander II

William the Lion's son, Alexander, became king in 1214 and the first years of the new king's reign saw him in conflict with the Church. Alexander had joined Louis IX of France and a number of rebellious English barons who were challenging the authority of the guardians of Henry III. The Pope considered himself the protector of the young English king and in 1216 Alexander was excommunicated and Scotland placed under an interdict. This should have meant that for the citizens of Edinburgh there would have been no Communion, no baptisms, no marriages and no funerals. However, it appears that the interdict was not published in Scotland until sometime later. This probably only aggravated the relationship between the Scottish Church and the papal legate, who sent his ambassadors north to receive the submission of the Scots.

The Black Friary

The first two orders of friars were given papal sanction at the beginning of the thirteenth century: the followers of St Francis became known as the Grey Friars, from their grey habits, and the followers of St Dominic were a teaching order who wore black. The Black Friars established a large friary on the south side of the Cowgate during the reign of Alexander II (probably in the 1230s). There is still in Edinburgh today a wynd leading down from the High Street to the Cowgate called Blackfriars Street. The friary was destroyed in the years of the Reformation.

Alexander III

Alexander II died in 1249, leaving his 8-year-old son as his only heir. The young king was quickly crowned at Scone and a power struggle began between Alan Durward, the Justiciar of Scotland, and Walter Comyn, Earl of Menteith. The earl and his supporters took control of the young king and his queen (a daughter of Henry III of England), keeping them in Edinburgh Castle.

Cardinal Bagimond

In 1274, Cardinal Bagimond arrived in Scotland to assess the various parishes and monasteries for a papal tax. The roll, drawn up by the papal envoy, provides us with a list of the parishes in Edinburgh during the second half of the thirteenth century:

St Giles of Edinburgh	Keldeleth (Currie)	Gogar
St Cuthbert's under the Castle	Hailes (Colinton)	Ratho
Duddingston	Lastelric (Restalrig)	

The parish of Cramond is not mentioned in the roll and, at that time, must have formed part of Gogar. The Church of St Mary's in the Castle and the chapels at Corstorphine and Liberton must have been assessed as part of the Abbey of Holyrood. The priests in these parishes were expected to pay a few marks, but the abbey was assessed at the huge sum of £42.

The Death of Alexander III

Alexander III died in 1286, to be succeeded by his granddaughter, Margaret, who was the daughter of King Eric II of Norway. She was the last direct descendent of William the Lion. Her death in 1290 led to a dispute over the Scottish throne. This in turn led to wars between England and Scotland as the English kings tried to gain control of much of the country. Within these struggles were two civil wars between the Bruces and the Balliols. It would be a long time before peace returned to Scotland.

EDINBURGH IN THE YEARS 1296–1399

The Wars of Independence

Edward I invaded Scotland in 1296. Berwick was taken and, after a week's siege, Edinburgh Castle also fell to the English. Walter de Huntercombe was appointed constable of the castle and Sheriff of Edinburgh. The leading men of the country were then summoned to take an oath of allegiance to the King of England.

William de Dederyk, described as burgess and alderman (provost), travelled to Berwick with James of Edinburgh, Walter Fitz Martin, Walter le Arblaster, Henry le Scot, William of Leicester, John Hog, William le Taillout, Walter of Rypon, Waldof de la Roche, Richard Fritz Wawter of Edinburgh and John Wyggemore. They took the oath for themselves and on behalf of the community of the burgh. This became known as the Ragman Roll – a list of all who gave their support to Edward I. These were the men who formed the first burgh council of which we have any record. Sadly, they are only names, but the mention of Leicester and Rypon (probably Ripon) gives the council wider connections than might be supposed for the end of the thirteenth century.

In November 1298, John de Kingeston was appointed constable of the castle and Sheriff of Edinburgh by Edward I. One of his first acts was to take the oath of allegiance from the canons of Holyrood Abbey. The sheriff took with him a Carmelite friar called William and they were received by Abbot Adam. The abbot and then William, the former abbot, both took the oath. They were followed by John, the prior, and Thomas, the sub-prior. The rest of the canons followed, including the precentor, the sacrist, the cellarer and the almoner.

By 1300, John de Kingeston had a force of 347 soldiers as well as 156 horses. The castle housed a considerable staff to support this garrison, including an engineer called Master Thomas. There were two brewers (it was safer to drink the ale than the water), two maltsters to look after the drink and a baker to look after the food. Other technical staff included two carpenters and two smiths.

Transport was provided by two carters, a water carrier and a sea coal carrier. Presumably they would bring supplies from the Port of Leith to the castle. The coal would have been used to heat the castle and provide fuel for the kitchens. The castle even had its own harper.

However, by the end of 1302 John de Kingeston was left with only thirty men and their officers. This was hardly a sufficient force to control the burgh, let alone the surrounding lands. It is, however, a reflection of the financial realities of a medieval state which had no organised way of raising money from a reluctant population. Armies were raised from those who owed military service, and these men served for a limited time before returning to their farms. A castle garrison would have needed professional soldiers who had to be paid.

Life in the Burgh in the Fourteenth Century

We know very little about life in the burgh at this time. The town and the castle were occupied by the English during the years 1296–1314 and 1335–41. Edinburgh was burnt in 1385 by the army of Richard II. Add to that the plagues of 1349 and 1362 and it is a wonder that the burgh survived. Yet it not only survived but prospered. Edinburgh merchants grew wealthy exporting wool and hides. Nothing is known of the craftsmen but the restrictions put on their attempts to organise during the first half of the next century suggest that they had little influence on the affairs of the burgh. However, their products must have played a part in the growing economy of the town.

The burgh was expanding beyond its walls. The Netherbow formed the entrance from the Canongate and the beginning of the road to Leith. The Bow was the gateway to the south and west as well as to the Burgh Loch. The Cowgate and Grassmarket were now lined with buildings.

The houses of the burgh were probably timber framed with infills of wattle and daub. Roofs thatched with straw or reeds covered them. They were easy to destroy, but also easy to rebuild. Behind each house would be an area of ground in which the householder would keep a few animals and hens. Vegetables like beans and kale (a type of cabbage) might be grown. The houses became known as 'lands' and the area behind as the 'enclosure'. Sometimes a small lane ran alongside the house leading into the enclosure. These lanes were to form the 'closes' and 'wynds' of the burgh. The enclosure behind the house would be used for business.

Merchants would have warehouses to store fleeces and hides. Craftsmen might keep some of their workshops away from their house; for instance, baxters (bakers) needed to have their ovens well away from the house for fear of fire. Chapmen (packhorse men who transported goods on roads which were unfit for horse and cart) would need stables and stores of fodder.

A poorer climate led people to give up farming arable areas on higher ground, and farms in the nearby Lammermuirs were abandoned. Scottish agriculture was dominated by oats and barley, and porridge, gruel and oatcakes formed the staple diet. Kale, fish, eggs and cheese would be brought in from the local area and sold in the markets along the High Street. Some meat, mainly mutton and offal, was eaten by the ordinary inhabitants of the burgh, and some householders kept pigs and chickens in the yards behind their houses.

The Lawnmarket, or 'Land Mercat', was where goods produced on local farms were sold. Traders would have their goods weighed at a 'tron' (weighhouse) and pay a toll before offering them for sale in the burgh market. The town houses of Scottish burghs were called 'tolbooths' because one of their early functions was as a place where traders paid their tolls

During this period the old burgh, excluding the Cowgate and Grassmarket, may have been surrounded by a stone wall. An excavation in 1833 revealed two walls, and outside the earlier of these was a cemetery.

The Years 1310–14

The second decade of the century began with a serious famine. The Scottish chronicler John of Fordun claims that people were reduced to eating horses and 'unclean cattle' – these were probably animals that had died from various natural causes. The citizens of the burgh would have suffered as severely as the rest of the community. The famine was not only confined to Scotland, one historian believed that 'for England this was the worst famine in recorded history'.

The English, with their headquarters in the castle, still controlled the burgh and the expense of keeping a large force in Scotland must have weakened the position of the English king. In the first nine months of 1311 the garrisons of the ten castles in central and southern Scotland were costing Edward II over £1,800. Leith was also important for the occupiers. Wheat, malt, barley, meal and canvas sacks were all shipped in to the port for the use of the garrison in the castle.

However, the English hold on Edinburgh was under threat. Local nobles were deserting Edward II as Robert Bruce's power grew. In March 1314 Thomas Randolf, Earl of Moray, led a surprise attack at night. Using ladders, the Scots climbed up the north side of the rock and took the castle. If you stand on Princes' Street and look across at the castle, you can see how difficult it would have been to get fully armed men up the rock and over the defences. The Scots had no heavy siege machines, so all recaptured castles were destroyed to prevent them being used by the English or any other enemy. The churches – St Mary's in the Castle and St Margaret's Chapel – appear to have been left untouched.

The End of the War

Bannockburn, fought in June 1314, was not the end of the war. The Scots launched attacks into northern England and across the sea to Ireland. Edward II was finally murdered by a group of nobles and peace was agreed. However, the opponents of Bruce, led by Edward Balliol, remained unhappy with the situation.

The Charter of Robert the Bruce, 1329

… by this our present charter confirmed to the Burgesses of our Burgh of Edinburgh our foresaid Burgh of Edinburgh together with the Port of Leith, mills and others their pertinents.

…pertained to the said Burgh in the time of Alexander.

This is not a new grant of lands and rights but a confirmation that the burgh possessed such in the time of Alexander III. At about the same time as this one, Bruce issued another charter confirming the possessions of the Abbey of Holyrood, as granted by David I; William the Lion had also given the abbey a similar confirmation charter. Thus, at least by the late thirteenth century, Edinburgh had control over parts of the Port of Leith. Which parts of Leith were possessed by the burgh is unclear, but it must have been on or near the Shore (the south bank of the Water of Leith, close to its mouth). Leith was very important to the merchants who ruled the burgh, since it gave them a port through which they could export their wool and hides; imports would have included wine, quality cloth and pottery.

The king, the burgh and the two estates of Restalrig and Holyrood Abbey had claims to sections of Leith. The charter is part of a longer story in which the merchant elite who controlled Edinburgh took power over Leith. Independent trading in Leith, or by the inhabitants of Leith, was vigorously put down. Only the captains, referred to as 'skippers', appear to have been accepted and allowed to carry on their trade without too much interference from the merchants of Edinburgh.

The charter also tells us that Edinburgh had its own mills. These mills were most probably situated in the present Dean Village. This, in earlier times, was called the Village of the Water of Leith. Since 'mills' is plural, there must have been a group of mills sharing a dam and a lade.

The charter does not go into details about other rights or marches. This must surely mean that to the king and the burgesses these were so well known and accepted by all that detail was unnecessary. Other properties would have included the Burgh Loch and the Burgh Muir.

The burgh had the right to hold a fair for eight days at the beginning of November. The fair would attract traders and visitors bringing money into the burgh. For all this, the burgh had to pay 52 marks annually – half was due at Whitsunday and the other half on Martinmas, 11 November (the medieval calendar was run on religious lines).

Edinburgh in the 1340s

John Wiggmer is recorded as Provost of Edinburgh in both 1344 and 1348. The loss of Berwick and the decline of Roxburgh left the Borders without a dynamic royal burgh and opportunities that had once been open to the merchants of Berwick now fell into the hands of the merchant elite who ruled Edinburgh. By the end of the century, Edinburgh was paying more customs for the export of wool and hides than the two next largest exporters (Perth and Dundee) put together.

Much of the wool and hides shipped abroad went to Flanders (modern Belgium). Scottish merchants based themselves in the Low Countries so they could trade with the local merchants, and special privileges were granted to these merchants to encourage this profitable trade. This was called the 'Staple'. In 1347 the Staple was situated in the town of Middleburg in Zealand, near the mouth of the Rhine. Scottish merchants were allowed to run their own affairs under the Conservator of the Staple. The following year they were negotiating with Bruges for privileges there.

The Recapture of the Castle, 1341

The English, supposedly in support of Balliol, recaptured the castle in 1341. The plan to retake it seems to have been hatched in Dundee. There, Sir William Douglas, William Bullock and William Fraser met Walter Curry, who had a ship in the port. They loaded the ship with 200 men, sailed for the Forth and put into the island of Inchkeith.

Walter Curry, in the guise of a merchant from Elie, visited the captain of the castle. He claimed to have a cargo of grain, beer and good wine which he wanted to sell to the garrison. Curry's servant brought in two skins containing wine and beer. Curry promised to return with a cask of wine, a cask of beer and two baskets of spiced biscuits. In return for this handsome bribe, the captain was to encourage the garrison to buy the rest of Curry's cargo. He must have gone to bed a happy man with such a good deal.

The Scots returned the next morning – twelve of them, all wearing armour underneath their cloaks. The three sentries had their throats cut. They drove a large stake in the gateway to prevent the portcullis being lowered, a trumpet was blown as a signal and Douglas led his men into the castle. The English offered resistance, but were unable to hold off the Scots and the castle was captured. Walter Bower, Abbot of Inchcolm and author of the *Scottichronicon*, commented, 'The burgesses rejoiced and returned to their allegiance to the king.' It would appear that the town had supported the English while there was a threat from the castle.

The Black Death

The Black Death arrived in Scotland in 1350. It was not known as the Black Death to contemporary chroniclers, however. John of Fordun, who died sometime in the 1380s, refers to it as 'a pestilence and plague among men'.

It is generally believed that the plague spread from central Asia. Fleas living mainly upon rats brought it along the trade routes from the East. Death rates were high. Even Fordun claims it killed one-third of the population. He does, however, point out that it was mainly 'the meaner sort and common people who suffered most'.

We have no idea how the burgh fared during this major disaster. Certainly the workforce would have been considerably reduced, leading to a drop in production. Yet by 1370 Scotland was exporting more wool and hides than at any time during the Middle Ages.

Edinburgh after 1350

In 1355 the Scots attacked Berwick and recaptured the town. The following year, Edward III marched north into Lothian. Edinburgh was set on fire, but again the shortage of food forced the English to retreat. They were now fighting not only in Scotland but also in France. However, an overwhelming victory at Portiers destroyed the French army and left the French king a prisoner of the English.

If matters were not bad enough, the plague returned in 1362 and the king and his nobles retired north to try to escape its effects. This appears to have been a repeat of the previous outbreak. Yet this does not give a true picture of life in the burgh at this time. Exports of wool and hides reached a peak in the early 1370s. Such trade brought considerable wealth to the merchant burgesses who ruled Edinburgh. Adam Forrester, who was provost in 1373, made enough money to purchase estates in Corstorphine and Nether Liberton. He was also Sheriff of Edinburgh in 1382. The family began the move from merchant burgess to landed gentry and then finally to government service.

Fish, packed in barrels of salt, were also an important export. Some of it would have passed through Leith. Edinburgh's port was now the only major outlet for exports in the south-east of Scotland.

A New Tron

In 1364, David II gave a piece of land measuring 100ft by 32ft to build a new 'tron'. Since it is described as 'on the west part of the old tron', it must have replaced that building.

Trons were weighhouses where goods being brought into the burgh's markets were first weighed and assessed for duty. This tron was built near the road leading to the castle. It was probably built at the top of the Bow, one of the main entrances into the town. No doubt this building was destroyed and rebuilt a number of times.

In 1458 Margaret Bertram received the tenancy of the 'Butter Tron' for £4 6s. As late as 1745 a tron stood at the top of the Bow. Bonnie Prince Charlie's troops used it as a guardhouse from which to watch the castle.

A Fair at Newbattle

This was the age of monopolies, and no one protected their rights more fiercely than the burgesses of Edinburgh. Trading was the special privilege of the burgh which, in return, paid their customs to the king.

A fair was set up illegally at Newbattle and this threatened to take trade away from the burgh. David II, then in Perth, wrote to the Sheriff of Edinburgh who, at that time, was Simon Preston. (His family were soon to acquire the castle and lands of Craigmillar.) Anyone caught 'buying or selling in that place or keeping any market there' was to be immediately arrested and held in custody in Edinburgh Castle. All goods found in the market were to be confiscated and become the property of the king. So, the king was no loser by this act, protecting his own burgh and gaining from anything the sheriff found.

The Rebuilding of Edinburgh Castle

In 1367, David II began a complete rebuilding of the castle's eastward defences. The rock provides sheer drops to the north, west and south. Only on the east side, where the burgh stood, could the castle be easily approached. To protect this, a huge L-shaped tower was constructed on the site of what is now the Half Moon Battery (in fact, the foundations of this tower are still under the battery). The tower covered the southern part of the eastern wall as well as providing apartments for the king.

David died in the castle in 1371 before he could finish the tower, which later became known as David's Tower. The king was buried in Holyrood Abbey in front of the High Altar. He was succeeded by his nephew, Robert II, the first of the Stewart kings.

A second, smaller tower was built to the north of David's Tower. This was called Constable's Tower and it was the home of the constable of the castle and guarded the entrance to the castle. A gate and a drawbridge added to the strength of this royal fortress.

The Port of Leith

The Black Death was followed by an economic boom. In 1332, the customs levied on wool and hides exported from Leith raised a little under £43. By 1379, these duties brought the king £2,420. Nineteen years later, forty-six ships left Leith, paying customs of over £2,000. Much of the foreign trade was still with the Low Countries where the strong cloth-making industry fuelled demand for wool.

In 1382 the last of the Restalrigs died. Their estate was one of the largest in the Edinburgh district; it included not only Restalrig but also most of South Leith. For over 200 years it had belonged to the family, but now it passed by marriage to the Logans.

Edinburgh in the 1380s

The Scots supported the French in their struggles with the English, and this led to several invasions of Scotland by Richard II's troops in retaliation. The one safe place in Lothian was the newly fortified Edinburgh Castle, so Robert II, the first Stewart King of Scots, granted a piece of land 8ft square within the castle to the Abbot of Holyrood for the use of himself and his canons. The canons, who also served the Church of St Mary's in the Castle, could live there in safety from any impending English attack. This grant was followed by a second one giving the burgesses of Edinburgh the right to build within the castle. They would be able to take themselves and their valuables into the fortress away from the invading English army.

Things looked brighter for the Scots in the summer of 1385. A strong French force of some 2,000 men landed at Dunbar and Leith. The French admiral, Sir John de Vienne, joined the Scottish nobles in Edinburgh. He also brought armour, weapons and 50,000 gold francs.

Sadly, even this force was not strong enough to stop the next English invasion and a retreat into the heart of Scotland began. Anything that could be used by the enemy was destroyed; cattle were no doubt driven into hiding places. The English marched into Edinburgh and set fire to the burgh. Even the Kirk (Church) of St Giles was burnt. Most of the citizens, knowing what was to come, had probably taken refuge in the castle or fled to the safety of remote areas like the Pentland Hills. Holyrood Abbey was spared by the intervention of John of Gaunt.

Since there was little left, the English were forced to withdraw, leaving the burgesses, yet again, to rebuild their town.

The Charter of Robert II, 1386

The king gave a grant of land on the north side of the street in the market place. It was 60ft by 30ft. The burgh was given the right to put up houses or buildings 'for the ornament of the said burgh and their necessary uses'. The charter does not tell us to what purpose the burgh authorities put this land. It has been assumed that the land was used to build the Tolbooth, and since it was a grant for the use of the community the assumption does not seem unreasonable. However, the Old Tolbooth was situated on the south side, not the north side of the High Street.

St Giles, 1387

The rebuilding of the burgh began soon after the retreat of Richard II and, as religion was very much the centre of life in a medieval burgh, priority was given to the parish church of St Giles. Only the four large central pillars remain from the mid-fourteenth century; the rest must have either been destroyed in the fire or been removed to make way for the new kirk.

Adam Forrester, one of the richest burgesses and the laird of Nether Liberton, together with Provost Andrew Yutson, employed some masons to build five chapels. Each of the first four chapels was to have its own window. The fifth chapel was built by the west door. The rebuilding probably began in the following year.

The five chapels were just the beginning and the new St Giles was to be developed constantly over the next 100 years. More and more patrons wished to support chapels and altars in the kirk, and private masses and prayers for the souls of the patrons were becoming an important part of religious life. Over the next century, the number of altars grew rapidly. They were supported by the rich merchants of the burgh and later by the craft guilds.

The Knighting of the Duke of Rothsay

Robert II died in 1390, to be succeeded by his eldest son, Robert III. The new king had two sons. The elder was called David and he took the title of Duke of Rothsay. His younger brother was the future James I. According to Bower, the knighting took place 'close to the north side of the town of Edinburgh where there is now a loch'. This is the area which is now occupied by Princes' Street Gardens. It would appear that this ground might have been a traditional place to hold tournaments.

The event took place in 1398. Abbot Bower died in 1449, and sometime between these dates a dam was built to control the little burn running from a spring near the castle. This dam created the Nor' (North) Loch. It was considered to provide a defence for the north side of the burgh.

The Charter of Leith, 1398

Growing international trade required an expansion of the port facilities in Leith. South Leith was part of the estate of Restalrig, which was owned by Sir

Robert Logan in 1398. He probably lacked the resources to develop the port and so granted rights to the burgesses. They were permitted to enlarge the port facilities – possibly along the Shore – and boats were now allowed to tie up along the Restalrig Shore.

The medieval coastline ran along the present St Bernard and Commercial streets (the modern docks stand on land reclaimed from the sea). The merchants were given the right to build a bridge linking North and South Leith. They were also given free passage to take themselves and their goods through the barony of Restalrig. The charter does not say how Sir Robert Logan benefitted from this.

EDINBURGH DURING THE
FIFTEENTH CENTURY

This century saw the rebuilding of the burgh after the destruction by the English in 1385. Although there was a general economic decline all over northern Europe, Edinburgh suffered less as it gained a larger share of Scotland's trade. Throughout the century, St Giles was extended, becoming a collegiate church.

It seems probable that the Old Tolbooth was built on land granted to the burgh by King Robert II. The burgh was situated on a ridge which fell away steeply to the north and south. Thus, no back roads developed parallel to the High Street. Some of the wynds which led down to the Cowgate had already acquired their names: Friars' Wynd (Blackfriars) was the road down to the Dominican Friary; there was St Mary's Wynd, Niddri Wynd, Peebles' Wynd and Liberton Wynd; Forrester Wynd may have been the site of the town house of the Forresters of Corstorphine. Most of the markets were held in either the High Street or the Lawnmarket.

Standing on the High Street, looking down George IV Bridge towards Greyfriars, it is hard to believe there is a steep valley between the two sites. Pass down Victoria Street and the Bow, cross the Grassmarket and climb up Candlemakers' Row, for only then can you get the feeling of how the land lay in the fifteenth century. By this time, the Cowgate and Grassmarket were built up and new developments were taking place to the south. The Franciscans began the building of their friary in 1460.

Beyond these new lands was the Burgh Loch which covered part of the land now known as the Meadows. Further south again was the Burgh Muir, which was a mixture of undeveloped forest and scrubland. On the north side of the burgh, sometime in the first half of the century a dam had been built to create the Nor' (North) Loch. This was to remain as the boundary of the city until the middle of the eighteenth century.

Danger from the English at the Beginning of the Fifteenth Century

Relations with England remained uncertain in the fifteenth century, leaving Edinburgh merchants at the mercy of English pirates. Even James I, on his journey to France in 1406, was captured by them off Flamborough Head, and three years later, Sir Robert Umfraville launched a raid in retaliation after Scottish pirates had taken English ships. He captured thirteen ships in the Forth. If these were seagoing vessels rather than coastal traders, the Firth must have been a busy place.

Leith was the chief port from which long-distance trading voyages were begun. By 1421 the English raids had become so bad that the monks of Inchcolm spent the summer on the mainland. Only when the winter storms drove the ships to port did they venture to return to the island.

The English were not the only danger facing the merchant exporters of Edinburgh. Storms could easily take control of the small trading vessels used in the early fifteenth century. The monks of Inchcolm lost three men while returning across the Firth to the abbey, and a Lombardy carrick, presumably making for Leith, was driven onto the shore near Granton – this is the first account that we have of merchants from northern Italy, then one of the most prosperous parts of Western Europe, trading directly with Edinburgh.

Acts of the Scottish Parliament in the 1430s

James I was concerned with his subjects' spending on clothes and drink. This did not, of course, lead to the king curtailing *his* expenditure. He used Parliament to bring in various restrictions on the lives of the less wealthy of his subjects; in Edinburgh, only members of the burgh council were allowed to wear fur, for instance. The king also banned our national sport – football! – while archery was to be encouraged because it produced trained men for military service.

Every man in the burgh was expected to join the army when they were summoned, although few had much training or proper weapons. However, we must remember that the king had no police to enforce his wishes and was dependent on the support of the local nobles, lairds and burgh councils.

Capital of Scotland

The term 'capital' means the seat of government. No Scottish king ever remained for long in one burgh or castle, and although government moved with the king some business needed to be conducted in one place.

The King's Chapel, or Chancery, drew up the documents required by the king. These may have been charters granting land and privileges, or orders given to some royal official. Possibly some of this work was done in Edinburgh Castle.

Parliaments met in many places over the years, although they were usually held in Perth, Stirling or Scone. Surprisingly, Parliament had only met in Edinburgh once, in 1328 when it confirmed the Treaty of Northampton. Parliament had been held at Holyrood in 1334 under Edward Balliol, and again in 1389. After the murder of James I, Parliament met in Perth but was then moved to Edinburgh. The king was normally crowned at Scone, just outside Perth, but the coronation of James II took place in Holyrood Abbey.

From then onwards, Parliament was to be held in the burgh – except for three parliaments held in Stirling during the 1350s – presumably because castles offered security in an age of uncertainty. We cannot be sure where these subsequent parliaments were actually held, and numbers attending were not large. For example, the Parliament of 1479 was made up of eighty-nine representatives of the clergy, the nobility and the burghs – this was considered a large meeting.

Edinburgh Castle in the Fifteenth Century

Throughout the fifteenth century, the castle remained a royal residence and an important centre of royal administration. The king, when he stayed in Edinburgh, lived in David's Tower (the remains of which lie beneath the Half Moon Battery), while the constable or keeper of the castle occupied Constable's Tower. James I added to David's Tower by building the Great Chamber. This is now referred to as 'the palace' and contains the Scottish crown jewels as well as the Stone of Destiny.

James II
At this time, Edinburgh was controlled by Sir William Crichton, who had been made keeper of the castle and Sheriff of Edinburgh by James I. After the coronation, Crichton took the new king into his care in the castle. In 1439 he became chancellor. That year, the Earl of Douglas died of the plague, leaving two sons, William and David.

In November 1440, young Earl William and his brother were invited to dine with the young king in Edinburgh Castle. The two brothers and their advisor, Sir Malcolm Fleming, foolishly accepted the invitation. During the dinner, Crichton placed a black bull's head on the table – a sign of impending death. The brothers were given a brief trial and then executed on Castlehill. This event became known as the 'Black Dinner'. In 1442 the burgh closed its gates and set up a night watch of six men.

James II was very interested in new guns – too interested! – the king was killed when one of his own guns blew up at the siege of Roxburgh. His wife's uncle, Phillip the Good, Duke of Burgundy, had sent him two large siege guns. One of these, Mons Meg, can still be seen in the castle. By the end of the century the castle had a gunhouse for the building and storage of these larger weapons which were changing the face of warfare. Castles were no longer just safe places of refuge for powerful nobles.

In the later part of the century vaults were built to raise the southern side of the castle and it was upon these that the Great Hall was eventually built by James IV.

The Rebellion of 1482–83

The castle was also a royal prison. In 1479, the Duke of Albany, James III's brother, was held in the castle, but escaped by killing his guards and lowering himself down the rock using a rope. Four years later, James III himself was held as a prisoner in the castle.

James III was taken prisoner by a group of nobles; the king's uncles, the Earl of Atholl, the Earl of Buchan and the Bishop of Moray, were behind the plot. Atholl was the constable of the castle and thus held the king. Events leading to the release of the king are shrouded in mystery. What we do know is that the Duke of Albany and the burgesses of Edinburgh all played their part. James was eventually freed from his captivity in the castle. As a reward for their help, the Provost of Edinburgh and his successors became Sheriff of Edinburgh. The bailies were then sheriff's deputies. The council now not only controlled the burgh but they were also the magistrates enforcing the law. The burgh also received a banner, known afterwards as the Blue Blanket.

James III was injured at the Battle of Sauchieburn. His supporters took him to an old mill before summoning a man dressed as a priest. This 'priest' murdered the king. After James III's death, James IV and his supporters searched the castle looking for his father's treasury.

The Defences of the Burgh

The valley to the north of the burgh (now Princes' Street Gardens) was open land and may have been an area used to hold tournaments and other military sports. Sometime before 1450, the stream flowing from a spring beneath the castle was dammed to form the North Loch. The Burgh Loch, situated in the present Meadows, was the South Loch. This new loch was designed to offer a defensive barrier against a possible attack from the north.

The original boundary to the south of the burgh was at the back of the yards of the houses lining the High Street. An excavation took place before the new Meal Market was built in 1832. It led to the discovery of two stone walls. The outer one was built over a cemetery, from which the excavators removed six skulls. The second wall was probably built at the time the North Loch was created, during the middle of the century, and the earlier wall may date from the time of David II. It ran across the slope between the High Street and the Cowgate. The southern gate into the burgh was in the Bow. However, by 1450 this defensive line was redundant. The town had grown beyond here long ago. The town council may have decided, under pressure from the king, to take the cheaper option and reinforce the existing town wall.

Plagues in Fifteenth-Century Edinburgh

At various times Edinburgh and Leith suffered from plagues, which were referred to as 'the pest'. Plagues occurred at the beginning of the century and twice in the 1430s. This seems to have been a lean time, with severe weather to add to the difficulty. Even the Earl of Douglas died of the pest in 1439.

In March 1499 villages on the south side – Currie, Swanston and Hailes (Colinton) – as well as on the north at Cramond, were 'infected with a contagious infirmity of pestilence'. People from these areas were not allowed into the town. By the end of the year all visitors to the burgh had to report to the bailies first. Later the next year, four brave men – Will Rae, George Stewart, James Galloway and Alexander Stobo – were paid 12d a day to clean the goods and houses of all those affected by the pest.

Strict rules were made that all must report an outbreak of the infection and washing was to be carried out, not in the lochs, but in running water. The Water of Leith and the Powburn (on the Burgh Muir) were generally used. However, the outbreak continued into the next century.

What caused the plagues? Was the same organism responsible each time? The answer to these questions is that we do not know and possibly never will. They were considered to be very contagious and the victims were isolated. Travel restrictions were placed on people, especially those arriving in the Port of Leith from more distant parts where the pest might have broken out.

While the exact nature and origin of the pests may be in doubt, conditions at the time must have encouraged their spread and effect. Hygiene was very poor, with few people ever washing themselves thoroughly. Clothing was not often changed or washed. Despite the fact that some claim the medieval diet to be healthy, with its low sugar content, it must be remembered that the inhabitants of Edinburgh in the fifteenth century were dependent on the seasons of the

year. Summer and autumn might have brought plenty, but winter was a hard season even in good times. During wet summers and hard winters food would be in short supply. Water was not reliable, and wells were the only source of comparatively safe drinking water. Unwashed bodies and unsanitary conditions offered a breeding ground for germs.

The Burgh Council

The records of the burgh council date back to the opening years of the fifteenth century, but they are not complete and are thus unable to give us a clear account of the workings of the burgh officials. The head of the burgh was the provost. He appears to have held the office for one year, although Patrick Cockburn (1446–49) and Thomas Cranston (1449–51) served longer. Cranston was also one of the king's collectors of customs in Edinburgh during the 1450s. Three generations of the Napiers of Merchiston also held the office.

In the early part of the century only William de Liberton, according to known records, held the office of provost at three different times (1425, 1429 and 1432). Towards the end of the century, John Murray (1485–87, 1493) and Sir Thomas Todd (1488, 1491 and 1493) served as provosts of Edinburgh.

In 1487 Patrick, Lord Hailes, was chosen as provost. As a lord, he was now called 'lord provost'. This was the first use of the title, but the right of any head of the burgh to be called lord provost was still some time off.

During this time, the provost was granted a payment of £20 a year. In 1482 James III granted the position of sheriff to the provost of the burgh. Thus, the provost was not only head of the burgh council, who made the laws of the burgh, but also chief magistrate who enforced these laws.

The main officers of the burgh were the dean of guild, the treasurer and the bailies. The guild was made up of wealthy merchants who were the real power in the burgh. The dean of guild was the head of the guild and a leading member of the council and all the councillors were probably members of the Merchants' Guild. The craftsmen were just beginning to organise themselves into guilds and would later gain representation on the burgh council.

The posts of treasurer and Bailie of Leith are mentioned as early as 1403, and fifty-three years later the election of three bailies is recorded. The bailie was responsible for a district of the burgh and when the provost became Sheriff of Edinburgh, the bailies acted as sheriff's depute.

During the fifteenth century, an important body in the burgh was the 'dusane'. In 1431, absence from a meeting of the dusane would bring a fine of 4d. This body appears in the records at various times throughout the century, and as early as 1436, listed at a meeting held in the Tolbooth, were 'the alderman [provost], bailies and council'. Was the dusane the council, or another body? It seems likely that the dusane was a larger body of merchants meeting either to support or influence the council. In February 1479, the provost is associated with 'the great dusane and various neighbours'. Two years later, it is the provost with the 'great dusane and the deacons'. The deacons were the elected leaders of the crafts. After 1500, the dusane disappears from our history.

In 1456, we hear of complaints about an irregularity in the election of the officers of the council for that year. Two days before Michaelmas, the dusane produced a list of names for the officers of the burgh. The next day, the bailies were chosen and on Michaelmas Day, the provost and dean of guild were elected. Unfortunately, we do not know who actually did the electing.

The town council itself met in the Tolbooth of Edinburgh, and in 1484 it is recorded that the council met every Wednesday and Friday at 9 a.m. within the Inner Tolbooth.

In 1469 the new council was chosen by the members of the retiring council, enabling the councillors to control the composition of the new body and therefore keeping the power to themselves. Thus, a wealthy group of Edinburgh merchants were able to establish perpetual rule over the burgh. This remained in place until the reform of elections and voting rights during the first half of the nineteenth century!

Trade and the Crafts Guilds

Leith and its Trade

Leith was the port through which the Edinburgh merchants exported their goods and brought in foreign products such as wine to sell in Scotland. The Teutonic Knights, who controlled large areas of eastern Germany, set up a Staple in Leith, and by 1414 the Edinburgh merchants acquired a piece of land for the purpose of building warehouses to store their goods in the port.

James I issued a charter to the burgh granting Edinburgh the right to collect duties on every ship and boat which docked in the Port of Leith. The money was to be used to maintain the harbour. The charter was later confirmed by James II in 1454. It infers that the burgh had control of much, if not all, of the Port of Leith. This would make little sense if there had been an alternative landing place free of these duties in Leith. In 1483 the burgh council ordered all merchants and skippers trading out of Leith to make written contracts. This was because English pirates and the severe storms made voyages risky, and skippers would ditch cargoes if they felt that it might save the ship (a lighter ship travelled faster). No doubt the merchants saw this as too easy an option for the skippers at a time when there was no insurance.

The development of a strong monarchy under James I enabled the king to spend nearly £200 on his 'house' in Leith in 1436. Even more money was spent in the shipyards: he paid £122 for a barge (possibly a ship with oars and a sail) and £43 for a small ship for the queen; a further £36 was spent on a vessel called *The Kele*. Work on the three ships suggests that Leith had a thriving shipbuilding industry by the first half of the fifteenth century. This would have provided work not only for shipwrights but for carpenters, blacksmiths and other tradesmen. We do not know where these early shipyards stood, but since most of the trade was carried out on the southern bank of the river they may have been in North Leith. Certainly, in later times (the eighteenth century) shipbuilding was centred on North Leith.

Fish (a considerable part of the diet of the wealthy in medieval Britain) remained an important part of life in Leith. We know that in 1438 they were salting fish to preserve it. The town council of Edinburgh set out the duties on herring in 1428 and 1445. Salmon were brought from Banff, Moray and the Spey, and may have been preserved before being exported.

Naturally, the wealth of the port attracted the good and the bad. Rich Edinburgh merchants bought property in the port. Alexander Napier, who was Provost of Edinburgh in 1454, 1455 and 1457, had a house in Ratoun Row (Rotten Row), while Alexander Forrester of Corstorphine, one of the wealthiest merchants in Edinburgh, owned a house in the town which he hired to the king as a store for holding food.

Piracy was a considerable problem to any peaceful trader during the wars with England. Scottish vessels carrying goods to the Low Countries were vulnerable to attack from ships based in ports along the east coast of England. However, the English did not have it all their own way. In 1449, Andrew Powety of Leith, master of an armed carval, seized an English fishing boat and its crew of eighteen men.

In 1450 the new queen, Mary of Guelders, landed in Leith and was entertained at the monastery of St Anthony before travelling to Holyrood to be the guest of the abbot. The event appears to have been organised by Alexander Napier, as he was given £39 from the customs to pay his expenses.

Less happy events were to overtake Leith in the middle of the 1470s, when rats destroyed the grain in Logan's Granary. The following year the king also lost goods, although rats were not named as the culprits. It was also a time when the plague struck the port. Throughout its history, Leith was vulnerable to such outbreaks being brought in by the ships which visited the port.

Booths: The Lease of Burgh Property

Trading was done from open stalls called 'booths', although the poorer traders probably just found a place in the market to set up their wares. It is unlikely that the sellers of vegetables, eggs or cheese were people of standing. More substantial traders were the burgh craftsmen, selling the products they had made in their own small workshops. These people sold their goods on the open stalls in the markets of the High Street and the Lawnmarket. Lawnmarket means 'Land Market', where products from the land – farms and country crafts – were sold. The poultry market, by the Cross, would be filled with men and women from beyond the burgh.

The two main council buildings were the Tolbooth and the Belhouse. The council owned the land and the booths situated around those buildings. In 1458, sixteen booths placed round the Tolbooth were up for rent. The eight on the north side in the High Street were let for about £2 each although, for some reason no longer known, Nicholas Spathy only had to pay 15 shillings for his lease, while Robert Murray received the two booths on the west side for the same price as one booth on the High Street. The council only managed to let half of the six booths on the south side and John Best was given his for nothing.

The Belhouse, which may have been an extension on the east side of the Tolbooth (no booths are listed on the east side of the Tolbooth), cannot have been much used. The council rented out six flats in the Belhouse; five booths by here were each leased for £2 each or more, suggesting that these too were in the High Street. The Fleshhouse was let 'to the fleshers' (butchers), who must have had some organisation (possibly a guild) in order to conclude an agreement with the council.

Margaret Bertrem paid the handsome sum of £4 6s for the lease of the Butter Tron. This weighhouse was at the top of the Bow. Adam de Cranston acted as surety for her, and may have been related to Thomas de Cranston, who had held the office of provost a few years earlier (1449–51). Margaret Bertrem was not the only woman in business; Janete Scott, a widow, rented one of the booths on the north side.

The records for 1481 show the council leasing seven booths on the north side. The price had doubled, with tenants paying £4 each, which might suggest a growing prosperity in the town. Allan Brown, who rented the first booth, is the only tenant whose name appeared in the list of 1458. Thomas Williamson's sixth booth was now occupied by Isobel Williamson – possibly the widow of Thomas Williamson, carrying on his business. The rest of the tenants of the seven north-side and ten south-side booths were new since the previous rent list of 1458. Again, the south-side booths, at £2 each, were half that of those on the High Street, but the cost had still doubled in twenty-three years. A year later, only Isobel Williamson and Andrew Bertram remained as tenants of the High Street booths. These booths still cost their tenants an annual rent of £4.

The records of 1482 list booths being leased to skinners. The council had recognised the Guild of Skinners in 1474, and from the list of skinners who had petitioned the council for recognition, Robert Lanerok and William Ramsay are recorded as renting booths from the council. On the south side of the Tolbooth, only Robert Fowler and John Currour continued their tenancies.

Medieval society has always been considered very static, with few people moving either physically or socially. Craftsmen generally had to serve a five-year apprenticeship, and outsiders were not immediately welcome. The Hatmakers' Guild required any member of the craft who had moved to Edinburgh to produce a piece of work to the required standard while being watched by an Edinburgh master hatmaker. He would then have to serve for a year and a day and produce two further pieces of acceptable work before finally becoming a Freeman of the Burgh. The wrights and masons were more welcoming to incoming members of their craft. They had to be examined by officers of the guild and pay a mark to the Altar of St John. The guild supported this altar in St Giles Church.

The Merchant and Craft Guilds of Edinburgh

Edinburgh was ruled by a group of rich merchants who had organised their own Merchants' Guild. Their dean of guild held an important place on the town council. Below them in the social scale of the burgh were the craftsmen. They carried on their trades in small workshops and sold their goods in the market. Merchants supervised their businesses, letting others do the physical work, while craftsmen, in contrast, worked with their own hands at their trade. They would train up apprentices who often lived with them.

The other influential groups in the burgh were the various craft trades. They wished to come together to regulate their trades and possibly to gain some say in the running of the burgh. However, the merchants, and even the government, feared this new power and an Act of Parliament in 1427 forbade crafts appointing deacons who would enforce the craft's rules and represent the craft in any negotiations. The holding of meetings by groups of craftsmen was also prohibited. Fear of rebellion, such as had happened in the Peasants' Revolt in England, might have been a reason. However, it is more likely an attempt by the merchant elite to keep their power.

Ultimately this served to cause only a delay, and by the end of the century the main crafts in Edinburgh had formed their own guilds and their status has been recognised by the burgh council, although the Merchants' Guild of Edinburgh still controlled the trade and the burgh itself. The first burgh record lists the officers of this guild, who appear also to be the officers of the burgh: Alexander Napier is described as 'prepositus', a term later translated as provost.

The crafts of the late fifteenth century associated themselves with the Church, and the guilds each supported an altar to their patron saint in the Kirk of St Giles. In 1451, seventeen skinners came together to jointly provide money to pay for a chaplain and for the upkeep of the altar of St Christopher in the Church of St Giles. This was the beginning of the move to bring members of a craft together and to gain recognition from the burgh authorities. Five years later, the baxters (bakers) were given the right by the burgh council to object to any member of their craft being made either a Burgess or Freeman of Edinburgh if they felt his work was not up to the required standard. All baxters had to pay a duty towards the maintenance of the altar of St Ubert.

It would appear that by the middle of the century, most of the craftsmen had formed themselves into guilds. These were run by a deacon, who was chosen from among the masters of the craft. Each craft had a monopoly of the work within their trade. No one could work in a craft unless he was a member of the craft guild and the deacon was responsible for inspecting the work of the craftsmen.

However, the guild had no way of enforcing their regulations, so they still had to turn to the burgh council. The first craft guild to go to the council were the hatmakers. In 1474 ten masters of the craft asked it to recognise their right to choose a deacon and to make their own rules. All apprentices had to serve for five years, except the sons of master craftsmen who had this reduced to only three years. To become a master, the journeyman (a man who had passed his apprenticeship) had to produce two pieces of work, unless his father was a master, when this was reduced to one. Later that same year, twenty skinners came together to regulate their craft and receive the council's approval. In the Seal of Cause, as the agreement was known, John Cranston is already named as deacon. This suggests that the organisation of the skinners was in place long before 1474.

In the following year, the wrights and masons (building workers) agreed to pay for the maintenance of the aisle of St John in St Giles Church. This grant was made by 'the provost, bailies, council, dean of guild [Merchants' Guild] and the deacons of the whole craftsmen within the Burgh of Edinburgh' according to the Burgh Records. It would appear that by 1475 the craftsmen of Edinburgh were already organised into guilds with their own deacons and only required the authority of the council to enforce them.

The wrights and masons were two separate crafts which had come together to control the building trade. Two members of each craft were to be elected to inspect the work of those in their particular craft. They also had the authority to examine those apprentices who had completed their training. The craft agreed to bury any of their members who left no money to pay for their burial. This is an early example of crafts looking after their poorer members.

The websters (weavers) received their recognition as a guild by the council in 1476. They expected each member of the craft to pay towards the upkeep of their altar in St Giles. In the case of the websters this was dedicated to St Severiane.

In 1483 a discontented Guild of Hammermen (blacksmiths, goldsmiths, leather workers, saddlers, cutlers, buckle makers and armourers) brought their complaints before the council. An experiment of the 1460s, minting copper coins known later as Black Money, had weakened the value of the coins which were used to buy the products of the hammermen. It also appears that metal goods which were not made by their members were being sold on the High Street and in the closes. They refer to 'unfree' hammermen, 'both booth holders and others', who were not members of their craft but were producing metal goods and selling them in the burgh – probably cheaper than the guild members. The council ordered that these men were to be brought into the guild, made to serve their time and reach the required standard of workmanship. They were also expected to pay their dues to the burgh, the guild and the altar supported by their craft.

In 1488 the Guild of Fleshers (butchers and fishmongers) came before the town council with a bill of complaint. Richard Furde, their deacon, and seventeen other masters of the craft, complained about the 'blaspheme' (slander), the devalued money and other injuries to the craft. The petitioners were asked to withdraw so the matter could be discussed by the council in private. Every inhabitant of the burgh, including the councillors, would have had to deal with these traders in the market. Again, the devalued money was a problem. The fleshers, for one reason or another (possibly much of the butchery was done in the street, causing unpleasant smells and considerable mess), must have been unpopular with some of the townspeople, which would account for the cursing and swearing. The council agreed there was a need to regulate the craft and invited the deacon and the principal masters to present their proposals. All members of the flesher craft were to serve a proper apprenticeship, and the guild was given the authority to check that all meat and fish was of good quality. No one was to sell meat or fish, except in the proper markets where it could be checked.

The Exile of Henry VI in Edinburgh

Continuing poor relations with England often led the Scots to support the defeated party in the long struggle between the houses of York and Lancaster. Lollards in London put about a rumour that Richard II (deposed in 1399) was alive and living in Edinburgh. There is no evidence to support this, and Abbot Bower makes the claim that Richard II died in Stirling in 1424.

The Yorkist victory on Towton Moor in 1460 forced Henry VI to flee to Scotland, where he spent the years from 1461 to 1464 in Edinburgh. His great-grandfather, John of Gaunt, had also spent a short exile at Holyrood. In a gesture of thanks for his hospitality, he gave the merchants of Edinburgh the right to trade freely in England. Since the king was never able to take hold of his country again, the grant unfortunately proved worthless.

The Mills of Edinburgh in the Late Fifteenth Century

The Water of Leith was the source of power which drove the burgh mills. These mills ground the grain for flour and malt to make bread and beer. All the inhabitants of Edinburgh and Leith had to have their grain ground in the burgh mills.

There were, however, other mills on the river. John Peny is recorded as taking over the fulling mill of Ballernoch in west Currie as early as 1376, and the name Waulkmill Loan can still be found leading down to the Water of Leith – waulkers (walkers) were fullers who washed the newly made cloth.

The tenants of Holyrood Abbey would have to take their grain to Holyrood's mills at Canonmills. In 1423 the town received a five-year lease of these mills from the abbey.

During the 1460s the burgh council had placed the revenues of the mills in the control of Alexander Turing. He was 'the farmer of the mills'. The mills were 'farmed' to a person of substance who would pay the town an agreed sum. The money coming in from the mills in rents would be his, but he also had to see that the properties were properly maintained. The farmer expected to make a profit, while the council were saved the job of collecting the money.

Fairs in Edinburgh

Fairs were events of importance, bringing in traders from great distances, and the fairs of medieval Europe played a central role in the economy. People came from near and far to buy and sell at them. The fair in Edinburgh began on All Saints' Day and lasted for eight days over the first week of November, although from 1447 James II granted the burgh the right to hold a second fair in May.

All those selling at the fairs had to pay for the privilege, and therefore added to the income of the burgh. The fairs gave opportunities for the inhabitants of the burgh to buy items not normally available at the town's markets. Entertainers would travel to the fairs; jugglers, acrobats, musicians and animal acts all brought colour and excitement to the event. Life for an inhabitant of medieval Edinburgh would have offered few chances of entertainment, so the fairs would be the biggest events of the year. No doubt much of the activity took place in the High Street.

Edinburgh Markets

A letter from James III to the burgh listed the places where particular markets were held. The market for the products of the metal workers, known as hammermen, was at the east end of the High Street next to the Netherbow Port. Further up the street, towards the entrance of Blackfriars Wynd, was the fish market and beyond that stood the salt market.

Continuing up the High Street we come to the tron, a weighhouse where goods brought into the town were weighed and a tax, or 'toll', would be paid by the seller. The Tron Kirk, built in the middle of the seventeenth century, stands close to the spot where the old tron stood. Here, in the later years of the fifteenth century, the fleshers (butchers) carried out their trade. After the tron came the skinners and hatmakers on the south side of the street, while the chapmen waited for their clients on the north side. Chapmen owned packhorses and possibly carts. They would be hired to carry goods to and from the town.

The Mercat (Market) Cross was always the centre for any town. In the days before newspapers, it was the place where news and council decisions were proclaimed. At this time, it was placed in the centre of the High Street, and here the poultry traders had their market.

West of the Tolbooth, where George IV Bridge stands today, were the markets of the meal (flour or grain) sellers, the shoemakers and cordiners (ropemakers). The Lawnmarket ('Land Mercat') was the home of the sellers of cloth, wool, butter, eggs and cheese. These were all goods produced on the land and hence the name Land Mercat. At the end of the Lawnmarket, by the entrance to the Bow, was the Butter Tron where such goods would be weighed.

Food, straw and hay for the many animals kept in the burgh, particularly horses, were sold in the Cowgate. This may have extended into the wide street we know as the Grassmarket, giving it its name. The second road into the burgh, bringing traders from the west and south, was the West Port. This stood at the west end of the Grassmarket. From there, travellers would wind their way up the steep slope and round the sharp turns of the Bow. Victoria Street has removed the Upper Bow, but it is still possible to see where the old road must have been. The visitor would have to pass through an arch in the burgh wall before coming out at the west end of the Lawnmarket.

The traders were not allowed to operate a market every day. In 1473 the council laid down that markets selling food were to be held on Monday, Wednesday and Friday. There were probably a lot more rules made by the town council to control the markets, and possibly even the prices, however our records of this time are very limited. We do know that in the following century the council regulated the markets and the prices of some of the goods, although these rules do not appear to have been strictly adhered to. The merchants, many of whom had become wealthy through the wool trade, complained that people were selling cloth in booths on the High Street and even from ('under the stairs of') their own houses. The council, controlled by the rich merchants, ordered this practice to stop.

The poultry market was held by the Cross, but obviously trade must also have been carried out elsewhere, because in 1494 the council enacted that poultry was to be sold *only* at the Cross.

Feus and Customs Duties

In 1425 the annual feus (rents) paid by the burgh to the Royal Exchequer were £34 13s 4d. Bailie William Fish was responsible for the collection, and £6 13s 4d from this was given to the Dominican Friary (Blackfriars) in Edinburgh. The Abbot of Dunfermline received £5, with the remainder going to Sir John Forrester, the chamberlain, who was responsible for the king's household. In 1446, £20 was donated to the Chapel of Corstorphine.

Much more important to the public finances (crown revenues) were the customs duties collected from the burgh. The collectors of these customs (known as the Great Customs), were generally important merchants of the burgh. Thomas Cranston was not only a collector of customs but also served the king (James II) as constable of the castle and master of the mint. He was Provost of Edinburgh in 1438, 1443 and 1449–51. Alexander Napier, another Provost of Edinburgh, collected customs in 1455 and 1457. The revenue from the Great Customs of Edinburgh varied from highs of £2,616 in 1426 and £2,522 in 1483, to lows of £1,098 in 1415 and £1,055 in 1478. The duties were paid on wool and hides exported mainly to the Low Countries.

The Staple

As early as 1348 the Scots had a Staple in Middleburg. Later in the century, the Staple had been moved to Bruges, but by 1467 there was dissatisfaction with this. Edinburgh merchants were the leaders in overseas trade and the special rights of the Staple would have been important to them. They had to compete with the Hanza (a group of northern European cities joined together by a trading league) and by the English, who were powerful competitors in the wool trade. Thomas Flockhart and Alexander Napier, both Edinburgh merchants, were sent to negotiate with Middleburg. In 1472 the Staple was again in Bruges, but five years later it returned to Middleburg.

Markets and Trade, 1482–99

The provost, bailies and council regulated trade within the burgh. After all, they were merchants themselves and purchasers of the goods sold in the burgh markets.

Wool and linen cloth were only to be sold on market day. Meal (grain for cooking) had to be sold at the proper market and no one was allowed to buy it in order to resell – burgh laws against the buying of products for resale were a constant theme of the council for years to come. They were also concerned with the number of pigs wandering through the High Street. For the first (recorded) time, but certainly not the last, the council ordered the pigs to be removed from the main street of the burgh.

The Water Court was to be held in Leith to prosecute those who tried to break the burgh's monopoly over trading. No inhabitant of Leith was allowed to buy directly large quantities of food or timber shipped into the port, but must purchase it from a Freeman of the Burgh.

Edinburgh wished to keep a tight control over Leith, through which much of its trade passed. Monopoly, not free trade, was the economic policy of the day. Therefore, baxters who bought flour in Leith (thus avoiding the cost of having grain ground in the burgh's mills) were to pay the money to the farmer of the mills. In February 1495, twenty-two baxters were convicted of buying French flour for resale. 'Regraiting', that is, buying to sell on, was considered a crime.

Sellers of wildfowl, it appears, had also been trying to deal privately with their customers. They were ordered to come to the poultry market which was held at the Cross. In addition, brewers, who used large quantities of water, were made to pay 12d per annum towards the cost of maintaining the burgh's wells.

In 1498 it was ordered that both the merchants and the craftsmen should keep weapons in their booths so that they could come to the aid of the town's officers to prevent disorder and violence occurring on the streets. Edinburgh had no guard or police force at this time. The provost and bailies were the magistrates, and they were expected to keep order in the burgh or answer for their failure to the king.

The Luckenbooths

The High Street was filled with booths which formed the markets, and it was about this time that the Luckenbooths were built. According to Chambers, the name means 'locked booths'. They were, thus, of a superior nature to the open booths. The Luckenbooths were built on the High Street between the north side of the street and the north side of St Giles Church. At their western end, they were joined to the Old Tolbooth. A narrow passage ran between the Luckenbooths and the church and this was, certainly in later times, crowded with booths. These buildings made the wide High Street very narrow at this point. The Luckenbooths and the Old Tolbooth were not pulled down until 1817.

Beyond the Burgh

The Logans of Restalrig

North of the burgh, along the shore of the Forth, were three large estates. To the west of the Water of Leith were the lands of Holyrood Abbey. These included North Leith, Newhaven, Bonnington and Broughton. East of Arthur's Seat were the estates of Duddingston, which were also abbey lands. In their case, the abbey was the Kelso.

Between these two were the lands of Restalrig. This had passed to the Logans by marriage in the previous century. In 1439, the Abbot of Holyrood granted Sir Robert Logan and his heirs the office of bailie of the lands of St Leonards in Leith. Sir James Logan agreed to 'maintain and defend the freedom of the town of Edinburgh' in 1455. This appears, in practice, to have been to defend the trading monopoly which Edinburgh merchants had gained in Leith.

The Grant of Greenside

In 1456, James II granted the burgh land between Calton Hill (called Cragingalt) and the road to Leith (Easter Road) 'for tournaments, sport and proper warlike deeds'. This is now called Greenside. The land perhaps replaced that which might have previously been the tournament field and had been flooded by the North Loch.

Towers

Situated around the burgh, and now within the boundaries of the modern city, were a group of fortified towers. To the west of the burgh, lying between Corstorphine and Gogar Lochs, was Corstorphine Castle. This belonged to the Forrester family, who were Edinburgh merchants grown rich in the wool trade. Later, they entered the king's service. Sir Adam acted as an envoy for Robert III to England in 1400 and Sir John Forrester was the first chamberlain depute in 1405; he later served as chamberlain. The Church of Corstorphine became a collegiate church in 1429 and was served by three chaplains.

North of Corstorphine, across the hill, stood the tower of Barnton, once owned by Sir George Crichton, who was Admiral of Scotland and Sheriff of Linlithgow, while Cramond Tower and the lands about it were the property of the Bishop of Dunkeld.

In 1450 Muirhouse Tower passed to a man called Scot.

Merchiston Tower, which can still be seen in the main campus of Napier University, was built by the Napiers sometime in the late fifteenth century. Alexander Napier was a wool merchant who served as provost in 1437. His son, Sir Alexander, probably purchased the estate in the middle of the century. Like his father, he also served as provost in the years 1453–56 and 1469–72. His son,

John Napier, also held that office in 1484. He may have been responsible for building the tower.

Another tower from the late fifteenth century built on the south side of Edinburgh is Liberton Tower.

Along the Water of Leith, to the west of Currie, stands a tower known to the locals as Lennox Tower. Its origins and its early owners remain a mystery. The ruins of this fortified house stand on a wooded ridge overlooking the Water of Leith.

The Exchequer Rolls of 1458 record that Andrew Balerno and Francis Knychtsoune paid the sum of £60 and the Knychtsounes began the building of Malleny House to the south of Balerno in the late sixteenth century.

In the middle of the century, the three baronies of Roslyn, Cousland and Pentland were in the hands of William Lord Sinclair, Earl of Orkney and Chancellor of Scotland.

The largest fortress outside Edinburgh Castle was Craigmillar Castle. It had been acquired by Simon Preston sometime in the fourteenth century. The outer walls were added in 1427, making it an impressive stronghold. In 1455 the castle was owned by William Preston and Thomas Oliphant acted as constable of the castle. To the north-east of it lay the large estates of Duddingston and Restalrig.

Duddingston was part of the lands of Kelso Abbey and rents from this estate helped to pay for the upkeep of the abbey. Restalrig was now in the hands of the Logan family. Their castle stood near Lochend Park and the estate stretched into South Leith and brought them in touch with the merchant burgesses of Edinburgh who used the port. In 1487 the church of Restalrig, the parish church for the whole estate, became a collegiate church; it was eventually destroyed by the orders of the first General Assembly of the Reformed Church in 1560.

Much of the area to the north – North Leith, Bonnington and Broughton – formed part of the lands of Holyrood Abbey. The abbey mills were on that part of the Water of Leith which we still call Canonmills. Possession of these lands by the canons of Holyrood dates back to the original charter of David I.

The Burgh Muir

Much of the land lying to the south of Edinburgh had once formed the ancient Forest of Drumselch. Edinburgh had been granted large parts of this land, which became the Burgh Muir. However, in the fifteenth century it remained a mixture of woodland and open glades. We do not know whether traditional forest occupations such as charcoal burning took place, but we do know that, at this time and for many years following, the Muir was the home of disreputable characters; lime and coal were being dug up at Gilmerton and, by the middle of the century, coal was also being produced at Duddingston.

Six

THE EARLY SIXTEENTH CENTURY

A New World

By the beginning of the sixteenth century, the great cultural change known as the Renaissance had begun in Italy. This was the age of Leonardo, Michelangelo and Raphael. Peace and prosperity enabled money to be invested in art, architecture and sculpture. Unfortunately, Edinburgh had to wait another two centuries before it experienced its own great cultural renaissance.

By 1500, Christopher Columbus and Sebastian Cabot had reached the Americas, while Vasco da Gama had rounded the Cape and sailed on to India. These first voyages of exploration were to lead the countries of Western Europe to establish huge empires and bring to them untold wealth. The Spanish Conquistadors would build empires for Spain in Mexico and South America, and gold, silver and emeralds were shipped back to enrich the Spanish crown. The Portuguese, and later the Dutch, chasing the spice trade, set up colonies in Sri Lanka and Indonesia (the East Indies). France and England were to build empires in North America, India and the West Indies. But Scotland, lacking strong leadership, failed to join this move to empire. In fact, it was not until the beginning of the eighteenth century that they tried to establish a colony in Darien.

In the meantime, the merchants of Edinburgh continued their trade with Europe through the Port of Leith.

The sixteenth century saw the break-up of the old unified Church in Western Europe. It was the Reformation, as this movement was known, coupled with internal instability that was to dominate life in sixteenth-century Scotland. The three monarchs who succeeded to the throne in this century were very young children; Mary, Queen of Scots, was only eight days old. Periods of regency only led to powerful nobles seeking to gain control and influence over affairs of state. In England, the Wars of the Roses had led to the destruction of many of the great ruling families. In Scotland, however, the Douglases, the Hamiltons, and the various branches of the House of Stewart were still forces to be reckoned with.

Although it had grown southward beyond its original boundaries into the Grassmarket and Cowgate, Edinburgh remained a small town. On the ridge above this valley stood the buildings of the Franciscan Friary (Greyfriars) and the collegiate Church of St Mary in the Fields. Both places were to be the scene of dramatic events that would shape the history of Scotland. Nothing remains of the medieval burgh today, except the pattern of streets and closes. Even St Giles, the burgh's ancient church, has been rebuilt and its many altars swept away.

Problems with the Plague

The plague continued its periodic outbursts at the beginning of the new century. The burgh council tried to control the spread of these outbreaks. It ordered that all goods of infected persons were to be washed in either the Water of Leith or the Pow Burn, and the bailies were expected to seek out the victims and take action. In 1512, it had reached the point where the bailies were meeting twice a day, at 8 a.m. and 3 p.m., to co-ordinate the work. Severe punishments, such as branding a mark on the cheek, banishment and destruction of property were threatened to discourage anyone from hiding an outbreak.

Cleaning the Town

Old Edinburgh had a reputation as a very dirty town. The streets were used for the disposal of waste and sewage. Animals, especially pigs, were allowed to roam the streets. Market traders, such as fleshers (butchers and fishmongers) and skinners carried on their trade in the open, leaving their waste on the street. In 1505 the council hired Thomas Glendunwyne to clean the High Street, from Castlehill to St Mary's Wynd. He was given two men and a cart, leaving the street traders to pay for this at the rate of 1d per quarter. The fleshers had to pay 4d per quarter, presumably because their trade created much more mess. The skinners were banned from working on the High Street due to the evil smell. In 1506 and 1513 the council ordered the removal of pigs from the street. However, pigs continued to be part of life on the High Street for many years to come.

One wonders how successful this first attempt at street cleaning in Edinburgh was – the Cowgate and the closes were omitted from it. You have to applaud the initiative, but ask whether three men and a cart were sufficient to clean up all the rubbish from the householders and the market traders.

Another Outbreak

The pest had broken out in Perth, Dundee and Couper in 1529. The council placed a ban on people and goods crossing the Forth. Nobody was to offer lodgings to travellers from these infected areas and all victims were to remain at home and report the infection to council officials.

By 1530, St Andrew's was the main area of concern, and a ban threatened the death penalty on those who had any connection with the people or clothing from that town. Failure to obey these rules could be terrible. In August 1530 William Miller, a tailor, was condemned to be branded on the cheek for throwing a sick woman out of his house. The authorities changed this to banishment from the town as they feared he too might carry the plague. David Duly failed to tell the officers about his sick wife and attended mass at St Giles. Despite being a poor man with young children, Duly was sentenced to be hung. However, luckily for him, the rope broke! The council agreed to banish him from the town instead.

Others were not so lucky. Marion Clerk, who had visited places where the plague was known, attended a chapel in St Mary's Wynd. She was ordered to be drowned in the Quarry Holes at the Greyfriars Port. Kathryn Heriot suffered a similar fate, being accused of bringing sickness from Leith.

Infected people were sent to the Burgh Muir where James Barfour had been appointed master and governor. Nothing further is mentioned of the pest as 1530 turned into 1531, and we can probably assume that the outbreak came to its end.

The Guilds

The Edinburgh craftsmen continued to organise themselves into guilds. They sought the approval of the burgh council so that they could enforce their regulations. The waulkers (washers of newly made cloth) and the tailors had their guilds recognised by the council. In 1505 the barbers and surgeons followed.

Each guild elected a deacon to supervise the trade and to see that the regulations were enforced. These organisations helped to ensure good quality of work, but as they held a monopoly they could also control prices. By the middle of the first decade of the century, the craft guilds represented a large and important group in the burgh. Naturally they began to seek power over decision making. In 1508, Thomas Hathowyne asked that six or eight craftsmen might be represented on the council – this was definitely optimistic! The merchant elite of Edinburgh had no intention of giving up its monopoly of power. This was the beginning of a long struggle by the craftsmen to gain seats in the burgh council.

From 1505 to 1506 Richard Lawson was provost. He was succeeded by Alexander Lauder, who held the office until his death at Flodden in 1513.

The Markets

Edinburgh was a major market centre in a world where commerce was based on monopolies. All goods had to be sold in the various markets that took place in the burgh. In the Lawnmarket, fleshers traded on Sunday and Monday; the Meal Market was held on Monday, Wednesday and Friday. The poultry market was held by the Cross and the fish market was now beside Trinity College Church (the site of Waverley Station today).

The council regulated the prices and even the quality of some of the goods sold in the markets. Whether this was for the benefit of the inhabitants of the burgh or themselves is open to question. Stables had to be properly kept, providing corn and hay. A sensible precaution was the banning of candles in buildings where hay was stored. In the early sixteenth century most of the town was built of timber and roofed with thatch, and fire was an ever-present danger.

Bread, wine and ale were the main products that the council watched, and prices were laid down for these goods. When pricing bread, it was the weight that changed and not the price. During the century, the 4d loaf was sold at various weights.

The candlemakers also felt the council's orders. Candlemakers Row, by Greyfriars, was their home, and in the early years of the century it was on the very edge of the burgh and separated from the High Street by the steep valley which is the Cowgate. At this time, of course, candles were the only means of lighting after dark. They were warned to sell 'good and sufficient stuff' and 1lb of candles was to cost no more than 3d.

James IV and Edinburgh

In August 1503, James IV married Margaret Tudor, the daughter of King Henry VII of England, in Holyrood Abbey. The marriage celebrations continued in the newly built palace in the abbey grounds.

James IV started the building of a second royal residence in Edinburgh (technically in the Canongate) at the beginning of the century. The palace, which at that time consisted of a single tower, was at the east end of the Royal Mile next to Holyrood. Today the palace dominates the whole area, but in the early sixteenth century the abbey with its church and many buildings would have been the more imposing site. As the century progressed the new palace became the main royal residence and the castle returned to being a defensive site from which to resist invaders. Nothing now remains of these buildings, save some foundations hidden beneath the ground.

James IV added the magnificent Great Hall to the castle. This created an inner courtyard with the steep drop of the crag on the south side and the Church of St Mary's on the north side. The main royal apartments were situated in and around David's Tower, which formed the eastern block of the castle and its chief defence. David's Tower has now gone, but some of the residence remains. Here today you can still see the Regalia of Scotland – Pope Alexander VI, one of the famous Borgia family, gave the sceptre to James IV, and in 1507, another pope, Julius II, sent the Sword of State as a present to the king. The crown itself was remade by John Mossman, an Edinburgh goldsmith, in 1540.

James IV carried on his grandfather's interest in guns, and wished to increase his power and prestige. Robert Borthwick, with the help of foreign craftsmen, had already begun the manufacture of artillery in Edinburgh Castle. However, James also wanted to build a navy. At this time, ships were built as trading vessels and were not specifically designed for war. *The Margaret* was built in Leith in 1504 and launched the following year. During the year in which she was built, the council had ordered the repair of the harbour channel. James had bigger ideas and he needed deeper water, so he came to an agreement with the Abbot of Holyrood. The king exchanged some land near Linlithgow for a strip along the shore to the west of Leith. This became the king's Newhaven. Here, James IV built *The Great Michael*, the largest ship yet seen in Europe. The small fishing hamlet would suddenly have been transformed into a busy industrial site employing many people with differing skills. In 1511, Edinburgh acquired control of Newhaven.

The Battle of Flodden, 1513

James IV decided to attack England in support of France. The king summoned his forces to assemble on the Burgh Muir of Edinburgh, and the grand army marched south to attack the Border castles at Norham, Wark, Etal and Ford.

Meanwhile, the Earl of Surrey, who was responsible for the defence of the north of England, collected his troops and met the Scottish army in a strong position on Flodden Edge. The earl moved his army away from Flodden, tempting James to leave the high ground.

The English carried 8ft spears with an axe on the end – these were called halberds, or bills – while the Scots infantry was armed with long pikes, which proved difficult to handle on the wet ground. The English bills smashed the pikes and the Scottish army, which lacked leadership – the king being in the middle of the battle – collapsed. Scotland lost her king, nine earls and many members of her leading families. It is estimated that 10,000 Scots died that day. Many a citizen of Edinburgh met his end on Flodden Field, including Sir Alexander Lauder, Provost of Edinburgh since 1505, and his brothers, Sir

George and James Lauder. Four of the town's bailies were also killed that day. Flodden was the worst military disaster to ever befall Scotland.

A Dominican nunnery dedicated to St Catherine of Sienna was founded in 1517, and some of the ladies who entered the convent were the widows of men killed at Flodden. Part of this nunnery survived into the nineteenth century, but all that remains today is the name of the district – Sciennes.

After the defeat at Flodden, the council decided to build a wall to defend the south side of the burgh which was beyond the old wall. The new wall enclosed the properties in the Cowgate and the Grassmarket and was called the Flodden Wall. Some of the wall remains in Infirmary Street and on the Vennel leading from the Grassmarket. New ports (gates) were also constructed.

It is doubtful whether all this effort would really have saved the burgh from a determined attack, and the English took Edinburgh in 1544 despite the wall, which was too long to be able to provide guards at all points. This was the age of artillery when trained gunners could easily breach a stone wall.

James V and the Struggle for Power

Edinburgh was caught up in the struggle for power during the minority of James V. With the end of the regency of the Duke of Albany (the duke preferred to remain in France), the nobles began to struggle for power. By February 1525 the Earl of Arran and Margaret, the queen mother and sister of Henry VIII, held Edinburgh Castle, while the Earls of Angus and Lennox controlled the town. The following year, Angus had custody of the young king and used his power to ensure that his uncle, Archibald Douglas of Kilspindie, became Provost of Edinburgh again.

Finally, in May 1528, James V escaped from Edinburgh Castle, only to return in force at the beginning of July. Angus withdrew from the town just before the king's army arrived. Eventually he was forced to go into exile in England.

The English Party
The 1530s were uncertain times, with continued fear of the plague and preparations against a possible English attack. Henry VIII wanted a marriage alliance to give him control over Scotland, but James V, having been a prisoner of the pro-English Earl of Angus, did not wish to encourage English ambitions and preferred a French marriage. In 1532 the council offered to raise 300 armed men to support the king.

The Palace of Holyrood

James V added to his father's work at Holyrood by building the large northern tower. The work was begun in 1528 and completed four years later in 1532. Further apartments were constructed to the south of the tower. It must have been a busy site, for it contained not just the palace but the abbey and its church. The foundations of the abbey buildings lie under the late seventeenth-century palace and the lawn behind it. The abbey church was to remain the place of worship for the residents of the Canongate until the Canongate Church was completed in 1688.

The Court of Session

The king and his council formed a Court of Justice, but this body was too busy to handle the workload before it. James IV had created a Daily Council, but this also proved inadequate for the job.

In 1532 the Court of Session was set up by James V. It consisted of fifteen judges, although the king, who chose all the judges, was also able to add three or four nobles to their number. The court at this time was thus only partly staffed with those learned in the law. It sat for two terms – from 13 November to 12 March and from 12 June to 12 August. The court was to meet in Edinburgh, although the king had the final say in the matter.

Mary of Guise

James V, who had always favoured a French alliance, finally married Mary of Guise. The Guises were one of the most powerful families in France. Her brothers, the Duke of Guise and the Cardinal of Lorraine, had great influence at the French court. After the king's death in 1542, the Earl of Arran held the regency, but eventually Mary assumed control and, aided by her French connections, resisted the growth of the Protestant Reformation.

The First Printers in Edinburgh

In 1507 Walter Chepman, an Edinburgh merchant, formed a partnership with Andrew Millar to set up the first printing press in Scotland. This was to be the beginning of a business still carried out today in the city. Printing enabled books to be produced at a price that the wealthier people could afford. In the same year, at Noyonne in France, was born a man who was to have more influence on Scottish life than any of his compatriots. This Frenchman was John Calvin, and printed books now helped to spread the ideas of the Reformers.

The Burgh Muir

The Muir was still a mixture of forest and scrubland. It was probably also the home of various undesirable characters. The council came to an agreement with the king and set about leasing out large areas of the Muir. The new tenants had to build houses, cow byres and malt barns by Michaelmas 1512, as part of their tenancy. It has been suggested that the council allowed the inhabitants of the High Street to extend onto the street with wooden frontages, thus creating a market for the timber which was cleared from the Muir. Whatever the arguments for and against this, it must be remembered that nearly all the properties of the burgh were still built of wood.

Education in Edinburgh

Little is known about education in the early centuries of the burgh. However, when the Guild of Surgeons received recognition from the council one of its rules stated that all those wishing to take an apprenticeship in the guild had to be able to read.

In 1517 the town grammar school was situated in St Mary's Wynd. The council, as in other matters, took a monopolistic view. In 1520 they ordered that there were to be no other schools in the burgh. This suggests that some people must have been setting up private schools, taking potential pupils away from the town's grammar school. The council appointed the staff and inspected the school, and rival schools were not permitted without its sanction. In Leith, after the Reformation, South Leith Kirk Session took control of education.

Prizes in Leith

In 1523, some French soldiers brought some ships they had captured in to Leith. These 'prizes', as captured enemy ships were known, were bought by Robert Bertoun and his friends. Bertoun was obviously an inhabitant of Leith, and the Edinburgh Council complained that the right to purchase these ships belonged solely to the burgesses of Edinburgh. The matter was taken to court and the burgh won the case.

Sir Robert Logan, who owned the estate of Restalrig and was probably part of the group who bought the ships, protested against the decision, and little good it did him! This was not the first time that Bertoun had tried to get round the burgh's monopoly on trade. In 1517 a case against him was heard by the King's Council. He had been trying to import timber directly into Leith. Edinburgh had control of the business in Leith and were prepared to go to court to protect their monopoly. It is not surprising that the inhabitants of Leith resented the control the burgh held over their affairs.

The Early Protestants of Edinburgh

In 1534 the king wrote to his lords of council to express his concern at the circulation of 'books and tracts in the Scottish tongue which were heresy in favour of the sect of Luther'. Knox blamed Cardinal Beaton, but the initiative may well have come from the king. The cardinal began to take action against Protestants in Edinburgh. Firstly, he summoned Sir William Kirk, Adam Davies, Henry Cairns and John Stewart to Holyrood. The men all came from Leith. They were joined by William Johnston and the Edinburgh schoolmaster Henry Henderson. Beaton ordered the burning of various works written by them.

Worse was to follow. Later that year, David Stratoun and Norman Gourlay were hung and their bodies burnt at Greenside. Jeronimous Russell, a Franciscan friar, and a man named Kennedy, were burnt on Castlehill. These were the first citizens of Edinburgh to die for their Protestant beliefs. Castlehill seems to have been the site chosen to punish religious crimes and 'witches' were to suffer there as well.

The Protestant Party in Scotland received encouragement from England when Henry VIII had broken with Rome. One of the leading Scottish Protestants at this time was George Wishart. In March 1546, while he was visiting John Cockburn at his home in Ormiston, Lord Bothwell arrived to arrest him. With Cockburn were his brother-in-law, John Sandilands of Calder, and Alexander Crichton of Brunstane. Wishart was taken to Edinburgh Castle and held in prison before being sent to St Andrew's, where he was put to death.

Eight weeks later, St Andrew's Castle was captured and Cardinal Beaton was murdered by a group of Fife lairds. One of these men was William Kirkcaldy of Grange, who was to play a prominent role in the Reformation and the Marian Revolt. Later, these men were joined by John Knox.

Cockburn of Ormiston was also arrested and taken to the castle. However, he managed to escape. Cockburn and Crichton were both banished in 1548 but Sandilands seems to have remained in Scotland as, during the winter of 1555–56, he opened his house in Calder to John Knox.

In 1550 Adam Wallace, whom Knox in his book on the Reformation describes as 'a simple man, without learning but one that was zealous in godliness', was arrested at Ormiston. The officers may have believed they had captured the laird. Wallace was taken to Blackfriars and tried for heresy. He was burnt on Castlehill.

Law and Order

The bailies of the town were not only expected to keep order in their districts but also to act as deputy sheriffs. Fear of riots on the busy streets and in the crowded markets led the council to insist that booth holders had weapons in their stalls so that they could come to the aid of the authorities if a disturbance took place. Even quarrels between groups of children were being drawn to the attention of the magistrates, who feared that they might get out of hand and people would be hurt. Fathers and masters (if the youngster was an apprentice) were to be held responsible for their good behaviour.

Banishment from the town was a frequent punishment used against those whom the magistrates considered to be vagabonds. David Christison was banished for begging when they felt that he could actually work for a living. So too was an Irishman who sang and begged for money – an early busker!

The Craftsmen and the Council

Records of council meetings often begin, 'The provost, bailies and council sitting in judgement' or 'order that'. However, there are times, although not very often, when the craft deacons are also associated with their decisions. The council was run by a group of wealthy merchants who kept power to themselves. The deacons, who represented a large number of the prosperous inhabitants of the town (small businesses), were looking for representation on the council. This struggle was to continue into the eighteenth century.

A considerable disturbance broke out in the burgh towards the end of 1539. The initial cause of the dispute is unknown, however Alexander Spens, one of the bailies, brought certain accusations against the Deacon of the Fleshers. Other craft members and their deacons (William Sineberd, Andrew Galloway and David Kinlock are named) held a meeting to protest. Since the only source for the dispute is the Burgh Records we only hear the council's side of the story, but the craftsmen were convicted for making an 'insurrection and convocation [holding an illegal meeting]'. Since the council were the magistrates as well as the prosecutors in this case, it would appear the craftsmen never stood a chance.

Streets and Markets

In sixteenth-century Edinburgh the markets were regulated by the council. They fixed the prices of beer, wine and bread. At this time, only the wealthy merchants would have drunk the wine and thus the councillors could be accused of having a vested interest in this item. However, this was an age of monopoly and control over trade and their actions were not uncommon for the period. Certainly, some regulation was necessary to ensure that buyers were not being cheated. In 1544 John Maxton, who had a booth at the top of Halkerston Wynd, was appointed to sell measuring containers with the town's official mark.

Concern was expressed about some of the people found in the Meal Market. Council records refer to them as 'a multitude of vile, dishonest and miserable creatures' and recommended that the market be moved to 'some honest and convenient place where inhabitants may meet to buy and sell'. The town had its share of 'vagabonds' and orders were often made to have them removed. Since the council had no proper police force, it was not easy to ensure that their orders were carried out.

One of the major crimes of these times was the buying of goods to resell elsewhere at a profit. We would consider this a normal business practice now, but the authorities passed Acts against such activities – all goods had to be sold in the markets. In 1548 the council brought in a list of punishments for those selling eggs, butter and cheese outside the market. A second offence could lead to the seller spending four hours in irons at the Market Cross. Claret and white wine could only be sold up to a maximum price of 16d per pint.

Regulating Taverns

Taverns were an important part of burgh life; they were the only public meeting places at the time. At the beginning of 1544 the council set about regulating measures, taking 'consideration of the great fraud by the taverners and others by their wrong measures'. This appears to be part of a wider move to control measurements. The council also ruled that only burgesses or guild members should run taverns and they should pay the duties for the upkeep of St Anthony's Altar. It seems that some people were setting up taverns in their own houses to avoid the duties and restrictions. Although the measures protected the customers, they also protected the monopoly held by the burgesses and the guild of merchants over trade in the burgh.

The New Calsay

The 'calsay' was a term used to describe street paving. In 1532, the council made the decision to start to pave the High Street. Sand and stones were laid on what was called 'the calsay'. Paving must have made driving in the High Street much easier. It would also have been a help to those trying to keep it clean as the High Street, together with the Lawnmarket, was still the market place of Edinburgh.

John Mayser and Bertraham Foliot were given the task. They were responsible for the quarrying and dressing of the stones while the town undertook to provide the sand and the transport. The records fail to say exactly how much of the street was to be paved.

In 1542 the council ordered huts, such as pigsties, to be taken off the streets. The following year, Morris Crawford was awarded the contract to improve the surface of the Calsay from the Over Bow to the West Port.

The Hertford Raid, 1544

Henry VIII was not a man to stand back and see his plans to marry his son Edward to young Mary being thwarted by the new pro-French party. On Saturday, 3 May 1544, a large English fleet entered the Firth of Forth and anchored opposite the city. The English admiral sent out boats to take soundings in preparation for a landing. The Earl of Hertford, Henry VIII's brother-in-law (brother of Jane Seymour, Henry's third wife, and later made Duke of Somerset), led the force. Mary of Guise and Cardinal Beaton remained in Edinburgh.

On Sunday morning, English soldiers climbed down from their ships and into small boats in preparation for a landing. By 10 a.m., Hertford had landed 10,000 men – probably along the shore between Newhaven and Granton. They met with no resistance. By lunchtime the English had moved east and entered Leith. There, according to Knox in his book on the Reformation, they 'found tables covered, the dinners prepared, such abundance of wine and victuals'.

Hertford was reinforced on Monday with the arrival of 2,000 horsemen riding up from Berwick. He continued to meet with no resistance, save from the guns of the castle. Wednesday brought disaster as the English captured Edinburgh and set it alight; Holyrood, too, was burnt. Sir Simon Preston was forced to surrender Craigmillar Castle. Only Edinburgh Castle remained in the hands of the Scots. The English put some guns at the Butter Tron at the top of the Bow, but they made no impression on the castle.

Finally, the English withdrew to their ships, having achieved nothing save for the destruction of the town. However, this was the last time that the city was destroyed by an invading army, although, as we shall see, it was not the last time it was *captured* by an invading army. The long process of rebuilding began and even as late as 1548 concern was expressed about clearing up the burnt lands.

The Watch and the Defence of the Burgh

Following the Hertford disaster, the council decided set up a guard, or 'watch'. In 1545, a nightly watch of eight men patrolled the city looking for thieves, vagabonds and those trying to return from the Muir. These last had been exiled because they had been in contact with the 'pest'. This sounds more like a policing measure than an attempt to defend the city as it was a pitifully small force to cover such a large area.

In 1546 the watch consisted of ten armed men led by an officer. Another fifteen, the merchants paying for twelve and the crafts for the other three, were raised to act as a bodyguard to the provost.

Edinburgh was a walled town, except on the north side where the loch acted as a barrier, and ports (gates) were always a weak point. In 1547 all these ports were closed except the Netherbow Port, the West Port and the Kirk of the Fields Port. The road from the Netherbow led through the Canongate, around Calton Hill and down to Leith. It followed the line of the modern Easter Road. From the West Port the road turned north to St Cuthbert's before travelling west to Linlithgow and Stirling. Both these burghs were important centres of royal government.

The Kirk of the Fields Port was the entrance to the burgh for those who travelled from the south. The gatekeepers (porters) were to be armed. A night watch of twelve armed men was to meet at the Cross at 8 p.m. This was presumably to check that they were all there, as this was a conscript body with some inhabitants paying others to take their place; patrolling the burgh on a cold winter's night would not have been much fun.

The next year, the porters were reinforced by a guard of twenty-four men – twelve for the Netherbow and six each for the West Port and the Kirk of the Fields Port. The inhabitants of the burgh (usually referred to as the neighbours) were selected by the bailies to provide the watch. Failure to attend (in 1548 the watch met at the Tolbooth) could lead to a fine of 40 shillings (£2). The burgh was divided into quarters – north-east, north-west, south-east and south-west. A bailie oversaw the activities of his quarter and would receive the keys of the ports when they were closed at night.

The Battle of Pinkie and the Arrival of the French

The Earl of Hertford, now Duke of Somerset, was Lord Protector for the young English king, Edward VI. The French had helped the Scots to recapture St Andrew's Castle from the Protestants and an English army numbering about 16,000 men advanced towards Edinburgh. They were opposed by a Scottish force at Pinkie, near Musselburgh.

The Scots suffered a heavy defeat, but the English failed to move against Edinburgh. Among those killed was Mungo Tennant, the father of Francis Tennant who was later to hold the office of provost. The English remained in

Haddington where they could easily move against the town and its important Port of Leith as the sea offered the easiest way to bring in supplies or extra men. To counter the threat, the Scots, led by the Queen Regent Mary of Guise, sought further military help from France.

In June 1548, a large French fleet, reported as '120 sail', although most were small ships, was sighted in the Firth of Forth. They landed some 10,000 men in Leith, of which only 2,000 were French; the rest were made up of Swiss and Germans.

However, tension between the Scots and the French eventually broke into violence. George Tod had been given a gun to repair by a French soldier, but another Frenchman claimed that it belonged to him. A fight began. The two were arrested, but a well-armed French force appeared, driving the poorly armed citizens back. David Risk and David Barbour were killed in the Bow. James Hamilton, captain of the castle, was also killed before the French retired to their lodging in the Canongate.

Adam Otterburn of Redhall had been provost in 1522, 1528–32 and 1543–44. He was again elected as provost in 1547, despite accusations that he had surrendered the burgh to the Earl of Hertford in 1544 (there was little else he could have done without the means to resist the English). He acted as an ambassador for James V, who made him a judge in the new Court of Session. In 1547 Otterburn continued his role as an ambassador for the Scottish government. In 1548 he appears to have been with the French and Scottish forces facing the English at Haddington. It seems unlikely that Otterburn would have been involved directly in the fighting. Sir Thomas Palmer, who commanded the English forces, forwarded a letter to the Duke of Somerset, Lord Protector of Edward VI. This had been delivered to him by a spy who came from the Scottish camp. This spy reported that 'Otterburn is sore hurt in the head and his servant slain as he helped, some think by the Governor's [Earl of Arran] orders'. Was Provost Otterburn assassinated, or was he killed in a skirmish with the English?

Mary of Guise

In 1554, Mary of Guise, the mother of Mary, Queen of Scots, returned from France and took up the regency. She was French and a supporter of the Catholic Church. The Queen Regent lived in a house on the north side of Castlehill. The building was pulled down in 1846 to make way for the college and assembly hall of the new Free Church of Scotland. Eventually, this site was to be the meeting place of the General Assembly of the Church of Scotland and, for a short time, the home of the Scottish Parliament.

Living in Edinburgh, the queen took a considerable interest in the affairs of the burgh. Mary was faced with a weak financial position at a time when the English threat remained considerable. Edward VI had died replacing the Protestant regime with a Catholic pro-Spanish one and Mary Tudor was eventually to marry King Phillip of Spain. Between them, they ruled Spain, Portugal, Flanders, the Netherlands, England, Wales and Ireland. France needed the Scottish alliance if she was not to be isolated along the coast of western Europe. Control of the Port of Leith was not something that concerned just the merchant burgesses of Edinburgh; if Mary required military help from France Leith was the obvious place to land them.

The Queen Regent needed extra money to control the growing debt and she asked the council for a loan. This does not appear to have been a popular move as it was reported that 'the neighbours are obstinate to lend the same'.

In 1556, the queen and the council crossed swords over the appointment of the Water Bailie. He was the bailie for Leith and, unlike the other bailies, he was elected for life. The queen ordered the council to appoint John Little, while the council proposed Alexander Barron, son of the previous Water Bailie. John Little was chosen, but the queen was unhappy at the resistance offered by some of the council. She demanded that those who had failed to support John Little be removed from the council. However, the council did its best to keep on the right side of the regent. In December 1555 they bought spices, wax (for candles) and wine, paying the huge sum of £80; this at a time when £1 would buy 30lb of candles or 15 pints of wine! These were given as a present to the queen. Other gifts of wine and spices were to be made in the years that followed.

A powerful and influential figure in Edinburgh during these years was Henri Cleutin, Seigneur d'Oysel. He was the French Ambassador and advisor to the queen. Presents sent to the queen also included gifts for him.

Newhaven and the Mills

James IV had wanted to increase the power and prestige of the kingdom of Scotland. Part of his plan was to build a navy. He persuaded Holyrood Abbey to accept estates near Linlithgow in return for land west of Leith. Here, he had transformed a small fishing village into a busy shipbuilding centre. Edinburgh had purchased Newhaven, probably to prevent it becoming a rival trading port, but with their facilities along the Shore of Leith the port was not required and went into decline. However, in 1555 the council set aside £500 for the rebuilding of Newhaven.

We cannot be sure how many mills the town owned at this time. Mills were situated in the Village of the Water of Leith and they would also have owned

mills in Leith. The mills were 'farmed out' by the council, and the farmer of the mills paid a fixed sum and recovered this by collecting the rents. The council was saved the trouble of collecting the money and the farmer looked to collect more money than he paid to the council, resulting in profit. However, he was obliged to keep the mills in good repair.

In 1556, the farmer of the mills was James Lindsay. He must have been a man of considerable wealth for he offered to build a mill for the town's use. The new mill, with a house for the miller, became known as Lindsay's Mill. James Lindsay was also a prominent member of the council.

All the inhabitants of Edinburgh had to have their grain ground at one of the town's mills. Grain was used to make flour for bread and malt for the brewing of beer. The poor quality of the water meant that it was safer to drink a weak beer. James Lock, an Edinburgh maltman, brought 20 bols to be ground in one of the town's mills. The miller delayed starting the work to the annoyance of Lock. On 1 December, twelve armed men broke into the mill and removed the malt. This was taken to a mill at Cramond.

John Knox

John Knox arrived in Edinburgh at the end of September 1555. He lodged with a Protestant merchant called John Syme. He met John Erskine of Dun (an Angus laird) and David Forrest, master of the mint. Knox also received a visit from William Maitland of Lethington, who was to play a major role in Scottish politics, mainly as Secretary of State, for almost twenty years.

Knox left Edinburgh to visit John Erskine in Dun before coming to Mid Calder to stay with Sir James Sandilands. He received visits from Lord Erskine, the future Earl of Mar, and Lord James Stewart, who was to be Earl of Moray. Both men were to act as regent to the young James VI. Another visitor was Archibald Campbell, who was to become the 5th Earl of Argyll. Thus, at this time, Knox was building up connections with the leading supporters of the Reform movement.

Knox made visits to Edinburgh, where he preached in private houses – he made no direct challenge to the religious authorities by preaching in a church. However, John Hamilton, archbishop of St Andrew's, set up a commission to try Knox for heresy. The trial was scheduled to be held in Blackfriars on 15 May. No one expected Knox to attend, so it was a surprise when he arrived in Edinburgh on the day before the trial. Mary of Guise feared that this might lead to riots and ordered the archbishop to drop the prosecution. So, instead of standing trial Knox preached in the house of the Bishop of Dunkeld in the Cowgate. He continued to preach there for the next ten days.

Knox married Marjorie Bowes, possibly in Edinburgh, before returning to Geneva. Marjorie was 16 or 17, while Knox was about 35 years old. Though there was much support for the Protestant cause, the Queen Regent remained opposed to them. The Catholic presence in the burgh was strong enough to burn an effigy of Knox after his departure.

Officers of the Burgh

The chief officer of the burgh was the provost, and two very different groups of men filled this post. Some were men like Francis Tennand and William Craik, who were burgesses. They and their families had held offices on the council. Others, such as Lord Maxwell and Lord Seton, were powerful figures in the government of the country.

There were five bailies, but they do not appear to have attended meetings together. The Bailie of Leith, known as the Water Bailie, was a position given for life. The other bailies were elected, along with the provost and other officers, at the beginning of October. They were responsible for policing the four quarters of the burgh – north-east, north-west, south-east and south-west.

In 1555, Francis Tennand, a former provost, claimed that he had been told that the bailies of the previous year had 'in the box £1,200 or £1,800 of money by their offices'. These were huge sums of money for the time and it does seem improbable that the bailies had the opportunity to gain much from their office. Tennand, it has to be said, did not believe this.

Another office was that of dean of guild. The guild in question was the Merchants' Guild, and every man who operated a business in the burgh had to be a member. Those who produced work with their own hands were craftsmen and belonged to their own guilds. Every member of the council, save the provost, if he was a nobleman, and the two selected deacons were members of the Merchants' Guild. Through the guild, the merchants were able to maintain their control of the council and resist pressure for greater representation from the craft guilds.

The dean held the list of guild brothers. In 1547, he was ordered to give the names of all owners of taverns who were guild brothers to see if anyone who was not a member of the Merchants' Guild was running a tavern. He also held the keys to the charterhouse, in which the charters and records of the burgh were kept.

The final officer of the burgh was the treasurer, who was responsible for the burgh's money. He carried out the council's wishes and, in the burgh's records, is frequently instructed to make payments.

The council employed a common clerk. In 1559, Alexander Guthrie was named in the records as common clerk. He had first appeared two years earlier, carrying out a mission for the council, and may have held the post as early as 1557. His son and grandson were also to hold the position, and the three Alexander Guthries acted as common clerks for nearly a century.

Inflation

Trade in the town was strictly controlled, with goods being sold only at places specified by the council. Thus, in 1551 traders were reminded that poultry and wildfowl must be sold at the Market Cross and 'at no other place'. It must surely have been easier to carry the birds around and sell to customers on their own doorsteps.

Of course, traders from beyond the burgh would have to pay for the right to sell their goods in the markets of Edinburgh. The council prohibited the buying of goods to be resold at a profit. For instance, Robert Likke spent three hours in irons at the Market Cross for reselling butter.

As already seen in the previous decade, they had come down on the taverns by setting standard measures. In 1551, they fixed prices and weights for the candlemakers. However, they also protected the candlemakers' monopoly by ordering the fleshers to sell their tallow only to the people of Edinburgh and their candlemakers, and not to 'strangers and inhabitants of other towns'.

The standard loaf cost 4d, but its weight varied. This was fixed by the council, who also stipulated that the bread brought into the burgh should weigh more than that produced by local baxters. Thus, bread from outside was actually cheaper, although this does not seem to have concerned the Edinburgh baxters who never raised this price difference with the council.

In the summer of 1551, the 4d loaf weighed 20oz, while the loaf baked outside Edinburgh was 4oz heavier. Ale – most people drank this rather than risk the water – cost 3d per pint. Prices continued to remain low, with the 4d loaf weighing 30oz in 1553. However, the warnings were already starting to appear, with a shortage of cheese and butter, and it was not long before other foodstuffs were affected. Even the Privy Council expressed concern when, in 1556, the 4d loaf was reduced in weight to only 14oz – they set the weight at 17oz. By 1560, the 4d loaf weighed only 15oz, although it did rise to 18oz, and ale now cost 4d a pint.

The trend was to continue, despite efforts to control prices. Eighteen years later, the price of ale had doubled and the humble 4d loaf had dropped to 12oz. By 1617, a pint of ale cost 14d and the 4d loaf was replaced by one costing 12d and weighing only 14oz.

Seven

THE REFORMATION

On 24 April 1558, Mary, Queen of Scots married Francis Valois, the heir to the French throne. Many people, particularly those looking to reform the Church, feared that Scotland might become just a province of France.

The following month saw a big meeting in the Tolbooth. The people of Edinburgh feared an imminent English invasion and asked the Queen Regent to appoint people of standing to order the burgh defences. Various names, including the Earl of Bothwell, the Earl of Morton and Lord Glencairn, were put forward. At this time the provost, Lord Seaton, was in France attending the wedding of the queen. He was one of the major opponents of the Reformers and a loyal supporter of Mary of Guise and her daughter.

The council ordered stone walls to be placed across the foot of the closes on either side of the High Street. The burgh sent its money to the castle for safety, and the Church of St Giles did the same. Both the merchants and craftsmen raised forces of over 700 men each for the defence of the burgh.

During the summer, the statue of St Giles was broken. A replacement was hurriedly made for a procession through the High Street on 1 September, attended by the Queen Regent. Banners were carried and tabors, trumpets and bagpipes provided the music.

On 17 November, Mary Tudor died and the Protestant Elizabeth succeeded to the English throne. Many Catholics did not recognise the Boleyn marriage and, thus, the legitimacy of the new queen. The next in line to the English throne was Mary, Queen of Scots.

The Church in Edinburgh

At this time, the burgh had two collegiate churches – St Giles and Trinity College. The collegiate churches contained altars where prayers and Masses were said for the souls of the founders and their patrons. In Edinburgh these were usually the families of rich burgesses or the members of the craft guilds.

The priests in the college were headed by a man holding the title of provost (but confusingly not the same position as the head of the burgh council).

There was also St Mary's Church in the Castle, but by the middle of the sixteenth century this was probably only used by the garrison and other employees of the castle. Two other churches were situated close to the burgh. St Cuthbert's, at the west end of the Nor' Loch, was an ancient foundation which included Macbeth as one of its patrons. Much of the northern part of modern Edinburgh belonged to the parish of St Cuthbert's, and the present church was built on the site of the old church. The other church was St Mary's in the Fields, better known as Kirk O' Fields. It stood close to the junction of South Bridge and Chambers Street, where the university is today. It was a collegiate church.

At the Reformation, the Reformers generally took over the old churches, and the burgh agreed to pay the former provost John Pennycuke £1,000 for Kirk O' Fields in 1563, but they were unable to close the agreement. The Hamiltons had their town house to the south of Kirk O'Fields.

Outside the burgh, the Church of St Columba, in Cramond, belonged to the Bishop of Dunkeld. While at Corstorphine, the church was supported by the wealthy Forrester family. It was dedicated to St John the Baptist, and at some time during the middle of the fifteenth century it became a collegiate church.

The ancient church of Duddingston was under the authority of Kelso Abbey, and Holyrood Abbey had been given the church at Liberton in its founding charter.

The Church of the Holy Trinity and the Virgin Mary at Restalrig was founded by James III and continued to receive royal support. Its parish included South Leith and the lands of the Logans of Restalrig. The well of the ancient Scottish St Triduana stood near the church. Other churches were taken over by the Reformers, but the first General Assembly of the Church of Scotland ordered its destruction and South Leith Church, founded sometime around 1490, became the parish church for South Leith and Restalrig.

A chapel was founded in North Leith in 1493 but only became a parish church in 1609. James IV had built a chapel at Newhaven dedicated to the Virgin and St James but it fell into ruins. Currie Kirk had belonged to the Archdeaconry of Lothian, and at the time of the Reformation the patronage fell into the hands of the Burgh of Edinburgh. Thus, the affairs of the parish of Currie fell into the hands of the burgh council.

The Virgin Mary was a revered figure in medieval times. Chapels dedicated to her were to be found in Portsburgh, Niddrie Wynd and St Mary's Wynd. Mary of Guise had her own private chapel in her palace which stood near what is today the top of the Mound.

A chapel dedicated to St Roque was built on the Burgh Muir. The Muir was used as a place to isolate plague victims. The cemetery of the chapel was the burial place of those who died of the plague while in exile on the Muir.

In these times, hospitals were not places for the sick but homes for the elderly poor of the burgess community. East of Greyfriars was the chapel and hospital of St Mary Magdalene. Arnot states that it provided a home for a chaplain and seven poor men of the 'hammermen craft'. The Hospital of Our Lady was situated in Leith Wynd near Trinity College Church. It was the home of twelve poor people. Later, the council used the property as a workhouse and it became known as St Paul's Work.

At the time of the Reformation, Edinburgh had three friaries. The Carmelite friary, situated at Greenside on the slope of Calton Hill, was founded in 1526. Greyfriars was the home of the Franciscans, and the largest and most important was the Dominican friary of Blackfriars, situated in the Cowgate. The friars were a particular target for the wilder elements among the Reformers. On 1 January 1559, notices to quit were placed on the doors of friaries throughout Scotland. This became known as the Beggars' Summons, since it demanded that the friars quit their buildings in favour of the poor and the sick. Friday, 12 May was to be 'Flitting Day'.

The wealthiest foundation in Edinburgh was the abbey of the Augustine canons at Holyrood. It owned large estates, especially in the north of the present city. Broughton, Canonmills, the Canongate and North Leith all belonged to the abbey. James IV had built a palace there and his son had added to it. The abbey church was the place of worship for the citizens of the Canongate until the reign of James VII, when it was used for Catholic worship.

Leith had a community of canons dedicated to St Anthony. Their monastery stood near the foot of Leith Walk. A new foundation was the nunnery of St Catherine of Sienna, which gradually fell into ruins after the Reformation. It is from this nunnery that the district of Sciennes received its name. Another nunnery dedicated to St Mary of Placentia – thus giving the name Pleasance to a district of Edinburgh – appears to be totally fictitious.

John Knox

The most famous minister of Edinburgh was John Knox. He had been associated with George Wishart and was one of those captured by the French when they took the castle of St Andrew's after the murder of Cardinal Beaton. There, he met Sir William Kirkcaldy of Grange, one of the leading Protestant lairds who had brought about the Reformation. Knox spent years in exile, before returning to Scotland as the crisis which led to the Reformation deepened. He was even corresponding with William Cecil, Queen Elizabeth's Secretary of State. In a

letter of October 1559, he used the pen name 'John Sinclair'. Sinclair himself was Dean of Restalrig and a leading opponent of the Reformation.

At the end of June 1560, the Lords of the Congregation entered Edinburgh, and on 7 July John Knox was installed as minister of the burgh. Any suggestion that the burgesses should choose their religion by vote was rejected by the Reformers. There was a strong Catholic Party in the burgh led by the provost, Lord Seaton. Once in Edinburgh, the Lords of the Congregation made contact with the English, and in particular with Sir Henry Percy and William Cecil, Queen Elizabeth's Secretary of State. Sir William Kirkcaldy of Grange wrote letters in July to both Percy and Cecil.

John Knox played an important part in the negotiations. In a fortnight, he wrote twice to Cecil and once to Percy. He even wrote to Queen Elizabeth, trying to heal the rift between them. In August, he attended a secret meeting on Holy Island which Sir Henry Percy described in his report to Cecil: 'Mr Knox arrived in Holy Island so without any secrecy that it is openly known in both England and Scotland'.

In 1562 Knox was joined by John Craig, formerly minister of the Canongate, as second minister. The return of Mary, Queen of Scots increased the tension between Church and State. There could be no meeting of minds between the young queen, who was a devoted Catholic holding Mass in Holyrood, and the man who had served the Reformers for most of his adult life. To Knox, the saying of the Mass was an outrage.

Where did John Knox live in Edinburgh? His first manse in Edinburgh was the former lodgings of the Abbot of Dunfermline. When he first came to town, David Forrester had paid his expenses, for he is recorded as being repaid by the council. Did Knox ever live in the house named after him? The house certainly dates from the right period, but it appears to have belonged to an Edinburgh goldsmith called James Mossman. It is possible that Mossman rented part of the house to the burgh as lodgings for their minister. There is no contemporary evidence connecting the house with Knox. It is not until the beginning of the nineteenth century that people began to believe this was the manse of John Knox. Twice, in 1561 and in 1564, the council ordered the treasurer to pay Robert Mowbray, the heritor of the house occupied by John Knox. In 1569, he is recorded as occupying John Adamson's house.

The Growing Crisis: Summer 1559

With the threat of disorder fermented by the Protestants, the Queen Regent, Mary of Guise, asked the provost and the council to ensure that order was kept. On 19 April, Alexander Barroun, one of the bailies, and Alexander Guthrie, the burgh clerk, were arrested and placed in the Tolbooth by the order of the provost, Lord Seaton. The council asked for an explanation, but the provost's reply that they were held 'in prison for certain reasons known to him' naturally failed to satisfy them. He sent a further message ordering them to put Adam Dickson and two sons of Thomas Thomson in irons. In May, Seaton had a second bailie, David Forrester (a known Protestant, as he later gave John Knox financial aid), arrested and placed in the castle. These arrests appear to be an attempt by the provost to weaken the Reform Party in the burgh. However, the removal of two bailies and the town clerk must have seriously weakened the administration of the burgh at a time when civil war threatened to break out in the country.

There were already murmurs of discontent on the streets. Matthew Stewiston was accused of throwing stones at the windows of the friaries. The Church officials were worried too. They asked John Charteris, the dean of guild, to take into his care the jewellery and silver ornaments of the high altar, but he refused as he only had his wife and women servants to protect them. They were eventually distributed among the councillors, although it would surely have been safer to send them to the castle.

It was decided to lock all the ports and restrict entry to the town to the West Port and the Netherbow. A guard of twelve armed men was appointed to keep order at these gates. They could certainly control entry into the burgh but would have been insufficient men to stop a determined assault. A company of twenty-four armed men were to patrol the streets at night. Towards the end of June these precautions were increased by setting up a guard of sixty men to protect St Giles.

By 20 June 1660 the Lords of the Congregation, as the leaders of the Reformers became known, had reached Linlithgow and a delegation set out from Edinburgh to negotiate with them. The bailies took charge of the keys of the ports – Netherbow, Water Yets (by Trinity College Church), Kirk O' Fields, Greyfriars, Cowgate and West Port.

The French remained secure behind their defences in Leith. The death of King Henry now made Francis II not only King of France but, through his wife, King of Scots. The French were therefore prepared to increase their forces in Scotland and Leith offered them a safe port. On 25 October, Knox wrote to Sir James Croft, Captain of Berwick, that any plans to attack the French in Leith had been abandoned through want of soldiers and money.

A new council was elected at the beginning of October, with Archibald Douglas of Kilspindie returning as provost. Three of the four bailies, John Preston, Adam Fullerton and Edward Hope, had served as members of Kilspindie's council of 1555–56. James Barroun, the former dean of guild from that council, returned to office. Only the treasurer, James Lindsay, remained

in place. This should not be seen as a purge on the council by the Reformers as bailies normally served for just a year. When Adam Fullerton left to visit England, John Spens, a bailie on the previous council, was summoned to replace him.

With a large well-trained force facing them in Leith, the Lords of the Congregation were forced to abandon Edinburgh. A report to Cecil by his agent in the burgh stated that the Queen Regent returned on 7 November, 'but most of the inhabitants have fled with bag and baggage and put their best stuff in the castle'. Lord Erskine, however, refused to give up control of the castle, claiming he had been appointed by Parliament and thus only Parliament could dismiss him.

The Siege of Leith, 1560

The English decided to intervene on the side of the Protestants. The Duke of Norfolk took overall command of the expedition, although he remained in England. Admiral Winter, on *The Lyon*, reached the Forth in the last week of January. Forts on Inchkeith and at Leith and Burntisland fired on the English ships, and by the middle of April his force had increased to twenty-nine ships, although most of them were probably quite small. He was considering an attack on Inchkeith, which he felt was poorly defended.

On 6 April, an English army estimated at 10,000 men entered Scotland. They advanced on Edinburgh. Four days later, the English established their first camp on the high ground above Leith at Restalrig. The Duke of Norfolk had given orders not to besiege the castle. He did not believe Queen Elizabeth would wish to put the dowager (Mary of Guise) in danger, nor did he wish to turn Lord Erskine, the governor of the castle, into an enemy. The Scots were more concerned with the French in Leith and would have been alienated by what they considered a diversion.

The following day, cavalry from both sides came into contact before the French withdrew behind their defences in Leith. The port was protected by a 30ft wall of earth and stone designed to absorb the cannonballs of any attacking force. The French had also placed guns on the steeples of St Anthony's and St Nicholas. The town was defended by 3,500 French and 500 Scottish soldiers.

The English set about constructing two fortified batteries linked with trenches. Mr Pelham and his pioneers built a battery on the rising ground south of Hermitage Place. The mounds on the Links appear to be natural features and not gun emplacements, as the Pelham Fort shown on a map of the siege is placed further south. The second battery in North Leith was not completed until 11 May.

After a week (probably 18 April) the English grew slack. Some of them even left their lines to visit Edinburgh. French cavalry and infantry broke out of Leith and drove the English from their trenches. However, they counter-attacked and the French were driven back into Leith. Both sides lost between 140–160 men killed or wounded. Obviously, there must have been some criticism of the failure to push home the attack on Leith, for Lord Grey informed the Duke of Norfolk, 'This opinion of our slackness is wrongful, for no day escapes or almost a night but we lose some blood and distress our enemies'.

On 30 April, a large fire started in south-west Leith, destroying as much as a third of the town. This appears to have been an accident and not due to enemy fire. It is credit to the defenders that they got it under control and continued holding the town.

Two assaults on Saturday, 4 May, using over 5,000 men, failed to make a significant breach in the wall. The French soon repaired the damaged sections of the wall. However, they did abandon the mills, which were situated outside their defences where the Water of Leith flowed into the town. Lord Grey complained that his men were 'raw soldiers without skill'. Most of the English soldiers were probably levies from the northern counties lacking the technical knowledge to handle a siege. The attack cost the English 1,000 men dead or wounded.

A massive attack was put in on 6 May. This involved using 2,700 men to attack the defences in North Leith while 3,750 men were deployed south of the river. The aim was to make breaches in several places on the upper parts of the wall and then to use scaling ladders to allow the soldiers to climb through these holes. The English made some breaches in the wall but their ladders proved to be too short to take advantage of the situation and the French drove them back. According to Knox, Sir James Croft was to lead an attack along the shore from the west. This he failed to do. In the official report, Sir James was to look after the artillery on the north side of the river.

The consequence for the attacking force was serious since they were reduced to only 4,500 men fit for action. Powder was so short that they had to borrow it from the ships. While Lord Grey was trying to assure Cecil that the losses were not as bad as rumour would have it, Sir Ralph Saddler was informing Norfolk that the men were 'more likely to mutiny or desert us than do good service'.

And what of the French? They must also have taken heavy losses, for they made no attempt to follow up their success. D'Oysel had a large force but they had to be fed; they would no doubt be low on ammunition and, unlike their enemies, they had no way of bringing supplies into the port. On 12 May, a group of French soldiers who were foraging for shellfish on the shore were caught by the English cavalry. That night an attack was made on the English trenches but it was repelled.

The English changed tactics. They gave up plans for a direct assault on the walls and began digging mines. Tunnels were to be dug beneath the walls and then the supports removed. They would cave in and hopefully the wall above would collapse into the tunnel. They began digging three mines. One was aimed at the area known as the Citadel (in North Leith close to where the later Cromwellian Citadel was built) but the ground proved difficult and progress was slow. A second mine was directed towards St Anthony's, at the most southerly point in the wall. The third mine was dug from the Pelham Battery under the Links and probably directed towards the wall near the kirk.

On 6 June, Sir Henry Percy informed Norfolk that he had contacted D'Oysel, who wanted him to come into Leith to begin negotiations. In the *Calendar of Scottish Papers* Vol. 1, D'Oysel complained of 'the ill treatment of our soldiers by Lord Grey', and continued by saying, 'I would rather we the nobility should fall into the hands of Sir Henry than taste the cruelty of Lord Grey'.

On 11 June, Mary of Guise died in Edinburgh Castle. She had given much of her life to the securing of the French cause and the succession of her daughter. It is one of the strange ironies of history that she should die in the middle of a war with the country that her grandson would one day rule.

June 17 brought a ceasefire, allowing negotiations to continue. Finally, on 6 July at a meeting in Edinburgh, a treaty was concluded. French and English troops were to withdraw from Scotland. leaving the Scottish nobility and the Reformers in charge of the country. On 5 December 1560, Francis II, King of France and husband of Mary, Queen of Scots, died. He had never been strong and his death was to mark the end of the 'Auld Alliance'.

Neither the French nor the English could claim victory in the Siege of Leith. The French had built a strong defensive wall round Leith using the latest technology. They were probably the more skilled soldiers, most of whom were professionals. However, with the English ships controlling the Forth and much of the country hostile to them, they were trapped in Leith. The English lacked soldiers of the same quality as the French and did not have the overwhelming numbers necessary to overcome the well-defended positions around Leith. The attack on 6 May showed a failure in leadership, since an attack on breaches using inadequate ladders can only be put down to bad decision making. In a letter to Queen Elizabeth written on 17 June, William Cecil places the blame on Sir James Croft: 'Sir James Croft, I am sorry to find so apparent matter, his neglect of duty was the principal [cause for] the loss of the town'. This seems a harsh judgement since it was Lord Grey, and not Sir James, who had overall command of the siege.

Edinburgh Under the Reformed Church

Parliament met in Edinburgh in August and the authority of the Pope over the Church in Scotland was brought to an end. It became illegal to celebrate the Mass.

A confession of faith was drawn up, and superintendents, elected for three years, were to be responsible for each diocese. Scotland was to have ten of these, and they were expected to travel throughout their diocese, preaching and supervising the ministers. Knox, however, claiming ill health, declined to become a superintendent. His wife, Marjorie, had died five or six weeks before the end of the year and he was left with a young family.

Before the end of 1560 the first General Assembly of the Church of Scotland met in Edinburgh, and the 'First Book of Discipline' was signed in January 1561.

Preaching became the centre of church life, so that large churches like St Giles had to be partitioned. Without modern sound systems, it would have been impossible for a minister to project his voice over such a distance in a long sermon.

Trinity College Church continued to serve the north-east parish. Other churches, outside the old burgh, were taken over by the Reformers, except for Restalrig; the assembly ordered it to be closed and the parishioners to attend the Church of South Leith. The collegiate Church of St Mary in the Fields (Kirk O' Fields) also appears to have also been closed.

Laws Against Immorality

Early in June, even before the Reformation Parliament met in Edinburgh, the Reformers on the council set about controlling morals. Those people found keeping idols (crucifixes, statues of saints, etc.), brothel keepers and prostitutes were to appear before the minister or the elders and promise to reform. The first offence led to the offenders being carried through the town in a cart. For a second offence, the culprit was branded and exiled from the burgh. A third offence was final, for those convicted could be hung. Persons caught swearing were to be set in irons. Strict rules for the Sabbath were proclaimed to ensure that everyone attended the morning and afternoon services to hear the sermons. Markets and other sales from street booths were banned on Sunday. Taverns and other hostelries were forbidden to serve food or drink during the times of the services. A strict warning was given to women serving in taverns who in previous years had offered more than meals and drinks.

The Sabbath and the Kirk

Sunday was to be kept for the study of the scriptures – both by attending sermons and studying the catechism at home. The council passed laws to control activities on the Sabbath. Markets and every kind of selling were forbidden. Everyone was expected to attend the morning and afternoon sermons. Taverns and hotels were to be closed during the time of sermons. The Sunday Fleshmarket was moved to Saturday.

The new Church may have come into conflict with the monarchy but, in Edinburgh at least, the ministers did not speak out against the rulers of the burgh who, it has to be said, called them to their churches and were responsible for their stipends. Inflation and food shortages led some ministers to ask for rises in their salaries while the council struggled to raise the money from the congregations.

The Riot of November, 1560

In November 1560, the first test of the new laws occurred when John Sanderson, the Deacon of the Fleshers, was caught in an affair with Margaret Lyell. Sanderson was sentenced to be carried through the town in a cart and then to be banished. The craft deacons objected and the affair led to a riot by some of the craftsmen of the burgh. John Rynd (a pewterer), John Sanderson, William Wycht (a cutler) and James Fraser (a saddler) were arrested for organising the riot. The Privy Council took action and ordered them to be imprisoned in the castle.

The representatives of the fourteen crafts were called before the council. They pleaded that they had taken no part in the riot, which they claimed was caused 'by wicked members'. They promised that in future all their members would keep the law. To show there was no ambiguity, the council brought in new laws. When a craftsman was accused of breaking the law the craft was forbidden from holding a meeting to raise support for him. Craftsmen were made responsible for their servants.

The whole affair illustrates two recurring themes in the governance of the town. The council wished to run the burgh on the strict ethics of the Puritan Protestants. For some two centuries they struggled to protect the Sabbath. The council itself was chosen from the merchant elite of the burgh. They had no wish to share their power with the representatives (deacons) of the craftsmen. In this they were to prove spectacularly successful, holding onto power until the Reform Act of 1832.

The 'Robin Hood' Riot

One of the popular activities of late medieval Edinburgh was the 'game' of Robin Hood. It was an opportunity for the apprentices and youth of Edinburgh to let off steam and enjoy themselves. This, to use modern terms, was not necessarily the image of the burgh the Reformers wished to project. Such events naturally led to some disorder. On Sunday (probably 9 May 1561) a band of craft servants and apprentices entered the Netherbow with banners, armour and weapons. They marched up the High Street to Castlehill and then marched down again, taking possession of the Netherbow Port. These high spirits led to some of the apprentices being locked up in the Tolbooth.

The following year, the council received a letter from the queen instructing them to ensure that no one was chosen as Robin Hood, Little John or the Abbot of Unreason. She considered it to be an excuse to cause a disturbance.

The Arrival of Mary, Queen of Scots

On 19 August 1561, Mary landed in Leith. She had made a fast passage from Calais and her early arrival surprised everyone. She was given hospitality by a rich merchant of Leith, called Lamb. This was not in the present-day Lamb's House, which was built some sixty years later. Eventually she entered the burgh and a small boy of 6 years old presented her with a Bible, a psalter and the keys to the town.

The Tolbooth

In 1385 Richard II had captured Edinburgh and set fire to the burgh. After this it is believed that a new tolbooth was built. A further destruction by the Earl of Hertford in 1544 may have damaged this building.

The summer of 1560 saw the Tolbooth used by the Privy Council as a place to hold its prisoners. The building was also used as a school, a tolbooth (a place where the council met and worked), a prison and the burgh clerk's chambers. If that was not enough, the Tolbooth had to provide room for the Court of Session.

Faced with this demand for more space, the council decided to use St Giles. James Barron, the dean of guild, was ordered to build a wall, a foot thick, partitioning off the west end of the kirk (in those days there was no great western door). It is thought that this might have had two storeys, for in 1560 there is a reference in November of that year to the council meeting in 'the Over Council House of the Tolbooth of this burgh'.

In June 1561, the youths involved in the craft riot were held in the Over Tolbooth, while in September of the same year the council met in the Tolbooth. 'The Tolbooth' refers to council business premises and not necessarily one building.

The situation was complicated when the newly arrived queen wrote to the council in February 1562. 'The Queen's Majesty understands that the Tolbooth of the Burgh of Edinburgh is ruinous' and ordered them to take 'down the said tolbooth' and to provide room for the Lords of Session, justice and sheriff courts. Action followed immediately with David Somer's appointment. He began to remove slates from the roof.

Six hundred marks was to be spent on the Tolbooth and on the other tolbooth at the west end of the kirk for the Lords of Session. Timber from the Old

Tolbooth was to be used to further this work. By April, work must have slowed down because the Lords of Session were threatening to move to St Andrew's. In July, the building seems to have been finished, as the council met in the new tolbooth. However, by now the work had stopped as funds were exhausted. In fact, it was not until December that William Currour received £100 for the land on which the new tolbooth was built as part of his payment.

Work started again in February 1563 when David Somer was ordered to use stones from the old chapel in the Nether Kirkyard. There is no mention of using stones from the Old Tolbooth. By June that year, the council were forced to borrow 1,000 marks to complete the building. The future income of the town mills was used as security. At the same time, there is an order to repair the tower of the Old Tolbooth and make it watertight. Thus, it would appear that by the mid-1560s there were three buildings used as a tolbooth.

The Old Tolbooth became increasingly used as a prison. In 1575, repairs were made to the tower, the jailor's house and the prison 'in the Old Tolbooth'. Hugo Arnot certainly believed the Old Tolbooth was built in 1561, but it seems improbable that in less than fifteen years it should be referred to as 'old' or those extensive repairs were required. It would appear that, faced with a considerable demand for space, the council did not pull down the Old Tolbooth but continued to use it mainly as a prison. It must be remembered that it not only housed those who were convicted of crimes in the city but also those seen by the Privy Council as enemies of the state.

So what did David Somer build? For what was the money raised used? There must surely have been a third building. This third building is referred to as the 'Councilhouse'. Regulating meetings in December 1576, it was ordered that the council should meet in the Councilhouse at two hours before noon. This was a separated building in the south-west corner of Parliament Square.

Greyfriars

By April 1561, the kirkyard no longer had space and a new burial ground was needed. The former lands of the Grey Friars were suggested to the council as a suitable place. James Watson, the dean of guild, was instructed to check the property and repair the walls. The council seem to have considered that the property belonged to the burgh and they could do what they wanted with it, but it cannot have been granted to them by the queen, as she did not arrive in Scotland until August. In fact it was not until August of the *following* year that the queen granted Greyfriars to the burgh as a burial ground.

Much of the repair work cannot have been completed, because Alexander Guthrie, as dean of guild, was asked to repair the wall and put a door on the front entrance. In fact, by the summer of 1563 there were plans afoot to build a hospital in the old Blackfriars. Things had gone so far that three men were appointed to oversee the work, while another group were asked to draw up plans.

The Council Elections, 1561

In October, the queen's government began to take an interest in the burgh's affairs. This may have been provoked by a proclamation of banishment against priests, monks, friars and other supporters of the Pope. The order of the council was read at the Market Cross. The queen's letter ordered the council and 'community of the burgh to meet in the Tolbooth and remove the provost, Archibald Douglas of Kilspindie, and the bailies from office'.

The new election became complicated because most of the deacons refused to be involved since they objected to the rights of the assessors to vote. However, such matters never affected the merchants on the council and they immediately went on to elect Thomas Makcalyeane as provost.

Having completed the election, Neill Laing appeared with a message from William Maitland of Lethington, the queen's Secretary of State. In it the queen proposed three names for the position of provost – Lord Seyton, Alexander Erskine and Simon Preston of Craigmillar. David Kinloch, Deacon of the Baxters, who had led the protest against the assessors, used the opportunity and claimed that he would obey the queen's will. It would appear on this occasion that the council had their way, because Makcalyeane remained in the post of provost.

William Robertson and the High School

In April 1562, the council expressed concern at 'the great corruption of the youth by Master William Robertson, master of the grammar school being an obstinate papist'. They wrote to Lord James Stewart (later Earl of Moray) asking him to use his influence to ensure the office went to a 'learned and qualified man and to try to persuade the queen to grant them the lands of the friars [presumably Blackfriars]'.

Three days later, William Robertson turned up with evidence that he had been given the office by the Abbot of Holyrood. The council wanted more information. The case dragged on until June when the council ordered him to be removed from his post.

However, William Robertson had no intention of going. On 22 July he came before them with his grant signed by the abbot, sealed by the chapter and dated 1546. He then handed them a list of names supporting his case. John Moscrop, counsel for the burgh, changed direction and began to question whether Robertson was qualified to hold the post. It would appear that the council was not only prosecuting the case but they were also judging in the matter. The odds were stacked against Robertson. A board of experts, which included John Craig, minister of the Canongate and later assistant to John Knox, were appointed to examine his teaching.

The case then moved on to a technicality. The abbot had been only 14 years old at the time of the gift and thus a minor. It was not until October that the council finally dismissed Robertson, claiming he had little knowledge of Latin or Greek. William Robertson had been in the post for sixteen years and it would have been extraordinary that, if this were true, no protest had arisen earlier.

However, filling the post was to prove difficult. In February 1563 they sent a message to James White, a Scotsman living in London, inviting him to take the post. The mission does not appear to have been a success because a year later, in the council records, William Robertson is still referred to as 'Master of the High School'.

The council employed a new tactic to remove this troublesome man – they stopped paying him. Robertson was not a man to give up, however, and by then he had found a new ally. Various letters arrived from the queen, and a stern letter of February 1564 pointed out that Robertson had a lawful grant from the Abbot of Holyrood and had by then held his post uninterrupted for eighteen years. She was concerned at the harassment of the master 'for what cause we know not'.

Neither side seemed willing to touch the real issue – William Robertson was a Catholic. The queen complained of them 'intending to put another in his place against our express mind and will'. Another letter arrived in December demanding that he should be paid. It was not until May 1565 that the council gave way and the treasurer was ordered to pay Robertson. In fact, he continued in office, as he is then recorded as being paid for the Whitsun term of 1566.

Nothing further is heard of the matter until July 1568, when Alexander Guthrie was sent to St Andrew's to offer the post to Thomas Buchquhennane. Had William Robertson retired, or had the new regime (the regency of the Earl of Moray) enabled them to remove him? We will never know.

The Kirk of the Field

In August 1562, the queen had promised to provide land for a hospital and a school once the council had money to carry out the building. The following March, Bailie John Spens, Andrew Murray, and John Preston, the town treasurer, were instructed to meet with John Pennycuke. Pennycuke was the former provost of the collegiate Church of St Mary's in the Fields. They were to discuss the position of the kirk and buildings, probably with a view to the town purchasing them.

The negotiations appear to have reached a conclusion in June 1563 when, according to the Burgh Records, Pennycuke sold the kirk and buildings to the council: 'John Pennycuke sells and disposes to the good town the whole building sometime called the Kirk of Field both old and new with kirkyard with lodgings, buildings, mansions, yard, duties pertaining to the provost and prebendaries'.

Despite this, Pennycuke appears to have acted as if he owned the property. In August 1564 no agreement had been reached, but the council were worried for they had heard that Pennycuke was dismantling the church and planning to sell off the stones. These, the council had hoped, could be used to build a hospital or college (university).

However, the plot thickened. In December 1566, according to the Register of the Privy Seal, the property was acquired by Sir James Balfour of Pittendreich 'by the resignation of William Pennycuke, the last provost'. Knox states that he bought the kirk and the houses.

All this would probably be of little interest but for the fact that in February of 1567 Lord Darnley, husband of Mary, Queen of Scots, was murdered there. Why *did* Sir James Balfour of Pittendreich want the Kirk of the Field?

The Markets

The whole main street, High Street and Lawnmarket was one market place. The council and many of the inhabitants of the burgh were concerned with the crowds congregating in the Lawnmarket during market days. At this time the main entrance to the town from the west was through the Bow and into the Lawnmarket. This passage was being blocked by the booths and shoppers. Since the lands around Niddrie Wynd were not inhabited at this time, the council decided to move the market for wool, skins and hides to that area.

The Poor

The queen wrote to the council noting the daily increase of the poor and instructing them to see that the inhabitants of the burgh pay their dues for the upkeep of the poor. The letter was presented by one of the burgesses, Adam Fowleston, who told them that they should not be offended if he complained to the queen and the Privy Council of their failure (a polite threat!). Interestingly, this discussion about charity took place on Christmas Day.

The council acted a fortnight later by ordering a tax on all the inhabitants to be collected quarterly. It was to be used to sustain the poor and those who worked in public services for the kirk until another solution could be found. Previously they had relied on voluntary contributions given at the church door or, as set out in 1561, a group of men visiting houses and booths asking for donations. The council had agreed that everyone must contribute, but set out no sum to be paid by each citizen. Before the Reformation the Church had been the main provider of relief for the poor, now the State, in the form of Edinburgh Council, had to take its place.

Archibald Douglas

In 1562, the queen informed the council that she wished them to elect Archibald Douglas of Kilspindie as provost. This was a remarkable turnabout, as he had been removed from office the previous year by the direct intervention of the queen.

Douglas had served as provost before and after the Reformation. His father, bearer of the same name, had also served as Provost of Edinburgh. He was a member of the powerful Douglas family, who were led at this time by James Douglas, Earl of Morton.

Archibald Douglas remained in office until August 1565 when George Drummond appeared before the council with a letter from the queen and the new king (LordDarnley), once again ordering them to remove Douglas from office. The letter claimed that they had 'many reasonable causes and considerations', but failed to name any. However, the council sent six members to the queen and the king intending to put their case concerning the removal of the provost and also the ban on John Knox's preaching. That afternoon the delegation must have come home empty-handed, because they declared that they would not silence Knox.

The very next day, John Spens, advocate for Their Majesties, informed the council that the queen and king wished them to elect Simon Preston of Craigmillar as provost instead. He was hurriedly made a burgess and a member of the Merchants' Guild, before being elected Provost of Edinburgh. Preston owned Craigmillar Castle and had been one of the three who were proposed by the queen for the office the last time Archibald Douglas had been removed.

The Chaseabout Raid

On 29 July 1565, Mary married Henry Stewart, Lord Darnley, whose maternal grandmother was Margaret Tudor, the sister of Henry VIII. They were thus cousins and heirs to the English throne should Elizabeth die. Most Catholics did not recognise the Boleyn marriage, and so denied Elizabeth's right to the throne. The marriage was conducted by John Sinclair, Dean of Restalrig, using the Catholic rite in the Abbey of Holyrood.

The marriage took place despite the objections of James Stewart, Earl of Moray, and William Maitland of Lethington, the queen's Secretary of State. Both these men saw it as a strengthening of the Catholic position. They had worked hard to form an alliance with England which, in the event of Elizabeth having no heirs, would lead to Mary or her heir inheriting the English crown. Certainly Elizabeth was not best pleased with this marriage.

Moray led a rebellion but failed to gain support from the Protestant lords and the English. Despite a lot of manoeuvring (or chasing about) neither side met each other. Eventually Moray fled to England. The episode became known as The Chaseabout Raid.

The Murder of David Riccio

At no time in her long history has Edinburgh witnessed so many dramatic events which were to lead to the end of the reign of Mary, Queen of Scots. Already the burgh had been occupied by the Earl of Moray and his supporters. The queen's government was becoming more and more unpopular with the ruling classes. Only a few nobles remained at court; most of them felt that their rightful place as advisors to the queen was being usurped by men who were neither noble nor Scots.

One man in particular was angered by his growing exclusion from power – the queen's husband, Henry Stewart, Lord Darnley. No historian, in nearly 450 years, has come forward with a favourable assessment of him. Despite being the son of the Earl of Lennox, he does not seem to have had any close friends among his peers. He wanted to be king in his own right and yet he showed little interest in the government of the realm.

David Riccio was the leading light of a new group that had formed round the queen. He became her private secretary and, as such, probably controlled access to her. A group of Protestant lords led by James Douglas, Earl of Morton, Patrick, Lord Lindsay, and Patrick, Lord Ruthven, plotted the death of the queen's new favourite. On the night of 9 March 1566, they entered the Palace of Holyrood with the aid of Darnley. They rushed into the queen's private rooms and seized Riccio. It was said that Riccio was stabbed fifty-six times – this was a particularly brutal murder performed in front of the pregnant queen.

The next morning, James Melville, one of Mary's ambassadors, was passing below the queen's window when she called down to him. She asked him to go up to the town and seek the provost's help. As he left the palace Melville was stopped by Nisbet, master of the Earl of Lennox's household. However, the ambassador claimed that he was going to St Giles to hear the sermon and was thus allowed to pass.

He found Simon Preston, who was willing to call the people together. However, he informed Melville that 'he expected no help from their hands because the most part of them were so discontented with the present government that all desired change'. It was only in August of the previous year that the queen had demanded the removal of the last provost, Archibald Douglas of Kilspindie.

The murderers fled to England, except for Darnley who had promised to protect them. These included James Douglas, Earl of Morton (Darnley's mother was a Douglas). On 24 December they were pardoned by the queen and returned to Scotland, forming one more group who held a grudge against Darnley.

The Murder of Henry Stewart, Lord Darnley, King of Scots

The English Ambassador, Thomas Randolf, wrote to the Earl of Leicester at the beginning of June giving an assessment of the situation. He was based in Edinburgh and had represented Queen Elizabeth since the early days of the Reformation. He quoted a general rumour, 'The hatred towards him [Darnley] and his house is marvellous great, his pride intolerable, his words not to be born', adding also, 'They find nothing but that God must send him a short end or themselves a miserable life'.

September 1566 brought better news. In Edinburgh Castle, Mary gave birth to a son – the future James VI. James was later to succeed to the English throne and to become the first person to rule the whole British Isles. But all that was in the future. His father withdrew to Glasgow, part of the Lennox lands, where presumably he felt safer. It was possible that Darnley was plotting to seize power but he had no allies to assist him.

It is believed that a group of nobles led by the Earl of Moray and Maitland of Lethington met in Craigmillar Castle, the home of the Provost of Edinburgh. There they formed a pact to remove Darnley. Another man deeply involved in the plot to remove Mary's husband was James Hepburn, Earl of Bothwell.

Darnley was ill; most historians believe he had contracted syphilis. In January 1567, Mary set out for Glasgow to see him and persuaded him to return to Edinburgh. The initial plan was for Darnley to stay at Craigmillar Castle, which would offer some security. This was changed – by whom is a matter of debate – and Darnley was taken to the Kirk O'Fields and placed in the Old Provost's Lodgings. This property had had been acquired by Sir James Balfour of Pittendreich a few weeks previously.

Early in the morning, about 2 a.m., on 9 February 1567 the inhabitants of Edinburgh were awoken by a loud explosion. The Old Provost's Lodgings had been completely destroyed and the bodies of Lord Darnley and one of his servants were found some distance away. They had either been strangled or smothered. A group of horsemen were seen close to the scene of the murder. Were they James Douglas, the Earl of Morton's men? It seems possible that in fleeing from one attempt on his life, Darnley might have fallen into the clutches of a second group.

The Last Days of the Reign of Queen Mary

Accusations were made against the Earl of Bothwell by Darnley's father, the Earl of Lennox. In April, a trial was held in Edinburgh, but the burgh was full of Bothwell's men. Lennox refused to attend the trial fearing that he might be attacked by them. The Earl of Bothwell was naturally acquitted but suspicions remained. Placards appeared in the burgh continuing to accuse the earl of Darnley's murder.

On 15 May 1567, Mary and Bothwell, who had only just divorced his wife, were married.

In June, a powerful group of Scottish nobles entered Edinburgh 'in arms for punishing of King Henry Stewart's murderer'. Among these men were the Earls of Athol, Montrose, Morton and Mar, as well as two of the Riccio conspirators, Lords Lindsay and Ruthven, and the future leader of Mary's party, Sir William Kirkcaldy of Grange. They came together in the Councilhouse to make a bond to pursue the king's murderers, dissolve the marriage, protect the prince and restore justice. The council promised to assist the lords.

On 15 June, on Carberry Hill, just to the east of Edinburgh, the two armies met. Negotiations began, but little was decided. However, most of the troops supporting Mary and Bothwell began to desert, leaving little doubt as to the result of any battle. Mary surrendered and Bothwell fled.

Eight

THE REIGN OF JAMES VI

The Town Wall

The council's first action at the beginning of the new reign was to hire two masons, Thomas Jackson and Murdo Walker, to repair the town wall by the old Blackfriary. You can still see the remains of this wall as it climbs up the west side of the Pleasance. At the same time, they were lending weapons to Sir William Kirkcaldy of Grange. He was preparing an expedition to Orkney in the hope of catching the missing Earl of Bothwell.

The council expressed its concern at the amount of violence in the burgh. Any bloodletting would produce a £5 fine on top of the punishment for the crime itself.

Trinity College and Other Building Work

Trinity College Church, which was founded by the widow of James II, and its yards and buildings was granted to the burgh by the new regent, James Stewart, Earl of Moray, as a hospital for the poor, and Adam Fullerton, one of the bailies, was placed in charge of the building works. The site was later to be used as the town's workhouse, which became known as St Paul's Work, and today the land is part of Waverley Station. In order to pay for this new hospital, the councillors were forced to visit the citizens to ask them for donations towards the work.

In addition, not only was the pier of Leith in need of repair, but the road leading from the burgh (over Abbeyhill and down Easter Road) to the port also required some maintenance. A storm in March had broken many of the windows of St Giles and caused considerable damage to the roof. The council had to borrow the money using their dues from the port and the rents of the town mills as security.

Even the Nor' Loch dam was in disrepair, causing the western end to dry up. Edinburgh was protected by a wall which had been extended on the south side after the Battle of Flodden. Its northern defence was the loch formed by a dam. Beyond this dam was Trinity College Church and the site of the new hospital. Fortunately for the burgh finances, John Harwood, the treasurer, was able to recruit twenty-four workmen from the town to do the job. It was an earth dam and further work had to be carried out on the defences at the east end of the loch.

Sir William Kirkcaldy of Grange

Kirkcaldy was one of the group of Fife lairds who had seized the castle of St Andrew's and murdered Cardinal Beaton. It was here that he first met John Knox. After the fall of the castle, Kirkcaldy was sent to serve in the French galleys. After he was released, Kirkcaldy served in the French army before returning to Scotland at the beginning of the Reformation. He fought in the Siege of Leith and became associated with the Protestant Party. At Carberry, when Bothwell offered to fight anyone who would challenge his honour, Kirkcaldy put himself forward. The earl wisely withdrew.

Kirkcaldy was a supporter of the Regent Moray, who made him keeper of Edinburgh Castle. He moved the guns held in Dunbar Castle and placed them in his keeping in Edinburgh. Like William Maitland of Lethington, the former secretary, Kirkcaldy was unhappy with the total exclusion of Mary from the government of Scotland. In October 1569 Kirkcaldy was elected as Provost of Edinburgh. Now he controlled both the castle and the town. The regent wrote to the council expressing his concern that the Laird of Grange had too much responsibility. The council, however, could find no reason to remove him from office.

Moray was determined to keep his grip on power. James Hamilton, Duke of Chatelherault, was taken from his house, which stood just south of the Kirk O'Fields, and placed in the castle. Lethington was to follow. He was lodged in a house on Castlehill and held there under armed guard. Kirkcaldy arrived and secured his release. The secretary was then taken to the castle for his own safety.

The whole matter might have come to nothing, but on 23 January 1570 James Stewart, Earl of Moray and Regent of Scotland, was assassinated.

Scotland was divided between those who wanted a government with Mary and those who had no wish to see her return. Kirkcaldy and Lethington favoured the queen. However, opposition was close at hand. John Knox would never countenance the return of Mary and was to break with his old friend. James Douglas, Earl of Morton, became the force behind those opposed to the queen.

The Summer of 1571

Edinburgh was now under the control of Kirkcaldy, with his troops and guns firmly secure within the walls of the castle. James McGill, who had been elected provost in the previous October, was expelled from the town. The provost and his bailies set up their headquarters in Leith. Kirkcaldy appointed his son-in-law, Sir Thomas Kerr, as provost, leaving the burgh with two councils. The supporters of the queen held a parliament in the Tolbooth, while the new regent (the Earl of Lennox, who was Lord Darnley's father) summoned a parliament to meet in the Canongate. Here, the members were in constant danger from the bombardment by the guns of the castle. It was necessary to move regularly to prevent the meeting being targeted. Thus it became known as 'the Creeping Parliament'.

The regent and the king's supporters withdrew to Stirling. Kirkcaldy decided on a daring raid to capture the leaders of the king's party. On 3 September, a cavalry force entered Stirling and within a few hours they had rounded up the nobles in the town. Only the Earl of Morton offered any resistance. Victory was almost complete when poor discipline and a counter-attack by the Earl of Mar from the castle enabled the prisoners to escape. The chief victim of the raid was the unpopular regent, who died from a gunshot wound.

Winter, 1571–72

Queen Elizabeth sent ambassadors north to try to obtain a settlement between the supporters of Mary in the castle and the new regent, the Earl of Mar. They had no success and the siege of Edinburgh Castle was tightened. Mar placed garrisons in Craigmillar, Corstorphine, Craighall and Merchiston. Ships entering the Forth were compelled to dock in Leith to prevent the castle being supplied by sea. The people of Edinburgh suffered the most, with anyone caught trying to smuggle food to those who remained in the town facing the ultimate penalty.

The Truce, 1572

The French and English arranged a truce which came into force on 1 August. This enabled the regent's men, led by Morton, to occupy the burgh. The ministers, including an ailing John Knox, returned. The English continued to hope for a compromise between the king's men, all strong Protestants, and those in the castle who were also Protestants but favoured the return of the queen.

Two events were to harden the opposition to Kirkcaldy and his men. On 24 August (St Bartholomew's Day) 20,000 French Protestants were murdered by their Catholic countrymen. The massacre, when the news reached Scotland, increased the fear and hatred of Catholics. This was followed at the end of October by the death of the Earl of Mar. The regent had done all he could to achieve a settlement, but now power fell to the new regent, James Douglas, Earl of Morton. Morton, from his base in Dalkeith, had been an uncompromising opponent of Kirkcaldy and his men. He saw only one way to end the matter.

The End

Eventually Morton persuaded the English to intervene. Siege guns were shipped north to Leith. A battery of these heavy guns was set up and the whole east end of the castle, including David's Tower and the Constable's Tower, was destroyed.

William Maitland of Lethington died a prisoner in the Tolbooth of Leith; Sir William Kirkcaldy and his brother, James, were hung at the Cross; and James Mossman, goldsmith and owner of the property known now as John Knox's House, with fellow goldsmith, James Cockie, met the same fate. The eastern end of the castle was reconstructed, with the famous Half Moon Battery built around the remains of the fourteenth-century David's Tower.

George Douglas

In October 1576 George Douglas, who was already Captain of Edinburgh Castle, was elected Provost of Edinburgh. George was the half-brother of James Douglas, Earl of Morton, who ruled Scotland as regent until March 1578 when James VI took control himself.

However, all was not well and James VI, in a letter to the Earl of Rothes, complained, 'There is action of hostility already entered betwixt the inhabitants of Edinburgh and the keepers of Edinburgh Castle under the Earl of Morton'. The king wanted the matter settled and Captain Hallyburton was ordered to set up a barricade to prevent George Douglas and his soldiers launching an attack on the town and the nobles who were in residence there. The Privy Council then demanded the removal of Douglas from his office of provost. Archibald Stewart was chosen in his place.

The years leading up to the union of the crowns were difficult times in Scotland. Various factions of the nobility attempted, often successfully, to seize power. In fact, during the years following the Ruthven Raid and during the Gowrie Conspiracy, James was virtually a prisoner. Edinburgh, as the largest and wealthiest burgh with its royal fortress, played an important part in these affairs.

Edinburgh and Scotland, 1578–85

James VI finally entered Edinburgh in October 1579, when the council presented him with a silver plate and 1,000 marks. He stayed at Holyrood.

The palace also housed the king's favourite, Esmé Stewart, Seigneur d'Augbigny. However, the English distrusted him, fearing that he was really

a French spy and the Kirk were worried that he was a Catholic intent on converting the young king and restoring the old faith. Stewart was the king's cousin (on his father's side) and became Duke of Lennox.

The following August, Lennox had the gates of the town closed while he searched for the Laird of Drumwhassell, who had been seen in the town. The laird was Captain of Dumbarton Castle and Lennox wished to gain control of it. Edinburgh Castle also came under his control, and later in the year he sent one of his French servants back to France to acquire shot and gunpowder for the castle.

John Knox, Edinburgh's first Protestant minister, had quite openly criticised the queen and the Catholics in her court. His successors were to prove just as stubborn in their hostility to the king's government when they thought it wrong. The Kirk was free from royal control and the Edinburgh ministers were not slow in expressing their opinions. This was a novelty at a time when freedom of speech was unknown.

Robert Montgomery, a minister from Stirling, was created Archbishop of Glasgow, but the Presbytery of Edinburgh excommunicated him, then the king annulled this. For a time, James was under the power of a group of strongly Protestant nobles known as the Ruthven Raiders. They were led by Lord William Ruthven, Earl of Gowrie and Treasurer of Scotland. They ruled the country until in June 1583 James escaped and a new group led by James Stewart, Earl of Arran, took control of the king's government. Arran was the brother of John Knox's second wife. He became chancellor in 1584 and later that year was elected Provost of Edinburgh. Although Arran was chosen again as provost in 1585, when the king rejected the choice of William Little, he was forced to flee the country by the end of the year. Thus William Little of Over Libberton finally became provost.

David Lindsay, Minister of South Leith

The Reformers, who now controlled Scotland, were concerned that an important town like Leith should have a sound minister. Thus they appointed David Lindsay to South Leith. He was a nephew of the 9th Earl of Crawford and a supporter of the new Protestant ideas. In 1568 he became moderator of the General Assembly (or Chairman of the Assembly), a post that he was to hold on another five occasions. His relationship with John Knox must have been good for, as he lay dying, Knox asked Lindsay to go to the castle and give Kirkcaldy of Grange a message which prophesised his doom, should he not surrender.

Lindsay became a friend of James VI, even though he opposed some of his reforms. He was the only minister to comply with the king's request that prayers should be said for Mary, Queen of Scots before her execution. James appointed him as King's Chaplain and they sailed together to Scandinavia where, in November 1589, he married the king to Anne of Denmark.

Lindsay continued his loyalty to James VI, while the ministers in Edinburgh opposed many of the king's policies. After the Gowrie Conspiracy the ministers in the capital refused to hold a service of thanksgiving, so Lindsay conducted his own at the Market Cross of Edinburgh. He was appointed Bishop of Ross, but continued to serve in South Leith.

In 1603 Lindsay went south with the king, presumably acting as chaplain. He returned later to Leith and continued as minister until his death in 1613. He had served as minister of South Leith for fifty-three years, a record unlikely to be surpassed.

The Town in the Late 1570s and 1580s

Problems for the Council

Ale and Water

The council began to take an interest in two groups of women working in the burgh. The first group was the women who were employed in the taverns; they were barred from selling drinks – no doubt from a fear that they might lead their drunken clients astray. However, an exception was made for the wives and widows of burgesses who were probably the owners of the premises.

The second group were the water carriers. The summer of 1580 proved to be such a dry one that the council had to ban those brewing ale from using the precious water from the wells. Many of the inhabitants bought water from the water carriers, who brought it from the wells to the lands. It was hard enough work hauling a barrel of water on your back without having to climb the stairs to the upper storeys of these tenements. Gladstone's Land is an example of a tenement from this period, although it was altered some years later. The council had received complaints about the strong language and the low morals of the women employed in this trade.

Hygiene

In November, complaints recorded in the Burgh Records were directed at the inhabitants of the burgh who 'maist filthly castes forth ... their closettis and pottis on the hie gaitt and headis of the vinellis'. If this were not enough, some were 'doing their ease at the said heidis as is maist uncomely to be sene'. Suffice to say that Edinburgh was a dirty place with animals, especially pigs, roaming freely.

Craftsmen

Each craft had a monopoly of trade and was responsible for the quality of the workmanship. Such a position could encourage some to keep their prices high – or so it might seem to their customers. In 1577 the baxters hired unfree masons because they considered that the members of the Guild of Wrights & Masons were overcharging. The burgh craftsmen tried to prevent these men from continuing, but the council intervened, allowing the work in Grey's Close to be completed.

One of the main targets of public discontent were the fleshers. In 1577 they were accused of causing scarcity by pasturing their animals in the park (Holyrood) and on the Burgh Muir. In 1585, two bailies were sent to the fish market. The fleshers in the fish market were accused of buying up stocks to resell at a profit and of hoarding goods to cause shortages. How they were able to keep the fish fresh in the days before refrigeration was not a matter that the council seem to have considered. All meat was supposed to be sold at the correct markets, but some appears to have been sold elsewhere, probably to avoid market dues and inspections. The council ordered that all 'beef, mutton, veal and such like to be sold in open market and not hidden in their booths to the dearth of the markets'.

The fleshers were a good target to blame for food shortages and rising prices and, sadly for them, not all fleshers were honest men. In August 1585, two of their members were convicted of selling rotten meat. They were paraded at the Cross with a paper tied to their heads.

The new constitution allowed the merchant members of the council to choose six of the fourteen craft deacons to be members of the council. The others were extraordinary deacons, called in if the council wanted wider support for a controversial decision. As far as the records show, no Deacon of Fleshers was ever selected to become a member of the council.

The Sabbath

August 1581 saw another attempt by the burgh council to control morals and Sabbath activities. The bailies, together with the ministers and elders, were to visit their own quarters of the town and 'purge ... the great multitude of harlots and vitious persons'. Bowling in the back yards, dancing, playing games and 'all manner of dissolute behaviour' were all banned on the Sabbath. Children were not even allowed to run down the High Street. The onus was placed on the heads of families to keep their children and servants in order.

Fines and imprisonment could be imposed on those who failed to obey. This was quite hard on the ordinary inhabitant of the burgh whose only day free from work was a Sunday. They would be expected to attend church services in the morning and the afternoon. The head of the house had a duty to see that the younger members of the family, and presumably the servants, knew the teachings of the Church.

A Merchant City

Edinburgh was a city of merchants. They dominated the burgh council and possessed much of the wealth of the town. When, in 1581, the French placed duties on imported Scottish cloth, the provost went to the king to seek his support. It took nearly three years (possibly because the Ruthven government was not acceptable to the French) before a delegation was put together. Walter Adamson was chosen to represent the town, but when Lord Seaton, who was to lead the group, objected the council threatened to withdraw its financial support.

The burgesses were seen by the king as a source of ready money. In March 1581, he asked them for a loan of 10,000 marks, but by June the council were still struggling to raise the money.

Wealthy individuals, like George Heriot, were able to help towards the expenses of the king and queen. Heriot began with a stock worth £200 (a considerable sum in those times) and his shop was close to the Tolbooth, facing the west end of St Giles. Robert Chambers tells a story about a visit made by Heriot to the king in the Palace of Holyrood. The goldsmith complemented the king on the agreeable smell coming from the burning wood. When the king boasted of the cost of such wood, Heriot invited him to come to his shop where he would see an even more costly fire. James duly obliged and was very disappointed to find an ordinary fire in the grate. Heriot then took out a bond worth £2,000, which he had lent to the king and placed it on the fire. Heriot was subsequently appointed goldsmith to the king in 1597 and jeweller to the queen in 1601. So important was his business that when the court moved south in 1603, Heriot joined them. He died in London in 1624 and left most of his fortune for the building of a hospital for the education of the sons of burgesses who had fallen on hard times.

Leith in the Late Sixteenth Century

During the early years of the reign of James VI, the inhabitants of Leith again tried to circumvent the restrictions placed on them by the town council in Edinburgh. Some members of the council were sent to the town to check on extensions put up illegally by householders; outside stairs and small shops were obstructing the streets.

An application by John Dalmahoy to convert a little house in Brand Wynd into two small shops was rejected, and a larger encroachment onto public property appears to have been made by John Logan of Coatfield, whose land bordered the Links. Stones were ordered to be placed there to mark the boundary.

Shipping presented its own problems for Leith. In October 1580, the *Bark Wynden*, arriving from Bruges, was quarantined. An outbreak of plague had appeared in Flanders. Possibly a bigger worry than the plague were English ships operating from the east coast ports, who took the opportunity to prey on Scottish merchants trading with Flanders. Complaints were made to the English Ambassador, but these did not lead to an improvement in the situation.

The English were doing it on an even grander scale in the Americas. The Lord High Admiral, the Earl of Bothwell, seems to have acted little better, seizing ships in the harbour during the emergency of 1588 (the Spanish Armada).

Vessels coming into Leith were subject to customs duties. One trick used by unscrupulous captains was to land the goods secretly at another port (Burntisland was one such place) before docking in Leith. An investigation into this practice was ordered by the council. Trading was not always easy. The French placed heavy duties on the importation of Scottish cloth in the 1580s.

In 1583 we get a rare glimpse into the working of the harbour. The Town Council of Edinburgh set the wages of the twelve stingmen whose job it was to take the wine to the cellars or storehouses. They also handled fish, which included salmon and herring. Eight polkmen were responsible for the unloading and removal of wheat, beer and salt, and two persons appointed as 'metters' measured the quantities of food passing through the port.

It is difficult to know how restricted the inhabitants of Leith were in carrying out their commercial activities. All imported cargoes were supposed to be taken to the markets in Edinburgh, and no one in the town was allowed to trade in these goods. However, with no regular police force (the bailie had *some* officers), the inhabitants tried hard to organise a black market. James VI had barely taken up the reins of government when Thomas Lindesey was found to be buying wine in the port. Since he claimed that he as acting as an agent for the king, the matter had to be referred to the Privy Council.

In January 1585, the town council received information of large 'black' markets selling butter, cheese, meal and other food stuffs, but there seems to have been a crackdown in 1591. Robert Uddert, whose nickname was 'Robin Hood', was accused of selling cloth in Leith and thus breaking the Edinburgh merchants' monopoly. Six other inhabitants were also prosecuted later in that same year for illegal trading. Uddert was in trouble again with the Edinburgh authorities in 1592 for buying barrels of tar and in 1595 he was fined for purchasing timber. His wife was among a group who were accused of selling wine without a licence. Towards the end of the year, Robert bought a licence.

It was a time of shortage and no doubt the council were looking to find someone to blame for the problem. However, there were obviously wealthy people in Leith. Andrew Lamb was a ship owner who provided passage for the king's special ambassador to France. He received 2,000 marks from the town council's share of the expenditure for this trip. No doubt his family was responsible for the construction of that imposing building known as Lamb's House which still survives today.

At the beginning of 1599 the council took action against Andrew Sclater, who was both Water Bailie and Leith's jailor. He was 'dismissed for oppressions and extortions in his office' and turned out of his positions and his home in the Tolbooth. However, Sclater had friends in high places, one of whom was Sir David Lyndsy, a senator in the Court of Justice. By the end of the year Sclater was back in his job.

The Ministers of Edinburgh

The post-Reformation Kirk in Edinburgh was forcefully led by John Knox, whose outspoken views on Catholicism and the Mass had soon brought him into conflict with Mary, Queen of Scots and her court. However, the exile of Mary and the death of Knox did not end the conflict between the ministers of Edinburgh and the Crown.

In 1580, Walter Balcanquhal, minister of St Giles, was summoned before the Privy Council for an attack on the 'French court'. Esmé Stewart, Duke of Lennox, was a French Catholic and the Kirk feared his influence over the king. Balcanquhal appears to have escaped punishment, but two years later John Durie, another of the ministers, was ordered by the Privy Council to leave the burgh. However, Durie's exile lasted less than six months and by November he was back in post. Bowes, the English Ambassador, reported to Lord Burleigh that 'a great number of the inhabitants' were 'singing psalms ... before the lodgings of the duke' – Durie was among them.

The Parliament of 1584 passed the so-called 'Black Acts' condemning presbyteries and confirming the power of bishops. Walter Balcanquhal and James Lawson fled to England. Lawson died in exile but Balcanquhal returned. James was generally willing to compromise to avoid conflict.

The year 1587 saw the appointment of Robert Bruce to the ministry in Edinburgh. He appears to have been popular among his colleagues and with the populace of Edinburgh. When the king left for Denmark, Bruce was made an Extraordinary Privy Councillor – not even Knox achieved that status. At the crowning ceremony of the new queen, Bruce anointed her.

The riot of 1596, which the king believed was caused by city clergy, saw the ministers of Edinburgh banished from the burgh. They all gradually returned but remained strong opponents of the Episcopal system (the riot will be discussed more fully later in the chapter). After the collapse of the Gowrie Conspiracy, the Church was ordered to give thanks for the safe return of the king. Some people, including the ministers in Edinburgh, had doubts about the king's version of the event. Robert Bruce refused to give wholehearted thanks for the king's delivery and was again banished from the burgh. He carried on his ministry until his death in 1631, but never returned to Edinburgh.

Balcanquhal continued the opposition to James' reforms in the Church and was summoned before the Privy Council in 1600 and 1610. He had been transferred from St Giles to Trinity College Church on his return and continued his ministry there until his death in 1616, having served the people of Edinburgh for a remarkable forty-three years. His son, another Walter Balcanquhal, was an executor to the will of George Heriot. He followed his father into the Church but served in England as Dean of Rochester and later Durham. Walter junior was a supporter of the king and died in Wales towards the end of the Civil War.

Inflation

The late sixteenth century was an era of inflation with the prices of basic foodstuffs rising sharply. In the early 1560s the light ale which everybody drank (as it was considered safer than water) cost only 4d a pint. A decade later, the price had doubled and it continued to rise, so that by 1603 a pint of ale cost 12d, after which the price appears to have remained stable.

Bread is more difficult to assess as price and weight varied. In the early 1560s the council fixed the maximum price for bread produced by the Edinburgh baxters at 4d for a loaf weighing 15oz. Prices continued to change, and in 1625 the council fixed the weight of the 12d loaf at 13oz.

A comparison of prices between 1553 and 1611 in the poultry and butter markets illustrates how rapidly the cost of living was rising. In 1553, butter cost 9d per lb and eggs 4d per dozen. By 1611, the price of butter was 40d per lb and eggs were 20d per dozen. A good hen which had once cost 10d had, by 1611, reached 72d. The cost of a pair of teal had risen tenfold to 80d.

The Constitution of Edinburgh

The uneasy peace between the merchants who controlled the town council and the craftsmen who were seeking greater representation came to an end with the 1582 election. The council had elected three of its own friends (John Sharp, Thomas Craig and Jon Preston) as assessors. A mob of some 200 assembled to prevent them entering the Councilhouse. Gilbert Primrose, the Deacon of the Surgeons, then opened the door allowing the mob to enter. Despite the council's efforts, the king's nominee, Alexander Clerk, was elected provost.

The situation could not continue in this disorderly way, so it was proposed that a committee approved by the king should draw up a constitution, which would satisfy all parties. A list of names was given to the king. In February 1583, a proposed constitution was presented to a meeting of 150 freemen of the burgh who met in the Councilhouse. It was rejected by the craft guilds. However, the new constitution was then imposed on the burgesses regardless.

The office bearers (provost, four bailies, the dean of guild and the treasurer) were all to be merchants who had served on the council for several years. There were to be ten other merchants who were to include the former provost, bailies, dean of guild and treasurer. This left three other merchants to be added to their number. There were fourteen craft guilds in Edinburgh, each with their own deacon. Six of these deacons were to sit on the council, while the remaining deacons were sometimes called upon to support controversial decisions. Two other craftsmen were given seats on the council, but they also had to be chosen by the council.

Power was placed in the hands of a small group of merchant burgesses who were able to impose their policies on the burgh. The election of the burgh's representative to Parliament (be it Scots or the United Kingdom) was carried out by these thirty-three councillors until the passing of the Reform Act (Scotland) in 1832. The king, or his representatives in Scotland, took an interest in the post of provost and often put forward a candidate for it.

The Barony of Broughton

David I had granted the lands of Broughton to the Holyrood Abbey and after the Reformation, Adam Bothwell, Bishop of Orkney, acquired the barony before it came into the hands of Sir Lewis Bellenden. He was a supporter of the government of the Ruthven Raiders and an opponent of the Earl of Arran. In 1587 Broughton became a free barony with its own tolbooth, bailie and court. Bellenden came into conflict with Edinburgh in 1602 when it was discovered that workmen from Leith were taking rocks from the barony's lands to use them as ballast for their ships.

The family gained a reputation of dabbling in witchcraft and the barony, according to Grant (a historian of Edinburgh), was notorious as a haunt of witches and warlocks who were frequently incarcerated in its tolbooth. In 1608, a group of women were burnt for witchcraft, despite their denials.

Sir William Bellenden appears to have been short of money and mortgaged the mills at Canonmills and lands in Broughton with George Heriot. The barony was eventually sold to the Earl of Roxburgh and in 1636 it was purchased by Heriot's Hospital.

Education at the End of the Sixteenth Century

One of the main policies of the new Reformed Church was the establishment of a school in every parish. The teachings of the Church were based on the written word so it was important that everyone could read. Edinburgh already had a high school, and a new building was begun in 1578, when William Bickerton was given a contract by the council to construct a new school in the grounds of the old Blackfriary in the Cowgate. William Robertson was appointed the first headmaster to this new school. He was followed in 1585 by Hercules Rollock, whose brother became principal of the college in the following year.

On 1 September 1587, a group of pupils locked themselves in the High School. They were armed with pistols, swords and halberds (a short pike with an axe attached to it). The provost and the bailies ordered the doors to be broken down. Nine pupils were arrested and fined 40 shillings (£2) each. They must have been quite young – probably upper primary age – because pupils started at the college aged about 12 years old. One of the ringleaders was Nicoll Bannantyne, whose father was a judge in the Court of Session. Another was Alexander Napier; his father was Laird of Napier and the inventor of logarithms.

This did not settle the unrest, which reached a crisis in September 1595 when pupils again locked themselves in the High School. It seems probable that the dispute related to the granting of holidays. Eight days were generally given in May and September. Pupils asked for the September holiday but this was refused. Discussions held that year, between headmaster Hercules Rollock and the Town Council, reveal concern over broken windows. The pupils may, or may not, have been to blame.

John McMorane, one of the bailies, was called to quell the disturbance. A shot fired by young William Sinclair rang out across the yard and struck the bailie on the head, killing him. The death of the bailie seems to have ended the affair. Sinclair was the son of the Chancellor of Caithness and appears to have escaped punishment, but Hercules Rollock, the headmaster, did not. He was dismissed but continued to fight against the decision in the courts until he died in 1599. This brought an end to the affair, and the council granted his widow and children the sum of 1,000 marks.

The council then set out to reform the school. Already they had employed William Fleming to teach writing. Now they made it a stipulation that all new pupils had to be able to read. Four men were employed to teach the four year groups, with the fourth-year teacher to hold the position of principal. The school was to have a monopoly for the teaching of grammar. In the first decade of the 1600s Robert Steven, a former high school teacher, set up his own grammar school in the Canongate. His popularity led to pupils leaving Edinburgh's High School for Steven's school. In 1608 he was arrested by the burgh authorities and fined the large sum of £100 and forbidden from continuing his work.

The Canongate, as a separate burgh, had its own grammar school. It was situated near the abbey and dated from pre-Reformation times. Other schools, teaching more basic education, were the responsibility of the Church Sessions and the heritors (the leading property owners of the parish). In Edinburgh, the council assumed these responsibilities. The burgh had two specialist schools – the French School and the Song School. In 1603 Samuel Henderson, master of the Song School, was given permission to break the High School's monopoly and teach grammar.

We know little about the session schools, save that girls and boys were taught separately. Three masters were named and given responsibility for teaching the girls.

Outside the burgh, the development of schools may have been slow because of the lack of qualified teachers and resistance on the part of the heritors to spend money on new schools. The Kirk itself was short of ministers. Information is lacking because few records survive from this period.

In 1591 Tobias Martin opened a school for the children of the parish of St Cuthbert. Since he only had twenty pupils it would not have made much progress in such a large parish. In 1598 South Leith Kirk Session gave James Hay and Daniel Blacklaws permission to set up schools in the parish, while Elspit Morton had set up a school without a licence from the Session and presumably this was closed.

In 1607 Robert Dunlop is recorded as a teacher of a school in Restalrig (part of the parish of South Leith). Mention is also made in the 1609 Session minutes of a grammar school in Leith.

The main achievement of this period was the opening of the town's college in 1583 on the site of the Kirk O' Fields. This small foundation was to develop into the University of Edinburgh. Its first ten years produced 259 graduates, of whom 103 were to enter the Church. This average of twenty-five graduates a year was to increase to thirty by the end of the reign of James VI.

The Riot of 17 December 1596

The relationship between the king and the town's ministers had never been good. The Kirk claimed the right to criticise James and his court, and the ministers

of Edinburgh were not slow to do that. John Drury had suffered banishment for his attacks on the Lennox regime in the early 1580s, and the reintroduction of bishops had angered those who were of a Presbyterian inclination. James' easy attitude towards the Catholic lords had made the ministers of Edinburgh suspicious of the king's plans.

On 17 December 1596, James joined the Lords of Session in the Tolbooth. What exactly happened next still remains uncertain. However, we do know that a large crowd appeared and surrounded the Tolbooth, trapping the king inside. There was a suspicion in the minds of some people, including the king, that the ministers in St Giles had roused the crowd. The provost was summoned from his sickbed and with assistance from some of the leading citizens he managed to bring calm to the situation and escorted James back to Holyrood.

The king left Edinburgh for Linlithgow and ordered the Court of Session to follow. He demanded the arrest of a number of persons, including the four ministers of Edinburgh. James considered the 'attack' on the king as an act of treason, putting the burgh council in a very weak position when they came to appease him.

By March, an agreement was reached. The burgh was to pay the king 20,000 marks. The new ministers – the former ones were never to serve the town again – were to live in their individual parishes and not collectively, as had been the case, in the Kirkyard of St Giles. Despite this, Robert Bruce, Walter Balcanquell, Robert Balfour and William Watson returned to their duties in Edinburgh.

Provost Alexander Seton, Lord Fyvie

Alexander Seton (sometimes spelt Seaton or Seyton) was born a few years before the Reformation. His father was a strong supporter of the queen and had held the position of provost at the time of the upheavals. Alexander was his fourth son and became an advocate. He was suspected by many of being a member of the Catholic Church. As an opponent of Regent Morton, he had made little progress.

Even after the earl's fall, Seton was still of little importance. However, with the disgrace of the Earl of Arran in 1585, his fortune changed. He joined the Privy Council and in the following year became a Lord of the Court of Session. The Kirk began to suspect him of favouring Catholics when he supported the return of the Catholic lords from exile, but he argued that it was easier to keep a watch on them at home than abroad.

Alexander Seton was clearly a man of great ability, and was soon one of the men looking after the royal finances. In 1598 he was created Lord Fyvie, and in the autumn of that year he became Provost of Edinburgh, a post which he held for the next ten years.

The death of Queen Elizabeth I in 1603 saw James departing for the south. The king was no longer at the mercy of noble conspirators and the burgh council did not have to maintain a strong watch against rebel members of the aristocracy. The ports no longer needed to be closed against the king's enemies.

Despite James' move south, Edinburgh remained the home of the Scottish Privy Council and the Court of Session. James ruled Scotland through men like Alexander Seton and James Elphinstone, who was created Lord Balmerino. Elphinstone acquired the lands of the Logans of Restalrig and built a large mansion in South Leith. Seton went on to become chancellor in 1604 and was made Earl of Dunfermline two years later. During all this time, he retained his position of provost.

Finally, in 1608 James wrote to the Scottish burgh informing them he no longer wished to have nobles elected to the post of chief magistrate in the burgh. Such powers, he believed, only led to mischief and it was better that a burgess should hold the post. Edinburgh ignored the royal instructions and in October 1608 Seton was again elected provost. However, the council were forced to climb down when they realised that the king was serious about the matter.

Constables

In 1611 James VI ordered Edinburgh to elect constables to maintain order in the town; Leith was included in this directive. The constables were to be chosen equally from both the merchants and the craftsmen. It could not have been a popular post, for the constables not only had to carry out their duties but would also have to continue to run their own businesses. The posts, therefore, were to be held for only six months.

Constables were now to deal with disorder in the burgh – previously this had been the duty of the bailies. They were given the right to enter private property to conduct a search. Part of their duty was to seek out Catholics and their priests, as well as to track down 'sturdy beggars'. They were also expected to enforce the ban on the carrying of pistols in the burgh. On the last Saturday of each month, they reported to the provost and the bailies. Added to all their other duties, the constables had to ensure their districts were kept clean – a near impossible job! Thirteen years later, the constables were sent to patrol the bounds to check for any who might have the pest.

However, the council considered that, despite the introduction of constables, crime and disorder had increased. Constables took turns to supervise a night watch from 9 p.m. until 5 a.m. This must have eased the workload of the bailies, who were normally responsible. Maintaining law and order in the growing burgh still remained in the hands of 'volunteers'.

Two hundred years after their introduction to the streets of the city, a proper police force was created for Edinburgh, but crime, disorder and street cleaning were still part of their responsibility.

The Growing Debt

In the twenty-two years following the union of the crowns the burgh treasurer only had a surplus on six occasions. Although the last three years of the reign brought a small surplus totalling some £9,000, in 1612–13 and 1618–19 the burgh had a shortfall in its revenue of over £13,000 for each year, and 1620–21 was a particularly bad time with the deficit reaching £15,042.

The town's income more than doubled in these years, but costs were rising more rapidly. The council was responsible for the ministers' stipends and the salaries of the High School staff. Church repairs and the building of the new Kirk of Greyfriars further added to the problem. A considerable amount of money was spent on the Netherbow Port prior to the visit of the king. A new hall for the college and a weighhouse helped to increase the burden of debt.

Edinburgh itself was expected to pay its share of taxes. In 1607 this amounted to £12,777 – more than Dundee, Aberdeen and Glasgow combined. The burgh was dependent on its market and the trade which passed through the Port of Leith. Shortly after the union of the crowns, some £11,000 was paid out to people like Lady Cassilis to ensure the superiority of Leith remained in Edinburgh's hands.

The restrictions placed on the commercial activities of the inhabitants of Leith were greatly resented, and Edinburgh also collected the duties from shipping using the port, which helped pay the cost of maintaining the harbour.

Buildings from the Reign of James VI

There are still a few buildings remaining from the time of James VI. Gladstone's Land in the Lawnmarket has been restored to show the cramped conditions in which even wealthy merchants lived during the seventeenth and early eighteenth centuries. In the close behind this land is Lady Stair's House, built by Sir William Grey of Pittendrum in 1622. He was the grandfather of the first Lady Stair. It is now a museum to honour the famous Scottish writers Burns, Scott and Stevenson.

On the south side of the Lawnmarket you can find Riddle's Close. Here is the house of Bailie John McMorane, who was killed in the High School Riot of 1595. Further down the Royal Mile is Blackfriars Wynd which links the High

Street and the Cowgate. Near the head of the wynd stands the town house of James Douglas, Earl of Morton and Regent of Scotland. It was Morton who began the rebuilding of the eastern part of Edinburgh Castle after the siege. The Half Moon Battery was constructed over the remains of the ancient tower built by David II.

In the Canongate, the Tolbooth was built in 1591. Further down, on the opposite side, is Huntly House, dating from 1570, although in fact it may have been created from three smaller buildings with earlier dates. It was known as Speaking House because of the words written on its front. Today these buildings are both museums.

Near the foot of the street is a small close which once contained the White Horse Inn. The beginnings of this close and the inn itself may date from the last years of James VI.

In Leith, not far from the Shore, stands the home of the Lambs. One of these wealthy merchants entertained Mary, Queen of Scots when she returned from France. Sadly, it was not in this house, which was probably built in the first decade of the seventeenth century. Roseburn House is even earlier; Mungo Russell, who served as treasurer to the town from 1575 to 1582, built it in the last year of his office.

Mary King's Close, which is now open to the public, probably dates from this period. The close fell into decay after the plague that struck Edinburgh and Leith in 1645.

The Craft Elections, 1615

It was customary for the council to choose the leet (list of nominees) from which the craft masters elected their deacon. All appears to have gone well until 1615, when Arthur Hamilton, Deacon of Wrights, refused to accept the leet and hold an election. He was an experienced deacon who had held the office on four occasions. The council was naturally angry and sent Hamilton to prison. David Brown, who had served as deacon in 1612 and 1613, also refused to accept the leet. He joined Hamilton in prison. The two former deacons were forced to apologise to the authorities. Despite all this trouble, Arthur Hamilton was re-elected deacon and the council accepted the decision.

When the election for the Deacon of the Baxters was described as 'disorderly', Mungo Ross, the former deacon, was told by the council to hold a second election in Magdalen Chapel. In order to ensure a fair contest the council appointed four men, respected deacons from the other trades, to supervise this election. The result saw Gavin Stevenson chosen as Deacon of the Baxters.

The Visit of James VI in 1617

In 1603, James VI and his court had gone south to receive the crown of England. It was expected that he would make regular trips back to his northern kingdom but this did not happen. Governing Scotland became the job of the Scottish Privy Council and no longer could various groups of nobles attempt to take the king into custody and assume control of the country. James now had a prison much more formidable than the Tolbooth of Edinburgh, or even its castle.

It was not until 1617 that James returned to Edinburgh. The burgh had already spent a considerable sum on the Netherbow Port and a temporary banqueting hall had to be built and then dismantled, thus doubling the cost.

The Netherbow Port separated the burgh from the Canongate and work on restoring this entrance had begun in 1615. Benjamin Lambert received £128 7s for his work during 1615–16. However, it was in 1616–17 that the real money was spent, with the visit of the king in mind. William Cockie was paid over £213 for paintwork, while William Rea, an Edinburgh merchant, charged £145 for 118 books of gold leaf. It must have been an impressive sight with all the gold. The whole cost for that year exceeded £1,000.

Food Shortages, 1622–25

Prices had begun to stabilise, but a food shortage in 1623 saw the cost of stronger ales reaching 20d per pint and beer 24d per pint. The 12d loaf, which weighed 20oz in 1620, fell sharply in weight and in 1623 was being sold at less than 10oz.

The position had become so bad that special collections were set up to aid the poor and guards were placed on the ports to keep out 'idle and sturdy beggars'. The next year, the ministers were given 1,000 marks to be divided equally between them to assist them during these food shortages.

The End of an Era

Edinburgh had passed through turbulent and troubled times at the beginning of the reign of James VI. The days when powerful nobles could bring disorder, not only to the country but also into the streets of Edinburgh, appeared to have gone. James had pushed through changes in religious worship but they had not challenged the heart of the Presbyterian Calvinist Church, which was the Kirk in Scotland. He knew from experience that there were limits to the power of the king and he was prepared to compromise to obtain a peaceful, if not always satisfactory, solution.

Nine

CHARLES I AND THE COMMONWEALTH

The Ministers' Stipends

Since medieval times a tax called teinds (tenths) had been collected for the upkeep of the Church and the stipend of the priest or, after the Reformation, the minister. Prior to 1560, much of this money was taken by the abbeys who had been given the parish churches. The right to collect the dues was farmed out to tacksmen who were often important local landowners (lairds). Naturally they peeled off a goodly amount in profit.

Local lairds were not the only ones to gain from the break-up of the medieval Church, which had been the wealthiest landowner in Scotland. Church properties came into the hands of the nobility by grants or purchases, probably well below market value. As in England, the Church settlement was backed by a considerable vested interest.

Charles I wished to see that the ministers in the Church were paid properly, and the king could have expected to receive the support of the clergy whose rights he was trying to secure. However, many of them disliked the new influence of the bishops and were not inclined to give him their support. Faced with this opposition, Charles made no progress in solving the problem of the payment of the ministers' stipends.

David Aitkinheid and John Hay

At the beginning of the reign of Charles I, David Aitkinheid was Provost of Edinburgh. He had served on the council since 1601 and had already held the position of provost from 1620–22. Aitkinheid supported royal policies during his second term in office from 1625 to 1629. After a short break, he was again elected provost in 1634 and continued to hold the office until his death in

August 1637 – a month after the riot in St Giles. He was buried in Greyfriars Churchyard.

His successor as provost was Sir John Hay. Hay had been appointed deputy town clerk and after 1619 he became joint town clerk with Alexander Guthrie. The council sent him to London as their representative in negotiations to sort out the will of George Heriot. Hay was also credited with persuading the king that building a fortress in Leith would infringe the town's rights in the burgh. Since the cost of this project might well have fallen on Edinburgh he had certainly done the town a good service.

Hay was apparently related to David Aitkinheid and in October 1627 Sir Robert Dalyell accused him of using his influence to stop Sir William Nisbet being elected provost.

Hay became a Lord of Session (high court judge) in 1633. A loyal supporter of the king, he joined Montrose and was captured after the Battle of Philiphaugh. For some time Hay was held in Dumbarton Castle before being released and allowed to retire to Duddingston, where he died in 1654.

George Heriot's Hospital

George Heriot left most of his money to build a hospital 'for the maintenance, relief, bringing up and education of so many poor fatherless boys, freemen's sons of that town of Edinburgh'. Heriot was not just a goldsmith but a banker to people of wealth and importance. His clients had included James VI and his queen, thus it was necessary to secure the money owed to Heriot and invest it to secure the future of the new foundation. Much of this money was used to buy land around Edinburgh.

Dr Balcanquall, the son of the former minister of Edinburgh, was chosen by Heriot just before he died to act as chief executor. Balcanquall lived in London and later became Dean of Rochester. The council appointed John Hay to act on their behalf in trying to reach a settlement. Eventually he was able to recover a sum of £23,625 for the hospital.

Edinburgh and Charles I

By 1630 Charles I had decided to rule without the financial support of the English Parliament. This forced him to gather as many duties as he could from his southern subjects while remaining technically within the law. In Scotland, he continued to call Parliament, which was managed by the Scottish Privy Council and failed to reflect the growing opposition to some of his policies.

The king's demands for money from his Scottish subjects rose rapidly in the 1620s, and the burden fell heavily on the capital. The king wanted a new house for the Scottish Parliament and this was built on the old kirkyard of St Giles, which sloped steeply down towards the Cowgate. It cost the town £127,000.

St Giles was to become the cathedral for the newly created bishopric of Edinburgh. The internal walls, which had been constructed at the Reformation to provide churches for three congregations, had to be removed. Two new churches were proposed for the displaced worshippers. The Tron Church was begun in 1637 and opened ten years later. A second church was planned for Castlehill, but nothing came of this. However, they were able to build another church using money given by Dame Margaret Ker, Lady Yester. It was built on land near the college (today, this is the north side of Infirmary Street off the South Bridge).

Charles I visited Edinburgh in 1633, adding £40,000 to the costs. In the first ten years of his reign expenditure had risen threefold. Income had failed to match this and the capital was faced with a growing debt problem. This was something that future councils failed to address, and it took a further two centuries before the crisis finally came to a head.

Street Cleaning

In April 1633, no doubt with the king's visit in mind, the council discovered that 'the high streets and public vennels of this burgh abound with all kinds of filth'. Orders were issued that all waste must be put out into the street before six o'clock in the morning. Men were to be paid to take this in wheelbarrows to the head of the close, where a man with a horse and cart would remove it. One cart for the whole town seems to be a rather inadequate response to the problem; Edinburgh was a crowded burgh and all waste eventually ended up on the street. At this time there was no piped water or means to remove sewage except by placing it on the street.

Trinity College and its Hospital

At the eastern end of the Nor' Loch, where Waverley Station stands today, was the collegiate church of the Holy Trinity. It had been founded by Mary of Guelders, and at the Reformation, Trinity College, as it came to be known, became the parish church for the north-east quarter of the burgh. Next to the church was the hospital – an almshouse for elderly distressed burgesses. It had been founded by Bishop Thomas Spens of Aberdeen in 1467. In 1528 it was referred to in the Burgh Records as the 'Hospital of St Paul beside Trinity College'. The church and the hospital were offered to the burgh by the Earl of

Moray during his regency. Simon Preston, the provost, gratefully accepted this. Bailie Adam Fullerton was immediately appointed to the position of master of works to the hospital. However, it was not until 1597 that the council issued instructions for 'Paul's Work to be repaired and poor children and others to be placed there and fed at the town's expense'.

The children were taught such skills as spinning and weaving. Bethea Guthrie, the widow of an Edinburgh merchant, donated some money to set up the teaching of drapery. Attempts to set up a broad cloth industry next to Trinity College failed.

In 1660 a council report attempted to tighten up the running of St Paul's Work. All legacies had to be put in the register and a man was to be appointed to test the children on their skills. At that time these were spinning, making of stockings and serge. There is no mention of basic literacy. Five adults were to live on the premises and supervise the children and see to their needs.

In 1632, the easternmost property on the site was given over for a trial period as a correction house. William Stanfield was paid £90 a quarter to run this prison. From that, he was expected to find the wages of his staff and also tools, irons (for restraining prisoners) and even beds. The experiment was originally to last for one year. The correction house was a useful place to put vagabonds and other petty criminals who would have crowded up the Tolbooth.

Ladies' Fashions: Plaids

It was not often that the Edinburgh councillors became involved with ladies' fashions. In July 1628 they banned the wearing of plaids by women in the burgh. It did little good, for they had to repeat the order in April 1631 and 1633. In November 1637 they complained that matrons were 'not being able to be discerned from strumpets and loose living women to their own dishonour and the scandal of the city'. These women were 'wearing their gowns and Pittiecottes about their heads and faces'. Despite these complaints they had to repeat the ban in April 1641 and again in 1645.

The College

During this period, the council set out to lay down regulations governing all aspects of life in the college. Students were forbidden from visiting taverns 'or any other unseemly place'. They were not allowed to carry weapons or to wear their hair long. All scholars were expected to speak Latin and not Scots. The day began early – 6 a.m. in winter and 5 a.m. in summer!

The four-year course commenced with Latin and Greek grammar in the first year. This was followed by arithmetic and more Greek. The third year added Hebrew grammar and anatomy to the course. Work for third-year students also brought in studies in logic, ethics and physics with theology on Sundays. In their final year, the students also studied astronomy. All students were to attend both Sunday sermons in the company of their regents.

The Church, in the form of the Edinburgh ministers, kept a sharp eye on the college. In 1626, the principal, Samuel Rutherford, was dismissed from his post after the authorities discovered he was having an affair with Euphame Hamilton. The following year, James Reid, who had served as a regent and later a professor for twenty-four years, was sacked because William Struthers, one of the Edinburgh ministers, disagreed with some of his teaching. To be fair to the Church, it must be remembered that many (probably the majority) of the students would go on to take up positions as ministers of the Kirk. Independent thought, particularly on religion (and politics), was strictly discouraged.

Broughton and the Canongate

In 1626, with the money coming in from the estate of George Heriot, the council bought property in Broughton from Sara Miller and Thomas Fleming. The money from the feus (duties paid to the owners of the properties) would help finance the new hospital. It was a move which would turn Heriot's Hospital into one of the largest landowners in the city. Ten years later, they purchased the Canongate, North Leith and the village of Pleasance. The agreement was not finalised until 1639 when a royal charter confirmed the sale of these lands. The charter also included an agreement made with the Earl of Roxburgh, allowing the town to acquire the Barony of Broughton.

The council wasted no time. Even before the sale was completed, they appointed Henry Bannatyne as a second bailie for the Canongate. Edinburgh now controlled the harbour of Newhaven and the lands on both sides of the Water of Leith. The acquisition of Broughton and the Canongate linked these lands to the town.

When the council was formed again after the capture of the town by Cromwell's troops they were soon reasserting their power over the Canongate. The inhabitants were informed that both the bailies and most of their council would be elected by Edinburgh. New burgesses were to be chosen by the bailies. The Canongate was given no option but to accept this 'agreement' dictated to them by Edinburgh Town Council.

The National Covenant, 1638

Charles wished to make changes to the Church in Scotland. The Scottish bishops drew up the New Prayer Book which was passed to the king for alteration and approval. The Scottish Privy Council were unable to take any decisive steps as major Acts of policy had to receive sanction from London. The distance not only led to delays but cushioned Charles from the reality of Scottish feelings.

On Sunday, 23 July 1637 the Prayer Book was used for the first time in Edinburgh at the morning service in St Giles. This led to a riot in the church when a vegetable seller called Jenny Geddes threw a stool at the minister. What part Jenny Geddes played in these events is open to question, but it is certain that this was no spontaneous outburst. Later rumour held that men disguised as women were the ringleaders.

Opposition to the changes in the service was very strong in Edinburgh. The town council were accused of failing to keep order in the burgh, but it is difficult to see what they could do without a proper police force. The Privy Council was faced with similar difficulties for they had no military force to call upon.

Disturbances in Edinburgh were not unknown, but resistance to the changes in worship began to turn into a movement to defend the Scottish Church. Throughout the autumn, ministers gathered in the burgh to express their opposition to the New Prayer Book. Even the Privy Council drew up a petition to the king to ask that the use of the book be discontinued. However, when it was learnt that they had failed to send this on to London, another disturbance in the town broke out on 18 October. The king's representatives in Scotland, led by the Earl of Traquair, had doubts about their ability to change the mind of the king.

Grievances were building up. Since August, after the riot in St Giles, the bishops had removed the ministers of Edinburgh, which prevented regular worship in the burgh churches. The Privy Council and the Court of Session moved to Stirling, leaving the burgh in the hands of those who opposed the king's policy. The clergy were joined by nobles who felt resentment that their views carried little weight with the king.

On 23 February 1638 Alexander Henderson and Archibald Johnston, an Edinburgh lawyer, drew up a draft copy of what was to become the National Covenant. The next day, representatives of the peers revised it before, on 28 February, it was brought before the ministers, lairds and nobility. On that day many of the most powerful and influential people in Scotland met in Greyfriars Church to sign the National Covenant. Soon copies were sent to all parts of Scotland to gain the signatures of those who were unable to come to the capital. Pressure was placed on people to sign. Robert Rankin and John

Brown, teachers at the college, were dismissed for their refusal to endorse the Covenant.

More ominously, the town treasurer, James Rocheid, was ordered to buy powder and matches, and in October 1638 William Dick of Braid replaced Sir John Hay as provost. Two months later, the council ordered 'training in military discipline for defence of the country if need shall appear but also for serving His Majesty'. An interesting turn of phrase, because the only force that they might have to defend themselves against would be one raised by the king.

The men who signed the Covenant did not see themselves as rebels. It was not the king whom they opposed but his ministers and the policies they represented. This fiction was maintained to counter any charges of treason that might be brought against them. In the New Year (1639), more powder, matches and lead for shot was being stored in St Giles' church. Appeals were made to the inhabitants of the burgh to contribute to this. Eighty muskets and forty pikes were lent by the crafts in case they should be needed if the king's troops were to invade Scotland. General Alexander Leslie, a veteran of the war in Germany, laid siege to the castle on 19 March and, five days later, he proceeded to blow up the gate to secure the fortress for the Covenanters. A boom was placed across the harbour at Leith to prevent the port being used for the landing of English soldiers, and a general muster of the town's forces was held in Greyfriars Churchyard on 26 March. However, when war finally broke out between the king and the English Parliament, the Scots remained neutral.

Markets and Streets

In both January and March 1642, the council received complaints about the high prices to be paid in the Edinburgh markets, as they were responsible for regulating prices in the markets. The usual suspects were blamed – buying for resale and selling privately (outside the market to avoid paying market duties). Action, however, was needed and the council appointed three inspectors each for the Lawnmarket, the Nether Market (poultry and fish) and the Meal Market.

Fleshers also came in for necessary regulation; they were using the streets and vennels as slaughterhouses. With the common passageways used as sewers, rubbish dumps and slaughterhouses, it is not surprising that outbreaks of disease occurred in the burgh. The council ordered that all animals were to be killed either outside the burgh or at the side of the Nor' Loch.

The town, like the country, was under the control of the strict Presbyterians who enforced the laws against all activities on the Sabbath which were not connected to the study of religion. Traders who lived some distance from

Edinburgh had to travel on the Sabbath so that they could reach the town in time for the start of the Monday markets. The council therefore stopped the Monday markets.

The Solemn League and Covenant

By the end of 1642 the Civil War in England had reached a stalemate. The Royalist Army had driven the forces of Parliament back at Edgehill but the king had been unable to challenge the strong defences Parliament had placed around London. Both sides now began to look for an ally who could offer military support.

The Scots had already proved that they could raise such a fighting force. Edinburgh had, until the signing of the National Covenant, been led by people who had given their support to the king's policies. In May 1643, Provost Clerk received a letter from the king in which he reminded the council of 'the many favours our town of Edinburgh has received from us'. Members of the council might have questioned the veracity of that statement. The town had been heavily taxed, and the costs of the alterations of St Giles and the building of the new Tron Kirk had had to be found by the capital. Edinburgh had also had to pay for the new Parliament House.

Parliament also sent commissioners to negotiate with the Scots. Religion remained the driving force in Scottish policy. They now wished to establish the Presbyterian system not only in Scotland but also in England and Wales. The Parliamentary side were willing to sign up to this. An agreement was drawn up between the Parliament of England and the Scottish leaders. This was known as the Solemn League and Covenant. Delegates were sent to Westminster to finalise the religious settlement while a Scottish army prepared to march south to join up with the Parliamentary troops. Edinburgh recruited a regiment of its own citizens under Colonel James Rae. Even some of the ministers of the town left their charges to serve as chaplains in the Scottish army.

In January 1644, Alexander Leslie led the Scottish army into England. The cavalry force was commanded by David Leslie (no relation). The Royalist town of York was the target of this force. Prince Rupert, the king's nephew, marched north to help the defenders of York while the Eastern Association sent an army north with a large troop of cavalry under the command of Oliver Cromwell. The two armies met on Marston Moor outside York. Parliament and their new allies won an important victory which led to the collapse of the king's power in the north.

The Plague, 1645

An outbreak of what is thought to have been bubonic plague reached Leith in May 1645. Lodgings for the victims were set up on the Links, their houses were cleaned and then closed up, and clothes were boiled in large cauldrons. Matthew Mitchell promised to lend his cauldron but the authorities requisitioned James Mathie's. These were very difficult times with people dying in large numbers.

In June, the authorities (bailies, minister and session) set about removing the middens of muck and dead pigs from the streets. The job was so big that the townswomen were called on to help clear up the mess. The work continued through into October when Bailie Barnes threatened to imprison any woman who refused to help.

Heather for kindling, and probably fumigating, was in short supply. John Charteris, the minister of Currie, informed messangers from Leith that the men of his parish would not supply any more until payment for previous stocks had been made. They then appealed to Sir William Scott of Malleny (Balerno, in the parish of Currie). This must have brought results, as five days later a man was sent to Currie to collect the heather.

John Aldinstone, one of the bailies of Leith, and James Crawford, an inhabitant of the port, travelled to the Scottish Parliament which was being held in Perth (because Edinburgh, too, was suffering from the plague). He told them that 'the plague of pestilence is such that the number of dead exceeds the living'. He went on, 'they were visited with a lamentable famine' – restrictions on movement and the deaths of so many workers would have led to a shortage of food.

The situation was so bad that even preaching, the centre of religious life, had been abandoned. The deaths continued through the autumn until a terrible storm of wind and rain struck the port on 2 November. This appears to have cleared the air, as the number of new victims began to decrease rapidly. A month later, they started to take down the camp on the Links. It is possible that Bailie Aldinstone's words were true and that half the population of Leith died in this plague.

The actions of the bailie and the Session in cleaning up the town may have made Leith a healthier place. Twenty years later, London was stricken by a terrible plague but this failed to spread to Leith, despite the port's links with the English capital.

In Edinburgh, the old nunnery of Sciennes was used to shelter some of the victims removed from the town, but the keeper of the property was found to be neglecting his duty. The council decided to abandon the idea of sending any more people to Sciennes. Things were so bad in the summer that a lot of inhabitants were considering leaving the town. Possibly some had already left, although they would not have found any escape from the plague which was well established in much of the country. The council stepped in to prevent the movement of people. Lodgings on the town's side of the Burgh Loch (the Meadows) were taken down and the materials burnt. Some debtors were even released from the Tolbooth in August and the office of the town clerk was closed. Only when the weather began to change towards the end of the year did the plague relent.

The Engagement and the Whiggamores

A group of Scottish lords saw the chances of carrying through the agreement put forward in the Solemn League and Covenant fading. If Parliament would not agree to establish the Church of the Covenant as the Church in Britain, maybe the king would do so. Led by Loudon, Lanark and Lauderdale, they made a treaty with Charles I in December 1647. This was known as the Engagement. Two months later this was rejected by the Commissioners of the Church. The supporters of the Covenant were no longer united.

Life in Edinburgh was already hard, with the burgh expected to pay £4,167 a month to support the Scottish army. The Presbytery of Edinburgh came out against the Engagement but Sir Archibald Tod, who had become provost in October 1646, supported the Engagement and it would appear that he was backed by most of the council.

Another army was raised and, led by the Marquis of Hamilton, it invaded England, only to be defeated in August near Preston. The opponents of the Engagers saw their chance; Loudon deserted them and joined Eglinton and Argyll in a bid for power. This was known as the Whiggamore Raid. Argyll took the castle and Edinburgh fell under the control of the extreme Presbyterian Party. Loudon, who now became lord chancellor, asked the town to provide 500–600 men to counter the Engagers, who had an army in Haddington.

The Committee of Estates ruled that no supporter of the Engagement was to hold any position of authority in the country. This led to a purge of the town council in the October elections of 1648. Sir Archibald Tod was replaced by Sir James Stewart, many of the council lost their positions, and William Thomson, the town clerk, was dismissed.

One example of the change was the fate of the Edinburgh merchant, Alexander Brand. On 30 June, his criticism of Hamilton and the Engagement led to him losing his burgess ticket. He had also been expelled from the Merchants' Guild. However, the victory of the Whiggamores led the new council (9 October) to restore Brand to his previous positions.

On 6 October 1648, a delegation which included two bailies and the old provost set out for Moray House in the Canongate. There they met 'Lord

Cromwell, Lieutenant General of the English forces'. He was eager to ensure that the supporters of the Engagement were excluded from power in Scotland.

The Town Guard, 1648

During the period of uncertainty which followed the seizure of power by the Whiggamores, the council decided to recruit a body of soldiers to be responsible for the guarding of the city. Sixty men were placed under the orders of Lieutenant Colonel Affleck. Two months later he was replaced by Major Thomas Weir, whose men were probably seasoned soldiers who had fought against the Irish rebels and the king's supporters.

Weir's religious views would have met with the approval of the new government. Many years later, he was to become one of Edinburgh's most notorious characters when he confessed to being involved in witchcraft.

The guard was paid off in the following May and the townsfolk resumed the watch duties. The Town Guard of 1648–49 should not be confused with the later body of men who were set up in the 1680s.

Portsburgh and Potterrow

In 1648 the town council purchased the superiority of Portsburgh and Potterrow. Sir John Wemyss of Bogie received 20,000 marks in return for the control over the streets which had grown up outside the Bristo Port and the West Port.

Later, on 4 April 1649, Portsburgh was given its own court and bailies. All appointments to the court and the office of bailie were to be made by Edinburgh Town Council. Negotiations were opened with James Boilands with a plan to add king's stables to the town. These were to drag on until the Restoration and were only completed in 1663.

The bailies of Portsburgh were allowed to use the Tolbooth prison until their own tolbooth was completed in 1652. This was to be the last expansion of the town for over 100 years, when Edinburgh obtained the property that created the New Town.

The Fall of Edinburgh, 1650

Charles I was beheaded in January 1649 by the orders of what remained of the English Parliament. The Royalists, and later the Presbyterian members, had been excluded. The real power in England lay with Fairfax, Cromwell and the army. With the death of the king, the Scottish leaders recognised his son,

Charles II, as the new king, and this brought them into direct conflict with the new rulers in the south. The situation was not eased by the arrival of Charles in Scotland.

July 1650 saw Edinburgh being put into a state of defence as Cromwell's forces (the 'sectarian army', as the Scots called them) approached the city. Supplies were requisitioned for the castle to withstand a four-month siege and the Spur, in front of the gate, was demolished. General David Leslie, in command of the Scottish forces, placed his troops on the high ground between Leith and Edinburgh, and Hermitage Hill, Hawkhill, Restalrig, Calton Hill, Salisbury Crags and St Leonard's were all prepared to resist Cromwell's push into central Scotland. Guns were placed on the town walls and the provost, Sir James Stewart, organised a barricade at the Cowgate Port. Even the hospital at Trinity College was turned into an infirmary for wounded soldiers.

Charles II arrived in Leith on 29 July. The next day, Cromwell entered Musselburgh. Throughout August Cromwell probed the defences but the Scots held firm. Faced with a shortage of food, the English army finally withdrew to Dunbar on the last day of the month, and General Leslie and the Scots followed their retreating enemy. The ensuing battle led to the complete defeat of the Scots, and on 7 September Cromwell's troops entered Edinburgh and Leith.

The town was left without a council, and troops were billeted in the houses of the local inhabitants. To prevent chaos and probable reprisals, a committee of seventeen merchants and thirteen craftsmen was set up to look after the affairs of the town. Among its members was Archibald Tod, who had been provost until the arrival of the Whiggamores. In November, a party of soldiers who were billeted in Holyrood Palace managed to set fire to the palace. Much of the building was destroyed in the fire, but fortunately James V's Tower survived. It was later rebuilt by Cromwell, but this proved only a temporary measure as the whole palace was to be redesigned after the Restoration.

Throughout 1651 the town was ruled by the troops and the Committee of Thirty. In November, Lieutenant General Lambert came to Edinburgh to prepare winter quarters for his soldiers. Finding no official body in charge he proposed to set up a town council. This time, there was to be no provost and two of the four bailies were to be nominated by the general, who was to be the governor. Ten councillors were to be chosen – half by the town and half by Lambert himself. This was not acceptable to the people of Edinburgh.

Lambert ordered – presumably the committee – to clean up the town streets and to ensure lights and candles were hung out at night to light the streets and closes. This order might well have been given to discourage poor discipline under the cover of darkness among the billeted troops.

Finally, on 9 March 1652, a new council was set up under the old Edinburgh Constitution. The army had not won that battle, and Archibald Tod was re-elected as provost. A new committee, supposedly of twenty, although twenty-one names are listed in the record, was elected by the council. They may well have continued to assist in the billeting of soldiers. Shortly afterwards, St Cuthbert's was damaged by the occupying soldiers and the congregation had to use the College Hall until the damage was repaired. The inhabitants of South Leith also lost their church, which was used by the army as a store for their supplies.

The Town Government Under the Commonwealth

With the restoration of municipal government, Sir Archibald Tod became provost again. He had held the post from October 1646 until he was replaced by Sir James Stewart after the defeat of the Engagers. William Thomson, who had lost his post after the Whiggamore Raid, was also reinstated as town clerk and then sent to London to act as a representative of the town.

One of the bailies elected in this new council in October 1652 was Andrew Ramsay. Two years later, Ramsay set out for London to ask the Protector's (Cromwell's) Council and the new Parliament for some relief from the burden of taxation. In 1655 the council elected him as provost.

That same year, Lord Broghill was appointed as President of the Council of State (for Scotland). In one of his first judgements he decided in favour of Edinburgh in the dispute with Leith. Broghill was made a burgess and was chosen by the council, along with Provost Ramsay, to be their Members of Parliament. This was the first Parliament to include representatives from all parts of the British Isles. John Nicoll commented in his diary that Ramsay was 'spending much of the town's money, which being resented by the town, they turned him out of his office of provestry'.

Sir James Stewart returned as provost. He was to hold the post until the return of Charles II, after which the new government imprisoned him in the castle. Sir James was eventually released and allowed to retire from town politics. Andrew Ramsay returned as provost in 1662.

Religion in the Burgh in the 1650s

The Scots had failed to achieve their main object of setting up a Presbyterian National Church in the whole of Britain. They had signed an agreement with the English Parliament (the Solemn League and Covenant), but during the years that followed the defeat of Charles I the army began to take control of the country. Most of its officers belonged to sects who did not want their churches controlled by bishops or presbyteries – they are sometimes known as the 'Independents'. Many of them were to form the Baptist and Congregationalist churches. Another sect, who in their earlier years proved to be a disruptive group, were the Quakers; they first appeared in Edinburgh in 1655.

The ministers of Edinburgh were opposed to the new regime ruling the burgh and the country after the defeat at Dunbar. Some of them had served as chaplains in the Scottish armies and had been put in prison by the 'sectarian' army. They refused to administer Communion during the occupation and continued their protest until July 1655. Edinburgh churches had not celebrated the sacrament for six years. This was not their only complaint, as the council was behind in its payment of the stipend. By 1655 the five ministers (George Hutchison, Hew McKail, Thomas Garvie, Robert Trail and John Stirling) were owed £8,160 13s 4d – enough to make any one protest!

Fires in Edinburgh, 1654

In the autumn of 1654 Edinburgh suffered two major fires. The first, in October, affected both sides of the Cowgate. There were a considerable number of casualties, both Scots and English (possibly soldiers quartered in the area), and after the fire had been extinguished more bodies were found under the rubble and charred timber. The second fire, in Kirkheugh, broke out in December, when a tall tenement collapsed. English soldiers assisted the people of the town to put out the flames.

At this time the council took a look at the trades who used fire as part of their businesses. The candlemakers were moved to the gateway in Leith Wynd, while baxters and brewers were made to carry out their work in the Society Lands, opposite Greyfriars Church. We do not know how strongly the council enforced these rules.

In 1656 a tack was given for a candlemaker's house and shop by the Society Port. Perhaps this area on the edge of the town (approximately the southern end of George IV Bridge and Chambers Street) was considered the safest place.

Down the Water of Leith

Passing through the West Port the road entered the burgh of Portsburgh, newly acquired by Edinburgh. From here, one route turned north past St Cuthbert's down to the village of the Water of Leith (now called the Dean Village). It was here that the burgh had built its mills.

Storms at the beginning of 1659 damaged the road, and the council, who were responsible for its upkeep, had to pay for the repairs. Two years previously the dam had been so seriously damaged that the flow of water to the five mills on the north side was restricted. Further down the river at Canonmills, John

Paterson was operating a paper mill. The stone bridge at Stockbridge and the wooden one at Silvermills had both been repaired in 1658. The river flowed down to the two corn mills at Bonnington and repairs had had to be carried out on the buildings. The council used stone from the old leper house at Greenside.

The Water of Leith now reached the port. A large fortress known as the Citadel had been built on the high ground above North Leith, and this had brought English traders north, leading to a conflict between the English butchers and those from Leith.

William Cowston, a skipper in Leith, may have been using the breakdown in authority to take over a shipyard in North Leith. It is possible this was the yard constructed by James Arnot as part of his agreement made with the council in 1638. It should have been handed over to the town in 1651, but William Cowston began a shipbuilding business relying on James Rae, a council officer, to turn a blind eye. Cowston was put in prison until he had seen to the demolition of his dock and James Rae was dismissed, but reinstated a few months later.

The End of the Commonwealth

The collapse of the Commonwealth came quickly. On the death of Oliver Cromwell, his son Richard assumed the role of Lord Protector. On 22 April 1659, he resigned, leaving the country at the mercy of the army and its leaders. General George Monck, a former Royalist officer and now commander of the Commonwealth forces in Scotland, assembled his forces in Edinburgh. The army marched south, encountering some opposition at Coldstream. Soon, Monck and his men were in London and moves were afoot to bring the king back to London from his exile in Holland.

Ten

RESTORATION AND REVOLUTION

Edinburgh and the Restoration of Charles II

The summer of 1660 brought an end to the Parliamentary Regime with the return of Charles II. In May, Edinburgh Council sent a letter to the king expressing their goodwill and loyalty, and the citizens lit bonfires to celebrate the king's return.

The provost, Sir James Stewart, was arrested and held in the castle. No charges were ever brought against him, but he took no further part in the affairs of the burgh. However, others who had served as provosts or bailies during the Cromwellian period were not excluded from office. Robert Murray became provost in October. He held the office for the next two years, after which Andrew Ramsay replaced him. Murray was an Edinburgh merchant who had previously served as provost from 1650–52 and as a bailie from 1652–54. Andrew Ramsay served as provost from 1654–57 and had the distinction of being knighted by both Cromwell *and* Charles II.

August saw the withdrawal of the English garrison from Edinburgh, although a sizeable force remained in the Citadel at Leith. One of the major problems facing the new government in London was the need to pay the army. Soldiers who had not been paid regularly had run up debts in the city and the council formed a committee to discuss the problem with the army's officers. One visible sign of change was the removal of the Court of Guardhouse by the Cross.

By November the new regime must have felt secure because General Morgan handed over 400 pikes and 400 muskets from the arsenal in the Citadel. These were to be used by the town's companies. However, not everyone accepted the changes. James Guthrie led a group of ministers who met in Edinburgh to protest about the restoration of episcopacy. Guthrie was charged with treason and was convicted and hung at the Cross. His head was placed on the Netherbow Port.

In 1663 the same fate befell another opponent of the regime. Archibald Johnston of Warriston, one of the men who had drawn up the Covenant of

1638, had fled to the Continent, but he was captured in Rouen and returned to Edinburgh. He too was tried for treason before being hung at the Cross.

The most prominent supporter of the Commonwealth had been Archibald Campbell, 8th Earl of Argyll: he was beheaded at the Cross on 27 May 1661.

John Maitland, Earl of Lauderdale

The most powerful man in Scotland after the Restoration of Charles II was the Earl of Lauderdale. John Maitland was born in 1616, the great-nephew of William Maitland of Lethington who had served both Mary of Guise and her daughter, Mary, Queen of Scots. As the conflict grew between Charles I and the Scottish Presbyterians Maitland threw in his lot with the Kirk. In 1643 he was one of the commissioners who travelled to London to negotiate with the English Parliament. The treaty they signed was called the Solemn League and Covenant. Lauderdale later joined those in Scotland who tried to make an agreement with the king. The failure of the Engagement forced Lauderdale from power.

After the execution of King Charles I, Lauderdale supported his son, Charles II. He took part in the invasion of England which led to the disastrous defeat at the Battle of Worcester in 1651. Charles II escaped, but Lauderdale did not. He remained a prisoner of the new government until the Restoration of Charles II in 1660.

Charles appointed Lauderdale as Secretary in Scotland. Despite attempts to remove him (Lauderdale had once been a committed Presbyterian which aroused suspicions among the new Episcopal elite) the earl, with the support of the king, increased his hold over the country. His family's fortunes had been ruined by the victory of the Cromwellian forces and Lauderdale did much to set that right. In 1662 he secured possession of the Cromwellian Citadel in Leith. Edinburgh had been forced to pay for the building of the fortress and now they had to pay to get it back.

A considerable amount of the burgh's revenue was paid out to the Earl (later Duke) of Lauderdale. He acquired the Citadel of Leith and the town had to pay £5,000 to secure its return. The council minutes in 1663 carry this interesting decision:

> Taking into consideration in time of this session of Parliament [Scottish Parliament held in Edinburgh] there will be a necessity to gratify those in public authority and other persons of quality by giving them a kindly welcome to the town and some of their servants and followers to the freedom of this burgh. Therefore the council finding it will be most convenient that the Lord Provost shall perform these things in the most decent and frugal way.

Lauderdale owned property in Musselburgh, which included some mills. They were given the right to sell their malt in Edinburgh, breaking the monopoly of the burgh's own mills. That same year, 1669, a pew seat was provided for him in St Giles and Maitland was created Duke of Lauderdale. In 1671 he secured a tax on wine for the burgh. In return he received the princely sum of £5,000, a timely present, as in the same year he married Margaret Kennedy, Countess of Dysart, just six weeks after the death of his own wife!

It was necessary not only to keep on the good side of the duke but also that of his wife and servants. Some believe that it was the duchess' influence that led to the fall of Sir Andrew Ramsay. Patrick Vaus, who was Keeper of the Tolbooth, asked 'permission to repair to London to visit his grace, the Duke of Lauderdale, his master'. The man obviously had two employers – the duke and the burgh council. One can guess to whom he answered first. The burgh admitted William Archibald, governor of the duchess' son (by her first marriage), and some of the duke's servants as Guild Brothers and burgesses. No charge was made for this honour.

Later the council expressed 'humble and hearty thanks for your grace's continued care of the general concerns of this city'. The duke had secured them the 2d per pint tax on ale and secured himself a gift of £320. Finally, in 1680, the city was granted a tax of 2 marks per bol on barley for twenty-one years. Lauderdale then received a gift from the council of £6,000. It proved to be the last gift; Lauderdale resigned that year for reasons of ill health and was replaced as commissioner by James, Duke of York, the future King James VII. Lauderdale died two years later (1682) in Tunbridge Wells.

Sir Andrew Ramsay and a Power Struggle

The Restoration years were not a period known for good government in the burgh. In October 1662, Sir Andrew Ramsay was elected provost, an office which he was to hold for the next eleven years. He had previously served as provost under the Commonwealth. His monopoly of the provostship naturally brought resentment from those who considered it their right to hold the office.

Although Ramsay held a firm grip over the town council in the 1660s, opposition to his rule began to grow. This was led by Francis Kinloch and James Rocheid, who was town clerk. Both these men were to play an important part in burgh politics in the years following the defeat of Ramsay.

In 1671 Sir Andrew Ramsay was made a member of the Scottish Privy Council and a Lord of the Court of Session. Some members of the council claimed that now Ramsay was a lord he was no longer eligible for the post of provost, since an Act of Parliament (June 1609) permitted only merchants to hold the office. However, this did not stop him from being elected provost again.

A protest was made by Dean of Guild Francis Kinloch, John Johnston, William Hay and James Dick. The election was further complicated when Walter Borthwick and Henry Barclay alleged that some members had been offered bribes. Members were urged to 'purge themselves by an oath that they had no manner of accession to such corrupt practices'.

Francis Kinloch, John Johnston and others (probably one of these was James Rocheid) went to court. Their council claimed that Ramsay 'sometimes most tyrannously threatened and abused any of the members that displeased him or offered calmly to debate with most scandalous and opprobrious language and commanding silence lest he would lay their feet fast [imprison them]'.

In 1658 the council had laid down that:

> It is unanimously agreed upon statute and ordained that in all time coming the Provost, Dean of Guild and Treasurer of this Burgh shall not be elected or continue in their respective office longer than on or at most two years together at one time.

The election seemed to favour Ramsay when, in September, the king ordered the dismissal of James Rocheid, the town clerk. Walter Binning produced a letter from the lord chancellor in which he claimed that 'so far as my memory serves me there was nothing done to incapacitate my Lord Abbotshall [Sir Andrew Ramsay] from being on the leet this year'. Ramsay was duly elected provost but events turned against him. On 1 December, Charles ordered the council to restore Rocheid to his post of town clerk. On the same day, Andrew Ramsay resigned. Five days later, James Currie was elected provost. He was followed by William Binning. Both men had served as bailies as well as holding the post of treasurer.

However, the support of the Earl of Lauderdale enabled him to cling on to power and the withdrawal of that support in 1673 led to his resignation. Ramsay was accused of threatening to imprison his political opponents, filling offices with his friends and relatives, as well as making his own son joint town clerk (at the time the lad was still a boy and unable to carry out the demands of the office although Ramsay pocketed the money).

In 1677 Francis Kinlock, long-time opponent of Sir Andrew Ramsay, became provost. He was succeeded by Sir James Dick of Prestonfield, grandson of Sir William Dick, who was provost from 1638–40, and later by Sir James Fleming. In 1683 the Privy Council informed the town that it was the king's wish that George Drummond should be elected provost.

In the following April, the High Treasurer of Scotland and his depute began to investigate the finances of the burgh. They did not take their investigations further back than 1674, thus avoiding looking into the activities of Sir Andrew Ramsay. Their main targets were Francis Kinloch, Sir James Dick and Sir

James Fleming. The three former provosts set out for London to defend their reputations. According to Sir James Lauder of Fountainhall (son-in-law of Sir Andrew Ramsay), 'this broke the Rocheid and Kinloch party on the town council'. The move did not turn out so well, because Drummond appointed his own son as town clerk and in 1685 he fled to the abbey to seek sanctuary from his creditors.

The Religious Settlement

The Restoration Settlement led to the return of bishops to Scotland and the Act of Conformity. Only one of the ministers of Edinburgh (Robert Lawrie) in 1660 appears to have remained in office. John Stirling of the Tron Kirk was even imprisoned for a short while. Robert Trail, who had preached at Charles II's coronation in Scone, was held in the castle under a charge of treason. He later fled to Holland.

The decisions of the new government seem to have been accepted by most of the citizens of Edinburgh. Only in the West Kirk (St Cuthbert's) was there resistance to the new minister, William Gordon. Supporters of David Williamson, the previous minister, shouted at him during services and even tried to lock him out. Williamson remained in touch with his parish, and two years after the Revolution he returned to his former charge.

The council was still responsible for the upkeep of the burgh churches. They also had charge of the town's cemetery in Greyfriars. Ministers of the town's kirks were appointed by the council. However, some people wished to worship in the old way and they held illegal meetings called 'conventicles'. The council had a duty to suppress them and would have to face the anger of the Privy Council should they fail.

A conventicle was discovered in 1669 at the house of the widow of Archibald Patone. Five years later, they became more daring, holding a conventicle in Magdalen Chapel. Two of the bailies, Swinton and Carmichael, were ordered to seek out these meetings. Despite their efforts, in March 1676 the authorities discovered four conventicles. At one of these, in Shoemakers' Land by Potterrow Port, the town officers met with resistance from John Nicoll who was the college (university) janitor. He managed to hold them off long enough to allow most of the worshippers to escape.

It is possible that conventicles were held in remote areas like the Pentland Hills but Sabbath rules restricted people from travelling any distance.

'The Pentland Rising'

Discontent with the changes in forms of worship was particularly strong in the south-west of Scotland. Soldiers were being used to force the religious settlement on reluctant congregations. In November 1666, a rebellion began.

The rebels marched on Edinburgh, but they received little support on their way. People living along the edge of the Pentlands were not involved in the rebellion despite it receiving the name 'Pentland Rising'. The rebels were caught at Rullion Green. Prisoners taken after the battle were brought to Edinburgh and kept in Greyfriars Churchyard. Many were transported, but a few of the leaders suffered a greater punishment. You can read the names of the nineteen men, who were hung for their part in the rising, on a plaque in the Grassmarket.

The Palace of Holyrood

Holyrood had ceased to be a royal palace regularly used by the reigning monarch after James VI departed for England in 1603. The visits of James VI (1617) and Charles I (1633) led to renovations being made at the palace. During the Cromwellian period, repairs were carried out which had been necessitated by the damage caused by the occupying forces.

After the Restoration, the Earl of Lauderdale set about rebuilding and Sir William Bruce, the King's Surveyor of Royal Works, designed the new palace. James V's Tower was retained and a second tower added to create a symmetrical design. Lauderdale was able to recruit skilled craftsmen like John Houlbert and George Dunsterfield, who were responsible for the plasterwork of the ceilings. He brought in Dutch artists to work on the interiors.

The Duke of York, who was to become James VII, used the palace when he acted as Secretary of State from 1679. Controversy followed, because the duke was a Roman Catholic and the Chapel Royal was set out for Catholic worship. James returned to London in 1685 upon the death of his brother, and the new palace was not used again by a reigning monarch until George IV visited the capital in 1822.

Racing and Other Sports

The town council sponsored the racing at Leith and also set out the rules. They provided a silver cup worth £20 (a large amount of money in those times). A saddle worth 50s was the prize offered in the other races. The Silver Cup Race was run twice a year in March and June. Members of the council clearly enjoyed attending the races, because in June 1678 when a council meeting clashed with the running of the Silver Cup it was the council meeting that was cancelled.

The racing continued even in winter, and a provision was laid down by the council that there must be more than one entry. Horses competing for the Silver Cup had to carry at least 8 stone, but there was no weight limit placed on horses running for the Saddle.

Horses entering these races had to be stabled in Leith. Entries for the Saddle Races were brought to the town two days before the race and those for the Silver Cup had to be in the stables ten days before the race. Was this to bring money to the Leith stablers, or to prevent cheating? Much more interesting – was there betting on the races?

Golf was a popular sport. Leith Links and Bruntsfield Links were used for this purpose. George Watson set up a shop in Leith Wynd to make and sell golf balls.

Archery continued to be practised long after it was of any military use, and the council ordered Bailie Neilson to find a convenient place to set up butts for archery on Leith Links. Neilson was appointed Water Bailie in October 1676.

The town also had tennis courts. John Nash, a rope dancer, was given permission to set up a stage on the tennis court 'for acting his plays and shows'. The court was 'opposite the Tron'. It would appear that some form of drama was available in Edinburgh during the Restoration years.

Major Thomas Weir

Thomas Weir was born in Clydesdale at the turn of the century. In 1641 he joined the Scottish Covenanter Army, sent to crush the rebellion in Ireland. Nothing is known about his service in the civil wars that were to follow. At the time, when the strict Presbyterians had ousted those seeking an Engagement with Charles I, Weir reappeared in Edinburgh. Major Weir replaced Colonel Affleck as commander of the Town Guard.

Weir was a strict believer in the old Puritan ways, although he does not appear to have come into conflict with the Episcopal Establishment that ruled Scotland after the Reformation. He spent his final years living in the West Bow with his sister, Grizel. The major was known both for his extemporary prayers and the black staff which he carried. So, in 1670, the citizens of Edinburgh were shocked to learn that he had confessed to practising witchcraft. Even the provost, Sir Andrew Ramsay, refused to believe it.

Major Weir was tried and found guilty. He was taken down the road to Leith where he was strangled and his body burnt. His poor sister was led to the Grassmarket and hung as a witch. Stories of the major continued to haunt the West Bow for many years after his death, and his staff, which was probably no more than a physical support for a man of 70, took on great significance.

Transport in the Burgh

In 1660 William Woodcock set up a hackney carriage service. He was given permission to build a coachhouse at the foot of Leith Wynd. This must have been close to where SMT (Scottish Motor Traction Company) built their motor works centuries later.

In 1673, it was decided to regulate the trade. Hackney coaches were to be licensed by the council and each one to carry a number. Twenty coaches duly received their licences and numbers that year. Fares were fixed at 4s for the journey between Leith and Edinburgh.

Even in the late seventeenth century, there was concern over road safety. The High Street and the Lawnmarket were filled with shoppers travelling to the booths and the markets. No vehicles – coaches, carts or sleds – were allowed to gallop or trot in the streets of the burgh. The owners of the vehicles were held responsible for the actions of their employees. Two years later, the bailies were given warrants to remove the coaches 'out of the city to some by place because they trouble the street' (note the use of the word 'city' when referring to Edinburgh).

Two years later, the council had to address complaints about 'furious driving' which endangered the lives of men, women and children. Considering the narrowness of the streets and the busy markets where pedestrians were not separated from the vehicles, it is surprising that anyone could drive 'furiously'.

In April 1677 William Home introduced a large carriage pulled by four horses. It could carry ten or more people between Edinburgh and Leith. Leaving from the foot of Leith Wynd, it provided an hourly service to Leith at much lower fares. Later, Alexander Hay set up a slower means of transport to the city in 1687, when the council gave him an eleven-year monopoly to operate sedan chairs. It was no doubt very useful for carrying ladies in their best dresses through the dirty streets.

The New Water Supply

Probably the most important step taken in the development of the city during the Restoration years was the improvement of the water supply. A full council meeting, which included all the deacons and fifteen other important burgesses, was held to discuss the financing of this project. They proposed to raise the money through a tax on hearths and they asked the members of the College of Justice (lawyers and judges), who were exempt from local taxes, to contribute since their members would also benefit from an improved water supply.

Two years later, in 1674, they hired the Dutch engineer, Peter Braus, to lay a 3in diameter pipe to carry the water from Tod's Well in Comiston to the High Street. Five cisterns were situated at the weighhouse, the top of Forrester's Wynd, the Market Cross, the top of Niddrie Wynd and one near the Netherbow. The cost came to £6,500.

A year later, problems were reported – not with the water, but vandalism 'by malicious base humoured vagabonds or by young children ore by apprentices'.

They had now expanded the supply with a cistern in the Grassmarket and a fire pipe in the West Bow. Such was the demand for water that the supply from Tod's Well proved inadequate and an agreement was made with the Laird of Mortonhall whereby a second well at Swanston was brought into use. Water was piped from Swanston to Tod's Well and hence onward to the city.

Coffee Houses

A note in the Burgh Records for December 1676 refers to 'coffee houses which have become very frequent in this town'. It is strange that such a remark could easily be applicable to the city 340 years later. Certainly in London at this time the coffee house was becoming a centre where one met friends or clients to discuss business, politics or literature. To obtain insurance for ships in London, the owners would go to Mr Lloyd's Coffee House – the name still continues today in the insurance exchange.

The burgh council had discovered that in other countries coffee houses were licensed and so ordered the owners to seek permission from them before opening a coffee house. It has been suggested that they wished to restrict the growth of these places since the town's revenue was dependent on the taxes on wine and ale. However, it is possible, as occurred in London, that customers were not just restricted to the purchase of coffee.

In 1677, James Rew's Coffee House in Parliament Square was closed down. We do not know the reason for this action, but his partner, Humphrey Clerk, appears to have been involved with conventicles. The order came not from the town but from the Scottish Privy Council. What was going on in a coffee house in the very heart of Edinburgh that attracted the attention of such an important body? A clue to their possible motive came two years later when the Privy Council ordered that all gazettes and newsletters read in coffee houses were first to be presented to the Bishop of Edinburgh or another Privy Councillor, 'thereby false and seditious news and slanders may be prevented'. It would appear that opponents of the government were using coffee houses to distribute their own views and no doubt counter government propaganda.

Edinburgh in Debt

By 1677, Edinburgh's debt had reached the staggering sum of £439,559 1s 4d. Every year, expenses exceeded income. The two largest creditors were the Lords of Session (judges) and the College of Edinburgh (university) who were owed £120,000 and £77,732 respectively. The university was about 100 years old and must have acquired some wealthy benefactors to accumulate such a large amount of capital.

Landowners who lived outside the city had invested in this debt. The Laird of Mortonhall and his sisters had lent £8,800 (it should also be remembered that it was their property that the burgh relied on for its new water supply). John Scott, who owned the estate of Malleny in Balerno, had invested over £6,666, while William Fairlie, the Laird of Bruntsfield, was owed more than £8,666. Sir John Wauchop of Niddrie was another creditor for over £6,000.

The college was not the only institution that had lent money to support the growing deficit. Trinity House in Leith, St Leonard's College in St Andrew's,

Trinity Hospital and Heriot's Hospital were all creditors of the city. Perhaps the strangest debt of all was the £22,000 owed for the purchase of stock to provide work for the poor in St Paul's Work.

Much of the problem had arisen during the reign of Charles I and the rule of the Commonwealth. Large amounts of money were spent on new churches, the Parliament House and the Citadel of Leith. From 1639 to 1650 the council were contributing money not only for the defence of the town but for the defence of the country.

The 1677 accounts for the town's debt appear to show sets of arrangements between the treasurer, who generally held office for only a few years, and individual creditors. Rates varied, but were generally around 6 per cent. The Sultees family and Sir John Lockhart were only paid at 3 per cent. The rectors of St Leonard's College did particularly well, receiving a rate of interest of about 30 per cent, but the highest rate of interest was given to Sir Andrew Ramsay who, for an investment of £1,514, was paid £681 annually. No doubt this arrangement was agreed when Sir Andrew was the town's provost. Other town officers did not do so well. Bailie George Reid had only £100 annually from a capital of £3,333. Later his widow received just £50 annually from this sum. It was a sign of the times that a council consisting of merchants (large businessmen) and trades deacons (small businessmen) failed to see the need to set up a department to organise the management of this debt.

Education in the Burgh

Even in education policy 'monopoly' was the key word. Latin, then considered the most important subject, was only allowed to be taught in the High School. Leith had its own grammar school. Thomas Blackburn was ordered to desist from the teaching of Latin or he would lose his right to run a school. Blackburn moved to the Bristo Port, but this did not keep him out of the council's control. In 1681 a number of Edinburgh school teachers who ran private schools were brought before the Privy Council. Some of them were ministers who had lost their livings at the Restoration and others were suspected of having views opposed to the present religious settlement. They were forbidden from teaching Latin without a licence from the bishop.

Various 'vulgar' schools are recorded. They taught reading, writing and some arithmetic. Opportunities for girls do not appear to have been forgotten. Mistress Christine Cleland was given permission to begin recruiting teachers. She appears to have offered a broad curriculum, adding sewing, embroidery, dancing, singing and French to the three basic subjects. Girls did not have the opportunity to take their education further, however, neither the High School nor the college (university – although those who attended were only secondary school age) would take girls.

All schools required the parents to pay fees, and it was only in 1699 that George Clerk, the presenter in the Tolbooth Kirk, with the help of his wife set up a free school. His wife added stocking making for girls to the basic curriculum.

Most surprising is the number of Frenchmen involved in education in Edinburgh. Even before the Revocation of the Edict of Nantes (1685), Jaques Bernadou was teaching French, dancing and fencing. Louis de Buisson offered reading, writing, arithmetic and spoken French. Dancing, despite the puritanical outlook of Restoration Edinburgh, was obviously considered an important skill in certain circles. Edward and James Fonconto taught dancing and fencing, while Lewis de France was granted a licence to teach music. In 1672 William Destrinbue opened a school for the teaching of French. These men, and presumably their families, were part of a large group of French refugees who settled in the city during the latter part of the century. Their numbers were large enough to enable them to employ their own pastors.

Heriot's Hospital offered an education to the sons of burgesses. Arnot records that in 1661 their numbers had reached fifty-two. The trust owned large areas of land to the north of Edinburgh.

In 1695 the merchants of Edinburgh raised money to set up a girls' school. Mary Erskine gave a donation of £12,000 to buy a building for the new school, which was later named after her.

The university continued to grow with the support of the town. This was an age of scientific discovery and Charles II became patron of what became the Royal Society. One of its most celebrated members during this period was Sir Isaac Newton.

A most interesting event occurred in June 1685 when Robert Blaw, a teacher in the High School, was imprisoned in the Tolbooth for keeping 'a disorderly school within the liberty of Edinburgh'. Sadly, we are given no details of the disorder and the matter must be left to our imaginations.

The Danger from Fire

Fire was always a danger in the crowded city, where wood and thatch continued to be used as building materials. Extinguishing fires was still carried out using buckets, and 100 of these required to be repaired after the 1677 Canongate fire. It was only in 1687 that the council purchased two fire engines which were kept in the Tolbooth Kirk (the western end of St Giles) – yes, the kirk was used as a fire station! Maybe this was just as well, since they stored the town's ammunition and gunpowder in another part …

A fire broke out on the south side of the High Street in April 1674. The council expressed concern about 'most part of the houses in the fore street being built mostly of timber' and 'the closes being so narrow and the houses so thick and joined together'. They therefore ruled that new buildings should be made from stone and vennels and closes were no longer to be obstructed by outside stairs. The ground floors of the tenements or lands were usually commercial premises with the inhabitants living in flats on the floors above. An outer stair would lead to the upper storeys without passing through any workshops.

However, making rules did not necessarily mean action on the subject. After the April fire, the owners of the destroyed property were reluctant to clean up the debris. Rubble on the street was restricting access for coaches, carts and even packhorses, and in the end the provost and bailies had to make a personal inspection and then allocate the costs for repairs.

The following year a fire broke out in Parliament Square. Archibald Law was killed helping to put out the fire and his widow and children were given a pension by the council. Mention of casualties at fires is very rare and this may indicate that although much property was lost most people managed to escape. However, casualties and damage were not the only hazards faced by the inhabitants after a fire: the 1677 Canongate fire led to some looting and a demand by the magistrates that the stolen goods be returned.

Offences and Escapes

Alexander Cowburne was convicted of murdering a licensed beggar in January 1682, the penalty for which was hanging. This must have presented the authorities with a problem as he was, in fact, the public hangman. The magistrates appear to have had trouble finding suitable people for the position. Two years later, Munro, Cowburne's successor, was dismissed for attacking a beggar. Further intrigue occurred in April when James Aikinhead, an Edinburgh apothecary, was summoned to appear before the Privy Council. He was charged with 'selling poisonous and amorous drugs and files to provoke lust whereby a woman had narrowly escaped with her life'. The following month, Ninian Paterson, the minister at Libberton, was dismissed from his charge for 'openly defaming the bishop and other misbehaviours'. He disappeared, and so too did the church Bible, the money for the poor, a Communion cup and the keys to the manse.

On the night of 15 September 1683 there was a mass escape from the Tolbooth prison. Twenty-three men, including John Dick, held as a prisoner of the Privy Council for his involvement with the Covenanters, cut through the window bars and lowered themselves down onto the street. How they obtained the ropes to accomplish this feat is not recorded. Dick was later captured at the home of Mr John Rae, and was hung for his part in the Covenanter rising. This must have been the 1679 Rising which collapsed after their defeat at Bothwell Brig. You can find John Dick's name on the Covenanter Memorial in the Grassmarket.

In the following year, a group of prisoners (eight to ten) escaped from the Canongate Tolbooth. They were all Covenanters held for their part in the rebellion. Sir Alexander Gordon made an attempt to escape from the Tolbooth but was caught on the roof. Gordon was sent by the Privy Council to Blackness Castle where he remained until the Revolution.

The Reign of James VII

On 6 February 1685, Charles II died leaving the crown to his brother, James VII. For the first time since the removal of Mary, Queen of Scots, Scotland had a Catholic king.

The reign began with two unsuccessful rebellions. The Duke of Monmouth was defeated at Sedgemoor in the south-west of England, while in Scotland the Earl of Argyle met a similar fate. Argyle was brought as a prisoner to Edinburgh. He entered under escort at the Watergate and was taken up the Canongate, passing Moray House where, many years ago, he had stood watching the Marquis of Montrose taken up to meet his death in the city. Other prisoners of less importance were held in the Tolbooth and Mr Ewing took twenty-four of them in his ship to the plantations of Jamaica. Later in the year, another twenty-three prisoners, some of whom had accepted voluntary exile, were transported by Captain Alexander to America.

Sir George Drummond, Lord Provost of Edinburgh, fled to the abbey to seek sanctuary from his creditors. The king refused the council permission to hold elections and then changed his mind, and Thomas Kennedy was chosen to lead the new council.

James VII was a Catholic and wished to give more freedom to those who did not wish to worship in the Established Church. Over the New Year (1685/86) there were demonstrations against those who worshipped in their own homes. The Duke of Gordon, another Catholic, was placed in command of the castle. Such an appointment required the recipient to take the Test Act Oath, but James issued a royal dispensation. The king appointed a Catholic, Anderson, as royal printer and turned the abbey church into a Catholic chapel. This latter move forced the inhabitants of the Canongate, who had worshipped there since the founding of the Canongate, to seek a new spiritual home. Lady Yester's Church was used until a new church was built.

Alexander Ogston, a bookseller in the city, soon fell foul of the new king's printer. Two books, Bishop Usher's *Sermons against Papists* and *The History of the French Persecutions*, were confiscated. Then the king's printer seized some Bibles which Ogston had imported from London.

In October 1687, the king ordered the council to elect Magnus Prince as lord provost. Prince had entered the council in 1677 as a representative of the merchants. During his time on the council he had held the posts of treasurer and dean of guild, and there is no evidence that he was chosen because he favoured the new king's policies. Shortly after his election, three French Protestant refugees were admitted as burgesses of Edinburgh. No elections were permitted in October 1688.

The Revolution, 1688–89

Whereas, a century previously, Edinburgh had been at the centre of affairs, now it was becoming remote from the great events of the moment. There were disturbances in the city in November but it was in England that the political establishment began to move against the king. On 10 December Holyrood, the centre of Catholic worship in the city, was attacked by a mob. Captain Wallace and the palace guard were overwhelmed. The abbey church, the private chapel and other buildings used by Catholics were sacked. The next day the magistrates called out the militia under the command of Colonel Graham. This resulted in a stand-off between the palace guard and the town's militia. Negotiations began, and Wallace attempted to escape from the trap. He was eventually caught and sent to the prison on the Bass Rock, off North Berwick.

News came through to the city of the victory of the prince. The council met on Christmas Day to prepare a loyal address to the Prince of Orange and his wife, which Bailie James Graham took to London. On the first day of the New Year, a proclamation issued by the prince and his wife was read at the Cross. It must have been one of the few revolutions in history where no one was killed.

In Edinburgh peace was quickly restored, although the Catholic Duke of Gordon held out in the castle until June. Yet it still remained a dangerous time. Government forces were defeated at Killiecrankie and only the death of John Graham of Claverhouse in the battle prevented James VII's supporters from following up the victory. In the west, attempts to secure the loyalty of the clans led to the Massacre of Glen Coe. In Edinburgh, and Scotland as a whole, the Episcopal ministers were forced out of their churches to make way for those who favoured Presbyterianism. There was little resistance, although the second minister at South Leith did his best to hold on to the church.

French Settlers

In 1685 Louis XIV of France revoked the Edict of Nantes which had allowed the Huguenots (French Protestants) freedom to worship in their own way. The withdrawal of this protection began a migration of Huguenots to Protestant countries, and some settled in Edinburgh.

Even before the Revocation, Frenchmen had set up schools in the burgh. These skilled French refugees received licences from the council to practise their specialist trades. In 1695 Daniel Labibele and Henry Heiss were given permission to carry out their business of gilding, burnishing and lacquering in the burgh, while Daniel Fabrot set himself up as a seller of perfume. The next year, John Beneist Barroneir, a seller and manufacturer of perfumes, was given a licence. David le Merchand, another French immigrant, was allowed to carry out his trade in the cutting and designing of ivory.

Some of these immigrants even became burgesses. As early as 1687 Abell Labibele was made a burgess. He was joined nine years later by Pierre Chaselon, who was a furrier. Mr Le Fevre and Mr Dupont, who were the ministers of the French Church in Edinburgh were made burgesses. By now there must have been a large and wealthy French community in Edinburgh for them to be able to support two ministers.

The Reign of William and Mary

Bruntsfield Links and the Meadows

The Meadows were the grazing lands that surrounded the Burgh Loch which, for many centuries, had been an important source of water for the city. These lands were farmed out by the council and the 'tacksman' would collect his money and profit from leasing the grazing rights. In 1695 work began to improve the area by digging more drainage ditches and planting trees. A walk was built, possibly improving access to the Links.

Pressure was building regarding the use of Bruntsfield Links. During the same year, as improvements began in the Meadows, Patrick Carfrae, Deacon of the Masons, and his partners obtained a tack on an acre of land to open a quarry. Before choosing the site for this new quarry, Carfrae had to consult the local golfers. Nine years later there were complaints, presumably from some of the golfers, that people were driving carts over the Links and spoiling the grass. It was planned to dig ditches and force the carts to keep to the roads but this failed to have the required effect and in 1713 all horses, carts and sleds were banned from the Links. Two years previously, the council had restricted golf on the Links by prohibiting it during the months of May, June and July. An exception was made for those less than fifteen years old.

In 1695, George Warrender purchased the estate of Bruntsfield including Bruntsfield House itself. Warrender served as lord provost from 1713–15 and won the disputed parliamentary election in 1715. His house still stands as part of James Gillespie's High School.

The Darien Scheme

In 1695, an Act of the Scottish Parliament set up the Company of Scotland Trading to Africa and the Indies. The company was given a monopoly of trade between Scotland and the Americas, Africa and Asia. It was so popular that English merchants bought up many of the shares. However, pressure was put on the English shareholders to withdraw their support for the company. This left the Scots to carry on alone, and a sum of £400,000 was raised in Scotland – no doubt a good part of this came from Edinburgh.

William Paterson was one of the leading men in the new company. He had made his money in London and then invested in the new Bank of Scotland. It was Paterson who proposed setting up a Scottish colony on the Isthmus of Darien in Central America (southern Panama). The colony stood at the eastern end of the narrow land bridge between the Caribbean and the Pacific. In the sixteenth and early seventeenth centuries, the Spanish had used the isthmus to transport gold and silver from Peru to the Caribbean ports. The climate was hot and humid.

The land they proposed to occupy had been part of the Spanish Empire for 150 years, but Spain was one of William's allies in his war against France and so he had no wish to be associated with the enterprise. In July 1698 three ships set sail for Darien but they failed to build a permanent settlement. Two other expeditions followed, with the same result. The failure of the scheme led to the loss of a great deal of money for the Scottish investors and created hostility towards the English.

Famine Years

The last years of the century were marked by a series of poor harvests which led to severe food shortages. The harvest of 1695 had already been poor, but this was followed the next year by a very bad harvest in the south of Scotland. After a reasonable year in 1697, 1698 proved to be another disaster, with a considerable number of people dying of hunger in both town and country.

The position in Leith appears to have been particularly bad. At a Session meeting in South Leith parish church on Christmas Eve (not celebrated by the Church of Scotland at this time), they noted, 'Several of the poor die daily'. By the spring of 1697 they had set up a committee to oversee the poor relief. In the autumn, the situation was so bad that the poor were begging at the church door before the services began. The town council were concerned for the 'poor of Leith representing their mean and low condition and that several of the said poor are starving and dying in the streets', and gave '£200 Scots to Water Bailie Cunningham to distribute on the advice of the Bailie of Leith'. During these years, the council spent £12,772 on poor relief.

Eleven

THE EARLY EIGHTEENTH CENTURY

The Great Fire of 1700

On Saturday, 3 February at 10 p.m. a fire broke out in the Cowgate. It spread quickly along the street and up both sides of the kirkyard of St Giles. The flames then took hold of the buildings bordering Parliament Close. The council recruited 206 men from various trades to assist them in bringing it under control. Much of the area between St Giles and the Cowgate was destroyed, although Parliament House appears to have remained untouched. After the fire, the city's constables were ordered to make a search for goods stolen from the damaged properties – a sad reflection on the honesty of the citizens!

Another fire broke out in the Lawnmarket in October 1701 which claimed the lives of several people. The collapse of some walls added to the disaster.

Probably as a result of these fires, the council set up a committee to find ways to improve the fighting of fires in the city. It consisted of councillors and twelve fire masters. The latter were mainly wrights, masons and slaters, all experts in the building trade. They recommended that each fire master should have six men at his command. Equipment for extinguishing fires was to be stored in four separate places along the High Street. These were to be by the weighhouse (the top of the Bow), at the guardhouse, in the back close by the Councilhouse and by the new well. The remaining equipment, twelve ladders and 300 leather buckets, were to be stored in St Giles. Everybody was expected to carry buckets of water to help with a fire. The council accepted these recommendations.

After a fire at the head of the Canongate in November 1707, private furnaces used for brewing, distilling and metal work were prohibited unless the owner had a licence from the council. The dean of guild was to investigate a complaint from the neighbours in Covenant Close that Mr John Cameron, a former Episcopal minister, was operating one such furnace in his cellar.

The Riot of 1700

In June, news reached the city that the settlers in Darien had successfully driven off a Spanish attack. A crowd gathered at the Cross Keys Tavern to celebrate this success. Soon they were demanding that everyone should be celebrating this victory by putting lights in their windows. The crowd came onto the streets and began to throw stones at those windows which did not show a light. Some of the mob then took a different tone. They marched to Lord Carmichael's house and demanded a warrant ordering the release of Paterson and Watson, two prisoners held in the Tolbooth. Others set off for the prison. They broke open the door and injured one of the warders before freeing the prisoners. At around this time the Canongate Tolbooth held a group of people who refused to recognise the teachings of the ministers of the Kirk. The Cotomuir Folk, as they were called, may have followed the beliefs of the extreme Covenanting Party.

The Northern Entrance

In 1681 a new port had been built at the foot of Halkerston's Wynd to give access to the Fleshmarket by the shore of the Nor' Loch. In 1702, Thomas Kincaid presented a plan to the council which would extend the road crossing by Trinity College. This would enable carts and carriages from Calton and Leith to have easy access to the north side of the town. The route would bypass the Canongate and the narrow entrance at the Netherbow. The plan was accepted by the council, who believed that trades, such as masons, wrights and smiths, who required large storage yards would be attracted to the north side of the town.

Mary Erskine

Mary Erskine was the widow of an Edinburgh pharmacist who carried on her husband's business after his death. She also acted as a moneylender and became a very wealthy woman. In 1694 she set aside a sum of money to be 'employed and expended for maintaining and educating at bed, board, clothes and school of young children of the female sex of the merchant burgesses'.

The merchants established a hospital (an almshouse, not a medical institution) in the Cowgate two years later. In 1704 they bought some property near the Bristo Port and three years later an Act of Parliament formed it into a corporate body. It was known as the Merchant Maiden Hospital founded by the Merchant Company and Mary Erskine. Arnot, in his history of Edinburgh, includes a picture of this hospital. The school, in a different form, still continues today.

Censorship

The Privy Council had ordered that nothing was to be published unless it had been properly vetted. They were unhappy with some of the material being printed in Edinburgh, so members of the town council were summoned to appear before them to explain their failure to control the publication of such articles. Therefore, in October 1703 the council issued an order forbidding printers and their employees from publishing any material 'not duly allowed by public authority'. All publications had to bear the name of the printer, who could thus be prosecuted if he failed to secure permission.

The Treaty of Union

The Riot Against the Union, October 1706
When the plans for the Treaty of Union (intended to unite Scotland with England and Wales) were revealed in October 1706, they were not welcomed by everyone. As night fell, a mob gathered and besieged the home of Sir Patrick Johnstone, a former lord provost and one of the Scottish commissioners who had drawn up the proposed Treaty of Union. One of the town's apothecaries alerted the Town Guard, but Captain Richardson refused to act without orders from the lord provost, Sir Samuel McClellan. When eventually the orders arrived, the guard marched to the scene of the trouble. The mob was dispersed and three or four men who had been caught trying to break Johnstone's door down were arrested and taken to the Tolbooth. The rioters continued to throw sticks and stones at the guard.

For a while the street became quieter until another mob arrived shouting such slogans as 'No Union' and 'English dogs'. The news of these disturbances reached the lord commissioner, the Duke of Queensberry, in Holyrood. He sent soldiers to secure the Netherbow Port. However, the mob received reinforcements from Leith using the unguarded gate at the foot of Halkerston's Wynd. At about midnight, the Duke of Argyle arrived at the head of a troop of horse guards. With this help the lord provost and the bailies were able to restore order.

A proclamation was issued, warning people that anyone who threatened the queen's business or her councillors could face charges of treason and the death penalty. The magistrates banned all meetings unless they had been licensed by themselves.

The opposition to the Treaty of Union also had a religious dimension. Some ministers, like James Webster at the Tolbooth Kirk, feared that an Act of Union would see the return of the Episcopalians.

The Union of the Parliaments, 1707

Any union between Scotland and England would allow Scottish merchants free access to the English colonies. Since James VI had succeeded to the English throne in 1603, little progress had been made on uniting the two countries, and only Oliver Cromwell had held a joint parliament. However, the situation changed remarkably in the early years of the eighteenth century.

The queen had no heir, so the English Parliament (which already included members from Wales and Ireland) had passed the Act of Settlement. On the death of Queen Ann, the throne was to pass to Sophia of Hanover or her heirs. Sophia was a granddaughter of James VI and wife of Ernest Augustus, Duke of Brunswick-Lüneburg and Elector of Hanover. The Scottish Parliament had not passed an Act to secure the settlement, and therefore should Scotland choose a different sovereign it could lead to the separation of the two countries. The prospect of an alliance between Scotland and France at this time of war (the War of the Spanish Succession was being fought, mainly against France, in the Low Countries) encouraged the English to seek an agreement.

Edinburgh had lost its royal court in 1603 and now it was faced with also losing the parliament. The failure of the Darien Scheme had further bred resentment of the English who had failed to offer support to the enterprise. Two riots in 1705 and 706 had demonstrated the hostility in the capital against the English and their agents in Edinburgh. The English government had their spies in the city, and one of these was Daniel Defoe, who was later to write *Robinson Crusoe*. Sir John Clerk of Penicuik, a Scottish Commissioner who had helped to draw up the treaty, wrote in his memoirs, 'He [Defoe] was therefore a spy among us but not known to be such otherwise the mob of Edinburgh had pulled him to pieces'.

This anti-Union policy was not necessarily the view of the political class in the city. Sir Patrick Johnstone, elected lord provost in 1704, had been chosen as one of the Scottish Commissioners to negotiate the Treaty of Union. He set out for London in early March 1706 with the council promising to pay his expenses. On 24 August, he reported back on the commission's success to the town council. The Scottish Parliament eventually passed the Treaty of Union, although there was considerable opposition, particularly from the crowds in the streets of the city.

Jacobites and Whigs

The Jacobites opposed the Union with England and looked for the return of the Stewart monarchy. Some of them were Episcopalians, who were unwilling to swear the oath of loyalty to the new monarchs (William and Mary, Anne and George I). They disliked the rigorous Presbyterian control of the Sabbath and society. A few dedicated supporters of the Pretender worked secretly. In March 1727, John Strachan, a Leith merchant, was arrested and sent to the Tower of London. Strachan ran a 'post office', passing letters between James, son of James VII, and his supporters in Scotland.

The main opponents of the Jacobites (*Jacobus* is the Latin for James) were the Whigs. This group took their name from the extreme Presbyterians (Whiggamores) who occupied Edinburgh in 1648. They were the loyal supporters of the House of Hanover and secured control over the government. After the accession of George I, most of the leading statesmen in England could be described as Whigs. They used government posts to secure loyalty. In Edinburgh, George Drummond, lord provost from 1725–27 held a post in the Department of Customs and Excise. During both rebellions, he raised volunteers to resist the Jacobites.

The Great Explosion

On 3 July 1702, in a storehouse close to the Links, thirty-three barrels of gunpowder exploded. It is estimated that as much as a third of the town suffered some damage. Roofs were blown off and windows smashed; even doors were torn off their hinges. The houses closest to the explosion were entirely demolished. The total cost of the damage was estimated at £35,935.

The Privy Council itself ordered a collection to be made for those who had suffered in the explosion. The town council placed restrictions on the storage of gunpowder of more than 4lb in weight. Some years later, in 1706, they moved their own stores to the steeple of Greyfriars. This led to the destruction of the church when it, too, blew up in 1718!

Immorality and the Sabbath

The council appointed particular days for the magistrates to deal with the prosecutions of those breaking the Act of Parliament for suppressing profanity and immorality. Patrick Middleton fell foul of these laws and was dismissed from his teaching post at the High School (sadly no details are given). The council even blamed the fire in the city, and the explosion in Leith as God's anger at the immorality in Edinburgh. In December 1704, the council ratified the Acts of the Presbytery of Edinburgh against immorality and Sabbath breaking. It later ordered a reprint of the Acts of Parliament on these subjects. Leith became a popular place from which to escape the rigours of an Edinburgh Sabbath, despite the efforts of the Session of South Leith.

Resistance obviously continued to the strict observance of the Sabbath. In 1720 the Presbytery complained that people were standing around idly or even leaving the city. Some were going out to the fields, parks, links and meadows, while others visited taverns and alehouses. Pressure against drinking was possibly not enforced as the Presbytery might have wished, as the council received 2*d* on every pint of beer and £50 per tun of wine. This formed a major part of the town's income.

Abbeyhill

The small hamlet of Abbeyhill was situated on the road leading out through the Water Gate in the Canongate. The road climbed the hill before dividing: one fork turned north to Leith and the other travelled east through Abbeyhill to Restalrig and beyond. Here in the first decade of the century Anthony Masson sold tickets for the Newcastle stagecoach. The journey took three days.

Food Shortages

During the years 1709–10 food was short and prices rose rapidly. The cost of wheat, oats and peas doubled in a year while barley rose by 50 per cent. The magistrates reminded the public of the laws against hoarding and constables were ordered to seek out those who might be storing food illegally.

The *Edinburgh Courant*

This newspaper was first published in 1705 by Adam Boig and printed by James Watson (although it was claimed in 1780 in an edition of this same paper that the late Mr Fleming, formerly owner of the *Courant*, had copies dating from the 1680s). Sometime in 1707 John Reid Jr, who lived in Liberton Wynd (demolished when George IV Bridge was built), took over the publishing of the paper.

The *Edinburgh Courant* at that time had a subheading of 'Authorised', suggesting that the government censored the content. Watson was also

producing an *Evening Courant* from his premises in Craig's Close and continued doing this work in the early 1730s. Five years later, after the death of Boig, the position was taken by Daniel Defoe, who had acted as a government agent in the city during the Union debate. In 1709 the council had authorised a payment of 15 guineas 'for his good services to the interests of the Good Town'.

The Escape of Robert Balfour

Robert Balfour was the eldest son of Lord Balfour. He had fallen in love with a girl from a lower class and was sent abroad by his family to end the relationship. He returned in 1707 to find his love had married a schoolmaster. Balfour shot the schoolmaster and went into hiding.

When he was finally caught and convicted of the murder, the sentence of the court was that Balfour should be lodged in the Tolbooth of Edinburgh until 6 January 1710, when he was to be taken to the Cross and his head cut off. Two days before the execution was to take place he was visited by his mother and two sisters. They arrived late in the afternoon and were let into the Tolbooth by Mr Forsyth, who was on duty at the outer door. The ladies were wearing plaids which hid their figures. Lady Balfour and her daughters proceeded to Balfour's cell. Once the staff were away, Balfour changed clothes with one of his sisters and the party left the building the way they had entered. It was nearly five hours before the authorities discovered the deception.

The Accession of George I

Queen Anne died on 1 August 1714 and the news travelled north, reaching Edinburgh around midnight on 4 August. Little time was wasted in proclaiming George I as the new king.

Most of the important nobles in the city, led by the Duke of Montrose, came together with General Wightman, commander-in-chief of forces in Scotland. They then set off up the High Street to meet with the Edinburgh Town Council and the Lords of Session. The Edinburgh militia had been called out to form a guard on both sides of the street as they made for the Cross where George was proclaimed king.

There was little chance of any disturbances with the militia in control of the streets and regular forces in both the castle and the palace of Holyrood ready to support them. The day ended with bells ringing, bonfires and, no doubt, fireworks. Later, a loyal address was drawn up and taken to the new king by George Warrender, the lord provost.

The Election of the Member of Parliament, 1715

Only the members of the town council and the rest of the deacons could vote for the Member of Parliament for Edinburgh. With an electorate of only thirty-three there was rarely the need to hold an election. The new reign meant a new parliament and George Warrender, the lord provost, faced two opponents.

Warrender was accused of entertaining members of the council at the town's expense. The provost's supporters also made allegations of malpractice. In the end, George Warrender was chosen and he set off for London. His stay, however, was brief, for the Duke of Montrose, who was the chief Secretary of State, ordered him to return as the city was threatened by the Jacobite Rebellion.

The 1715 Rebellion

A rebellion against the new king, George I, began in the Highlands under the leadership of the Earl of Mar. In August, the town raised 400 men, paying them 6d per day. The sluice on the Nor' Loch was shut, raising the water level and making it difficult to attack the town from the north. Some of the gates of the city were walled up to reduce the number of weak points that might be targeted by the enemy.

Perth fell on 14 September, and a plan to capture Edinburgh Castle had already failed. A small group of sixty to seventy handpicked men were to climb up the south-west face of the rock and scale the wall aided by a rope lowered by Sergeant Ainsley, one of the garrison. However, the plan came to the ears of Lord Ormiston, who informed Lieutenant Colonel Stewart, the deputy governor of the castle. The sergeant was caught in the very act of lowering the rope and the raiders fled.

Brigadier McIntosh managed to ferry a Jacobite force across the Firth of Forth and landed east of the city. McIntosh captured Leith and the Jacobites then fortified themselves in the old Citadel. As the government army prepared to bring guns from the castle, McIntosh, possibly realising that he could be trapped in Leith, withdrew eastwards to Seaton Castle.

The Duke of Argyle marched out of Stirling and the two armies met at Sheriffmuir on 13 November. Although it was not a decisive victory the duke held the field, forcing Mar to retreat. The rebellion quickly collapsed but the Jacobite movement, which looked to return a Stewart to the throne, went underground. Links between Scottish sympathisers and the exiled Jacobite court continued to carry on in secret.

The Destruction of Greyfriars Church

The town's munitions, which included a large quantity of gunpowder, were now stored in the steeple of the Kirk of Greyfriars. This, of course, was the church in which the first signatures were placed on the National Covenant in February

1638. The dangers were clear: in 1702 a huge explosion at a powder store in Leith had caused massive damage to the port.

On 7 May 1718, the powder stored in Greyfriars exploded, destroying the whole church. The cause of the explosion is not known, but a spark must have set off the powder. No deaths were reported. Gradually a new church was built which was divided, creating the congregations of Old Greyfriars and New Greyfriars. That building itself was destroyed by fire in 1845.

The Lawnmarket

This wide street was still used as a market in the eighteenth century. At the top of it was the Bow which led to the Grassmarket and the West Port. The Butter Tron stood at the head of the Bow.

In 1725 a large fire caused considerable destruction in the street. A fund was set up for the relief of those who had lost everything in the fire and it reached over £938. The magistrates (lord provost and the four bailies) distributed the money as they saw fit – a future MP for the city received £124 and another gentleman, who was later to serve as lord provost, was given £225, while a poor Episcopal clergyman received only £4 from the fund. Hugo Arnot, at his most sarcastic, stated, 'A great part of it was disposed of in this upright and equitable manner'.

James Brownhill built James Court in the years following the fire, and Riddle's Court and Close were also rebuilt at this time.

George Watson

George Watson came from a merchant family who had fallen into distressed circumstances. He spent some time in Holland and when he returned in 1676 he took employment with Sir James Dick. In 1695 he joined the newly formed Bank of Scotland as an accountant. Watson died in April 1723, leaving the sum of £12,000 with which to found a hospital to maintain and educate the children and grandchildren of distressed merchants. The building began on the land opposite George Heriot's Hospital in 1738 and the first twelve boys were admitted in 1741.

Forgery

The middle years of the 1720s saw a series of forged bank notes appearing in Edinburgh. The authorities made several arrests. John Gibson was pinned by the ear to the pillory for an hour with a note pinned to his chest, while Mrs McLeod was convicted and executed in the Grassmarket. Presumably the court considered her the ringleader, although she pleaded her innocence to the end. The third member of the gang, named Currie, was whipped and then pinned by the ear to the pillory. He was finally ordered to be transported to the colonies.

The Presbyterian Establishment and Dancing, Music and the Theatre

The city at this time was ruled under strict Calvinist lines. Music, dancing, assemblies and particularly the theatre were banned. Work was restricted on Sundays and everyone was expected to attend the morning and afternoon sermons. Leisure activities, including travelling, were also prohibited.

The fear of 'the wrath of God' came from the pulpit. After a fire in Canongate head, Reverend Moncrieff of Trinity College Church told his congregation:

> That God's voice was crying to this city, and that he was coming to the very ports, and was crying over the walls to us that we should mend our ways lest he should come into our city and consume us in a terrible manner.

According to Robert Chambers, the first public dancing in Edinburgh began in 1710 under the name of 'The Assembly'. Strict Presbyterians opposed such activities. The Assembly was held in the Bow, before it moved on to Assembly Close. By 1728 the Assembly had become so well established that the Board of Trustees for Improving Manufactures wrote to the directors asking them to encourage the ladies and gentlemen attending the dancing to wear clothes made in Britain.

In December 1732, the Honourable Company of Hunters gave a ball which was attended by 'a great number of persons of distinction'. Dancing was attracting wealthy and influential people, and the Church was slowly losing its grip over life in the city. The next year some 'nobles and gentry' who attended the Ladies' Assembly in November went dressed wearing cockades declaring 'Liberty, Property and No Excise'. This was an attack on the import duties (excise) which made smuggling profitable. Such was the growing interest that a Mr Downie was able to advertise his dancing school.

The theatre met with even more opposition than the Assembly. The Taylors' Hall in the Cowgate was used by visiting companies but they faced 'the incessant hostility of the clergy'. Allan Ramsay was involved in trying to set up a theatre in Carrubber's Close during the autumn of 1736. He had already met opposition from the town council when he had set up a circulating library. Not long after the Rebellion, a theatre began in a close (Playhouse Close) off the Canongate.

In the early years of the century, several gentlemen had met in the Cross Keys Tavern to play the harpsichord and the violin. Gradually the audience at these meetings grew until in 1728 it reached seventy. This group of enthusiasts then decided to form the Musical Society of Edinburgh and its first meetings were held in St Mary's chapel.

Sporting Activities

While the Presbyterians opposed cultural activities such as dancing and drama, sports were permitted provided they were not played on the Sabbath. Golf was played on the Links at Leith and Bruntsfield and a company of archers shot each year for the Silver Arrow. Presumably they held other less formal sessions to practise their skills.

The council itself continued to support horse racing on the Links of Leith; three races were held in the month of June, with the Hunters' Plate being run in November.

The Royal Infirmary

Plans to build an infirmary to provide medical help for the poor of Edinburgh were drawn up in 1725. That year, George Drummond was first elected to the office of provost. He took a considerable interest in the project, even paying off a debt of £156 to James Johnston of Gilmerton for building materials. The infirmary opened in 1729 in a building at the top of Robertson's Close. It had only six beds and Elizabeth Sinclair was its first patient.

On 25 August 1736, the infirmary received a royal charter. During this period, a larger building had been constructed and it was to remain the home of the infirmary until the 1870s when new property was bought on the south side of Laureston Place.

Small Pox, 1733

Edinburgh was still a small town in the early eighteenth century. The total number of deaths for 1731 and 1732 were 950 and 949 respectively. Over 40 per cent of these were children, who also suffered worse when diseases such as smallpox struck the town. In October, 120 deaths were recorded, of which ninety-one were children, most of whom died from smallpox. The numbers for November reached 163, which included 123 children. None of these figures can compare with the plague that had visited Edinburgh and Leith in 1645, when thousands died.

The Secession Churches

The Revolution of 1688 established the Presbyterian Church in Scotland. This was followed in 1690 by the Patronage Act. Formerly the patrons – lairds or other wealthy landowners – held the right to appoint the clergy and Edinburgh Council was the patron of the city churches and also of the Kirk of Currie. However, this Act enabled the congregations, led by the Church Sessions, to choose the new minister.

Patrons received no compensation for the loss of their rights, although these were restored by another Patronage Act in 1712. Although there were no differences in doctrine, congregations held different views in their approach to religious worship and observance. If the patrons' views on matters of worship and Sabbath observance were not the same as the congregations' conflict might occur. In the 1730s the situation became so bad that some congregations withdrew from the Established Church and formed the Associated Presbyteries. This led to the founding of Bristo Church with Adam Gibb as their minister. An Associated Presbytery chapel had been set up in the city by 1742.

Two years later, the Associated Presbytery had itself split over whether it was right for members to take the burgess oath. Hugo Arnot, who lived in Edinburgh at this time, claimed 'the seceders are, to a man, a set of fanatics' and suggested that a tax on their meeting houses might curb their growth. Opportunities for growth were considerable in the expanding south side of the city. The whole district was still part of the parish of St Cuthbert's, and to counter this problem they set up a Chapel of Ease where members of St Cuthbert's might worship in the Established Church without going to the West End.

A third group of seceders was formed in 1761. The Presbytery of Relief was more moderate than the Burghers and Anti-burghers. A split over the appointment of a minister to Lady Yester's Church led to a group in the congregation breaking away and founding the first relief church in the city. They set up a meeting house on the south side, in what is now South College Street.

The Episcopalian Church

The Revolution of 1688 which brought William III and Mary to the throne had led to the ejection of all the Episcopalian ministers from the churches of Edinburgh. The Episcopalians believed James VII was the head of their Church, although as a Roman Catholic he was not a member. Many refused to offer prayers for King William. Not unnaturally, the new government viewed the Episcopalian Church as the religious arm of the Jacobite movement. For much of the next century the fortunes of the Church had been closely linked with the failures of the Jacobites.

The Episcopalians in Edinburgh set up meeting houses, but we know nothing of their size and membership. In the 1690s there were meeting houses (probably halls let for a Sunday meeting rather than permanent buildings) in Bailie Fyve's Close, Barrenger's Close, Blackfriars Wynd and Hart's Close. Bishop Rose, who had been removed from St Giles, set up at Old St Paul's in Carrubbers Close. At South Leith, the first minister, James Waugh, was deprived of his position in 1689, but Charles Kay, the second minister, refused to go. Since he had the keys of the church it was difficult for the authorities to act. Finally, in 1692 the burgh officers broke into the church and changed the locks. James Waugh continued to minister to the Episcopalians of Leith – probably from his own house in Yard Heads.

A group of Episcopalians in Edinburgh invited Mr Greenshield, an Episcopal minister from Ireland, to set up a meeting house. The Presbytery of Edinburgh, supported by the burgh council, closed it. An appeal to the Court of Session went against Greenshield. However, this was not 1700 but 1710; the Act of Union had been passed, which meant that the House of Lords was now the highest court in the land. Greenshield appealed to the Lords, who were all Anglicans and naturally produced a judgement in his favour. The government were forced to act and produced the Toleration Act 1712 allowing Episcopalians to meet for worship providing they used the English Prayer Book, which was published in Edinburgh that year. This was not a popular decision with some, possibly many, Episcopalians.

However, worse was to come with the 1715 Rebellion. Episcopalian support for the Jacobites led to the closure of their meeting houses and the Abjuration Oath. In 1720, Bishop Rose of Edinburgh, the last of the pre-Revolutionary bishops, died.

Hugo Arnot tells us that two new chapels were founded in Skinner's Close and Carrubber's Close around 1740. In both cases they were qualified chapels with the ministers taking an oath of loyalty to the Crown. He describes them as 'mean, inconvenient apartments, too small for their congregations'. The Jacobite Rising of 1745 led to many distancing themselves from the Church.

Smuggling

One of the major sources of revenue for the government was from the taxes on imported products. This led to organised gangs trying to land goods without paying the excise. Leith was the base from which the revenue officers set out to patrol the Forth. Goods seized by them were taken back to their warehouses in Leith and auctioned in lots. The chief product smuggled into the Forth was brandy. Other cargoes seized by the customs officers included tea and tobacco. In January 1730 they even discovered three hundredweight of chocolate in a ship docked at Leith.

Customs raids also took place beyond the harbour. In June of that year, a cargo of brandy was seized by excise men on Leith Links. Two months later, a raid on a house in Leith produced 5lb of tea and a cask of coconuts.

Leith was not the only place targeted by the revenue officers. In December 1728 they confiscated a cargo of brandy in Newhaven. In 1702, the council complained of people bringing smuggled goods into Edinburgh via the North Loch. Properties in the parishes of Currie and Colinton provided safe havens for goods smuggled from the west coast, so smuggling was clearly not confined to a few men living outside society.

The Porteous 'Riot'

The story begins across the Forth in Anstruther, where a group of men met at a tavern in the village. They decided to rob the local excise officer. The smugglers set off for Pittenweem where they broke into his lodgings and relieved him of a considerable sum of money. The raid was successful, but one of the smugglers, William Hall, who came from Edinburgh, panicked and informed the authorities. Andrew Wilson and George Robertson were arrested and, with William Hall, were brought to Edinburgh for trial.

All three men were sentenced to be hung in the Grassmarket, but Hall's sentence was transmuted to transportation since he had given evidence against the others. They were placed in the Tolbooth. It is said that they tried to escape, but Andrew Wilson became stuck in the opening, thus preventing his comrade from gaining his freedom. On the Sunday before their execution they were taken to church. Wilson suddenly grabbed the guards, allowing Robertson to escape; he disappeared into the congregation and was never heard of again. This gallant act by Wilson in saving his friend only increased his popularity.

On 5 April 1736, he was taken from the Tolbooth by the Town Guard to the Grassmarket. Captain Porteous, the commander of the guard, suspected trouble and had ensured that his men's guns were loaded. Wilson was hung. Some of the mob threw stones and Porteous ordered his men to fire on the crowd. At his trial, it was claimed that he called to his men, 'Lower your pieces and be damn'd!' Four people were killed and two died later of their wounds; another eighteen were wounded. Witnesses said that Porteous shot Charles Husband, one of the dead, three times. The town council removed Porteous from his office and in July he was convicted for the deaths caused at the hanging of Wilson.

However, rumours began to spread in the city that the government might issue a pardon to Porteous. On the night of 13 September, a group of people, probably heavily disguised, met in Portsburgh. They seized the Portsburgh drummer and then marched through the West Port banging the drum. At this signal, others secured the city gates to prevent troops reinforcing the City Guard, many of whom had been dismissed or even arrested. This crowd then came to the door of the Tolbooth. Kindling and a barrel of tar was brought to them and they proceeded to burn down the door. Captain Porteous was dragged out and taken up the Lawnmarket. The mob turned down the Bow, where they broke into a shop and took a rope (money was left in payment – this was no ordinary group of thieves). They hung Porteous on the 'dyer's cross-trees'. His body was eventually taken down and placed in a churchyard and he was later buried in Greyfriars' cemetery.

When news of these events reached the government in London they were furious and threatened to take away Edinburgh's privileges. The lord provost and the magistrates had to act. Fourteen tradesmen were arrested, but eleven were soon discharged and the other three only remained in custody a little longer. A £50 reward was offered which was soon increased to £200, but no progress was made. The *Caledonian Mercury* produced the poor excuse that since no one identified them, 'it is generally believed no citizen acted any principal part in this tragedy'. More arrests followed, including that of John Crawford, the bell ringer of St Giles. The council went as far as collecting a list of all servants and apprentices lodging in the town. Not one member of the so-called 'Porteous Mob' was brought to trial. The whole event suggests a well-organised conspiracy by people of standing in the town.

Lord Provost Alexander Wilson was arrested and a bill was brought before Parliament to punish Edinburgh by removing the city gates and abolishing the guard. The bill met resistance in both houses. Although it passed the Lords, the Commons reduced the most severe clauses, leaving the city with a £2,000 fine. The following year the council passed a bill prohibiting the throwing of stones at public executions.

1740: A Hard Winter and Food Shortages

The frost was so bad at the beginning of 1740 that there was ice on the Firth of Forth. At Queensferry, even the sea had a light covering. The Water of Leith froze, thus preventing the mill wheels from turning. Some people in the town even died from the cold.

This was followed by a bad harvest. Prices increased so that people were struggling to pay for what corn (wheat, barley and oats) was available. This led to attacks on the storehouses and then to the use of troops to restore order. The council bought grain with which to stock the markets, and money was lent to them interest-free by the banks. Mr Coutts and other merchants involved in the importation of grain sold it to the authorities at cost price.

Bodysnatching

Bodysnatching was not a crime confined to the nineteenth century, for on 5 January 1721 South Leith Session ordered an examination of the grave of Ann Wright. The body was missing.

In 1739, they recorded the setting of a watch in the churchyard after a burial. Complaints were made to the Session in 1745 and again in 1747 about the behaviour of the watch. They had been firing off guns in the churchyard.

They were not the only ones against whom the good citizens of Leith brought complaints. George Carkettle, the gravedigger, was suspected of selling dead bodies. Robert Henderson, a custom's house porter, accused him of selling the body of his child. This nearly started a riot, but the excavation showed that the body was still in the grave. Carkettle was also accused of drunken and abusive behaviour and lost his job in 1743.

The Occupation of Edinburgh, 1745

Prince Charles and his army approached Edinburgh from the west. He set up his headquarters at Grey's Mill by Slateford. Representatives of the town council came out to negotiate with him but reached no successful conclusions, and a few citizens, like former provost George Drummond, collected volunteers to resist the Jacobites.

Two companies of dragoons rode out to Coltbridge to block any move towards the city by the prince's men. Upon the approach of the Highlanders they rapidly withdrew east and took up a position beyond Leith, leaving the town exposed to the advancing army.

In Edinburgh, the ports had been closed but the guards opened the Netherbow to allow a carriage to enter from the Canongate. A group of the prince's soldiers lay in hiding near the port and seized their chance. Once the gate was in their hands, the city was defenceless and soon the prince had occupied Edinburgh.

Prince Charles set up his headquarters in the Palace of Holyrood. Some of his officers were quartered in the nearby White Horse Inn. Queensberry House was taken over and later used as a prison and infirmary. There appears to have been no serious trouble between the citizens and the occupying force. Any

conflicts would surely have been reported after the defeat of the prince, if only to show that the citizens were loyal supporters of the government.

The main problem facing the prince was the force in the castle. General Guest's garrison was too small to launch any counter-attack and the occupying army lacked the big guns to reduce the defences of the castle to rubble. The prince placed a guard in the old weighhouse at the head of the Bow. It began as an uneasy peace, with both visitors and supplies passing through to the castle. When the prince's men decided to stop this, General Guest ordered his men to fire on the town.

After Sunday, 15 September, the day when the prince seized Edinburgh, no services were held in the churches. The strict Presbyterians probably suspected that Prince Charles might try to restore the Catholic Church in Scotland.

Not everyone in Edinburgh supported the Jacobite Army. One week later, news came that a government army led by General Cope was approaching Edinburgh from the east. Most of the prince's men were in a camp around Duddingston. They advanced on Cope's men. The battle was soon over and the government soldiers who were not captured, killed or wounded fled back towards Berwick.

Throughout October, the prince and his army remained in Edinburgh planning their next move. Rear Admiral Byng brought a squadron of ships into the Forth; this move cut communications with supporters in Fife and, more importantly, prevented any reinforcements coming from France. The lack of support from the French, who were at war with Britain at this time, played an important role in the eventual failure of the prince's mission.

On 1 November, Prince Charles left Edinburgh for his march into England. He would never return. We do not know how many inhabitants of the city joined his army. It appears not to have been many. In April 1746, the *Caledonian Mercury* reported that there was 'no acting magistracy' in the city. The constables organised a guard to patrol the streets and maintain order. After the final defeat of the prince's army at Culloden the government took control. George Drummond, a former lord provost and a supporter of the Hanoverian government, became lord provost.

Archibald Stewart, who had been lord provost at the time of the Jacobite invasion of the city, was arrested and placed in the Tower of London. Charges were brought against him, but the government were unable to prove them so Stewart was allowed to retire from politics. Only Archibald Blair, an Edinburgh solicitor, and Andrew Wauchop of Niddrie were excluded from the Act of Indemnity.

Poor Children in Edinburgh

Poor or orphaned sons of burgesses could be placed in Heriot's Hospital where they would receive board and some elementary education. George Watson had provided another hospital for these boys.

The Merchant Company and the Incorporated Trades founded two other hospitals for girls with the financial assistance of Mary Erskine.

However, those children whose parents were unable to support them ended up in the charity workhouse by Bristo Port. They were usually orphans. In February 1747, fifty to sixty boys and a similar number of girls were inspected by the Lords of Session. The children were smartly turned out in uniforms made in the workhouse.

Twelve

THE LATE EIGHTEENTH CENTURY

George Drummond and the Town Council

Since the accession of George I in 1714 the Whig Party had held control over the government of Britain. Patronage – government appointments given to their supporters, relatives and friends – had helped them maintain their grip on power. The chief of the Edinburgh Whigs was George Drummond, who was elected lord provost in 1746 and was chosen again in 1750, 1754, 1758 and 1762 (no one could hold the office for more than two years in a row).

The council consisted of the lord provost, four bailies, the dean of guild and the treasurer. Added to this group were the former holders of these offices, giving them a majority of fourteen votes on the twenty-five-man council. The rest of the members consisted of three merchants and two trades councillors, as well as six out of the fourteen deacons of the incorporated trades. The trades presented a leet of six to the council, who reduced it to three from whom the trade chose their deacon. It was the council who decided which of the fourteen deacons then served on the council. The rest (extraordinary deacons) had the right to vote for the Member of Parliament for the city. The system was designed to ensure that only those candidates who could be relied on to support the office bearers on the council were selected.

During these years, a number of people appeared regularly on the town council. George Lind was a bailie in 1754 and 1758. He was chosen as old provost in 1759, which was unusual as he did not become lord provost until the following year and eventually became the Member of Parliament for Edinburgh, although he stood down when he received the government post of Conservator of Scottish Privileges in the Netherlands. John Carmichael served as a bailie twice before becoming dean of guild in 1758–59.

James Rocheid was a bailie in 1753 and 1755 then served as dean of guild in 1756 and 1757. After this, he was appointed treasurer to Heriot's Hospital. During 1762 it came to light that the treasurer had embezzled the large sum of £1,000 from the hospital. His dismissal did not stop the Incorporation of Cordiners (shoemakers) asking their members:

> To concur with the Merchant Company, the Incorporated Trades and Societies in the city and the burgesses in calling the Magistrates, Town Council and Governors of Heriot's Hospital to account for their mismanagement and the loss sustained by the Hospital through the conduct of James Rocheid, Treasurer.

The skinners and furriers claimed that Rocheid was appointed despite it being widely known that he was having financial problems.

The three suburbs of Canongate and Calton, Leith and Portsburgh (which included Potterrow) had their own bailies chosen by the town council. Their senior bailie was always one of the old bailies.

The town council was a tight-knit and secretive group. The *Caledonian Mercury*, published in Edinburgh, recorded the activities of Parliament in London, but remained silent about the affairs of this town council until fierce opposition arose over the council's failure to consult the ministers and Session on the appointment to Lady Yester's Kirk (the council appointed a new minister without consulting either the city's ministers or the Church Session). Opposition to this procedure came not only from the trades but also the merchants. However, the Court of Session upheld the council's right to appoint the minister. As a result, many members left to form Edinburgh's first relief church in Potterrow.

The Press Gang

With the approach of yet another war with France (the Seven Years War began in 1756), the government needed to increase the size of the armed forces. At the end of February 1755, the navy, reinforced by 100 soldiers from the castle, searched Leith for potential seamen. Skilled men such as brewers, carters, bakers, weavers and shoemakers were all vulnerable to being taken up.

Naval discipline was enforced with considerable brutality and the men were tied to their ships in the same way a medieval serf was tied to the land. Those who volunteered received money (known as 'the bounty') and the town council offered them an extra one and a half guineas. The need was considerable. The fleet at Spithead alone consisted of thirty-five ships manned by 15,000 seamen.

On 19 May 1755, the press gangs were found waiting at the church doors. At the same time, they turned their attention to Edinburgh and its suburbs, although pressure seems to have eased in the later months of the year.

However, the press gangs returned in March 1756, taking up more men in Leith and Newhaven. Their return on a Sunday to Edinburgh resulted in two days of rioting. The magistrates (the lord provost and the bailies) had to call on all their resources, including soldiers from the castle. As loyal supporters of the government they were obliged to stand firm. However, even the Whig oligarchy who ruled the city were frightened by these demonstrations. Only one man, Alexander Fletcher, was prosecuted 'as the principal hand in the riot'. Concessions were made to ensure peace in the city and press gangs operating in Edinburgh now had to be supervised by a constable or law officer. Men who were taken by the press were brought to the guardhouse, where a magistrate examined them to prevent 'men of good character' from being taken.

The Royal Infirmary

This institution continued to grow, offering free medical help to the poorer members of the community. In 1756 they proposed to open two new wards for 'sober and industrious servants when seized with fever and other acute diseases'. Donations, supported by a collection at the church doors, were to be passed to Gilbert Laurie, their treasurer, who was to become lord provost. Later in the year the trustees appointed Mr Willhousie, a Minister of the Gospel, as their chaplain. His duties were composed of visiting the sick and preaching at the Sunday afternoon service.

Charity Workhouses

Edinburgh's Institution, built in 1743, was situated by Bristo Port to the south of Greyfriars Church. By June 1751 it housed 582 inmates at a cost of £2,760. The numbers rose to 725 by June 1757, with a similar increase in cost. The managers had to use up money from legacies to meet the deficit. The last public collection, in June 1752, had raised the large sum of £1,626 and it was felt necessary to appeal for more funds. Twenty-two more rooms were also required for the insane.

In 1759 the first stone was laid in the West Kirk's (St Cuthbert's) Parish Workhouse, and the Canongate built their workhouse in the yard behind the church. Both buildings were completed by 1761.

The Water Supply

As Edinburgh began to grow the shortage in the supply of water became a recurring problem. A drought in 1755 brought the problem to the fore and the town council proposed to take water from the springs at Swanston. An Act of Parliament in 1758 gave them the right to pipe water from these springs to the city. Henry Trotter, who owned the land, tried to resist this move in the Court of Session without any success.

The town council now had such a plentiful supply for the wells that in May 1762 they were able to offer piped water to private households. They charged £1 per annum, to be paid in advance. Bakehouses and taverns were offered a similar service at £2 10s per year. All installation costs had to be met by the owners of the property.

French Prisoners

In October 1759, a large body of French prisoners was marched through the High Street. It was reported that many of the inhabitants were moved to tears by the pitiable state of these men. Of the 362 French prisoners held in the castle, 331 had no shoes, 238 no shirts and 301 no jackets. In this state, few would have survived a Scottish winter.

Proposals were put forward by the public to raise funds to purchase clothing for these men. Three city merchants, William Alexander & Sons, Mansfield & Hunter and James Seaton, offered to receive the donations. This support for the prisoners met with some opposition, but by the end of November they had gathered sufficient contributions to be able to close the fund.

Nine French prisoners escaped from the castle at the beginning of December using ropes to climb down the rock. Seven were caught within a few days by a company of dragoons.

The Deacon of Masons & Wrights

In September 1763, the incorporated trades presented their leets (lists) containing the names of six persons from whom the deacon of the incorporation would be chosen. The town council then reduced the number to three. From the three accepted by the council, the Incorporation of Masons & Wrights chose Alexander Miller to be their deacon for the coming year. Miller received forty-five votes, while his nearest rival, Alexander Nicolson, gained only twenty-eight.

Nicolson claimed that as Miller did not live in the city he could not be a deacon. The council (though not the incorporated trades) agreed with him and so Alexander Nicolson became Deacon of the Masons & Wrights instead. Immediately objections were raised to this decision on the grounds that the town council had sanctioned Miller's name by keeping it on the leet. Miller had a business in Edinburgh and had been a member of the incorporation for twenty-five years, and he actually lived in the Canongate.

Why did the town council majority wish to anger the incorporated trades over the election of a single deacon? The Masons & Wrights believed they knew the answer, 'But the plain matter of fact is, that our present rulers are resolved to unmask entirely and stick at nothing to stop the tide of opposition which they perceive is now well nigh ready to overwhelm them'. A little optimistic perhaps, for it took another seventy years and an Act of Parliament before the town council of Edinburgh became more accountable for their actions.

The Meals Riots, 1763

The summer of 1763 did not appear to have been bad nor, according to Arnot, were prices particularly high. However, the public believed that a shortage was caused by speculators hoarding grain. On the night of Monday, 21 November, after a shortage of meal in the market for some days, a mob broke into the market and the tacksman's house. John Mowat had his furniture stolen.

Similar trouble occurred in Leith and the magistrates held a meeting with the Justices of the Peace for the county. They promised to use their influence to secure more meal for the market. Three men were charged with offences connected to the riot. At their trial the following August the jury decided the case was not proven. To prevent further trouble, the magistrates took severe action against hoarding. One retailer in December 1764, who was convicted of hoarding grain, received a fine and eight days in prison.

Crime on Our Streets

Towards the end of the 1760s, Edinburgh and its suburbs suffered a crimewave on its streets. Gangs, and even individuals, took advantage of the dark nights to commit a series of robberies. One correspondent of the *Caledonian Mercury* in November 1767 asked, 'Is it not amazing that no steps have been taken to put a stop to the frequent robberies which have of late been committed in the open streets and about the suburbs.'

The first weekend of December 1769 saw three of these attacks – one near the West Kirk and two others in the Canongate. A journeyman, Smith, was also held up and 6 shillings stolen from him. He pleaded with his attacker to return one of the coins to help him support his wife and four children. The robber handed him a coin which turned out not to be a shilling but a guinea worth 21 shillings. The smith no doubt went away happy, but many were not so lucky.

In September of the same year, a warning was given to the citizens to beware of strangers coming into their premises. A landlady was robbed when she left the room to fetch refreshments. A shoemaker suffered a similar fate as he was diverted by a 'customer'. The country had no proper police force to organise resistance to the problem and although Edinburgh had the Town Guard, they were not a large body of men.

The Theatre Royal

The Presbyterian Establishment looked with suspicion on cultural activities which they feared might lead to a lowering of moral standards. Gradually, dancing (called 'assemblies' in Edinburgh) and music became part of the social scene in the city by the 1730s. Theatrical performances were banned by the authorities, but drama companies put out programmes which included music. They then charged for the music but performed the plays free of charge. By this means they were able to avoid the restrictions.

In 1747 a new concert hall was opened in the Canongate but it continued to meet with opposition from the clergy. Ironically, their big hit of the 1756–57 season was 'The Tragedy of Douglas', written by a Presbyterian minister. The theatre received a royal patent in 1767, becoming the Theatre Royal, and so became legitimate. In 1769 a new theatre was also opened in Shakespeare Square by the new North Bridge.

Building Developments in the 1760s

The Netherbow Port, the western entrance leading to the Canongate, was demolished in 1764. It was proving to be a bottleneck for coaches and carts travelling between the Old Town of Edinburgh and the Port of Leith.

Demand for better housing from the more prosperous citizens led to the building of Brown's Square. A short lane linked it with Candlemakers' Row. It stood for over 100 years before the properties were pulled down to make way for Chambers Street.

In 1766, George's Square (now called George Square) was begun and became the home of many influential people. Henry Dundas, Viscount Melville and the Edinburgh solicitor Walter Scott all owned houses here. His second son became an advocate, but is better known as the author of *The Waverley Novels*. Sir Walter spent much of his youth in George Square.

This decade saw the initial developments which were needed for the setting up of the New Town. The Nor' Loch was drained and work began on the

building of North Bridge to link Prince's Street with the High Street. In 1767, Lord Provost Gilbert Lawrie signed the council's acceptance of Craig's plan and the passing of the Edinburgh Extension Act secured the town council's ownership and jurisdiction over the land for the New Town.

Sir Lawrence Dundas

Sir Lawrence was born in 1710. His father owned a drapery business in the Luckenbooths. However, he did not follow his father's trade but became a contractor supplying goods to the army. Not all government contractors were honest men: the practice of sending a smaller quantity but charging the full price was common. Such men were never fully accepted in the aristocratic society of the eighteenth century.

During the Seven Years War, Dundas made a vast fortune and was created a baronet in 1762. Two years later, Sir Lawrence entered Parliament for the constituency of Newcastle-under-Lyme and was chosen as governor of the Royal Bank of Scotland. As a Member of Parliament, he took a leading role to ensure the passing of the Edinburgh Extension Act.

In October 1767, Lord Provost Gilbert Laurie, with a delegation 'representing the majority of the town council', visited Sir Lawrence in his house in Stirlingshire. They offered him the parliamentary seat for Edinburgh, which he duly accepted. A year later, he took his seat as Member for Edinburgh, a position which he held until his death in 1781.

Criticism is made of Dundas, who was prepared to use his money to support both his own position and the political clique who ruled Edinburgh at this time. The conflict began in earnest in 1776 as both Henry Dundas and the Duke of Buccleuch tried to capture the parliamentary seat. A second election in 1780 was eventually decided by a parliamentary committee in Sir Lawrence's favour. However, they were probably no worse in their dealings than their contemporaries in other parts of the country. The political system was ripe for reform and pressure began to grow after the failure in the American War of Independence.

As the feuing of the New Town began, Sir Lawrence secured the important site on the east side of St Andrew's Square where he built his town house. This fine building can still be seen today, although it is now a branch of the Royal Bank. Ainsley's Map (probably 1780) shows large formal gardens at the rear of the building.

Sir Lawrence was disliked as an ambitious upstart and has met with considerable criticism, both in his own time and from modern writers. The *Caledonian Mercury* in November 1780 accused him of making more profit from the Edinburgh Regiment, which he had set up with his own money (by selling positions), than he gave to the public charities in the city. However, James Boswell, who knew him in his later years, gives this description of him in his *Edinburgh Journals*: 'He appeared to me not a cunning shrewd man of the world but a comely jovial Scotch gentleman of good address but not bright parts'. Later he wrote, 'I like Sir Lawrence more and more. There was a kindliness and even simplicity in this man.'

Sir Lawrence died in 1781, but no notice or obituary appeared in the *Caledonian Mercury*. He was succeeded as MP by Sir James Hunter Blair.

Gilbert Laurie

Gilbert Laurie owned an apothecary's business at the top of Niddrie Wynd, where he also sold tickets for the assemblies. He became treasurer of the Royal Infirmary. Laurie served as town treasurer in 1757 and as a bailie in both 1759 and 1764. It would appear that upon the death of George Drummond, Gilbert Laurie and his friends took control of the town council. He was elected lord provost in October 1766, then, like George Drummond, the government made him a Commissioner of Excise.

Laurie served again as lord provost in 1772. This era saw the development of the New Town. Contemporaries seem to be divided about the achievements of the council at this time. Hugo Arnot, whose history appeared in the late 1770s, wrote:

> From the year 1763 till 1776 the city continued to be peaceably governed, conform to the rules of the constitution. At this time the chief magistrate of the place was a person to whom the citizens gave credit for liberality of ideas and for taste, judgement and attention in conducting the affairs over which he presided.

On the other hand, 'a Burgess and a Guild Brother' (an anonymous pamphleteer) accused Laurie and his supporters of squandering the city's revenue, giving jobs to their supporters and obstructing the city's development. The harbour of Leith, he claimed, was in a ruinous state.

The ruling group on the council were even blamed for the structural failure of the North Bridge which led to the collapse of one of the piers. It was said that 'if a man makes a foolish remark or if a stupid fellow be mentioned it is instantly replied that he is ripe to be an Edinburgh Magistrate'. A small minority of citizens were able to control the affairs of the city, since they were able to choose the office bearers for the following year. The members of the council, together with the extraordinary deacons, were the only citizens allowed to vote in the election of the Member of Parliament.

The Elections of 1776 and 1780

In 1776, Lord Provost James Stoddart proposed Alexander Kincaid as his successor and Thomas Elder as dean of guild. He also hoped Francis Brodie, father of the infamous Deacon Brodie (more about whom later in this chapter), should retain his place in the council. For once, things did not go to plan. When it came to choosing the new council, neither side appears to have covered themselves with glory. Thomas Sommers, one of the deacons, was being held in the Tolbooth for debt. The lord provost (James Stoddart) determined that he should stay there despite a writ to free him issued by the Court of Session. He was therefore unable to take part in the election. Kincaid was elected, much to the delight of the mob, who demanded lights be placed in windows to celebrate. Those who refused suffered the consequences – broken windows!

The writ for the election of a member for the new parliament in 1780 was sent to Lord Provost Hamilton, who appears to have had a nervous breakdown. Mr Thomson, the senior bailie, was left to call a meeting of the town council, at which the extraordinary deacons were present. They forced through a motion opposing any delay in the election. Dean of Guild John Grieve protested because the extraordinary deacons had voted, enabling the motion to pass by eighteen to fourteen votes.

The opposition to Sir Lawrence had originally been divided between James Craig and William Miller, but pressure behind the scenes led to Miller becoming the official 'Tory' candidate. They called the voters to an entertainment in Fortune's Tavern after the writs were called for the new parliament. Fortune's was the headquarters of the Opposition; the majority of the town council met at Walker's Tavern.

Sir Lawrence Dundas' supporters boycotted the election, enabling William Miller to claim the seat by eighteen votes to none in September. However, the matter did not end there. In November the majority on the town council, led by James Hunter Blair and John Grieve, prepared a protest against the legality of the election of William Miller. The House of Commons passed it to a committee who found that Sir Lawrence Dundas, Bart. was duly elected.

The American War of Independence

In 1779, John Paul Jones raided the Scottish coastal trade, even threatening Leith. Two years later, with the Dutch in the war, groups of Edinburgh merchants began to invest in privateers. They received a letter of marque allowing them to attack the king's enemies (in peacetime this would have been piracy).

They were a diverse lot. *The Enterprise*, which set out from Leith at the beginning of February 1781, was described by the *Courant* as 'a bundle of boards'. On the other hand, Robert Moodie's *Resolution* was 250 tons and carried twenty-two 24-pounder (even frigates, usually 400 tons, were normally only armed with canon firing shots of 12lb). She was considerably overloaded.

The most successful people in this trade were the Royal Navy. It is likely that they captured the two French frigates which were sold as prizes in Lawrence's Coffee House, Leith. On the other hand, French and Dutch privateers operated in the North Sea, attacking the coastal trade as well as ships travelling to the Baltic – not every ship was able to join a convoy.

Trade and Shipping

The American War saw both French and Dutch privateers operating against shipping from Leith. Britain again replied by forming convoys protected by warships. Coastal ships visiting Leith came from as far north as Shetland and as far south as London, which was probably the most important destination for cargoes from the port. International trade with Baltic cities such as Danzig, Hamburgh, Memmel and Christisund had to run the risk of enemy cruisers. Trade links with Oporto continued, bringing wine for the wealthier citizens of Edinburgh.

Facilities in the harbour of Leith were limited to the quays along the river. In 1785, as many as 1,721 ships used the port – an average of four or five each day. This led to overcrowding in the harbour and even accidents.

In 1789 the *Juno* and the *Peggy* both sailed for Portugal. This was the year the Revolution broke out in France. A few ships even sailed into the Mediterranean, and the *Princess Royal* completed the round trip in 1790. However, war eventually broke out with Revolutionary France, making such trips very dangerous. In February 1795, John Lawrie's ship, *The Molly*, was taken by a French frigate. She managed to escape bringing her cargo of wine safely into Leith.

A few ships sailed to the West Indies. Robert Liddell brought back cargoes consisting mainly of sugar, rum and coffee. The war forced him to join the West Indian convoys for protection.

The London trade was important to the merchants of Edinburgh. The Edinburgh Glasshouse Company (based in Leith) had their own ships to carry their bottles safely. At the end of 1792, the *Phoenix*, one of the company's ships under the command of Captain Neilson, completed the voyage from Leith to London in four days.

Another fast sailor was *The Ceres*; Captain McIntosh was also able to complete the trip in four days, although the weather must have dictated the speed. A growing rival in this trade was the Union Shipping Co. of Berwick-on-Tweed. By the middle of 1795 they had a sufficient number of ships to offer three departures a week from Berwick to London, as well as a similar number for the return voyage. They even organised a carriage to take passengers from Edinburgh to Berwick. Soon they established themselves in Leith from where their ships, fast sailing smacks, offered frequent departures for London.

Increased Taxation

The failure in the American War led to the resignation of Lord North in 1782. Britain passed through a phase of political instability, with first the Marquis of Rockingham supported by Charles James Fox and then Lord Shelbourne forming Whig ministries. The next year the Tory, Lord North, and the Whig, Fox, formed an alliance which shocked people, even in those times. However, they failed to gain enough support and by the end of the year a young William Pitt was leading yet another new government. In Scotland, Pitt had the support of Henry Dundas.

The war had not only been a political and military failure but it had also been a huge drain on the financial resources. Taxes had to go up – something that was not just unpopular in Edinburgh. The window tax was increased, but proposals to place 1s 3d tax on every cart of coal was successfully blocked; even the town council petitioned against this. Other duties were placed on dogs, horses, hats and even shops.

Education in Edinburgh, 1760–99

Edinburgh, the Canongate and Leith had their own high or grammar schools. Each of them was inspected by the local magistrates and ministers. In 1762, the magistrates and ministers of Edinburgh were so pleased with the teaching that the rector and his teaching staff were made burgesses and granted the freedom of the city. The school had five classes made up for the five year groups.

On 24 June 1777, the foundation stone was laid for the new High School. Matters were not so happy when the lord provost (Sir James Hunter Blair) visited the school in February 1786. Two boys had been expelled; the first had stabbed another pupil with a knife while the second had attempted to shoot a teacher with a pistol. The *Evening Courant* reported that the lord provost had made 'a suitable speech', adding that 'it is to be hoped it will have a proper effect on their future behaviour'.

Henry Cockburn, later a judge in the Court of Session, commented on his time at the High School, 'I doubt if I read a single book or even 50 pages voluntarily when I was at the High School'. The boys, at this time, wore round black hats and shirts, presumably white, fastened at the neck by black ribbons. Breeches (knee-length trousers) were made from brown corduroy, with worsted stockings in winter and blue cotton ones in summer. Coats and waistcoats were brightly coloured – grass green, bright blue and even scarlet.

Four 'English' schools licensed by the magistrates were opened in the mid-1760s providing tuition in reading, writing and arithmetic. All lessons were in English and no Latin was taught. These continued to function throughout the rest of the century, although the masters (and their homes) changed over the years. In 1776, Mr Williamson ran an English school in the Canongate. That year, the inspecting magistrates were 'pleased with the rapid progress of the youngest boys and girls in reading and spelling'.

Mr Ruffin ran an academy in Nicolson Street where French was the only language spoken except, no doubt, in Italian lessons. Besides writing and arithmetic, he offered riding, fencing, dancing and military exercise. Mr Darling of Warriston Close gave lessons in geometry, geography, architecture, surveying and bookkeeping, as well as writing and arithmetic. Alexander Ewing, in Bishop's Land, also included algebra and astronomy in his curriculum. These private schools, and there were a considerable number in and around the city, offered a much wider curriculum than the high schools, where Latin and entry to the university were the main priorities.

Mrs and Miss Mary Jackson advertised their boarding school for young ladies in Prince's Street in 1782. Thirteen years later, Miss Heron moved her establishment to Prince's Street but, in the following year, she found more spacious premises in St David's Street. Most of her young ladies were boarders who may have come from well-to-do country families. Her curriculum included English, French, writing, geography, drawing, music and dance. Girls were not allowed to enter the high schools or the university.

Most children were dependent on the schools run by the Church Sessions. Parents were expected to contribute towards the lessons to help pay the salary of the schoolmaster. Mr Michie at Currie was teaching ninety children in the parish school in 1795. Praise was especially given for his work with church music.

The children of burgesses who could no longer afford to support their children were boarded in the hospitals. Heriot's and George Watson's provided basic education for boys while the Merchants' and Trades' hospitals did the same for girls.

Those children in the workhouse were less fortunate. In 1790 some seventy boys and girls were sent to work in the cotton mills of the Clyde Valley. Another forty-two came from St Cuthbert's Parish Workhouse. Some of these went to Mr Dale of New Lanark, who described their living conditions in a letter to Mr Baylay of Manchester. Children, some as young as 8, worked solely for their education and board until they reached the age of 15.

A charity school was opened in 1778 in Blackfriars Wynd for the 'poor and destitute children in the city of Edinburgh and its suburbs' (*Edinburgh Herald*, June 1791). By June 1791 Mr Mcfarlane had sixty pupils.

The University of Edinburgh

In the late eighteenth century, the university was divided into four faculties – Theology, Law, Medicine and Arts. The patronage of the university – the right to appoint the professors – was in the hands of the town council. In 1762, they chose William Robertson to be principal. He was a leading Church moderate and minister of Old Greyfriars. Robertson had gained academic recognition with his *History of Scotland in the Reigns of Queen Mary and King James VI.* He served as moderator of the General Assembly. His other leading work was a history of the Emperor Charles V. He retired as principal of the university in 1792 after thirty years' service.

The university was still dominated by the Church of Scotland. David Hume, one of the greatest philosophers and historians of the Enlightenment, was never a member of staff as his religious views were suspect, and Adam Smith taught at Glasgow University, before retiring to Panmuir House in the Canongate. However, the university did contain Joseph Black, William Cullen and Dugald Stewart.

On 16 November 1789, the first stone was laid on the new university building. Robert Adam was the architect. The cost, estimated at £30,000, was to be met by donations from the public. By the end of the year over £13,000 had been raised but after this initial burst of enthusiasm the money proved harder to find. By September 1793 the money had run out and men were laid off. Unfortunately, much of the eastern front had no roof, leaving it open to the elements.

The Canonmills Riot, 1784

At the beginning of June, a mob marched down to the distillery of Mr Haig in Canonmills. Rumours had spread through the city that a large quantity of grain was stored there. Led by the beat of a drum played by William Anderson they descended on this village by the Water of Leith. The employees prepared to resist but the mob soon broke through the gate. David Smith and John Lumsden, workers in the distillery, fired shots, killing Robert Gray, who was one of the mob.

Sheriff Cockburne (Canonmills was part of the county and not the city) arrived with a company of dragoons led by Captain Sykes. The mob was broken up, but they rallied and set off for Leith. The magistrates there had already taken measures to stop people going to Canonmills. When the mob entered the port they found no support for their actions.

Smith and Lumsden were arrested and taken to the Tolbooth. They were released a few weeks later as His Majesty's Advocate was unwilling to prosecute.

Mr Haig offered to pay for the funeral of Robert Gray as well as providing his parents with a pension.

A few days later, a second mob headed for Canonmills but the military reached the distillery first. The mob then threatened to attack the sheriff's house and the authorities placed a guard around it. Various people were arrested in the disturbance and William Anderson and James Paul (a tanner) were convicted for their part in the riot and were whipped through the city.

Coal and Salt

Whereas the workers on the land and in the burghs had become free from serfdom, the 1606 Act of the Scottish Parliament tied the miners and salt panners to their places of work. They could not leave without the permission of their masters. Only in the last years of the eighteenth century was legislation put on the statute book which led to the freeing of these workers.

During the century coal was mined in Duddingston and by 1790 around 270 men, women and possibly children were employed in the Earl of Abercorn's mine. Unfortunately in March of that year the mine flooded, and not even the steam engine was able to clear the water. Another pit, in nearby Brunstane, continued to work three seams of coal.

Salt pans which used coal to evaporate seawater were to be found along both shores of the Forth. The pans at Joppa relied on the local coal, and employed forty women to carry the salt to Edinburgh and neighbouring villages. They would sell it, presumably like the fishwives of Newhaven sold fish, although their burdens would have been much heavier.

Gilmerton, in the parish of Liberton, was an important centre for mining. They had, by the end of the eighteenth century, been extracting coal for over 200 years. Carters were employed to carry the coal to Edinburgh. The building of the Edinburgh & Dalkeith Railway provided a direct link between the Midlothian mines and the capital. A spur took the line to Leith where the coal could be transhipped to other industrial sites along the Forth.

Cramond Iron Works

In the middle of the eighteenth century, five mills operated on the banks of the Almond at Cramond. Most water-powered mills served a variety of businesses in their lifetime. In 1752, the Smith & Wright Works of Leith purchased Cockle Mill. They probably used it to produce agricultural implements. Seven years later, they were bought out by John Roebuck, a partner in the Carron Iron

Company. The iron works came into the possession of Cadell & Edington in 1770. Fairafar and Dowie's Mills were also added to the company's assets.

Iron imported from Sweden and Russia, and later from the west of Scotland, was turned into hoops for barrels, pans, pot handles and nails. Dowie's Mill produced spades and shovels. Fairafar possessed a forge and a furnace. By 1796, Cadell & Edington owned three forges, two furnaces and two slitting mills along the river at Cramond. As competitors grew in size Cramond Iron Works struggled to keep up with them. Peggie's Mill was turned into a papermill, but the paper was of a poor quality because the water was polluted, and Dowie's Mill became a sawmill.

Snuff Milling

The Act of Union in 1707 opened up the English colonies to Scottish merchants. The merchants of Glasgow established prosperous businesses importing tobacco from the North American colonies and thus became known as the 'tobacco lords'. Much of it was re-exported to countries like France. By 1760 they controlled much of the trade in tobacco. At the same time, the taking of snuff – finely ground tobacco breathed in through the nose – was becoming popular among the wealthier classes. It was carried in small ornate boxes which today are collectors' items.

A snuff mill operated in Gorgie as early as the 1750s. The picturesque little snuff mill at East Mills in Currie was built by Ferrier & Thomson in 1749. Downstream from here, three more snuff mills were opened. Watt's Mill began to grind tobacco for snuff in 1763, and close by stood Wright's Grain Mill. Nothing now remains of these two mills except the exit of a double lade leading back into the Water of Leith.

James Gillespie began manufacturing snuff at his Spylaw Mill in 1759. He sold his product directly to the customer from his shop on the High Street. Money from the profits of his trade enabled him to build a large mansion attached to his mill (which can still be seen in Spylaw Park, Colinton) and leave money in his will to found a school which still bears his name.

A rival mill at Upper Spylaw had been converted to grind snuff by William Reid. This had once been a papermill. It was also used as an inn, which gained a reputation as a haunt for smugglers. Much of the government's revenue in the eighteenth century came from taxes on imports. A raid by excise officers found nothing in the way of contraband but it did enable them to view the new machinery which Reid had brought into the mill. He suspected that some of the 'officers' were really men who worked for James Gillespie – a case of industrial espionage. Another search in 1776 did lead the excise officers to discover tea and brandy.

Henry Dundas and the Town Council

Thomas Elder was re-elected lord provost in October 1789. Shortly after this, the town council met with Henry Dundas of Arniston, later Viscount Melville, and agreed to choose him as the next member for the city. The years after the 1745 Rebellion had seen Edinburgh governed by a Whig oligarchy led by George Drummond. In 1780 the Tories, led by Henry Dundas and the Duke of Buccleuch, had tried to secure the election of a man who would support the Tories in Parliament. The town council had resisted the pressure, but in 1789 they turned to Dundas. It would appear that the ruling Whig clique on the town council had turned into a Tory one – a position which was to continue until the great Reform Acts of 1832–33.

Yet the change was not as dramatic as it would first appear. Drummond and the town council of his time were loyal supporters of the king's government and the constitution which gave them a monopoly of power in the city. In the 1780s the prime minister, William Pitt, was a Tory, and the Whigs, led by Fox and Sheridan, had proposed measures to enlarge the franchise. This threatened the position of the small group who controlled the council. It was now the Tories who supported the government and opposed reform.

Another point in their calculations must have been the influence that could be exerted by Henry Dundas, who was an important member of the government. All town councils required Parliament to pass Acts to further their development. The New Town and the improved water scheme of the 1760s had been created through Acts of Parliament.

From October 1788 until the end of the century, only two men, Thomas Elder and Sir James Stirling, held the office of lord provost.

William 'Deacon' Brodie

By 1762 Francis Brodie had established a thriving business with a showroom in the Lawnmarket where he sold cabinets and chairs as well as brass and iron fittings for the house. He also possessed a yard in the Cowgate, opposite Magdalene Chapel. Brodie's men carried out joinery work 'done in the best manner', according to the advert in the *Caledonian Mercury*. Francis became Deacon of the Incorporation of Wrights and a member of the town council. He died in 1780, leaving his business to his son, William.

In September 1781, William Brodie was elected by the wrights as their deacon. He was then chosen by the town council as one of the council deacons. Unfortunately, he also led a double life – gambling in various establishments in the city and Canongate. In the course of his business, Brodie gained access to homes in the Old Town and was able to copy the keys. These duplicates enabled him to access the property secretly.

Brodie and his gang planned to rob the Excise Office in Chessel's Court. They entered the building, but James Bonnar, the deputy solicitor, returned to the office unexpectedly. He was unaware that a robbery was in progress. The thieves panicked and fled the scene. They were arrested, but Brodie could not be found anywhere in Edinburgh. He was eventually picked up in Amsterdam and brought back to Edinburgh. Brodie was tried for his part in the robberies and was hung outside the Tolbooth in Edinburgh (the Grassmarket was no longer used for public hangings at this time).

The French Revolution

Few events can have had a greater influence in the long history of Europe than the French Revolution, which brought to an end the royal monopoly of power. At first, the Revolution was welcomed by many people in Britain, but as the violence increased a reaction set in. Louis XVI was executed on 21 January 1793 and, within a fortnight, Britain had joined a coalition against Revolutionary France.

Power in France fell into the hands of the Committee of Public Safety, dominated by the Jacobins. For a year, Maximilien Robespierre denounced opponents of the regime. Marie Antoinette was guillotined in October 1793. Even supporters of the Revolution were not safe from the Jacobins' attempt to free France of her enemies at home and abroad. Thus began the Reign of Terror, which only ended with the execution of Robespierre and his friends in the Paris Commune.

The news from France, even before war had been declared, frightened the British political establishment and turned them against reform. In a vote in the House of Commons in June 1797, the Whigs could only muster ninety-one supporters, leaving the government with a massive majority of 165 against a proposed reform bill.

Friends of the People

Pressure to reform the House of Commons began after the government's failure to bring the American War of Independence to a successful conclusion. In Edinburgh, a city containing many wealthy and influential men, only the thirty-three members of the town council had the right to select the Member of Parliament. A bill had been introduced in the House in 1789 to enlarge the franchise in the Scottish burghs. It received no support from the Scottish Members. The *Edinburgh Evening Courant*, not known as an opposition paper, commented, 'The greater part of them [MPs from Scottish burghs] owe their seats to those very self-elected magistrates at whose arbitrary power the bill is directed'.

The French Revolution initially stimulated the movement for reform. All over the country, groups known as the Friends of the People were formed. Unlike their French counterparts, they were not revolutionaries prepared to use violence but people who looked for reform of the franchise through Parliament. Friends of the People had three separate societies in the Canongate. The Lawnmarket, the Cowgate and Bridge Street in the Old Town had their own groups. George McIntosh chaired a society in the New Town.

In the suburbs of Portsburgh and Potterrow, the Friends had formed groups. Calton, Lauriston, Abbeyhill and even the Water of Leith (Dean Village) had their own societies, along with Leith itself. They consisted mainly of members of the middle class, although some aristocrats like Lord Daer gave their support. They even had their own paper – the *Edinburgh Gazetteer*. 'One of the People', who described himself as a 'working man', viewed them with suspicion: 'Some of the superior crafts, or classes, have been forming themselves into societies, professing to be Friends of the People.' He claimed, 'The societies are really our enemies under the mark of friendship.' His programme demanded action on issues such as housing, clothing, food and provision for the sick and elderly. This was a socialist programme far removed from the views of the reformers.

The Riots of June, 1792
The celebrations at New Year and on the king's birthday brought large crowds onto the streets. This could occasionally lead to disturbances fuelled by drink and high spirits. Food shortages, leading to high prices, could also bring a mob onto the streets to attack anyone suspected of hoarding.

A crowd gathered in the High Street on 4 June, which was the king's birthday. They attacked and set fire to a sentry box close to the guardhouse. There appears to have been no specific target except possibly the Town Guard itself.

The next day, a mob marched to George Square where they burnt an image of Henry Dundas. Stones were thrown at the windows of the home of Robert Dundas, the lord advocate (the chief government officer in Scotland). Eventually, at 7 p.m., Sheriff Pringle arrived, followed shortly afterwards by some soldiers (George Square was in the county's jurisdiction). The crowd withdrew.

However, a message arrived from Bailie Creech warning of an attack on the Lord Provost's house in St Andrew's Square. This proved to be a false alarm. The troops were moved to the New Town, allowing the crowd to return to George Square. The sheriff brought the soldiers back to restore order in the square.

On the third day, Sir James Stirling's house was attacked by the mob. Windows were broken before, once again, soldiers from the castle arrived to restore order. The lord provost had no doubt where the blame lay:

The favourers of reform and innovation … have, by their late intemperance and zeal, overshot the mark, and given an alarm to the sober and well minded part of the community which they did not intend.

Although the targets of the mob were the homes of the lord provost and the lord advocate, there are no reports to suggest this was a serious disturbance aiming to alter the constitution of the city.

The Conventions of the Friends of the People, 1792

On 21 November, the Friends of the People held a meeting in James Court, off the Lawnmarket. Its title of 'convention' came directly from Revolutionary France. Hugh Bell was elected to the chair. Demands were made for equal representation in Parliament and for more frequent elections. Thomas Muir, a Glasgow advocate, was given a vote of thanks for all his work for the Friends of the People. At the end of the meeting a communiqué was issued warning members that they faced expulsion if they were involved in any riots or sedition. It went on to warn the authorities that the Friends would support any member who was persecuted for their support of the movement. The letter was signed by Hugh Bell (chairman) and William Skirving (secretary).

A second general convention met on 11 December. Thomas Muir proposed Colonel Dalrymple as chairman instead of Hugh Bell. The colonel refused, until Lord Daer proposed that the convention should have a different chairman each day. They wanted free elections with equal representation, and these were to be held more often so that Parliament was more accountable. The Friends still saw Parliament as the means of achieving reform, but in contrast the Edinburgh Merchant Company came out in support of an unreformed constitution.

The Crackdown on the Reformers, 1793

The authorities began to take action against those suspected of 'revolutionary' motives. They set out to arrest James Tyler, an Edinburgh chemist, but he had vanished. Three journeymen printers were prosecuted for trying to seduce soldiers at the castle to desert their posts. They each received nine months in prison. William Stewart, a merchant who lived in Leith, was summoned to appear before the magistrates for printing Thomas Paine's *Rights of Man*. Before he could be arrested, Stewart fled to France where he later joined the French army.

In March, the Faculty of Advocates expelled Thomas Muir, but it was not until August that he was arrested and placed in the Tolbooth. At the same time, William Skirving was also arrested. They searched his home, but in the end Skirving was released. Muir, however, was brought to trial and convicted of sedition. The court sentenced him to be transported to Australia together with

Reverend Thomas Palmer, who had been president of the Lawnmarket Society of Friends of the People.

The Convention, November–December 1793
These actions failed to quell the reformers and they met again in the last week of November. No move was made against them, so they continued their deliberations into a second week. It was not until Thursday, 5 December that various members of the convention were held for questioning. The matter seemed over when they were released.

That evening they met again, but their discussions were interrupted by the lord provost (Thomas Elder) and the bailies. He declared the meeting illegal and ordered the members to leave. When they refused, the constables were called in to clear the hall. The lord provost personally dragged the chairman from his seat.

They met again on the following day, with Maurice Margot in the chair. The sheriff's substitute arrived with the magistrates and closed down the meeting.

In January 1794, William Skirving, Joseph Gerald and Maurice Margot were brought to trial. They were found guilty of sedition and ordered to be transported to the colonies (Botany Bay) for fourteen years.

The Pike Plot, 1794
During a search for embezzled goods the authorities discovered twelve pike heads in the home of Robert Watt. Another twenty were found in Orrock's smithy. The two men were arrested, together with David Downie. On 3 September both Watt and Downie were convicted of high treason. Watt was executed on 15 October, but Downie eventually received a royal pardon. There appears to be little evidence of a widespread movement against the government, but the discovery of the weapons helped to alienate the majority of people who feared the French 'Terror'.

Road Transport in the Eighteenth Century

By the middle of the eighteenth century, toll bars had been established on most of the roads leading out from Edinburgh. The job of collecting the tolls was farmed out by the trustees of the turnpike who were also responsible for the bridges. A toll was taken from those crossing the Almond Bridge at Cramond.

Later in the century, fast fly carriages were introduced on the important routes. In April 1777, the carriage departing from John Robertson's Black Bull in the Pleasance boasted 'Newcastle in a day', with London in four days. It was an early start – 2 a.m. Unfortunately these light carriages carried only three people.

Many of the carriages departed from the Grassmarket, which produced a busy trade for its inns. The Stirling Fly left three times a week from Mrs Gibson's inn. The Glasgow Fly operated six days a week from George Warden's inn in the Grassmarket. It was pulled by four horses. However, as late as 1789, most coaches still took a fortnight to reach London – twice as long as the new, fast sailing vessels.

Winter, 1795

The year 1795 began with a long cold spell. Temperatures in Edinburgh plunged to 12°F at the end of January and storms brought heavy snow, which disrupted communications. The Thames remained frozen for ten days. A slight thaw was followed by more snow on 10 and 12 February. The hackney carriages were forced to employ four horses to handle the difficult conditions. At Liberton Kirk, a burial had to be postponed as the deep snow prevented the burial party from reaching the graveyard.

The weather prevented labourers from carrying out their work, leading to a financial crisis for many poor families, and the town council asked the wealthier citizens to contribute to a fund to aid the labouring poor. By the second week of February, relief had been given to 2,314 families in Edinburgh and the suburbs. Three of the city banks – Forbes, Hunter & Co., Mansfield & Ramsay and the British Linen Bank – each contributed £50 to the fund. So too did Henry Dundas, the Member of Parliament for the city.

March began with a thaw, but more snow and frost returned in the second week. However, after that temperatures began to rise, heralding the coming of spring.

Crime in the City in 1795

A shopkeeper in the Grassmarket was concerned at the disappearance of small amounts of money and a few low-priced goods. An inspection of the premises added to the mystery. He could find no signs of a forced entry. In the end, his friends formed a guard inside the building. They were disturbed by the appearance of a 13-year-old boy who had climbed down the chimney.

The new Bridewell was opened in September. It was a joint venture to provide a correction house for both the city and the county. It stood on the south side of Calton Hill near where the government offices stand today. Janet Symmington became its first prisoner. The Bridewell was not the only choice open to the magistrates. Two carters who had assaulted a watchman on South Bridge were sent aboard a frigate in Leith Roads with the hope they would apply their skills against the French.

In October, a woman servant came back from the country to a house in James' Court. She had been sent ahead to prepare the house for the family's return. Unfortunately she had lost the key. However, with the help of some neighbours a smith was found. She got into the house and set about laying the fires. This 'servant' then left early next morning with some goods from the house.

The Royal Edinburgh Volunteers

The threat of a French invasion led to the creation of a defence force known as the Edinburgh Volunteers. They were the equivalent to the Home Guard of the Second World War. Unlike the Home Guard however, all volunteers had to be between the ages of 17 and 40. A minimum height of 5ft 6ins was also stipulated. They wore scarlet uniforms to distinguish them from the French, who wore blue.

Each regiment consisted of some 500 men (the 1st Regiment was 540 strong). By the summer of 1797 the whole force consisted of one cavalry and four infantry regiments. These included the Edinburgh Royal Highland Volunteers and the Royal Leith Volunteers.

Volunteers from Edinburgh were only expected to serve in the Lothians and Berwickshire and they appear to have received payment for their services. In October 1797, the Edinburgh Royal Volunteers gave one week's pay amounting to £75 19s to the fund to support the widows and orphans of the sailors killed in the victory over the Dutch fleet.

French Prisoners

Prisoners taken in the war with France were held in the castle. Sometimes they were exchanged for British prisoners held by the French. A ship would anchor in Leith Roads and take those released by the exchange agreement to Dunkirk. On the night of 11 March 1799, Jean Baptiste Vandevelle and Jean Jacque Japple escaped from the castle. They sought refuge in the home of Reverend William Fitzsimmons in Chessel's Court. He was the minister of the Episcopal Chapel in the Cowgate. Fitzsimmons may have done pastoral work among the prisoners held in the castle, because on the very next day two more Frenchmen arrived – Rene Griffon and Hippolite Depondt had both broken their parole.

The prisoners remained hidden in Chessel's Court until 15 March when Fitzsimmons smuggled them down to Newhaven. He hired two boatmen – Neil Drysdale and Philip Jarvie. Rather than risk taking them out directly to the French ship which lay off Leith preparing to receive exchange prisoners, the boatmen landed the French on the island of Inchkeith. Next day they were put on board the ship. Questions were asked of the master of the ship by the French authorities, who would not wish to breach the agreement to exchange prisoners.

When the ship returned to Leith at the end of April the information was passed to the British authorities and Fitzsimmons and the two boatmen were arrested. At his trial in July, Fitzsimmons pleaded not guilty, but the crown secured the verdict. He argued that this was an act of common humanity but the prosecution warned that the action would lead to a tougher regime for the prisoners in the castle and mean that some British prisoners would miss the chance of being exchanged.

THE GROWING CITY, 1800–40

Trade and War, 1800–1802

At the beginning of the century, most of the ships passing through the Port of Leith were involved in the coastal trade. The Union Shipping Company had armed its packet boats for London, however, the Old Shipping Company (formerly the Berwick Old Shipping Company), which was also involved in this trade, continued to rely on the speed of its smacks to avoid French privateers operating in the North Sea, as heavy cannons would have added to the weight. The companies offered regular departures to and from London. These small smacks relied on their speed and their owners did not wish them to be tied to convoys.

Poverty and Crime

Poverty was a very serious problem in nineteenth-century Edinburgh. The population of the city was growing rapidly: it almost doubled in the first forty years of the century. The charity workhouse was aided by collections taken at the doors of the churches. In March 1800 alone, five babies were found abandoned in the city. Kitchens providing soup and bread were producing 7,700 meals every week. By the middle of May they claimed to have served up 200,000 meals.

One of the nastier crimes in the city was stripping the clothes off very young children. In August 1800, Betty Forbes and Margaret Smith were sentenced to twelve months' imprisonment but this failed to discourage others.

A more daring crime was committed in the autumn of 1802 by two soldiers. James Clark, who used the name Alexander Stewart, and Robert Brown attacked the rider carrying the mail near Wester Sighthill. Clark was found hiding in a shop in Rose Street with some of the stolen money. Both men were eventually convicted and executed. At this time, public hangings took place at the east end of the Lawnmarket.

The Industrial Suburbs

Portobello

It is generally believed that the name 'Portobello' was given to the first house by its owner, who had served in Admiral Vernon's fleet which had captured that town in Central America. George Hamilton, who may or may not have been that sailor, was a shoemaker, but began to sponsor horse races in the nearby Figgate Whins – an area once notorious for robbers who presumably preyed on travellers using the coast road. There had been some industry in the area. Coal was mined near Duddingston until the shaft was flooded. The coal provided fuel for the salt pans at Joppa. The discovery of a large vein of clay led to the establishment of at least two brickworks at Portobello. A small harbour had developed at the mouth of the Figgate Burn, the main imports being coal and white clay.

In 1813 the lease was advertised for the brickworks at Joppa, lying between the beach and the London Road. It was claimed that this business could produce 18,000 bricks every week. The property included a large building (110ft square), two horse-powered mills and a well with a pump. A spin-off from the clay seam was a growing pottery industry, although it never developed into a major producer. During the first decade of the nineteenth century there were at least two companies making pottery in Portobello.

An extra boost to the economy of Portobello was the growing popularity of bathing. Reverend William Bennet, in his *First Statistical Accounts of Scotland* (1796), ascribes the rise in the population of the area to the manufacturers and to the 'migratory colony of bathers, summer lodgers ... upon the same coast, continues every year to increase their numbers'. In 1806 new baths were opened and by August of that year they had increased the supply of hot and cold water, as well as providing a waiting room. In the same year, a regular stagecoach linked Portobello with the city.

Iron and Paper

Further west, at the mouth of the Almond, was the village of Cramond. William Caddell had set up an extensive iron-manufacturing business using some old water-powered mills in 1771. Iron was shipped in, firstly from the Baltic but later from Wales and the west of Scotland. These mills produced nails, spades, bolts and hoops, as well as iron rods. By 1815, Peggie's Mill had been turned over to the manufacture of paper.

Edinburgh was a growing printing centre and this created opportunities for the manufacture of paper. Nisbet & MacNiven opened a paper mill in 1788 at Kinauld in Currie, by the Water of Leith. Another mill, which later became the largest on the river, was built at Kinleith before the turn of the century. It had twenty houses for workers, as well as a home for the overseer. The lease would have cost the prospective purchaser £800.

Balerno began to grow at the beginning of the century when three small paper mills were built on the Bavelaw Burn (a tributary of the Water of Leith). Success was mixed, and Brynie's Mill was soon turned over to woodcutting and Balerno Bank Mill took over Townhead. Above Balerno on the Bavelaw Burn, Leith Ropery opened a sailcloth manufactory in 1805. Flax was soaked and then beaten to separate the fibre before being spun into yarn. One of these mills, the Glen, can still be seen at the top of Harlaw Road.

Two Unusual Offences and a Murder Committed in 1806

Two carters were brought before the magistrate in the police court. Each one had been stopped for driving three carts at the same time!

How did they do it? The driver rode in one cart while also holding the reins of the horse pulling the second cart. The horse hauling the third cart was tied to the first cart. It is not surprising that driving in this manner through the streets of Edinburgh was considered dangerous.

Meanwhile, William Gordon and his associate, James Bisset, were both brought before the court. Gordon, who could neither read nor write, had disguised himself as a minister to perform wedding ceremonies and Bisset wrote out the certificates. It is hard to believe in a town with a small number of ministers that anyone could be fooled – the imprisonment of Gordon and Bisset suggests that they were not.

The Murder of William Begbie

On the afternoon of Thursday, 14 November, William Begbie, a porter with the British Linen Company, left Leith with a sealed parcel in a yellow canvas bag. This package contained notes to the value of £4,392. This was an enormous sum when you consider that, in January of that year, a house in Prince's Street was offered for sale at a fixed price of £2,000. It is difficult to believe that a porter could be sent alone on foot carrying (at today's prices) over £20 million.

He was last seen in the company of a man coming up Leith Walk. Begbie then crossed to the Old Town. Around five o'clock, he entered Tweeddale's Close, where he was attacked by a person carrying a common bread knife with a wooden handle stained red. This weapon had been sharpened to a point. Begbie was stabbed and the money stolen. This was an unusual crime for Edinburgh because of the amount of violence used; there was no need to kill the porter to secure the money.

Begbie left a wife and four children. A reward of 500 guineas was offered for information but it brought no results. It was not until the following August that the bag was found by three workmen in the grounds of Bellevue, between the customs house and Broughton Toll. It contained over £3,000, made up of the larger notes stolen from Begbie. They were still held together in their bands although they were now in a poor state. Nothing further was discovered and the murder of William Begbie remains one of the great mysteries in the history of the city.

Who killed William Begbie? The appearance of the weapon, deliberately sharpened, suggests that his assailant was intent on murder and not just robbery. Why murder Begbie unless he could identify his attacker? The Close, which is very narrow, is the only place on the porter's route where he could have been attacked without anyone witnessing the crime. It might be the only place where Begbie's killer could be sure to meet him. The Close is straight and short, with the offices of the company at the end of the close facing up towards the High Street. Anyone waiting in that short passage would surely have been seen. A man could have followed him off the street into the Close unseen, but he would have had to wait in the street for the porter's arrival. With such a large reward available someone would surely have come forward to describe a suspicious character hanging around. It does seem that Begbie's killer was aware of his movements, although he may not have realised the enormous quantity of cash the man was carrying.

Race Week

The end of July was Race Week, an important event in the city's social calendar. On Monday they raced for the City's Purse, a prize of 50 guineas, but Tuesday brought the richest event of the meeting. The competitors rode for His Majesty's Purse worth 100 guineas. The Subscription Purse on Wednesday was followed by the Hunters' and Ladies' Purses on Thursday and Friday, while Saturday's race was only for horses who had not won a prize during the week.

At the same time, a competition was held for pipers. Bagpipers and Highland dancers performed for prizes paid for by the admission money. Dances were held in Edinburgh and Leith. In 1808, two concerts were given at the end of the week in which Mrs Mountain, a famous actress and singer of the time, entertained the audience with songs and recitations.

A Crimewave in 1808

The *Evening Courant* expressed concern about a crimewave that seems to have broken out in 1808. Thieves broke into the shop of a tinplate worker in the West Bow stealing 4–5 shillings in halfpenny coins; a grocer in Blackfriars Wynd, a brushmaker in Advocates' Close and a jeweller in Parliament Square were the next victims. The New Town, probably the wealthiest area of the city, experienced vandalism: iron railings were broken and defaced; sign boards were pulled down.

The police launched special patrols at unexpected times and this achieved some initial success, with arrests and successful prosecutions following. However, in November, the *Courant* complained that 'we are sorry to understand the depredations under night are still going on in and about this city'. A new gang of robbers was at work. They applied for positions as servants, using fellow members to provide references, in order to rob the houses.

The next year, another gang appeared to be targeting shops in the Old Town. They were caught when they broke into the premises of Gibb & MacDonald on South Bridge. The suspects escaped punishment when the owners and the shopkeeper, who were all Quakers, refused to take the oath in court. The leader of this gang, William Thorpe, had been arrested in Warwickshire during 1804 and sentenced to be transported. Thorpe had escaped and made his way to Edinburgh in 1807. He settled here under the name of William Harris and was soon involved in criminal activities once again. He was finally caught and locked up in the Tolbooth. The English authorities found out about this and were anxious to bring him to justice.

After a number of assaults during the night had occurred on Leith Walk, the *Evening Courant* suggested, 'as Leith Walk has now become a very dangerous thoroughfare at late hours, especially to people who are strangers, measures ought to be adopted for having the Walk protected by an armed patrol'.

Lord Provost William Creech

In the middle of the eighteenth century, Allan Ramsay opened a bookshop at the eastern end of the Luckenbooths. The business was taken over by Kincaid & Bell and William Creech had worked for this firm before he left to work in London in 1766. The partnership of Kincaid & Bell broke up in 1771 and Creech came back to Edinburgh to join Kincaid in the business. When Kincaid retired two years later, Creech became the sole owner of the firm. He published works by David Hume, Adam Smith and Robert Burns. His account concerning the changing lifestyles in Edinburgh during the latter part of the century, was published in the *First Statistical Accounts of Scotland*.

Creech, like many other prosperous citizens of the time, moved to the New Town, where he set up house at 5 George Street. He was a well-known figure in the town: Chambers describes him as wearing 'black silk breeches and a powdered head [presumably a wig]'. Creech served as lord provost from 1811 until 1813. His death came two years later.

Post-War Edinburgh

In June 1815, a joint force of British and German troops defeated Napoleon and brought a long period of peace to Western Europe. The years following the end of the French War produced a series of depressions.

Unemployment was high and the council, despite its Tory principles, sought to bring some relief. Men were employed to improve paths and roads. The distress probably led to increased criminal activity despite the harsh sentences often given out at this time.

The poverty was made worse by the high price of corn imposed upon the country by the unpopular Corn Laws. These were first introduced in 1790 and prohibited the import of grain until the prices of homegrown grain had exceeded a fixed price. In 1813, Parliament, dominated by landowners, proposed to double the price above which corn could be imported into the country. The town council, normally loyal supporters of the government, set up a committee to consider the matter. They reported back to the council:

They regarded the expedient recommended by the Select Committee [of the House of Commons] as calculated to afford encouragement to agriculture at an unnecessary expense to the great body of the nation.

A motion to petition both Houses of Parliament was carried unanimously.

Low wages led to riots and government repression. In 1819, an attempt to break up a large meeting by the use of cavalry with sabres at St Peter's Field near Manchester led to several deaths and to hundreds of people being injured. The event has gone down in history as 'the Massacre of Peterloo'. Fortunately, Edinburgh lacked a large industrial base around which discontent could rally, neither was the city drawn into the problems of Catholic emancipation and Irish immigration, even though like other parts of Scotland it received its share of Irish immigrants. Two of these were to become the most infamous characters in the city's long history, as seen later in this chapter.

The Cases of Elizabeth Sinclair and Janet Douglas

Police raided the house of Elizabeth Sinclair in September 1806. Four girls were found locked up in the house, and a fifth one had escaped before the police arrived. Sinclair was 'charged with keeping a disorderly house to which she seduced young girls and kept them locked up and in a state of intoxication for the purposes of prostitution'. She was found guilty in the police court and given the maximum sentence available to the court – sixty days in the Bridewell (the town's correction house).

Janet Douglas was a 20-year-old coal bearer from Gilmerton colliery. In 1817 she lost her job and came into Edinburgh. In King's Stables Road she took young Margaret Reach, who was between 3 and 4 years old. Janet headed for Fife and found a job in another colliery before the authorities caught up with her. She was charged with kidnapping but pleaded that she was only using the child to gain sympathy in order to get a job. This is a sad comment on these times when 17-year-old girls were forced to earn a living carrying heavy sacks of coal round a mine.

Janet was found guilty and sentenced to be hung. By contrast, Elizabeth Sinclair had kidnapped five girls whom she was using for the purposes of prostitution and had received a sentence of only sixty days. Janet Douglas had kidnapped one girl, whom she had not harmed, and she had received a death sentence.

Even in the Edinburgh of 1818 there was considerable shock at such a harsh sentence given to a girl who was obviously not afraid of hard work. Few jobs for women could be more physically demanding than hauling coal around on their backs. The *Evening Courant* reported that the 'case has excited considerable interest in this city'. It must have reached people of influence for, using the royal prerogative, the sentence was suspended and Janet Douglas was transported (probably to Australia) for life.

Edinburgh: A Growing City

There was a steady movement of wealth away from the cramped quarters of the Old Town to the spacious properties of the New Town. Evidence that the wealthy burghers were now in the New Town is illustrated by church-door collections taken in 1815 for the Magdalene Asylum. The largest donations came from St George's (£90), St Andrew's (£62), the Episcopal Chapel (£42) and the West Kirk (£40), all based in the New Town.

By 1817 the New Town had been completed and building work continued to the north. At this time, houses were being built in Heriot Row and Northumberland Street. Plans for the Royal Circus were also being laid out.

To the west, the estate of Coates and the land of the Earl of Moray were built up during the 1820s. To the east, Bellevue, the villa of General Scott, had been bought by the town as early as 1802. Queen Street flowed through York Place and Picardy Place into Leith Walk. Some of the houses from York Place have been pulled down, including the home where Sir Arthur Conan Doyle was born.

The new prison had been built on Calton Hill, leaving Lord Cockburn to reflect, 'It was a piece of undoubted bad taste to give so glorious an eminence to a prison'. It could have been worse, for there had been plans to build it in the east end of Prince's Street Gardens! A grant from the government of £10,000 in 1813 assisted the development.

Regent Bridge was begun in 1815 and opened four years later. The Union Canal opened in 1822 linking Edinburgh, via the Forth Clyde and Monklands Canals, with the Lanarkshire coalfield. Port Hopetoun (on Lothian Road) became the terminus, with a second basin close to the Lochrin distillery. To the south of this were a ropeworks (on Gilmour Place) and the Drumdryan brewery. Two other distilleries could be found at Canonmills and in the Dean Village. Proposals to extend the canal to Leith, passing round the south side of the town, came to nothing.

By 1817 the Canongate was beginning to take on an industrial air. There were three breweries and Mr Cartrae's coach works. Mr Younger had a brewery on the Abbey Hill. The Edinburgh Gas Light Company was founded in that year and they built a large plant behind the Canongate Tolbooth. Gas from this company lit up the shops on the North and South Bridges the following year.

Gas was not without its problems. In 1822, one of Edinburgh's strong winds blew out all the street lights on the North Bridge. Three years later, a young servant smelt gas in the cellar of a house in Shandwick Place. Sadly, he went to search for the fault with a lighted candle and was killed in the resulting explosion.

The Edinburgh Oil & Gas Light Company was founded in 1822 and established its works at Tanfield (Canonmills). Sir Walter Scott acted as chairman. The company was taken over in 1828 by its rival, the Edinburgh Gas Light Company.

East of Leith, between the Links and the sea, were roperies and glass works. Two large wet docks lay near the mouth of the river in North Leith; the eastern one was completed in 1806 and the other was opened in 1817. They offered enough space for 150 ships and the complex also included three dry docks.

Much of the land between Leith and the city had not yet been built over. A considerable area belonged to nurseries, who no doubt sold their produce in the markets of Edinburgh.

Controversial Buildings

In 1817 the ancient Luckenbooths were finally taken down to widen the High Street by St Giles, and plans were soon to be produced to reconstruct the church itself. The most famous of the shops to be destroyed was Creech's Land, which stood at the east end of the Luckenbooths. Here, William Creech, publisher and lord provost, carried out his business. At the west end stood the Old Tolbooth, known as the 'Heart of Midlothian'. This too was soon to be demolished, but not before Sir Walter Scott secured the door for his house at Abbotsford.

A proposal was made that year to erect a monument to Scotland's most famous poet, Robert Burns. This was rejected by the council on moral grounds. Some of Burns' escapades did not gain the approval of the strict Presbyterians on the council. In response others rightly pointed out that monuments had been raised to Lord Nelson and Lord Melville.

The most controversial group of buildings stood at the east end of Prince's Street where the Balmoral Hotel stands today. They had been described in a report by Sir John Playfair as a 'specimen of modern vandalism'. *The Scotsman*, no lover of the Tory-dominated council, suggested that they should remain as 'an everlasting monument to the incurable mischief inflicted on this city by a self-elected and irresponsible junta'. They record the tale of two men who had come from Glasgow 'to consult certain wisemen of the east [it was just before Christmas and no doubt they were seeking legal advice]'.

'What's that big new building there for, John?' one asked.

'Hoot man dinna ye ken that Edinburgh expects to thrive greatly now for the magistrates are gieing premiums for building cottonworks; that ane o' them.'

This may be the first recorded humour based on the rivalry of the two cities (20 December 1817). The buildings in question had been reduced in height and so had flat roofs resembling large factories.

Opposition to the Council

The year 1817 brought the first publication of *The Scotsman*. It was a Whig newspaper dedicated to achieving reform of the burgh and parliamentary franchises. The council was the main target of its wrath. The only councillors who were not totally elected by the council were the deacons of the crafts. Even then, the council, or rather the merchant members of it, supervised the leets and chose those who would serve as full councillors.

A fierce critic and general nuisance to the council was Alexander Lawrie, the Deacon of Bonnetmakers & Dyers. He raised a successful action in the Court of Session to declare that the 1817 burgh election was illegal. The court declared that it found 'the whole of the said election of 1817 illegal, contrary to the set laws and constitution of the burgh and the laws of the land and absolutely null and void'. Laurie retired from the council in October 1819.

James Paterson, Deacon of the Hammermen, took a different tack by trying to inquire into the finances of the burgh. He produced a motion asking the council to present accounts of its funds, debts and annual expenditure. The motion was defeated by twenty-three votes to three. Concerns over Edinburgh's debts were beginning to grow, particularly with a projected figure of £15,000 for the rebuilding of St Giles.

In December 1818, the lord provost assured the council that the city's debt to the bankers was only £11,000. As events were to prove, this was far from the truth. However, motions against the ruling group on the council rarely received more than a few votes and sometimes those opposing the lord provost found it hard even to find a seconder for such a motion. Some of the trades' corporations held meetings at which they criticised the council, but they and their deacons were unable to make any progress against the determined group who held control.

The Crown Jewels

A group of commissioners, who included Walter Scott (he was not yet knighted), visited the governor of the castle on 4 February 1818. Their purpose was to examine the Crown Room. At 1 p.m. the king's smith and carpenter removed the locks on the outer oak door. The inner door, made of iron grating, was opened for the first time since 1794. The room was empty except for an oblong chest. This was opened to reveal the Scottish crown, sceptre and sword. A report was then made and forwarded to the Prince Regent (Prince George had, for a number of years, acted for his father). Four years later, he would visit the capital as George IV and see the Scottish Royal Regalia for himself.

Captain Brown, Superintendent of the Edinburgh Police Force

Various changes were made to the Police Act (Edinburgh) in 1812 and 1817. These increased the number of *ex officio* members of the commission, although the members elected by the assessment payers in the wards formed the majority. However, the power to dismiss the superintendent lay with the lord provost, the Sheriff of the County of Edinburgh and the President of the Court of Session.

Allegations of corruption in the force in 1820 led one committee of the commissioners to complain that most of their time was occupied investigating abuses. Mr Murray, the clerk for the police, was dismissed when it was discovered that wages were being paid to non-existent police officers. These were known as 'straw men'. Captain Brown claimed that this money was used to pay for secret work. In January of 1821 the police commissioners carried a vote of no confidence against the superintendent.

The lord provost refused to take action. During the summer, the commissioners separated the police duties. Lighting and street cleaning became a department of its own and was placed under the charge of James Logan, who had been dismissed for drinking on duty! Captain Brown encouraged his men to make life difficult for the new Head of Lighting and Cleaning, and two sergeants, Witherspoon and Mackenzie, received a warning from the commissioners.

At the turn of the year a new police bill was being prepared for Parliament. To be strictly accurate, two new police bills were being prepared – one by the council and one by the commissioners. By now the lord provost, William Arbuthnot, and most of the *ex officio* commissioners were boycotting the meetings of the Police Commission. This was becoming a battle between the council, who were mainly self-elected, and the commission, who were elected by a wide franchise. In their new bill, the council wished to decrease the number of those who could vote for the police commissioners. Deacon Field complained that if this went ahead he would be able, as a town councillor, to vote for the Member of Parliament but not for his local police commissioner. However, only seven members of the council voted against the bill prepared by the lord provost.

Suddenly, on 13 April 1822, the announcement came that Captain Brown had resigned from his position as police superintendent. A few days earlier, Sergeant Mitchell had absconded with the wages – £40. He was picked up trying to board a ship in Newhaven. Whether Brown's resignation was due to the growing pressure – every meeting of the police wards backed the commissioners and demanded his dismissal – or to the possibility that he might have been involved in the Mitchell case, we do not know.

The Visit of George IV, 1822

This was the first royal visit to the Scottish capital since Charles II had arrived in those momentous days that ended with the Battle of Dunbar and the occupation of the city by Cromwell's troops. The palace, which had been rebuilt under the directions of the Duke of Lauderdale, was now to receive a reigning monarch. The king was trying to rebuild his popularity after the disastrous

attempt to divorce Queen Caroline (who had died in 1821). The Royal Regalia was removed from the castle and taken to the Palace of Holyrood.

Advice was given to those ladies fortunate enough to be introduced to the king:

> The lady will drop her train [about 4 yards in length] when she enters the circle of the king. It is then held up by a lord-in-waiting until she is close to His Majesty. She curtsies. The king raises her up and salutes her on the cheek. She then retires always facing the sovereign until beyond the circle.

This was the difficult bit, for walking backwards wearing a long train was no easy matter. Ladies 'who have never worn such dresses should lose no time in beginning to practise this'.

The king's yacht entered Leith on Tuesday, 20 August, and at noon the royal barge set out for the quay. At a quarter past twelve a gun sounded, signalling that the king had landed. He made his way up Leith Walk (much of the Walk was bordered by nurseries with only groups of buildings) to be welcome by the Lord Provost of Edinburgh, who presented the keys, sword and mace of the city to the king. The procession continued into York Place before passing through St Andrew's Square into Prince's Street. Here it turned east, travelling along Regent Bridge towards the palace. It proved to be a fine day and large crowds assembled on Calton Hill to watch the king's progress.

Walter Scott, who took some credit in persuading the king to visit the city, presented His Majesty with a silver cross from the ladies of the Lothians. The considerable amount of tartan worn during the events which followed was probably due to Scott's romantic vision of ancient Scotland. A Highland Ball was held and even the king dressed in a kilt. The visit was considered a great success, especially for Scott, who afterwards received a knighthood.

Duddingston Loch and the Royal Park

The cold winters of the 1820s led even the larger lochs like Duddingston to freeze over. At the beginning of January 1830 *The City of London*, a steam packet which was used in the Leith–London trade, was trapped by ice in the Thames. Large numbers – although possibly the 5,000 claimed by *The Scotsman* for January 1826 is exaggerated – took to the ice. Bands from the military entertained the skaters and curlers. There was a cavalry barracks at Piershill by Jock's Lodge. In 1830 a sledge pulled by a pony was drawn across the ice. However, there were dangers, and in the same year a young man drowned when he fell through the ice at Lochend in an attempt to rescue a boy.

Conservationists were concerned that the quarrying in the Royal Park threatened Salisbury Crag. The Earl of Hamilton, as Keeper of the Royal Park, was able to profit by the enterprise. Claims were made that this was the cheapest source of rock available in Edinburgh: rock from the crag cost only 5s 9d per cubic yard, while rock from Ratho was nearly double the price at 9s per cubic yard. This brought a protest from John Crow who held the lease for the Ratho Quarry. He claimed that Ratho stone carried by the canal to Port Hopetoun cost only 3s 3d per cubic yard and that even with cartage it was little more expensive than the rock from the crag. Later that year (1826) the king intervened and quarrying on Salisbury Crag was stopped.

The Great Fires of 1824

The first fire broke out at Gunn's, a spirit seller, in Royal Bank Close on Thursday, 24 June. It appears to have begun in a wooden extension at the back of the building. By 3 a.m. the second tenement east from Parliament Close had collapsed. John's Coffee House and Thomas' Tavern were both destroyed. The magistrates, the military and the police were all involved in containing the fire. Even the poor children helped. Fortunately, only one man was injured.

The fire raised the problem of organising resources in the face of such a big blaze. The new water supply was credited with having saved the buildings to the west, which included the Advocates' Library, the law courts and Sir William Forbes' bank. One act of bravery was performed by a Mr Smith who broke into a tenement, removing stock from the shop and rescuing people who were still asleep. On the down side, one woman was arrested for trying to lure a child into a close with the intention of stealing its clothes.

The second and larger fire broke out on Monday, 15 November in a tenement at the head of Old Assembly Close. It is believed to have started at the premises of Mr Kirkwood, an engraver. By 10 p.m. the fire had become established in the upper storeys which were beyond the reach of the fire brigade. The flames spread west to Old Fishmarket Close, destroying the offices of the *Evening Courant*. Buildings behind the High Street all the way down to the Cowgate were caught up in the destruction. It took until 11 a.m. the next day to bring the fire under control.

An hour later, the fire broke out again, this time on the steeple of the Tron Kirk, destroying the wooden parts. It took four hours to bring this fire under control, but they did manage to save the church roof. At 10 p.m. yet another outbreak began in a tenement in Parliament Square. This building had nine or ten storeys and by 3 a.m. on Wednesday morning it was burnt to the ground.

The lord provost, the magistrates, the police and the surgeons were all praised for their actions. Those whose homes had been destroyed were sent to Queensferry

House. By the middle of Wednesday, the fires were all extinguished. The army remained on duty to keep people away from the dangerous ruins of three tall buildings. Their demolition was a priority because it was feared they might collapse, causing more devastation. A suggestion was put forward that artillery should be brought in and used to bring the remains to the ground.

Much of the south side of the High Street was affected by the fire. Four large tenements from Old Assembly Close through Borthwick's Close to Old Fishmarket Close were destroyed. Fortunately, in such an inferno, only six people were reported to have died in the fire. However, 400 poor families lost their homes and belongings.

Education in Edinburgh

The new Edinburgh Academy was founded in 1823, with its home in Henderson Row. The council saw it as a rival to the High School. The academy's board contained such distinguished figures as Lord Cockburn and Sir Walter Scott, both of whom had been pupils of the High School. In both the new academy and the High School pupils were admitted between the ages of 7 and 8. They would study for six years before passing on to the university at the age of 14. Some parents thought this was too young to enter the university and so in 1826 the academy offered a seventh year with courses in Latin, Greek, Mathematics and French.

The council responded by replacing the old High School in the Cowgate with a splendid new building on the south side of Calton Hill. (This building is now used as government offices, although at one time it was seen as a possible home for the new Scottish Parliament.) Plans were begun for this development in 1825 and the new High School opened four years later.

Many teachers set themselves up in the New Town offering classes in various specialist subjects. Mr John Christison, at 50 George Street, advertised lessons in French, Italian and Spanish. Native speakers like Mr Demarchi (an Italian) and Monsieur Le Dieu (French) also provided language teaching. Classes could be found for the teaching of dancing, drawing, painting and singing. Even the famous Mrs Eliza Paton, who always received glowing reviews from *The Scotsman*'s theatre critic, advertised singing lessons from her home in Frederick Street. On a more practical level, Miss E. Junior and Miss Watson both offered classes in dressmaking.

By 1830 there was already established in the city a school for infants run by Mr Witherspoon. It was situated in the Vennel above the Grassmarket. This school had a roll of 260 pupils, of whom sixty-four had been newly admitted that year. Education for such young children was still at the experimental stage.

Stockbridge

Stockbridge was an ancient crossing point over the Water of Leith. Council records for the year 1658 note that the stone bridge required to be repaired. Stockbridge's most famous son, Sir Henry Raeburn, was born in the village in 1756. The family owned considerable property in the area. Between 1813 and 1817 Raeburn Pace, Dean Street and Ann Street were built for people looking for homes on the edge of the New Town. India Place and St Bernard's Crescent were begun a few years later. In the eighteenth century the village was also famous for its waters. Lord Gardenstone, a judge at the Court of Session, built a small Greek temple over St Bernard's Well.

St Bernard's Church was built in 1823 and the next year a new bridge (St Bernard's Bridge) was taking traffic across the Water of Leith. In that same year, a large market was opened in the village which was now becoming a prosperous suburb of Edinburgh.

However, not all was well in Stockbridge, for a woman from the village was brought before the court charged with neglecting a 3-year-old girl. The child had been left alone from morning until midnight without food and in a room without any furniture. The case was dismissed by the court, but it shows that extreme poverty existed in an area which contained the homes of many wealthy people.

Opening Up the Access to the Old Town

Access from the new suburbs to the south and west was a major problem affecting businesses in the High Street and Lawnmarket. The deep gorge on the line of the Cowgate and the Grassmarket forced people entering the city to use the narrow and winding Bow. Improvements were needed, but there was also opposition on the grounds of cost and conservation. Lord Cockburn only went along with the proposals when it was agreed to prohibit building on the eastern part of what today is Prince's Street Gardens.

The first bill failed to be approved by Parliament, but a pressure group continued to push for these improvements. A large public meeting chaired by the lord provost was held on 18 December 1826 in St Giles: the supporters of the new proposals forced them through. A second bill was presented to Parliament, but in committee stage the clause which would permit building on the Meadows was rejected. The bill continued without this clause and received royal assent in 1827. This led to the building of the southern approach – George IV Bridge – and a western entry round the castle – now Johnston Terrace.

In 1830, residents on the High Street complained that by ten o'clock it was crowded with barrows, baskets and portable booths. They offered shoppers dried fish, shellfish, confectionary, vegetables and a variety of other goods. Vagrants mixed with the shoppers, lowering the tone of the neighbourhood. The residents were certain that such activities would not be allowed in 'other streets superior in fashion'. The Bridges and George Street contained the better shops and provided for the wealthier citizens of the burgh.

Bodysnatching

The Edinburgh Medical School created a demand for bodies to be used by the staff and students during lectures. Since members of the school were prepared to pay good prices for each corpse and were not prepared to ask any questions, a trade in the stealing of newly buried bodies began.

The business was not just confined to the Edinburgh area, as the Currie poet, Jamie Thomson, was to witness in January 1821. He dedicated his work, 'Poem on the Raising and Selling of the Dead', to Mr William Elliot, an excise officer whose prompt action led to the apprehension of two bodysnatchers. Some roadworkers breaking stones on the Lanark Road at Kinauld saw a cart which they suspected contained more than the peats with which the bodies were covered. They stopped it. The Balerno Paper Mill being nearby, they sought the help of Mr James Craig, the overseer. Since William Elliot was also at the mill he came out and offered his services. He then arrested the two men on the cart, suspecting that they were smuggling alcohol or tobacco from the west coast.

Still on they drive to Currie near,
But how they fared you'll quickly hear.
They were suspected on the road,
For having far too light a load,
To pay expense of man and beast,
It raised suspicion in the breast.

Near Currie town, brave Elliot met them,
And as fit farder wadna let them;
Fast by the reigns he seized the horse.
Craig searched the cart and a' by force.
O Elliot! Why is this sae handy,
Nae whisky here, nor smuggl'd brandy,
Nae tea, nae 'bacco for excise
Nor maut for you to make a prize.

The search was to reveal two bodies which had been dug up from the churchyard in Lanark:

'Twas no for these ye search'd awa
But to restore the lifeless two
Back to their graves, their place of rest
Sic thought your gen'rous mind possest.

Three years later, articles appeared in various papers and magazines which led people to believe that the medical school was still having difficulties in obtaining bodies. *The Scotsman* boldly contradicted this: 'We are assured, on good authority, that a very inaccurate statement appeared in the *Edinburgh Literary Gazette* and some other publications, respecting an alleged scarcity in Edinburgh of material for anatomical or surgical lectures or dissections'. Certainly during this time watches and even guard houses were placed in cemeteries – you can still see the one in St Cuthbert's on Lothian Road.

Burke and Hare

On Friday, 31 October 1828, while William Burke was purchasing some whisky from a grocer's shop he met an old woman begging for money. She appears to have been known by various names – Campbell or Docherty. Since they were both Irish, Burke was able to strike up a conversation with her. He took the poor woman to his nearby flat in Portsburgh. This consisted of one small room which he shared with his friend, Helen McDougal, and also with James and Ann Gray. The Grays were sent away to Hare's house in Tanner's Close. The old woman, generally referred to as Mary Campbell, was given a large amount of whisky to make her incapable of resistance. Then Burke lay on top of her face until she stopped breathing.

The next morning, James and Ann Gray returned to find Burke, McDougal (she acted as Burke's wife, although he had a wife back in Ireland) and a carter called Broggan. Eventually, all three left the house and Mrs Gray began to search for her child's stocking. It was then that she found the body of the old woman. On leaving the room, the Grays were intercepted by McDougal and Mrs Hare, who tried to persuade them that the woman had died through drinking too much. When they returned to the flat the body was gone.

The Grays then set off to report their findings to the police.

The police arrived at the flat and, of course, found nothing. However, a servant girl who lived nearby had seen Burke and Hare with their wives and a porter (John McCulloch) taking a tea chest stuffed with straw into the house. When the Burkes returned to their flat they were immediately arrested by the police. On Sunday morning, Lieutenant Paterson and Sergeant Major Fisher were sent to the dissecting rooms where they found David Paterson. He was employed by Dr Robert Knox, a lecturer of anatomy. Only one body was discovered but the Grays later identified it as that of Mary Campbell. Captain Stewart set out for Portsburgh with some other officers and arrested Mr and Mrs Hare.

The investigations continued, with William Hare and his wife agreeing to give evidence against Burke in return for immunity from prosecution. Burke was eventually charged with three murders. The first of these had taken place during April when Burke and McDougal were lodging in the house of Constantine Burke (no relation to William Burke), a street cleaner who lived in Gibb's Close. The victim was Mary Paterson, who was also known as Mitchell. She was aged between 18 and 20 and had been lured by Burke with the offer of free drink. Her friend, Janet Brown, managed to get away and had a lucky escape. The second charge against Burke was for the murder of James Wilson, known as Daft Jamie. This murder, which had been committed in Hare's house in Tanner's Close, had probably occurred in September. The third charge which was brought against both Burke and Helen McDougal was the murder of Mary Campbell.

When the trial began there was much legal discussion which led to William Burke and Helen McDougal being tried only on the third indictment – the murder of Mary Campbell. The jury return a verdict of 'not proven' in the case of McDougal but Burke was found guilty. *The Scotsman* reported:

The scene was altogether awful and impressive. The prisoner stood up with unshaken firmness. Not a muscle of his features was discomposed during the solemn address of the Lord Justice Clerk, consigning him to his doom. The female prisoner was much agitated and was drowned in tears during the whole of the melancholy procedure.

It was while under sentence of death that Burke gave a fuller account of his activities. In the previous October, an elderly lodger in Hare's house had died from natural causes. A funeral was arranged and the body was taken to Greyfriars Churchyard, after which Burke and Hare spirited it away to the anatomist.

The first victim appears to have been Abigail Simpson, an old woman from Gilmerton. Two men who lodged with Hare – an English peddler and Joe, a retired miller – were murdered and their bodies sold. Burke and Hare preyed on the poor unfortunates who were generally found in the Grassmarket and other deprived areas of the Old Town. Mary Haldane was one of these, and, later on, so was her daughter, Peggy.

The list continues: from February to their arrest in November, the two men were responsible for sixteen murders. Public anger continued after the trial and the family of James Wilson tried to secure a private prosecution against William Hare but the court ruled against them. The Hares and Helen McDougal were released and fled from the city. It is thought that the Hares made their way separately back to Ireland while Helen McDougal was last seen in County Durham. Others too, like Dr Knox and his assistant, escaped the courts, although the courts must have suspected that all was not as it appeared. Thomas Ireland, an Edinburgh publisher, produced an account of the murders and Burke's confession in the year of his execution (1829).

The Markets of Edinburgh

Much of the food purchased by the citizens of Edinburgh was done so at the markets. In an age before freezers, goods had to be brought into the city and sold quickly. In July 1830, the Butter Market at the head of the High Street consisted of fifty-six carts selling butter at 7d–9d per lb and eggs at 6s 6d per hundred.

In the Green Market, early fruits such as strawberries, gooseberries and blackcurrants were for sale. More exotic fruits – cherries, melons, grapes, peaches and nectarines – could also be purchased there. The main vegetables sold in the market at this time were peas, potatoes and cauliflowers. All these crops would have been grown in local nurseries close to the city.

The Fish Market was selling salmon at 2s per lb. Haddock was popular, with the local newspaper reporting that 'fishwives were paid whatever they were asked'. This proved true, with prices varying between 3d and 8d per fish (this may have depended more on the size of the fish). Edinburgh benefitted by its proximity to the sea and trout, mackerel and lobster could all be bought in the market, although no mention is made of oysters which had once been very fashionable.

Poor sales were reported from the poultry market which sold ducks, pigeons and chickens.

One of the main problems facing shoppers was the unscrupulous traders who sold their goods under weight. The markets were supervised by inspectors, but that did not prevent six people in 1830 being convicted of selling goods below the required weight. You were no safer in the shops, for some grocers appeared before the court charged with selling parcels of sugar under weight.

Parliamentary Reform

The early years of the century were dominated by the Tories and the war with France. They were led in Scotland by Henry Dundas of Arniston (later Lord

Melville) and reform of the electoral system was not part of their political agenda. Lord Cockburn in his *Memorials* wrote, 'A country gentleman with any public principle except devotion to Henry Dundas was viewed as a wonder or rather a monster'.

Dundas died in 1811 and the French threat ended at Waterloo in 1815. William Dundas, a nephew of Henry Dundas, continued to be elected as MP for the city until 1831. In 1820, John Mansfield was proposed in opposition to him but Dundas was re-elected by twenty-five votes to three. James Abercromby, an MP for an English constituency with interests in Edinburgh, raised the matter in the House of Commons in 1826. He told members of the House, 'An election of a Member of Parliament for Edinburgh by only thirty-three voters was not a state of things which could be openly defended' (Edinburgh and Leith had a total population of over 138,000, some of whom were wealthy businessmen or lawyers in the courts). His proposals were defeated by 122 to ninety-seven votes. William Dundas was one of those who voted against him.

Some of the leading citizens had set up a Reform Committee. They drew up a petition demanding a reform of the burgh's franchise. The council were asked to endorse the petition. The old bailie, John Smith, expressed the attitude of the members of the council to change, calling the petition 'a gross insult to the council and he trusted it would not be allowed to be seen on the face of the records'. Deacon Paterson failed to find a seconder for a motion to support the petition. At the same time, the lord provost with some members of the council were battling to secure control of the newly formed Docks Committee.

By 1830 attitudes, except on the council, had changed, with a new government at Westminster in favour of reform. A meeting of the leading citizens of Edinburgh, chaired by James Gibson-Craig of Riccarton, criticised the self-elected council and drew up a petition in favour of reform. The council were asked for their support but they refused to become involved. Even as late as January 1832, the council passed a motion by nineteen to thirteen votes that 'the magistrates and the council cannot give their support to the bills for parliamentary reform'.

In May, a rally was held in Holyrood Park. The trades supporters met on the Mound and marched down Prince's Street to the park. Numbers were said to have exceeded 60,000. William Dundas, the city's MP, claimed that there were anti-royalist slogans on display – an attempt by him to discredit and divide the reformers. However, after some resistance from the House of Lords, the Reform Bill was passed. A second bill, for Scotland, soon followed. Edinburgh was to have two Members of Parliament, with a third member for the County of Edinburgh (mainly those areas which today comprise the suburbs of the city – Duddingston, Libberton, Gilmerton, Colinton and Currie – but also stretching to Dalkeith and the Calders). The coastal towns of Newhaven,

Leith, Portobello and Musselburgh were formed into another constituency to be known as Leith Boroughs (or Burghs).

Only those men who owned property worth £10 or more were entitled to vote and there was no secret ballot. Although the leaders of the reform movement had achieved their own objectives, this was just the beginning of the struggle to give the franchise to all adults which would last for nearly a century.

Today we grumble about the length of time spent on campaigning before an election. In 1832 the candidates for Leith Boroughs were already in action by the end of June. Of course 1832 was exceptional, since the new voters had to register. Candidates often raised objections against those whom they believed were committed to their opponents.

August saw two huge rallies celebrating the success of the Reform Bill, held in Edinburgh and Leith on the same day. Edinburgh's parade was made up of seventy-one different groups displaying 120 flags and 300 banners. It culminated with fireworks on the Mound.

The election held in December proved to be a massive victory for the Whigs, who had led the reform movement. In Edinburgh, the lord advocate, Francis Jeffrey, received 4,036 votes and James Abercromby (who had proposed a motion for reform in Edinburgh in Parliament) gained 3,843. The Tory candidate, Mr Bair, only picked up 1,519 votes, while in Leith Boroughs, the Tory candidate withdrew before the votes were counted. The result was much closer in the County of Edinburgh, with Sir John Dalrymple, one of the leaders of the reform movement, defeating Sir George Clerk by 601 to 536 votes.

Municipal Elections

For the first time, the power of choosing members of the town council was removed from the small group who had clung onto power for so long and handed over to householders who owned property valued at £10 or more. The city, old and new, was divided into five districts. With the passing of the Royal Burghs of Scotland Act in 1833, meetings began to take place in the wards as potential candidates sought nominations.

In October, the fourth ward held its meeting in Rose Street Chapel. Other ward meetings followed. The struggle for election had begun. Each of the five wards chose six councillors and the elections took place in the last weeks of December.

At the first meeting of the council, Mr Spittal was chosen as lord provost. The new councillors included Adam Black, Duncan McLaren and William Chambers, all of whom were to serve as lord provosts. For the first time in its history, Leith became an independent burgh with its own elected council. Adam White was the first Provost of Leith. The other areas which now form Edinburgh came under a separate authority – the County of Edinburgh.

The Cholera Epidemic, 1832

At the beginning of the year the first cases of cholera were reported in Haddington. It then moved to the coast, so that by 3 February there had been 299 cases in Musselburgh resulting in 126 deaths.

The first death in Leith occurred on 26 January and the disease spread into the city through February with a few cases reported in Leith and Duddingston, although Portobello was hardest hit. By the end of August the number of cases of cholera in Edinburgh had passed 1,000. Another peak was reached at the beginning of October, with 112 new cases in three days. By 12 October, 912 people had died from the disease in the city.

Fortunately, the end of the month saw a dramatic drop in new cases. There were only seven reported between 10–16 November. In the space of a year over 1,000 people had died from cholera in Edinburgh and, if we count Leith and the modern suburbs like Portobello and the Dean, the total was probably around 1,500. Corstorphine escaped the disease entirely.

A public health board was set up and an attempt was made to improve cleanliness. A House of Refuge was opened to give aid to the poor. The cholera outbreak of 1832 appears to have affected the poorer classes who inhabited the Old Town while life for the more affluent members of the community seems to have carried on as normal.

Meetings and marches in support of reform and the celebrations which followed brought hundreds and possibly thousands of people together. In the autumn, the electors appear to have turned out to hear the candidates without fear of catching the disease.

Coach Travel in the 1830s

In 1830 two major coach companies dominated the trade from Edinburgh. The National Coach Co. was based in Leith Street, while Croall's had their offices in Prince's Street. They both offered services to the main Scottish destinations.

Croall's Chevy Chase left Prince's Street for London at 5.45 a.m. on Mondays, Wednesdays and Fridays. While this coach travelled on the east coast route, the New Times and the Defiance coaches went west to Carlisle and Manchester before continuing on to the capital. The National Coach Company used some patriotic names for their coaches – Wellington for London, Waterloo for Glasgow and the Royal Bruce for Dumfries. By 1838 Croall's were advertising their Royal Independent Edinburgh to London service. The trip now took only fifty-four hours (just over two days!). The cost was to be £5 for a seat inside and £3 for a ride on the outside.

By the summer of 1830, the trip to Glasgow was reduced to four and half hours. There, passengers could catch packets for Ireland. However, the busiest coach route was from the city centre to the ferries at Newhaven. It was estimated in June 1830 that 50,000 passengers used Newhaven and the Chain Pier at Trinity.

The struggle for trade between rival coach and steam boat proprietors sometimes led to violence. In 1830 the situation was so bad that the town council appointed Robert Steele, a former coach guard, as Trustee Conservator of the Peace of Newhaven. In July 1835, a fight broke out at the stone pier between a coach proprietor and one of Croall's coachmen. Security had to be improved, so a constable was placed at the Chain Pier and a barrier erected to prevent the entry of those who were not planning to catch a ferry.

However, despite the considerable amount of business available to the coach and packet ship owners, all was not well. A new rival was already entering the market – the railway.

'Edinburgh Bankrupt!'

It sounds like a scary headline, but in 1833, despite earlier denials, it came true. In 1826, at a meeting in which the lord provost's salary was raised to £1,000, Deacon Pattison commented (possibly with some sarcasm) that he was 'very happy to hear that the town's finances were in such a thriving state'. *The Scotsman*, a fierce critic of the old council, complained, 'The system of economy in the town council like tropical plants in Iceland perish before they have time to fix their roots'.

Debt, for Edinburgh, was nothing new. During the reign of Charles II the burgh had to support a large overdraft and this had only increased as time went on. New churches, the expansion of Leith Docks and improving the access to the Old Town had added to the problem. By 1833 the sums owed by the council had exceeded £400,000.

The situation was now so grave that the lord provost held meetings with the chief creditors and with the government. Sir James Gibson-Craig, leading the creditors, was pleased that the council had finally come into the open. Negotiations between the town council, led at first by its new treasurer, Adam Black, and its creditors began. The council proposed to hand over the docks to the government as security for a loan. Naturally the Dock Commissioners who represented an independent Leith were opposed to such a move. Tempers flared at the meeting of the commissioners. The lord provost and the two bailies representing the interests of Edinburgh prepared to leave but Mr Crichton stopped them, saying, 'We are not going to break up this meeting for your lordship. We are not going to be treated as the creditors of Edinburgh are treated.' The meeting continued.

The Dock Commissioners were not the only body worried about the possible solutions to the city's debt. The Merchant Company were opposed to giving too much power to the committee who would handle the debt. Despite all the doubts, James Abercromby, MP for Edinburgh, introduced the Edinburgh Community Estates Bill in the House of Commons. Some weeks later, however, he expressed concern that more consultation was needed with the citizens of the capital. The bill was eventually passed in 1834, placing the finances of the city under trustees for the creditors.

New Churches and the Annuity Tax

In February 1833 the Edinburgh Voluntary Church Association (representing those churches that were financed by voluntary collections from their congregations) met in Broughton Place Chapel. The speaker, the Reverend Dr Ritchie, called for Christian groups to work together. He expressed his disappointment that 'it was said they [the ministers of the Church of Scotland] mean to decline all intercourse with us'. The dissenting churches in Edinburgh had nearly 15,800 members and they resented public money being used to build new churches for the Establishment. St Stephen's in the New Town had cost £21,000; other churches, the Dean in 1836 and Greenside and St John's in 1838, were to be built at a cost to Edinburgh citizens, many of whom would never use them.

Many in the Established Church, although welcoming aid to build new churches, resented that the control over the appointment of ministers lay in the hands of wealthy patrons or, in Edinburgh's case, the town council. Candidates for vacant benefices were chosen because their views were in line with those of the patron and not the congregation. It would appear that this was not a problem in Edinburgh where the town council was the patron. Despite this, dissenting churches, particularly on the south side, continued to grow.

They were not the only people concerned with the growing cost of church buildings. In 1826 a trades' councillor expressed concern that seat rents were too expensive. The lord provost promised that some seats would be set aside for poorer families at a low rent, and some seats were to be provided at no charge. He then added that some wealthy people wished to pay for good seats and had joined the Episcopal chapels because of a lack of them. A pretty thin excuse for charging high rents, but obviously rising costs were giving concern.

Opposition to the 'annuity tax', as the money raised for the payment of the Church of Scotland ministers' stipends was called, continued to grow. The legality of it was tested in the Court of Session but the decision came in favour of the tax and a punishment of imprisonment for non-payment. In September 1833, William Tait, a bookseller who lived in Walker Street, was sent to prison for non-payment. He was the brother-in-law of Adam Black. On his release, he was met by a large crowd who unhitched the horses from his carriage and pulled it themselves. The next prominent non-payer to be imprisoned was Councillor Thomas Russell for a debt of £7 5s 6d.

New Harbour Facilities and Steam Power

Until this time, the harbour consisted of the quays along the Water of Leith. At the end of October 1791 the *Ariadne* had lost her bowsprit in an accident in Leith due to the packed conditions of the port and so the new East Dock was opened in 1806, although the West Dock was not completed until 1817. Shortly after, some of the shipping companies began to experiment with the new steam-powered ships. These were driven by large paddle wheels which limited their use to the coastal trade.

In 1821 the Chain Pier was opened at Trinity. It became an important destination for ferries crossing the Forth from the Fife ports. It was not until 1838 that the new harbour at Granton was completed and much of the packet trade moved there from Leith. Queen Victoria and Prince Albert landed in Granton on their first visit to Edinburgh in 1842.

As early as 1824 two steam-powered ships, *Velocity* and *Brilliant*, sailed from Newhaven to Aberdeen making stops at the small fishing towns en route. In the other direction, the Newcastle & Newhaven Steam Packet offered passage to Dunbar, Berwick and Newcastle. The London & Edinburgh Steam Packet Co. ships also began to challenge the sailing smacks.

The London, Leith, Edinburgh & Glasgow Co. launched their first steam vessel in Leith during March 1832. The *Royal Adelaide* was 175ft long and had a maximum breadth of over 44ft. The *Royal William* and the *Royal Victoria* soon joined their fleet.

The Arthur's Seat Coffins

In 1836 a group of schoolboys discovered seventeen miniature coffins buried on Arthur's Seat. Each one contained a fully dressed doll. Who made them? Why were they made? There are various theories, which even included black magic. The most interesting idea relates to the number of the coffins – seventeen was the number of victims of Burke and Hare, none of whom had received a Christian burial ...

Fourteen

EARLY VICTORIAN EDINBURGH

Two great political movements played an important role in British politics in the early years of Victoria's long reign – the Anti-Corn Law League and the Chartists.

The Anti-Corn Law League

The Corn Laws, which prevented the importation of grain until prices were high, protected the rural economy but met with strong opposition from the new and powerful industrial lobby. Times of economic depression with the resulting unemployment brought considerable pressure on the authorities. In the middle of the 1840s the Irish Potato Famine and an outbreak of cholera added to these difficulties. In 1846 Sir Robert Peel, despite the opposition of many of his own Tory supporters, repealed the Acts.

The Chartists

This movement wished to pass through Parliament the six demands of the People's Charter, which was drawn up in 1838. These were:

1 Universal adult male suffrage.
2 A secret ballot.
3 Annually elected parliaments.
4 The abolition of the property qualification for MPs.
5 Payment of MPs.
6 Equal electoral districts.

Today, these would not seem very radical demands, but in 1840s Britain they were seen as revolutionary by many of the political classes. Support increased in periods of economic depression (1842 and 1848 were two such years). The Chartists were more aggressive in their demands and felt that the Anti-Corn Law Leaguers were distracting attention from the main issue.

Duncan McLaren

Duncan McLaren came to Edinburgh and worked for John Lauder & Co. In 1824 he opened a small shop on the High Street opposite St Giles. He was a Dissenter and joined the Bristo Street Chapel of Dr William Peddie. The reform of the town council allowed him to take his first step into politics. This was led by Sir James Spittal, who McLaren described thus, 'There never was a man who more devoted himself heart and soul to the duties of office and gave his whole time and thoughts to it as he did' (from J. Mackie's *Life and Work of Duncan McLaren*).

McLaren earned his reputation from his spell as town treasurer. The trustees of the creditors were reluctant to compromise with the council. In the twenty years before the reform of the burgh councils (1813–33), Edinburgh had accumulated an extra £264,595 of debt. There was doubt as to the legality of this newly acquired debt and McLaren suggested that the burgh was not liable for this problem:

> If the burgesses would compel the old corporators to refund to the extent of their delinquencies during the period of 15 years prior to the Reform Acts there would be ample funds and to spare with which to pay the creditors in full.

An Act of Parliament in 1838 passed with little opposition despite opposition from the Presbytery of Edinburgh. During his time as treasurer, McLaren was able to acquire some of the huge amount of money produced by George Heriot's trust to found and run the Heriot Outdoor Free Schools.

Duncan McLaren left the town council. He was a Radical Liberal opposing the Corn Laws, and the Whigs who still controlled Edinburgh were able to defeat him. In November 1851 McLaren became lord provost and went on to top the poll for Edinburgh in the 1865 general election. Three years later, he was returned unopposed along with another Radical. The Independent Liberals believed in free trade but differed from the old Whig Party in wanting an increase in the franchise.

McLaren was a vehement opponent of the annuity tax and refused to accept any compromise, demanding total abolition. He resigned his seat in January 1881 in the hope that his son, John McLaren, might succeed him. John had been chosen as lord advocate.

Duncan McLaren lived latterly in Newington House, where he died on 26 April 1886. He was widowed twice. His third wife, Priscilla Bright, was the sister of the Radical leader, John Bright. Priscilla was an advocate of women's rights and in 1870 became the first president of the Edinburgh Society for Women's Suffrage. She died in 1906.

Granton

In 1838, the Duke of Buccleuch began to build the harbour at Granton to the west of Leith. By the middle of the next decade most of the packet boats running regular services along the east coast called at Granton. Steamships, powered by paddles, provided regular services to London. Others travelled north to Dundee, Aberdeen and the ports of the Moray Firth. By the 1850s ships out of Granton were sailing as far north as Orkney and Shetland. Travel until the 1840s in Scotland was restricted to carriages or ships.

Adam Black and the Election of the Lord Provost, 1840

Adam Black was a publisher who, with his nephew Charles, founded A & C Black. They bought up the rights to publish the *Encyclopaedia Britannica* after the collapse of A. Constable & Co. In 1851, they bought the rights to publish the works of Sir Walter Scott.

Some members of the council proposed to put up Adam Black to challenge Sir James Forrest. Black had been master of the Merchant Company in the late 1820s, an active advocate of reform and a member of the first reformed council. However, he failed to gain enough support and lost the vote by a majority of only three. Many suspected that the Church of Scotland majority on the council did not want to elect a Dissenter. He was chosen as lord provost three years later.

Black served as lord provost from 1843–1848 and as a member for the city from 1856–65. He died at his home, 38 Drummond Place, in 1874 at the age of 90. A statue of him can be found in East Prince's Street Gardens.

The Disruption, 1843

A century after the first groups had left the Established Church, the controversy over patronage remained unsolved. By now, the Court of Session and the General Assembly were deeply involved in moves to remove ministers whose views were unpopular with their own congregations. Considerable resentment built up among members of the Church against the interference of the courts in Church matters. A petition drawn up by the 1842 General Assembly asked the government to stop the Court of Session from encroaching on spiritual jurisdiction. They also requested that they abolish patronage in Scotland. The reply, when it came on 4 January 1843, showed that the government were unwilling to involve themselves with such matters.

In 1843 the General Assembly met in St Andrew's Church in George Street. Of the 1,200 ministers present, 470 marched out. They were led by Thomas Chalmers, who took them to the Tanfield Hall in Canonmills. Here they formed the Free Church of Scotland. It remained 'free' from the interference of the state but retained the same doctrines and forms of worship as the Church of Scotland.

In Edinburgh, this breakaway or 'Disruption' received considerable support. A majority of ministers in the city, as it is today, joined the Free Church. So too did many members of their congregations. In a letter to the *Edinburgh Evening Courant* in May 1859, Edinburgh MP and former lord provost, Adam Black, quoted these figures for church attendance in the city:

Church of Scotland	8,674
United Presbyterian	15,235
Free Church	15,922
Others	12,105

Duncan McLaren, another former lord provost and later one of the city's Members of Parliament, was also a Dissenter (United Presbyterian).

The Government of Sir Robert Peel

Sir Robert Peel became prime minister for the second time in 1841. It was a time of economic depression, often called 'the hungry forties'. The Irish Potato Famine caused many Irish migrants to come to the city seeking work and a better life, and the reappearance of cholera added to the difficulties faced by the people of Edinburgh in this decade.

Lord Ashley (later Earl of Shaftesbury) sought social reforms. He supported the move to provide education for the poor and in 1847 visited Edinburgh to speak to the leaders of the Ragged or Industrial Schools Movement. Lord Ashley told his audience that he saw 'before him a body of ladies and gentlemen who really did know something of the wants of the great mass of the population'.

Edinburgh was more a commercial city by this point and in January of that year the Early Shop Shutting Movement held its first meeting, with Lord Provost Adam Black in the chair. He told the meeting of a letter he had received from a boy who worked in a whisky shop from 6 a.m. until 11.30 p.m. Dr Wilson remarked that many grocers' assistants also worked fourteen or fifteen hours a day. It was agreed to campaign for a 7 p.m. closure, following the example of other cities. In August 1853 drapers, haberdashers and those in the hosiery trade agreed to close their shops at 5 p.m. on a Saturday 'for the benefit of those in their employment'.

Paper manufacturing was an important industry in the suburbs along the Water of Leith. In 1853, nearly six years after the Ten Hours Act, girls aged 10–13 were still working as pickers in the paper mills from 6 p.m. until 6 a.m. They were given just a ten-minute break at midnight. The pickers removed any unsuitable material from the vats and received only 6d for a twelve-hour nightshift.

The Visit of Queen Victoria, 1842

On the evening of Wednesday, 31 August, the royal yacht, towed by the steamers *Black Eagle* and *Shearwater*, reached the mouth of the Firth of Forth. Winds were unfavourable and the royal couple had suffered from seasickness. At 2 a.m. the squadron anchored close to Inchkeith, but plans to transfer the queen to a steamer had to be abandoned because of the weather. Meanwhile, crowds had been gathering in the city all through the day, with an estimated 8,000–9,000 travelling by train from western Scotland.

Thursday saw the royal yacht enter Granton Harbour and by 9 a.m. the queen and the prince were ashore. They then set out for the city, travelling along Inverleith Row and over Canonmills Bridge. It was here that the lord provost and the magistrates were waiting to present the queen with the keys to the city – the first reigning queen to do so since Mary, Queen of Scots. Unfortunately, as the queen and Prince Albert entered the city there was no sign of the lord provost or the bailies. The royal carriage continued its long climb up Pitt Street and on to Hanover Street before turning into Prince's Street.

The lord provost and the town council began to assemble in the council chambers at 9 a.m., expecting the royal party to leave Granton at 11 a.m. Guns from the castle warned them that the queen had already entered the city. This embarrassing situation now turned to farce as they raced off to try and intercept the royal party, who were heading for Dalkeith. One group turned down onto the North Bridge, only to be swallowed up by the crowds hoping to see Her Majesty. Another group headed down the Canongate in the hope of intercepting the royal carriages near Abbeyhill.

Meanwhile, the queen's carriage entered Waterloo Place where she passed beneath a huge garland of flowers hung over the road. A little further along, outside the Waterloo Rooms, the Celtic Society, dressed in their own clan uniforms, waited to greet the queen and the prince. They continued through Abbeyhill, making for Dalkeith where they were to be the guests of the Duke and Duchess of Buccleuch. The lord provost and the bailies had to set out directly to Dalkeith in order to meet the queen and the prince, who agreed to alter their plans and make an official entry into the city on Saturday instead.

So, two days later a group of carriages, one of which carried Prime Minister Sir Robert Peel, left Dalkeith and passed through Parson's Green before entering the Royal Park. There they were met by the Royal Company of Archers (the queen's official escort in Scotland), who took up their position beside the royal carriage. They then moved on to Holyrood, stopping outside the palace to give the royal couple a view of the frontage. The procession turned into the Canongate and the High Street which were thronged with crowds. From a balcony at Milton House (then a seminary for the Sisters of Charity), children threw flowers to the royal couple.

The carriage eventually came to a stop near the site of the Cross and the lord provost presented the queen with the keys of the city. Further up the street, boys from Heriot's and girls from the Merchants & Trades' Hospital were joined by a few boys from George Watson's to watch the procession. On the north side of the High Street the Celtic Society were again lined up in their uniforms. The queen noticed a group of women in traditional costume and she was informed that they were fisherwomen; she expressed her pleasure at their clean appearance.

The royal party reached the entrance of the castle where they left their carriage. After inspecting the castle, the queen and the prince were driven along the Lawnmarket and down the Mound to Prince's Street. One sad note on this otherwise joyful occasion occurred in Prince's Street when a stand collapsed, causing many injuries.

The royal couple rode on westwards to visit Lord Rosebury. On their return, they passed through Leith where they were greeted by the provost, James Rioch, and large crowds. James Rioch, only the second of Leith's provosts, learnt that the queen proposed to return to Dalkeith via Leith on the day before the visit. He immediately called a meeting of the heads of the public bodies. They decided to build a triumphal arch in Great Junction Street opposite Dr Bell's School. A force of special constables was sworn in to maintain order.

Saturday afternoon turned out to be very wet. The ringing of the bell of North Leith Parish Church warned them of the approach of the royal party. The guns of Leith Fort fired a salute. The queen's carriage turned into Great Junction Street to 'the most deafening cheers'. The provost and the council, wearing their robes of office, met the queen and Prince Albert. They drove on to the Links, which was 'one mass of carriages extending over the whole space'.

The prince commiserated with one of the officers of the Royal Archers, who were by now thoroughly soaked. The officer replied that they did not mind as it was such a satisfying duty. The prince, who had never visited Scotland, remarked that 'he supposed this was what they called a Scotch mist'.

The City Wall

The building of the new station meant that the ancient Church of Trinity College had to be demolished. The church had been founded by Mary of Guelders, the wife of James II, in the middle of fifteenth century. Before this happened, the body of the founder was reinterred in Holyrood Chapel. Lady Glenorchy's congregation were also faced with an unpopular move to Roxburgh Place Chapel. The Presbytery of Edinburgh had to take the trustees to court to secure this.

Another monument under attack was the city wall, which had been built after the disaster of Flodden. The Kirk Session of New Greyfriars had set up a school to educate and look after some 200 poor children from the Grassmarket and the West Port. They felt that the wall along the Vennel was inconvenient and the cause of the dampness in their school. The Session faced considerable opposition which included the Antiquarian Society of Scotland since this section of the wall contained one of the ancient towers of the city. The town council unanimously rejected the request to remove the wall, which can still be seen today.

In October 1860, a committee led by Sir William Johnston, a former lord provost, and William Chambers, the publisher, was formed with the aim of raising money to return the Market Cross to the High Street. At first they met with encouragement from the town council, but soon the opposition to such a move began. Duncan McLaren told the council, 'To call it a restoration of the ancient cross was a hoax on the credulity of the public of Edinburgh'. Faced with the opposition of the council, the committee abandoned the plan and returned the money that had already been donated.

Education in Edinburgh

Education at this time was provided by three groups – the churches, private schools and charities. The first of these three required the parents to make a payment, which generally depended on the subjects taken. Education beyond the basic or, as it was known, 'normal' curriculum was provided by the High School or private academies.

Edinburgh Academy had been founded on the north side of the city in the 1820s. A Southern Academy operated for some time in Buccleuch Place. By the 1860s it had moved to Park Place. It offered higher (secondary) education to children on the south side of the city after the High School had moved to Calton Hill.

The Reformers of the sixteenth century had planned to set up a school in every parish controlled by the Kirk Session. By the nineteenth century, this aim had been achieved in Edinburgh and its suburbs. The Session School for the churches in Edinburgh was originally in Leith Wynd, but in 1824 they had found new premises in Market Street. A final move in 1841 took the school to Johnstone Terrace, where they also trained teachers to work in Church of Scotland schools. Other parish churches, like St Stephen's, St Mary's and St Cuthbert's, had their own Session Schools. St Stephen's was particularly large, providing education for as many as 600 children in the 1830s.

Other churches also provided the 'normal' curriculum for the children of their congregations. An Episcopal school was opened in Orwell Place, Dalry. The Free Church founded their own school and teacher-training establishment at Moray House in 1848. Today, it is completely turned over to the training of teachers. The Roman Catholic Church and the newly formed United Presbyterian Church also had their own schools.

There were many privately run institutes and schools in Edinburgh. The *Evening Courant* in September 1863 carried adverts for two dozen, and the *Edinburgh Directory 1867–68* listed ninety-three private schools.

The Edinburgh Institute was founded in 1832 and it found new premises in Queen Street (1853), where it offered 'a thorough education in classics, mathematics, English and modern languages'. The six-year course prepared children for university, business or the public service examinations. The Scottish Institute of Civil, Commercial and Military Education in Hill Street had an extensive curriculum which included Hindustani, fortification, civil engineering and bookkeeping. Education for 'young ladies' was offered by the Scottish Institute (Moray Place), the Edinburgh Institute (Charlotte Square), the Royal Circus Institute and the Institute (Great King Street). This last also took boarders.

The city had charitable hospitals like George Heriot's and George Watson's, which provided free board and education to the children of burgesses who had fallen on hard times. Today they are part of the private schools of the city. George Heriot's Hospital was a very wealthy institution, and in 1836 the council – with the authority of an Act of Parliament – used some of the surplus revenues to set up 'outdoor schools'. By 1862, when the schools were visited to give anti-small pox vaccinations, there were twelve schools providing free education to over 3,000 children. The ragged, or industrial, schools offered some education and sustenance for the very poorest children in the city.

Thomas Guthrie and the Ragged Schools

Reverend Dr Thomas Guthrie was the minister of St John's Free Church in Edinburgh. One day he visited Anstruther, the birthplace of the famous Free Church minister, Robert Chalmers. He and a friend took refreshment at a local inn where he was inspired by a picture of James Pound, a Portsmouth cobbler who had rescued 500 ragged children. In his own words, Dr Guthrie said, 'I felt ashamed of myself. I felt reproved for the little I had done.'

With the aid of patrons, Dr Guthrie set up the Original Ragged School Movement in Edinburgh. Not only did they offer teaching to children who had virtually been abandoned but they also kept them off the streets and away from crime. Typical of the type of children he hoped to help were the five boys who came before the magistrate in 1847:

[They were in a] deplorable state of dirt, disease and raggedness and appeared to be part of a gang of neglected uncared for youth who prowl about the streets living on what falls in their way and who, having no home, take possession at night of any place they can find.

A sad reflection on the times and the reality behind Charles Dickens' story *Oliver Twist*.

The children would arrive at 7.30 a.m. (an hour later in winter) and their clothes taken away to be fumigated. Then they were scrubbed in long baths before being given a breakfast of porridge and milk. Dinner at 1 p.m. consisted of bread and soup. During the morning and afternoon sessions they were given a basic education (reading, writing and arithmetic), as well as some craftwork in the hope of training them for a job. They received a supper of porridge and milk at 6.30 p.m., before their clothes were returned to them.

By 1848 three schools had been established – one for boys, one for girls and a third for infants. Of the 369 children attending these schools, 189 (nearly half) were of Irish parentage. The death rate was higher among the pupils attending these schools than other establishments in the city. A new ragged school building was opened in Ramsay Lane near the castle, bringing the various departments together, and their total roll was 310.

In the same year, the rival united industrial school was opened. Their aim was 'uniting under one roof and educating in common'. Both the united industrial and ragged schools gave secular instruction to all and only religious training was taught separately for Protestants and Catholics. The first united industrial school was in Gray's Close.

There was no love lost between the two movements. Some thirteen years later, Dr Guthrie questioned the achievements of the movement, while a report by the united industrial schools claimed that their former pupils were earning a total of over £11,500. Two-thirds of the pupils were Catholics and this may have aroused animosity among the Free Church supporters of the original ragged schools. The board of the united industrial schools defended themselves. A letter of support from Dr Hunter, minister of the Tron Kirk (Church of Scotland) read, 'I have great pleasure in bearing my testimony to that admirable manner in which you construct the religious instruction of the Protestant pupils in the United Industrial School'.

There were certainly success stories to boast about. Owen Fairly, who, with his sister, had been a member of the very first class, was now a teacher in the school with a recognised qualification. James Kelly, another member of that class, had joined the army and won the Victoria Cross – probably the first Edinburgh citizen to receive that award.

New Greyfriars Parish Church set up its own school for 'ragged' children during the mid-1840s. The schoolhouse was in the Vennel. They offered education, as well as providing food and some clothing. The whole project was financed by the congregation. They may possibly have been the first group to tackle the problem of the destitute children found in the streets of Edinburgh during the nineteenth century.

The Railway Boom

During the middle years of the century, a large number of companies were formed to build railways linking the major cities of Britain. The Edinburgh and Glasgow line opened in 1842. Three years later, another line was being constructed with the aim of connecting Edinburgh to the ports of Granton and Leith and on, by ferry, across the Forth.

The North British purchased Trinity College Church and the adjoining property for their new Waverley Station. The Caledonian Railway, who also ran trains to Glasgow, were excluded from this venture and had to build their own terminus in Lothian Road. As lines joined up, people were able to travel further. Queen Victoria and her family made the journey north to Balmoral by train. They alighted at St Margaret's Station and spent the night in Holyrood Palace.

In June 1851 the Caledonian Railway was offering a £4 first-class return to London to visit the Great Exhibition.

The New Steamships

Up to 1850, all the steam-powered vessels working out of Leith and Granton were driven by paddle wheels, but the newest steamships were fitted with the screw propeller. Competition became more intense as the railway lines linked up and competed for much of the long-distance trade. Even Newhaven fishwives, it was reported in May 1855, were taking the train to Glasgow to sell the port's catches.

The London & Edinburgh Shipping Company had introduced five new screw steamers in 1852. The first one of these was the *Oscar*, which sailed from Victoria Dock in Leith. The new ships soon entered the international trade

routes and the *Osborne* was a two-funnelled, 800-ton steamer which sailed between Leith and Rotterdam. She had accommodation for first and second-class passengers and cargo could be loaded and discharged using her two steam cranes and her steam winch.

In March 1866, the General Steam Navigation Company introduced the *Granton*. She weighed over 1,000 tons and could carry 600 passengers. This screw-powered steamship boasted a top speed of 12 knots with no vibrations to disturb the passengers.

The Edinburgh & Leith Shipping Co., which already operated the *Stork* and *Heron* out of Granton, introduced their new steamer *Iona* in the summer of 1866. At 250ft long, she had berths for over fifty first-class and fifty second-class passengers. The *Evening Courant*'s reporter was so impressed that he wrote, 'There seems little difference of the sleeping accommodation on board and that which is furnished at a respectable hotel on shore'.

The Case of Charles McDouall

The religious problems facing the town council did not end with the Disruption of 1843. Adam Black was now lord provost and a majority of the council were no longer members of the Established Church. In October 1847, they decided to appoint Charles McDouall to the chair of Hebrew and Oriental Studies.

McDouall had left the Church of Scotland in 1843 to join the Free Church. The matter then came before the Presbytery of Edinburgh. After a two-hour debate in private, they agreed to send the problem to a committee which later advised them to make a challenge in the courts to the council's appointment.

Meanwhile, the minority on the council, led by Bailie Mach, did not remain inactive. They produced their own reply in writing. Councillor Russell, referring to it, explained, 'That document displays an assumption of ecclesiastical power worthy only of the dark ages. I am surprised such language should be used in the nineteenth century in a Christian country.' The majority group on the council then consulted the lord advocate and Mr Ingles, the city's solicitor, from whom they received a favourable report of their right to appoint Mr McDouall.

Three groups now opposed the appointment – the minority on the council, the Presbytery of Edinburgh and the senate of the university. The case came before Lord Robertson and he decided in favour of the town council, who immediately installed Charles McDouall. However, the supporters of the Established Church took the matter before the full Court of Session, who reversed the decision. Since the new professor refused to take 'the test', he was forced to resign.

The Cholera Epidemic, 1847–49

Fever patients at the Royal Infirmary during May and June 1846 totalled 102. For the same two months in the following year the numbers trebled, with 613 patients being admitted. Mr Charles Baillie reported to the town council, 'The cases of fever were found chiefly to prevail among the poorer classes of Irish located in different parts of the city, many of whom had only recently come to this part of the country'. The Irish Potato Famine had driven many people out of Ireland seeking food and work, and some of these refugees had come to Edinburgh where work could be found building new railway lines and reservoirs. As in the outbreak of 1832, it was generally the poorer people living in the overcrowded and unsanitary tenements of the Old Town who suffered from this epidemic.

Typhus, smallpox and scarlet fever were also prevalent in the city, and in December 1847 Sheriff Spiers died from typhus at the age of 51. Serious pressure was placed upon the infirmary. The army lent four large tents and three more doctors offered their services free of charge. The figures tell the story:

Patients admitted:

1846	3,895
1847	7,846
1848	7,763
1852	4,736

In 1848, 1,108 of these patients had been sent by the parochial council, who were responsible for the poor in the city. Two-thirds of this number were Irish immigrants. It was fear of another epidemic that began to alert the authorities to the overcrowded and unsanitary condition of much of the Old Town.

1848 – A Year of Discontent

The first trouble began in Edinburgh on the High Street at about half past eight on the evening of Tuesday, 7 March. It appears to have taken the form of vandalism – street lights and windows were the main targets of the mob. A second night of disturbances followed, but the lord provost had recruited a force of 200 special constables. Troops from the castle and Piershill Barracks were also placed at his disposal. A mob of some 600 people had gathered on Calton Hill but they were dispersed by the special constables. Similar action was taken against a group which had gathered on the Mound. About 500 lamps were broken in the streets and ninety-four people were arrested.

The action of the special constables and the rain prevented further trouble on Thursday night, but fear of more disturbances on Saturday evening when many labourers came to town led the lord provost to continue with the use of special constables. No particular motive appears to have brought about this unrest, and Edinburgh was not the only town in Scotland to suffer during the first two weeks of March.

In April, a group of men targeted the Relief Committee which had been set up to distribute funds donated to aid unemployed men. They provided manual work at 6d a day for unmarried men, 9d for a married man and 1s (12d = 1s) for married men with more than one child. Naturally the unmarried men were unhappy with the situation. About 100 of them gathered in the Lawnmarket and marched down the steps to the Relief Committee headquarters in Victoria Street. They then turned down the West Bow and entered the Grassmarket where they stole some straw from the carters. The mob continued up the Vennel and on to the new cattlemarket. Here, the straw was used to stuff an effigy of ex-bailie Gray, who was a member of the Relief Committee. They then marched back to the Lawnmarket parading their new standard. Sheriff Gordon and Superintendent List of the County Police intervened. The rioters then made for the High Street where Superintendent Moxey (City Police) captured the effigy. Mr Wigham, a member of the Relief Committee, appears to have calmed the situation by offering work with the Caledonian Railway which was constructing a line between Edinburgh and Glasgow. Other men were to be employed breaking stones, which would then be used to make and repair the roads around the city.

A Chartist meeting on Bruntsfield Links proved to be quite a small affair. Chartists from Leith looking to join the protests marched up the Walk to be met by special constables, who drove them back with what appears to have been excessive force. The authorities, looking around at the disturbances taking place across Europe, were in no mood to be lenient.

If these problems were not sufficient, the old issue of the annuity tax again raised its head. Two small city businessmen – Henry Darlington, an upholsterer in Frederick Street, and Mr Sword, who sold furniture in Hanover Street – had their goods impounded for non-payment. Many Dissenters and Free Churchmen resented paying money to support the Established Church. Some of these, like Bailie Stott and Councillor McLaren, who was to become lord provost, were also 'Independent Liberals' or Radicals.

In October, charges were brought against four Chartist leaders in the city. They were accused of 'conspiring to affect an alteration of the laws and constitution of the realm by force and violence'. The prosecution turned into a remarkable failure for the authorities.

The Charitable Institutions of Edinburgh

In November 1851, former lord provost Sir William Johnston gave a report to a select committee of the House of Commons on the charitable institutions of Edinburgh. George Heriot's Hospital, with a revenue of £16,000 a year, was the wealthiest of these. The town council and the ministers of Edinburgh (Church of Scotland only) acted as governors. At this time, 180 boys were being boarded and educated in the hospital. An Act of Parliament in 1836 had allowed the governors to use the surplus funds to set up 'outdoor schools' and by 1851 there were ten such schools, educating 3,000 boys and girls free of charge.

Of the other charitable hospitals for the care and education of children, George Watson's, managed by the Merchant Company, took boys from 7 to 10 years of age; John Watson's provided care and education for 120 destitute children between the ages of 8 and 14; and the Orphan Hospital, financed by legacies and subscriptions, took children from all parts of Scotland. At this time, they had on their role 100 boys and girls. Cauvin's Hospital, set up by a French teacher, looked after twenty-six boys and was situated in Duddingston. Sir William described it as 'a very excellent institution'.

There were two institutions for the education of girls. Both of these had been partly financed by Mary Erskine. The Merchant Maidens' Hospital had ninety-six girls, the daughters of merchants fallen on hard times. They were between the ages of 7 and 11. Sir William told the committee, 'They were so well instructed in that house that the greater portion of them are sent out ultimately as governesses'. He also pointed out, 'They are treated in a very ladylike way'. A similar institution set up by the trades held forty-eight girls.

At this time, parents had to pay for their children's education. The High School and the Academy were the main schools for the senior boys but those who could not afford to pay for education and had some connection with the city might apply for a place in one of the hospitals. The churches also had parish schools; but students were expected to contribute to their education.

Trinity College had a hospital (almshouse) which looked after forty-two (generally elderly) men and women, but since the property had been bought by the North British Railway to build a station (Waverley), they were boarded out. As this proved to be a cheaper option the numbers had been increased to 100.

James Gillespie, a snuff merchant from Colinton, had left money to look after forty-five men and women over the ages of 55. He also provided money to set up a school for 200 boys.

Donaldson, a printer in Edinburgh, had left £210,000 for a hospital for children. The governors had only recently set this up and they had taken the opportunity to provide places for ninety-six children (evenly divided between boys and girls) who were deaf and dumb. All of these institutions except Trinity

College still operate today, although not in the same form. Donaldson's is still a school for the deaf and dumb, but it is no longer in the original building.

There were other institutions dependent on the charitable giving of the citizens of Edinburgh which Sir William Johnston did not mention. The largest and busiest of these was the Infirmary, handling thousands of patients each year (4,736 in 1852). The House of Refuge was opened in 1832 during the cholera epidemic, in Morrison's Close off the High Street. The growing demand for its services led the trustees to purchase Queensberry House in 1853. Associated with the House of Refuge was the Night Asylum which was opened in Old Fishmarket Close in 1841. The Magdalen Asylum was founded in 1799 to give help to distressed women and the Lunatic Asylum had moved to its new home in Morningside during 1842 – this had provoked an argument over the funding of the new asylum.

No. 5 Frederick Street housed the offices of the Servants' Institute and Female Home. Their aims were to assist their members in finding jobs and offer help in difficult times. Part of this building was used as a home for unemployed female servants, who raised funds to provide for themselves in old age.

Local Government

Local government was very complex, with responsibility for providing services divided between a number of bodies.

The town council had control over the Old Town and the New Town. Those who broke the law were brought before the magistrates – the four bailies of the town. The Edinburgh Extension Act 1856 abolished the Police Commission and its responsibilities (policing, street cleaning and lighting) were then transferred to the town council.

The baronies of Calton and Canongate and Portsburgh became part of the city and the number of bailies was raised from four to six. The County of Edinburgh and Leith had their own council, police and sheriff's court, administering much of today's outer suburbs.

Parish boards had control over the welfare of the poor and sick. Edinburgh, the Canongate and the West Kirk (St Cuthbert's) had their own poorhouses. Dr Littlejohn's 'Report on the Sanitary Condition of the City of Edinburgh' recommended the removal of the very poor from the centre of Edinburgh. The City Parochial Board responded by building a new poorhouse to the south of Edinburgh. The report suggested, 'The citizens should insist that it should be extended to the other parishes of St Cuthbert's and the Canongate and that the city should be wholly relieved of their paupers'. Such a move, put forward in 1867, was particularly opposed by some influential members of St Cuthbert's board led by Sir James Baird.

Edinburgh in the 1850s

The city, which since 1832 had been a Whig stronghold, now gave its votes to the Liberals. A struggle for power between the Moderates and the Radicals began, and Duncan Maclaren became Edinburgh's first Radical lord provost. Many of them were Dissenters or Free Churchmen who were completely opposed to the annuity tax which paid the stipends of Edinburgh's Established (Church of Scotland) ministers. The Tories, now calling themselves Conservatives, failed to put forward a candidate for the city in the parliamentary elections although they did have some success in the county.

Crime

Concern was expressed as early as 1840 about a new kind of gambling called 'Thimblerigging'.

One man lost £2 and his watch when he came to the aid of 'a lady' who appeared to have lost some money. She was really a decoy for the fraudsters.

During the holidays, many people in the wealthy New Town visited relatives in the country, leaving their homes vulnerable to burglars, and February 1847 brought a spate of robberies in which excessive violence was used. Concern at the lack of progress by the police was expressed at a meeting of the town council. By the end of the month, two men had been charged with some of these crimes.

Much of the magistrates' court's time was taken up with cases involving drunkenness. Figures for the five years from 1847 to 1851 show a marked increase in the numbers brought before the court. While in 1847 they prosecuted 1,802 people, the figure had risen to 2,795 in 1851.

The Court of Session handled more serious cases and many of these were civil disputes, sometimes between landowners and the railway companies. There were also sad cases which reflect the poverty and morality of the time. In November 1855, Agnes Cameron (also known as MacDonald), an unmarried woman of 25, gave birth to a girl. Ten days later, she was charged with murder by throwing the baby into Duddingston Loch. The jury returned a unanimous verdict of 'not proven'.

The Meadows

In 1849, Bailie Stott tried to open up the eastern Meadows for the public so that they could use them to bleach and dry their clothes, as well as for recreation. A petition was presented to the council. The Reverend Begg claimed, 'Prince's Street Gardens had been usurped by the rich.' Pressure had increased as people were being turned out of Queen's Park. The council rejected the proposal because they received £200 a year from leasing the ground for grazing.

In 1855 the police commissioners looked at thirty-eight different designs for improving the Meadows. These ranged in cost from £583 up to a staggering £12,031. Plans for and against a drive through the Meadows became the centre of the controversy. In August, a Mr Gourlay collected his supporters at the east end of Prince's Street and they marched up the Bridges to Hope Park, where they knocked down the stone pillars that prevented carriages driving onto the Meadow Walk. Eventually the police arrived and Mr Gourlay, with three of his supporters, was arrested.

The Meadows was also the home of the Royal Company of Archers (the queen's bodyguard in Scotland). In 1861 they sought to enclose their shooting range to protect the public. The park appears to have been at least partly enclosed because the inhabitants of Meadow Place asked for an opening to be made so that they could access the park.

The Adelphi Theatre Fire, 1853

Fire broke out at the Adelphi Theatre (in Broughton Street) which led to the complete destruction of the building, although they managed to save the stock in the neighbouring shops. Police and soldiers were used to contain the crowds. Mr Wyndham, who held the lease, escaped with his costumes and luckily he had just secured the lease of the Theatre Royal so his company were not left without a home.

The Forbes MacKenzie Act

The purpose of the Forbes MacKenzie Act was to restrict the sale of alcohol. Every premises had to possess a licence, however, the Act also covered other groceries and the police began to prosecute restaurants who sold food to take away.

David Doull of The Restaurant at 60 Prince's Street was convicted of selling five tarts worth 10*d* to a boy who had been sent by Mr Bryson, a local shopkeeper. Bailie Cassels, in his summary, 'Felt it a hardship that that he should be constrained to convict such a respectable citizen as Mr Doull'. He was followed in court by Councillor Ridpath, the keeper of the refreshment rooms at the North British Station. His counsel claimed that the whole station was part of his sales area, where passengers needed to be able to purchase refreshments which were not available on the trains. The bailie, while sympathising with the councillor, fined him £1 5*s*.

The Annuity Tax

The Reform Act of 1832 had opened up the town council to the Dissenters, who were naturally unwilling to pay the annuity tax which was used to pay the stipends of the ministers of the Established Church. The lord advocate, Francis Jeffrey, had introduced a bill in 1834, but it failed to pass through Parliament. Further attempts in 1835 and 1837 fared no better.

The position of the Established Church was weakened by the Disruption in 1843. Now it could no longer claim that the majority of the citizens of Edinburgh were members of the Church of Scotland. Further attempts to solve this problem met with no success. However, new plans were put forward. A tax was to be placed on property with a rental value of £5 or over, to be paid by the owners or tenants. Money from the Trinity College fund and the Deanery of the Royal Chapel would ease the burden and the ministers would receive an annual stipend of £600, reduced to £550 for new incumbents. The two ministers of the Canongate fared worse, as they only received £250 each. The High Church, the Tron and St Andrew's Church in the New Town were reduced to single charges. The Edinburgh legal profession, who had been exempt from the annuity tax, would have to pay the property tax.

The two MPs for the city, Adam Black, a former lord provost, and James Moncrieff, the lord advocate, brought in a bill to abolish the annuity tax. It set up a body of ten ecclesiastical commissioners who took over the town's rights over the fifteen churches in Edinburgh. The council was to provide three commissioners, the Kirk Session three and the ministers, two. The remaining two members were to come from the Merchant Company and the legal profession in Edinburgh. The Established Church in Edinburgh was to be financed by a property tax based on the police rate, with the queen's auditor in Scotland providing £2,000 annually.

The passing of this Act did not end the controversy. The Radicals, led by Duncan McLaren who became MP for Edinburgh, were determined to pursue the matter. However, gaining support in Parliament for this local issue became very difficult. McLaren continued to bring forward bills to abolish the whole system. Finally, in 1870, Lord Advocate Young set out a government bill based on Duncan McLaren's proposals

Bailie Alexander Cassels

The city now had six bailies. During 1859, Councillor Cassels was appointed to a vacancy and after the November election the former treasurer, Councillor G.E. Russell, was proposed for the post of bailie in place of Cassels. Bailie Forrester said he understood 'that all party or sectarian feelings were to be laid aside and toned down'. One councillor criticised the former treasurer, who had been involved in the collapse of the Western Bank.

In the end the council voted twenty-two for G.E. Russell (there was also a Bailie T. Russell) and fourteen for ex-bailie Cassels. Councillor Cassels was a Conservative and a member of the Church of Scotland. Some felt this was the real reason for the unwillingness of the majority on the council to retain him as a bailie. He then resigned his position on the council and St Stephen's ward chose Major Mair to replace him.

Mr Cassels returned to the council, and in November 1862 he took up his duties once more as a bailie of the city. This appears to have been a period when more moderate views dominated the council, led by Lord Provost Lawson. During the absence of the lord provost in January 1865 Cassels, as senior magistrate, stood in for him, presiding over council meetings and representing him at the funeral of George Lorimer, the dean of guild.

Councillor Neil Macnish

Councillor Macnish, described by *The Scotsman* as 'a party on his own', entered the council in 1860 as a representative of St Leonard's Ward. Two years later, he was returned again for one of the two seats available:

Marshall	373
Macnish	339
Jamieson	330

A letter of protest was sent to Mr Marwick, the town clerk, complaining of irregularities in the election. It was claimed that some electors had voted twice while others, who had no right to vote, had declared for Macnish. The matter came before the council in February 1863.

However, the councillor had serious domestic problems. His wife had left him, alleging that he had assaulted her. She took with her the children from a previous marriage and their 3-year-old daughter, Jane Macnish. She asked the court for custody of the child and access to her clothes. Meanwhile, Macnish raised his profile even more by forcibly entering a private hotel in Prince's Street in an attempt to find his wife and daughter.

In an era when high moral standards were expected of leading citizens, members of the council demanded his resignation. He resisted for some time before resigning and promising to clear his name.

The 1860s

Industrial Disputes

A dispute broke out in the building trade as workers sought to reduce their hours from ten to nine each day. The strike continued through the summer of 1861 as both sides looked for a solution. In the autumn of that year, the scavengers (men who kept the streets and public gardens free from litter) threatened to strike. The council intervened and instructed their officials to pay them 15*s* a week. The carters also came out demanding a rise of 2*s* on their weekly wage of 16*s*. Most carters worked a twelve to fourteen-hour day, beginning at 7 a.m.; others had to start earlier in order to catch steamers leaving Granton Harbour.

Sewage and the Water of Leith

Dr Macadam reported that the Water of Leith 'as it leaves Edinburgh contains fifty times the quantity of organic matter which is found in the Thames at London Bridge'. Some 100,000 people in Edinburgh and Leith discharged their waste into the river. An Act of Parliament in 1864 gave sanction for the creation of a main drainpipe to collect this sewage. Thirty years later, a new sewer extending from Balerno to the Forth at Leith was completed. This pipe proved inadequate and failed to take into account the pollution (particularly from the papermills) on the upper Water of Leith.

The Theatre Royal Fire

On Friday, 13 January 1865, at 4 p.m., smoke was seen rising from the Theatre Royal at the top of Broughton Street. It was a new building, having only been opened in 1855. The theatre was soon ablaze and although they got the fire under control the building was left in a dangerous state. George Lorimer, the dean of guild and Convener of the Fire Engine Committee, arrived to inspect the damage. While he was inspecting the ruins with some workmen the north wall collapsed killing him and some of the men. Once the property was made safe a total of six bodies were recovered.

Proposed Improvements in the Old Town

Dr Henry Littlejohn, Edinburgh's first medical officer, produced his 'Report on the Sanitary Condition of the City of Edinburgh' in 1867. It highlighted the problems of poor sanitation and overcrowding in the Old Town. The narrow closes and wynds not only restricted the circulation of air but also prevented easy access for the emergency services in case of fire.

In the previous August, the town council had divided the Old Town and some of the nearby suburbs to the south into fourteen separate districts, identifying many of the problems found in each one. Unfortunately the Free Trade Radicals who controlled the council failed to tackle the real heart of the problem – the landlords who crammed people into their tenements but failed to carry out proper maintenance or improve the sanitation. One five-storey tenement in the Cowgate contained sixty rooms in which 179 people lived. The building possessed only two sinks and one toilet!

Water Shortages

The growing city continued to place pressure on the supply of water. Public complaints about its inadequacy led the town council to propose the setting up of a Water Trust to take over from the Water Company. The company claimed that there was sufficient water and blamed the public for wasting it. One accusation raised by them was that toilets were fixed to produce a constant flow of water. Cisterns too were, according to the company, too small.

Opponents of the Radical majority on the town council feared that the new trust would be packed with Radical members. The shareholders of the company had to be compensated. Both sides eventually took their cases to a committee of the House of Commons. They began hearing evidence on 20 April 1869. The matter dragged on until the company's shareholders and the town councils (Leith and Portobello were also involved in this) came to an agreement, with the shareholders receiving an annual payment of 6 per cent on their stock.

The trustees held their first meeting on 2 September 1869. They were composed of representatives of the councils of Edinburgh, Leith and Portobello. The supply problem had not gone away, but now the responsibility for solving it was placed firmly in the hands of the three councils.

The Infirmary and George Watson's Hospital

The Royal Infirmary had outgrown its site and the search for new property had led the trustees to the grounds facing George Heriot's Hospital in Laureston Place. The land was occupied by George Watson's Hospital. The governors of George Watson's were suspicious; if the infirmary acquired the hospital it might lead to its closure. This, of course, had happened to Trinity College.

The purchase was finally concluded and George Watson's moved into the Old Merchant & Maiden Hospital. In the meantime, the university had their eyes on the Old Infirmary site. They had been freed from the patronage of the town council by the passing of the Universities Act in 1858. Their estimate of £20,000 was considerably lower than that proposed by the infirmary trustees.

Fifteen

LATE VICTORIAN EDINBURGH, 1870–1901

Council Workers

In April 1870, a delegation of scavengers presented a petition to the city council for a rise of 1s a week. Councillor Cranston reminded the town council that while ordinary labours worked fifty-one hours a week, the scavengers' hours were sixty-five – no half-day was given to the scavengers on Saturdays. There were 136 men involved and the total cost of the rise would not have been much over £350 in a year. However, this rise was refused by a majority of two votes, although this decision was later reversed.

The city council could, however, be generous with some of their employees. One of them was given an increase in salary of £50.

The Merchant Company Schools

The Endowed Hospitals Act 1869 enabled the Merchant Company to turn their hospitals (charitable, not medical institutions) into large private schools. George Watson's admitted 800 pupils in their first year, but unfortunately their premises were to be sold as the new site for the Royal Infirmary (Lauriston Place). George Watson's took over the Old Merchant Maiden Hospital while they, in their turn, moved to Queen Street. In 1870 this school admitted 1,200 girls and it was now called the Edinburgh Institute for Young Ladies. Daniel Stewart's School provided places for boys only, while James Gillespie's admitted both sexes.

The creation of these large schools represented a serious threat to the many small private schools and their staff. One governor of Heriot's Hospital, at a meeting in October 1872, commented, 'They knew very much teachers had been injured by the abrupt and wholesale movement which was made in connection with the Merchant Company'.

John Gould

On 14 January 1872 the death was announced of John Gould in the poorhouse of St Cuthbert's Parish at the age of 83. Gould had been a tailor but he struggled to cope, both mentally and physically, as he grew older. In his youth he had served with the Royal Scots Greys in the Battle of Waterloo.

Female Medical Students and the University of Edinburgh

In 1869 it was agreed that women could study medicine at the university. However, the medical faculty refused to offer mixed practical classes. They were also unwilling, owing (they claimed) to lack of resources, to provide separate classes for women. This meant that no woman could qualify for a medical degree.

A group of lady students took the university senate to the Court of Session. The senate claimed that they did not have the power to force the faculty to alter its position, and the court accepted this argument. Professor Crum-Brown explained that 'separate classes for women' were 'not practical'. Most of the medical staff opposed the change and Professor Lister (a real hardliner) put his views to the university council: 'The medical profession was one for which women were unfitted both by physical organisation and by mental and moral qualities'. Professor Christison, the most senior member of the medical school, was also opposed to the entry of women to the profession.

There then followed a series of 'indecent circulars against mixed classes' purporting to come from male medical students. One correspondent of *The Scotsman* wrote, 'I have scarcely ever met anything so bad, so gratuitously nasty'. A riot nearly occurred when a large group of male medical students tried to prevent the small number of lady students from attending classes in November 1870.

One of the women trying to attend the medical school was Sophia Jex-Blake, who came from Hastings. She continued to study, but in 1872 the Court of Session ruled that the university senate did not have the power to force the professors to accept female students. A series of public letters appeared (published in *The Scotsman*) between Miss Jex-Blake and Dr Paterson. Miss Jex-Blake argued that some women, especially nuns, preferred women doctors. After failing to break the male domination at the University of Edinburgh she set up the London School of Medicine for Women in 1874, commencing with fourteen students, twelve of whom were from Edinburgh.

Eventually she returned to Edinburgh and set up a practice in Manor Place. Sophia also lectured in midwifery for the extra-mural department of the university and founded the Edinburgh School of Medicine for Women. Sadly, her authoritarian manner led to clashes with her students and even a case in the Court of Session. One student, Elsie Ingles, with the aid of her father's money, formed the rival Scottish Association for Medical Education for Women. Gradually Sophia Jex-Blake lost her students and the Edinburgh school closed. In 1898 she retired to Sussex.

Education: School Boards

The Education Act (Scotland) 1873 placed the city's schools into the hands of elected school boards. Leith and Portobello had their own boards, so too did the smaller parishes like Colinton, Currie, Duddingston and Corstorphine. Women who possessed the right property qualifications could not only vote for members but were able to stand themselves and three women sat on Edinburgh's first school board. By August 1876 they had some eighteen schools, as well as the High School, providing education for 7,600 children. The Heriot's outdoor schools continued to operate under the trust. Fees were charged in the board's schools while the outdoor schools were free.

Attendance rates were the biggest problem facing school boards in these early years. Money from the government depended on the number of pupils in attendance (not on the roll) at each school. One committee interviewed parents who failed to send their children to school and sometimes it was necessary to take them to court. In most cases, poverty (lack of clothing and funds for fees) were the main problems. One of the worst cases was a girl who worked for John Morrison, a lodging-house keeper in the High Street. Her parents were dead and Morrison claimed they owed him money. It was said, 'She was kept in such a dirty condition that no teacher could allow her to mix with other children.' He told the board they could 'go to the d ...' and stormed out. The case was referred to the sheriff. Morrison returned later and agreed to place her in the custody of Mr Robertson, the head teacher of North Canongate School, until either relations or interested ladies could be found to take her.

The board and Heriot's schools were not the only educational establishments in the city. The Merchant Company ran its own schools. The industrial schools remained independent of the board but they were now taking only the most poorly behaved children. In 1877 the United Industrial School on Blackfriars Street, admitted thirty children; twenty-seven of these were sent to them by the courts. The city still possessed a good number of small private schools.

The 1874 General Election

At the beginning of 1874 Gladstone called a snap election which rebounded on the Liberals when Disraeli and his Conservatives were returned with a comfortable majority. In the city, the Liberals continued to dominate the polls. The two sitting members, Duncan McLaren and Thomas Miller, were joined by the lord provost, James Cowan, while J.H.A. MacDonald, a Conservative, was the fourth candidate. Duncan McLaren easily topped the poll, followed by the lord provost who immediately resigned his position on the city council. James Falshaw was chosen to be the new lord provost. He was a Yorkshireman, a Methodist and the first Englishman to hold the office.

The Conservatives held the county, despite a spirited challenge from the Liberal candidate, Lord James Hay. In the Leith Burghs, a local man, Donald Macgregor, defeated the sitting member, Robert Macfie. Both men were Liberals.

Fires and the Edinburgh Fire Brigade

On 16 January 1874 a fire broke out at Tods' Flour Mills in Leith. Most of the premises were destroyed, although they were able to save some of the stock. Four years later the City Paper Mill, situated in the Old Granaries of the Dean Village, caught fire. They had only been in operation for thirteen months, producing 20 tons of grey paper and mill board. Investigations later led the authorities to suspect arson.

A fire in Brandon Street at the properties of Mr Murray and Mrs Marr brought unwelcome criticism of the brigade as well as a police investigation. The fire was quickly extinguished, but Mr Murray accused them of theft when brandy, wine and jewellery could not be accounted for. Although seven men were temporarily suspended, the firemen denied any wrongdoing. However, Mr Williams, the firemaster, was dismissed as he had only turned up after his men had put out the fire.

Any doubts about Edinburgh's Fire Brigade must have been quelled by the bravery and persistence shown by them at the Greenside disaster on 19 December 1877. A fire broke out in the laundry of Milne's Commercial Hotel, 24 Greenside Street (part of Leith Street). This five-storey (at the front) building contained three shops on the ground floor. At the back, there were three sunken floors which were divided into flats. The poor quality of the timber supports, further weakened by the fire, led to one of the upper storeys collapsing, bringing down another five floors.

Mr Wilkins, the new firemaster, and his men dug into the ruins to try to rescue the families trapped under the rubble. They worked all through the night supervised by Mr Fraser, the burgh engineer. Dr Littlejohn remained to give medical assistance. Among the six dead were Mary Topping, her daughter Mary and her son Andrew, who was only 12 months old. Robert and Harriet Topping were rescued by the firemen. The last man out was Walter Purves, who had survived under the ruins for twelve hours.

Paper Making

The upper Water of Leith Valley from Slateford to Balerno was dominated by the paper mills. Paper tends to bring an image of wood pulp, but certainly the two largest mills, Kinleith and Balerno Bank, used esparto grass imported through Leith from North Africa.

Balerno Bank and Townhead Mills (both using the same mill lade in Balerno) opened in the first decade of the nineteenth century. Townhead was taken over by the owners of Balerno Bank and a small papermill downstream, close by Malleny House, was turned into a sawmill. The curiously named Balerno Mill (it is actually in Currie) began life as a papermill before becoming a glueworks. In the nineteenth century, first George Lang and then J. & W. Durham used it again for the manufacture of paper. Henry Bruce's Kinleith Mill was the largest on the Water of Leith.

The industry, for its manufacturing processes, required large quantities of clean water gathered from streams flowing off the Pentland Hills. The mill owners encouraged the Caledonian Railway Company to build the Balerno Branch Line and Kinleith had its own sidings while Currie and Balerno had goods yards (you can still see the old goods shed at Currie). Balerno's yard is now occupied by its high school.

Chemicals used in the manufacturing process, particularly lime, ended up polluting the Water of Leith. Towards the end of the century, the Water of Leith Purification Scheme met with resistance from the papermakers who were reluctant to contribute their share to this enterprise. They even commissioned their own report claiming their chemicals neutralised the sewage. The scheme went ahead anyway and a large pipe was laid from Balerno to the sea, collecting the waste produced by businesses and homes along the river.

Fire was always a danger. In 1870 Balerno Papermill was damaged by fire. Eight years later, the newly opened City Papermill in the Dean Village suffered from a severe fire, causing damage totalling £15,000. This mill only produced 'grey paper' and cardboard. Bonnington Mill had a fire in 1887, when two girls had to jump from the second storey to escape the flames.

Fortunately there were no fatalities, although Maggie Dowie was injured in the fall.

As with many industries in Victorian times, work was hard and the hours long. During the century, Parliament passed various Factory and Mines' Acts forcing the employers to reduce the hours worked, particularly by women and children. Workers (women and young people) in the paper industry appear to have been omitted from the 1850 Factory Act, which limited a day's work to ten and a half hours with only seven and a half on Saturday. The actual shift was still twelve hours, but one and a half hours was given for a meal break. Girl pickers aged 10–13, who removed unsuitable material from the vats, began their work at 6 p.m. and worked through until 6 a.m. They were given only ten minutes' break around midnight. For this they received 6d per night.

The Economic Depression

From 1876 the whole country suffered from an economic decline, culminating in 1878 with the collapse of the Glasgow City Bank. The debt of over £6 million included £400,000 of Western Union Railway stock which was found to be worthless. Six directors and two senior staff were arrested. On Saturday, 9 November a meeting in the music hall set up a fund to help those who had lost money in the collapse of the bank. By the middle of the month it had raised £64,000.

Trade had also suffered, leading to a sharp decline in the revenue of Leith Docks.

The Leith Libel

The *Leith Herald* published an article in their column called 'What Leith Folk are Saying', which ended with the newspaper and its editor, Mr Ebenezer Drummond, being brought before the court. This was not surprising when one considers the accusations made:

> That the grass widow near the Shore is on the lookout for another partner.
> That the two young sprats prove a great annoyance when they call her 'ma'.
> That the Sunday steamer is the best place for meeting suitable swains.
> That the tall lady who divorced her husband thinks of divorcing her sons.

May Letham, a tobacconist on the Shore and a widow with two sons, sued Ebenezer Drummond. She claimed to have lost £300 in takings over the year, as people were frightened to enter the shop for fear of appearing in the *Leith Herald*.

In court the editor pleaded ignorance. He did not know Mrs Letham; he did not know who wrote the article nor who had given permission for it to be published. Not surprisingly, the court refused to accept this and Drummond was fined £50, a very large sum for those times.

The General Election, 1880

In 1880, Edinburgh again returned its two Liberal members, Duncan McLaren and James Cowan, with a massive majority over the Conservative candidate:

D. McLaren	17,807
J. Cowan	17,301
J. MacDonald	5,651

The member for Leith Burghs, Andrew Grant, faced no opposition.

The election is best remembered for Gladstone's campaign in Midlothian. He arrived in Edinburgh towards the end of March as the guest of Lord Rosebery. On Thursday, 18 March, he spoke in Corstorphine and then Ratho, followed by speeches the next day in Davidson's Mains and Dalkeith. Saturday afternoon brought him to Juniper Green and Balerno, where he spoke in the United Presbyterian Chapel. In the evening he continued his campaign in Mid-Calder. It was unusual at this time for political leaders of Gladstone's calibre to take such an active and demanding part in an election. Gladstone secured the seat, but only by 211 votes.

Edinburgh Town Council and Local Elections

Local elections were not so eagerly fought. In fact, it was becoming difficult to find men who had time to give to council business. Meetings were held in the afternoon (during working hours) which prevented many people from putting their names forward as prospective councillors. The increase in the franchise therefore did not lead to stimulating local politics. In November 1876 (all local elections were held in November at this time), only three of the city's fourteen wards were contested. Two years later, there was not a single contest in the city and only two in Leith.

National political allegiances did not dominate local councils as they do today. Most Edinburgh councillors were Liberals, but that party was composed of a wide spread of political views. In the 1880s the Irish Home Rule question began to dominate national politics and divide the Liberals. In 1886, Gladstone

introduced a Home Rule Bill but it was defeated when ninety-three Liberals joined the opposition. Charles Parnell, the leader of the Irish Party, used his voting strength in the House of Commons to push for an Irish Parliament in Dublin. In April 1889, Bailie Walcot proposed that the council should offer Parnell the Freedom of the City. Bailie Turnbull led the opposition, concerned about Parnell's possible links with terrorism and his obstruction of Scottish legislation. Walcot, a leading member of the city's Liberal Party, secured a majority of twenty-four to twelve. Lord Provost Boyd voted with the minority.

Accusations were made at the time, and in the months following, that this was a political move. The Conservatives organised a plebiscite, sending out 42,971 postcards. Although they gained a massive vote against Parnell little notice was taken of the result. Lord Provost Boyd and Councillor Roberts, the senior bailie, refused to take part in the ceremony, leaving Bailie Walcot to present the Freedom of the City to Parnell in July.

William McEwan

William McEwan was the son of small shipmaster from Alloa. At the age of 30, William came to Edinburgh to work for Messrs Jeffrey who were brewers based in the Grassmarket. He remained with the company for only five years before setting up his own brewery in Fountainbridge. The business expanded rapidly and began to export to India and Australia, making William McEwan a very wealthy man.

The Liberal Party split over Irish Home Rule brought William McEwan into Edinburgh politics. The Edinburgh Central MP, John Wilson, opposed Gladstone's Home Rule policy. The Liberal Committee began to search for a man to stand against Wilson. McEwan offered to finance the campaign but when no candidate came forward McEwan himself stood for election to the constituency. In 1892 he was returned as Member for Edinburgh Central. William McEwan never sought honours, although he became a Freeman of the City and a Privy Councillor. Some of his money went to supporting the Working Man's Club and Institute. He paid the fees of many young apprentices attending the Heriot Watt College. His company was a regular supporter of the Royal Infirmary. The University of Edinburgh were the recipients of his largest donation when McEwan gave the sum of £115,000 for the building of a hall for the university which bears his name.

William McEwan died in London in April 1913. He was buried in Bookham, Surrey and a memorial service was held in Old Greyfriars.

The Tramways

The 1871 Edinburgh Tramways Act gave the company the right to lay lines on selected routes in Edinburgh and Leith. The trams that ran on these lines were still pulled by horses. A tramway driven by a moving underground cable was built, linking Golden Acre with the top of the Mound. The cable car travelled at 6mph and could carry sixty passengers.

Crime in the City

The crime figures for 1880 showed 7,351 persons had been arrested, although some may have appeared more than once in this list. Only 225 were described as 'well-educated', while 1,267 (one in six) were totally illiterate. In September of that year, three men assaulted John Sweeny in the Grassmarket on a Sunday morning. Sweeny was a Catholic who played for Hearts and the motive appears to have been sectarian.

To handle all this crime, the city had a force of 360 officers. There were only three lieutenants, three inspectors and twenty-six sergeants. Leith had its own police force, while Portobello and the rural districts surrounding Edinburgh were the responsibility of the county.

William Chambers

William Chambers, who came from Peebles, was born in the year 1800. He was an apprentice with John Sutherland, an Edinburgh bookseller, before opening his own shop, an open-air stall in Leith Walk. He was joined in Edinburgh by his brother, Robert, and they founded W & R Chambers Publishers. Robert had already produced his *Traditions of Edinburgh*. In February 1832 the first edition of the *Chambers' Edinburgh Journal* sold over 30,000 copies. This weekly paper, costing one and a half pence, had an educational as well as entertaining content. The company continued to grow, producing the *Chambers' Encyclopaedia* in the 1860s. Robert died in 1871 and was succeeded in the business by his son.

William Chambers was chosen as lord provost in 1865, an important time for the development of the city with the Littlejohn Report and the Improvement Act. Chambers visited the closes of the Old Town, reporting, 'In the ground floors the dwellings are dark, even at noon, and the inhabitants may literally be said to be living in the "Valley of the Shadow of Death"'. Streets were widened and new ones cut through old properties, and George IV Bridge was linked to the South Bridge by Chambers Street, named after the lord provost. Although he was elected again by the council as lord provost in 1868, he resigned the following year.

Chambers was created a baronet and the university awarded him an honorary LLD (Doctor of Law): he was always known afterwards as Dr Chambers. Much of his time in retirement was spent on the restoration of St Giles. He was determined to return the building to its pre-Reformation splendour by removing the partitions and forming a single church. It is estimated that he spent between £20,000–30,000 of his own fortune on this project. William Chambers died in 1883, just before the opening of the newly restored St Giles.

Destitute Children

Despite the work of the industrial or ragged schools, child poverty remained a serious issue throughout the nineteenth century in the city. Flora Stevenson told the school board of an encounter with a young child begging in the street. She asked the girl if she would like to go to school. 'No, mam,' came the reply. 'I'm not yet five.' In March 1883 the Destitute Children's Fund was set up with William Skene and Flora Stevenson as joint treasurers. The *Edinburgh Courant* took an interest in the scheme, even referring to it as the '*Courant* Fund'. By May of that year over £100 had been received in gifts. They were now able to give out 300 meals daily, although, 'Strictly speaking, the number 300 represented the number of separate meals rather than the number of children as many of them divided their breakfasts or dinners with their brothers or sisters who had not received tickets'.

By 1885 they had raised over £1,140 and two shelters had been set up in the Cowgatehead and in Carrubbers Close. In the latter, they provided Sunday lunch for over 300 children, 'a large portion bare headed, bare footed and with ragged clothes'. At the beginning of February, James Cowan, formerly lord provost and MP, told the children how he had earned his first sixpence. He had had to give evidence before the Sheriff of Selkirk concerning the death of a lad injured by a horse. Young Cowan was 'in such a state of terror he could barely speak but the pleasant look and kind conversation of the sheriff soon put him at his ease'. The sheriff who gave him sixpence was none other than Sir Walter Scott.

Mr Robertson, headmaster of New Street School in the Canongate, reported that some children 'fell off their seats from sheer hunger' having had no breakfast and some not even supper the night before. It is no wonder that the Edinburgh School Board was concerned about the wellbeing of their children. The Edinburgh and Leith Children's Refuge opened in 1884 in Stockbridge. Miss Stirling was the guiding light, rehoming fifty-three children in Nova Scotia.

The General Election, 1885

Electoral reform had led to changes in constituency representation. Gone were the multi-represented constituencies like Edinburgh with its two members. The city now had four members and four constituencies – North-West, Central, North-East and South. The county (Midlothian) electoral role was increased. Liberton, which had 288 electors, now had 792. In Cramond the electorate rose from 144 to 526.

Despite these changes, the political dominance of the Liberal Party in Scotland continued. A correspondent in the *Edinburgh Courant* put the position clearly: 'It is the misfortune of a Scottish Conservative to find his political faith shared by such a small minority that his mission is very much in a par with Christian missions to the Hindus'. He went on to explain:

> Toryism in Scotland is unfortunately associated in the minds of the common people with rank, privilege and landlordism, and the mistakes of former generations, from Pitt to Peel, have never been forgotten, but have been handed on as a tradition in Scottish politics.

In November, the Liberals' preferred candidates (sometimes more than one Liberal stood) secured the new seats, with Gladstone gaining a huge majority of 4,636 in Midlothian. The constituency consisted of many of the present suburbs like Davidson's Mains, Corstorphine, Balerno, Colinton and Duddingston. Sadly, Sir George Harrison, the former lord provost and newly elected Member for Edinburgh South, died suddenly in December of that year.

The International Industrial Exhibition, 1886

The Exhibition was opened by Prince Albert Victor on 6 May 1886 and ran until the end of October. The site, in the West Meadows, was divided into over thirty separate courtyards. The centrepiece was the Grand Hall with its glass dome surmounted by a statue of Fame with her trumpet (unfortunately, this broke off and fell through the roof, leading to a temporary closure of the hall). Over 2.7 million people visited the Exhibition during the six months it was open.

Machinery, from locomotives to manufacturing engines, went on display. The textile industry of Scotland was also well represented. Coats of Paisley produced a model of Paisley Abbey with over 6,000 spools of cotton with greenish stone-coloured thread wrapped round card to make the roof. Not to be outdone, Clark & Co. of Anchor Mills, Paisley, brought 25,000 spools which they made into two 18ft-high pyramids. Mr Thomas of Rose Park, Trinity, exhibited the work of the weavers and knitters of Harris, and girls from Shetland and Fair Isle, wearing local costume, demonstrated their knitting skills.

One of the star attractions was a working electric railway. The two carriages, one open and the other covered, came from London. Three girls of the Flower Girls' Mission (London) made muslin flowers watched by many interested visitors.

Special events and competitions were put on each Saturday. In October, they even had manned balloon races. One balloon actually travelled across the Forth and landed in Milnathort, Kinross. There was a Highland Games which included tug of war, hammer throwing and a three-legged race.

On the final Saturday, the crowds were treated to a brass band competition which nearly degenerated into a farce. The judges scored the bands from a list of numbers which proved to be incorrect. Hawich, who had not competed, were placed fourth. Eventually, after some boos from the audience, the correct results appeared giving victory to the Bess o' the Barn Band from Lancashire.

The ladies had their own industrial court with examples of embroidery and lace making. A large artisans' display consisted of work from 400 exhibitors. This included model ships and buildings as well as glass and cutlery from Sheffield.

Glasgow then hosted an exhibition in 1888, before another was held two years later at Meggetland. The organisers were dependent on the railways bringing visitors from the city centre.

Professor Sir Henry Duncan Littlejohn MD

Henry Littlejohn was born in 1826. His father, Thomas Littlejohn, was a wealthy master baker in Leith Street. Henry studied medicine at Edinburgh University before going on to study surgery in Vienna, Berlin and at the Sorbonne, Paris. He returned to the city and set up in private practice as well as assisting in post-mortems at the Royal Infirmary.

The fear of another outbreak of cholera (1832 and 1848 had seen epidemics in the city) and the deaths of thirty-five people in a collapsing tenement spurred the town council to appoint a Medical Officer for Health. In 1862, Dr Littlejohn took the post on a part-time basis. His 'Report on the Sanitary Condition of the City of Edinburgh' in 1867 led directly to the council asking Parliament to pass the Edinburgh City Improvement Act. At this time, the mortality rate for the city stood at 3.4 per cent.

The authorities needed to prepare for the outbreaks of infectious diseases, especially when the infirmary informed the council they would be unwilling to take any cholera patients, and in 1870 the old Canongate Poorhouse became the city's fever hospital. Fifteen years later, the Old Infirmary was turned into a second hospital.

Dr Littlejohn pressed for the compulsory reporting of infectious diseases but Edinburgh doctors resisted this necessary reform. Eventually the Edinburgh and Municipal Police Act of 1879 put it into law. Leith had resisted this change (doctors received 2/6d per report) but in January 1893 had introduced this for smallpox.

Dr Littlejohn also acted as police surgeon. He remained on duty as the fire brigade dug out the victims of the Greenside fire in 1878. He was responsible for the post-mortems carried out during his period in office. The government appointed him to the Board of Supervision in 1873 in a part-time capacity (the board supervised medical health problems in Scotland). In 1897, at the age of 78, he was appointed to the chair of forensic medicine.

Sir Henry Littlejohn finally retired in 1908. He spent his final years in Arrochar, where he died on 30 September 1914.

Jessie King, the Stockbridge Baby Farmer

Large numbers of young women were employed in domestic service. They were provided with room and board, but they had to remain single and any illegitimate children born to these household servants had to be found homes. Some women, known as 'baby farmers', would adopt them for a pittance. With their mothers unable to keep them, the babies would be neglected and probably die. In 1881, Barbara McIntosh of Portobello was prosecuted over the deaths of several children in her care. She was sentenced to fifteen months in prison.

Jessie King (real name Kean) was born in Glasgow in 1861. Her mother died when she was 18 months old. She spent some time at the Magdalene Asylum in Edinburgh, where she learnt laundry skills. Jessie appears to have moved back to the west but eventually returned to the city where she found work at Causewayside Laundry. In her lodging house, she became attached to a labourer named Thomas Pearson, but she had to move out when the women he was living with objected to the relationship. Jessie took new lodgings in Sciennes where Pearson continued to visit her in the guise of an older brother.

Pearson and King eventually set up home together, firstly in Anne's Court, Canonmills, and later in Cheyne Street, Stockbridge. Their daughter, Grace Pearson, was born in May 1887. The child was last seen in September of that year. No body was ever found. In October of the next year, some boys found the body of a young child in Cheyne Street. Two detectives, James Clark and David Simpson, on a tip-off from a Mr and Mrs Banks, searched Jessie King's home and discovered a piece of cloth similar to that found on the baby.

Jessie King was arrested on 5 November 1888 but she refused to make a statement. The following day, most unwisely as events turned out, she confessed to causing the deaths of Alexander Gunn (aged 12 months) and Violet Thomlinson (aged 6 weeks) but she refused to say anything about Walter Campbell (aged 5 months). Jessie had received £3 to adopt Alexander and £2 for Violet. She had been unable to support the babies.

The jury took six minutes to come to a unanimous verdict and Jessie King was condemned to death. She made three attempts to kill herself in twenty-four hours and a suicide watch was set up. Many people were horrified by the sentence, but despite a petition and an appeal to the Secretary of State for Scotland, the sentence remained. The authorities brought Mr Berry from Bradford to carry out the execution. His verdict: 'Well you don't think yon was satisfactory. In all my life I tell you truly I never saw a woman meet her death so bravely. Such bravery I never met in my life before.'

Cleaning up the Water of Leith

If improvements were to be made in the quality of water in the river it would require a joint effort by the county and city councils. Currie, Colinton and Corstorphine parishes all contributed household sewerage, although the major problems came from the mills. Professor Crum-Brown and Mr Robert Reid, a civil engineer, recommended the construction of a pipe running from Balerno to the sea with branches to take sewerage from Craiglockhart, Corstorphine, Murrayfield and Longstone. The papermakers countered the Crum-Brown/Reid Report with one of their own. Their report claimed that the chemicals discharged from the mills neutralised the sewage, but this failed to gain acceptance with the authorities.

It was later decided to raise the levels of the compensation reservoirs at Threipmuir and Harperrig. The work was eventually completed in autumn 1892 at a cost of £200,000. Rises in the cost of materials and modifications (washing tanks for skinners, etc.) had led to a considerable overrun.

The Schools' Strike, October 1889

No, not the teachers, but some of the pupils! It appears to have begun in North Merchiston School when some boys called a 'strike'. They may have been imitating the seamen who were in dispute with their employers at this time. According to the *Evening News*, 'Dalry School was this morning "stormed" by about 50 schoolboys strengthened by about the same number of message boys and "casuals"'. The headmaster, who confronted the boys, received their demands:

1 Shorter school hours.
2 No more homework.
3 Free education for all.

Others apparently cried, 'Hurrah for the dockers!' and 'Let the ladies out!' Some head teachers, like Mr Bell of North Canongate who had some of the roughest youths in the city, took precautions against further trouble. A group of boys from Fort and Bonnington Road schools marched to the centre of Leith but received no support.

This appears to have been a national problem with outbreaks in other parts of Scotland. The next day, many parents at North Merchiston escorted their boys to the school. After just two days of disruption the schools returned to normal.

County Councils

The establishment of county councils in Scotland began with an Act of Parliament in 1889. Midlothian County Council took power over the area surrounding Edinburgh and Leith. The new authority was elected by the ratepayers. It controlled many of the districts like Granton, Cramond, Corstorphine, Colinton, Currie and Liberton, which are suburbs of the city today. Mr Dundas of Arniston was chosen as its first convenor.

The General Election, 1895

The Liberals remained split over Irish Home Rule, leading to the Unionist Liberals who opposed this to stand against the official Liberal candidates. In the country as a whole, the Conservatives and their Liberal Unionist allies won a huge majority (152). Surprisingly, at a time of such intense rivalry only two of the city's four seats were contested. Lewis McIver (Unionist) in the West and William McEwan (Liberal) in Central were returned unopposed. The remaining two seats were won by Mr Wallace, a Liberal, and Mr Cox, a Unionist. The Liberals hung on to Leith Burghs and Midlothian, although Gladstone did not stand again.

The Gilmerton Play

Possibly as early as 1500, Gilmerton had its play, based on the story of Robin Hood. The riotous behaviour connected with Edinburgh's Robin Hood Play had led to the government of Mary, Queen of Scots banning the event. However, in Gilmerton the tradition continued until it fell foul of the government of James VI.

The play was resurrected in a simpler format by the Gilmerton Senior Friendly Society in 1787. The society continued to organise the event for the next 100 years. Prior to the Disruption, Dr Begg was Minister of Liberton and he objected to some of the activities connected with the play. This led to changes, although the Laird of Moredun advised him to draw down the manse blinds instead.

The Gilmerton Junior Friendly Society picked up the mantle when the Senior Society dissolved itself. The procession began at 9 a.m. and proceeded to collect the flag and banner bearers from their homes. At midday the society met in their hall while the people held a dance in the streets. The procession resumed after the meeting. The day ended with dinner in the hall, followed by an auction for the rights to carry the flags in next year's procession.

The Dalry Reformatory

Trouble had been brewing for some time at the Reformatory for Girls in Dalry. Prior to 1896, two girls had absconded but were soon returned to the Reformatory. The lady in charge had resigned her post because of the growing indiscipline.

In June, six girls ran away from the Reformatory and, after their recapture, were taken to court. Mary Ann McGonnigal and Beautrix Day, who had also been involved in the previous escape, were sentenced to forty days in prison. Maria Burgess and Jemima Hamilton Findlay, who were found in the company of a man on Calton Hill, received fourteen days. The other two, Catherine Coupe and Jane Ann Aitken, who remained out all night, were each given ten days in prison. The judge intended to set an example and deplored the leniency that had been shown the previous year.

The Edinburgh Underground

At the end of 1889 the Caledonian Railway Company put forward a proposal to build an underground line linking their Prince's Street Station with the Port of Leith. They planned to run their line beneath the south side of Prince's Street to a station at the top of Leith Street. Soon objectors began to hold meetings while the company put down boreholes.

The Lord Provost's Committee commissioned Sir John Fowler and Benjamin Baker to report on the Caledonian's plans. They raised concerns about damage to property and the difficulties of ventilation. It was claimed at the same time that the burgh engineer, John Cooper, had given a favourable report to the committee. The controversy raged on, but a large majority of the city council led by Lord Provost Boyd remained opposed to the scheme. Supporters were mystified as to why the council should turn its back on such an amenity.

The main opponent to the Caledonian's plans was the North British Railway Company. They had no intention of allowing their rivals from the west of Scotland into the east of Edinburgh. A select committee of the House of Commons removed the proposed underground from the bill. One observer, present at these meetings, thought that the opposition of the city council was representative of the people of Edinburgh.

Ice Cream Shops

The Medical Officer of Health, Sir Henry Littlejohn, placed a report on ice cream shops before the Public Health Committee. There were now seventy-eight such shops within the boundaries of the city (including twenty-eight in the New Town and forty-five in the Old Town). Twenty-three of these shops had no toilets. The storage of ice was generally unsatisfactory. The chief constable had complained, 'The great majority of the keepers are Italians and I learn that many of them are persons of very low character who had to leave their own country for their country's good'. Some of these shops remained open until the early hours of the morning encouraging children to stay up very late. However, nothing was found to criticise the quality of the ice cream, and in Portobello, an important summer holiday resort, all four shops were deemed satisfactory.

In September 1900, the council decreed that all shops selling ice cream must be licensed. This Act came into force at the beginning of November and the first prosecutions came before the court in January 1901. Nicola Ferri was charged with selling two 1d ice creams at 106 Lauriston Place without a licence. Her counsel successfully argued that although the law came into force on 1 November 1900, licences were not due to be issued until the following May. The case was dismissed and the other prosecution, against Francesco Rossi of 158 High Street, also fell.

Prostitution and Drunkenness

A crackdown in the early 1880s led many prostitutes to cross the border into Leith. Falshaw, Colston, Buchanan and Crow Streets comprised 243 houses, of which forty-eight were known to the police as 'irregular'. They were also keeping a watch on another seventeen properties in the district. Property fell in value, with sixty-six houses empty as the reputation of the area scared off potential tenants.

By 1896 the Edinburgh authorities could boast, 'At one time Todrick's Wynd, Hynford Close and Foulis Close in the High Street and Rose Street, Clyde Street and Street Terrace were simply nests of houses containing such women. They are now practically cleared out.' They claimed that the number of these 'unfortunate' women had been reduced to a quarter of what it had been. The police now knew of about 300 women.

However, as we all know, pride goes before a fall. When, in 1899, the Reverend Dr Isitt visited the city he saw an 'alarming amount of soliciting which goes on apparently unchecked'. He went on to complain, 'There are few places where open soliciting is more rife than in that street' (*Evening News*, April 1899). Swearing and drunken behaviour on this particular street had shocked him. The street in question was not one of the closes of the Old Town but the pride of the city – Prince's Street.

On the question of drink, in the same article Mr Lewis, a former bailie, wrote, 'Personally I regard the policy which certain magistrates have pursued of closing small public houses and underground cellars and substituting enormous gin palaces with vastly increased capacity to blame for the problem'. There was a strong temperance movement in Edinburgh and the country as a whole. Carrubber's Close Mission on High Street was an important meeting place for them. The city also had several temperance hotels where drink was forbidden.

Crime figures for the last quarter of 1884 reveal 2,473 convictions, of which 1,019 were for drunk and disorderly behaviour, while another 626 were just for drunkenness.

Theatre, Music Halls and the Circus

Cooke's Circus had opened during 1835 in Lothian Road before moving to nearby Grindly Street. It had to close in February 1883 because the site had been acquired by the new Lyceum Theatre. They eventually reopened in 1886 in East Fountainbridge. The programme consisted of mainly 'circus' events such as acrobats, clowns and the popular equestrian displays. Music hall acts also appeared there and in the 'Christmas season' a pantomime was added to the list of events.

H.E. Moss took over the Theatre of Varieties, as well as some adjoining property in 1877. Fifteen years later, he moved to a new site in Nicholson Street. This new Empire Palace Theatre had a capacity of 2,500. The *Evening News* reporter described it, 'An Indian designed domed ceiling and richly decorated copper arches are features of the entrance hall'. At the top of the marble staircase, 'a grotto is formed with water flowing over rocks into a large basin. An exceedingly pretty effect is given by palms and ferns and a ceiling painted to represent the sky with birds and fairy electric lights.' The programme for Monday, 23 November 1896 (and the following days) included Gus Elen (comedian and singer), Austin Rudd (vocal comedian), Victoria Daggmar (gymnast), Mlle Angeline (juggler), as well as a dance troupe. Their pantomime for that year was not well received by the critic of the *Evening News*, who described it as 'deadly dull ... "Santa Claus" is not a piece which will appeal to the adult male mind but it may be remarked that the ladies of the audience, adult and otherwise, were loud in its praise'. The famous music hall star Marie Lloyd appeared at the Empire Palace in 1900.

The Lyceum Theatre was more upmarket in these years and opera and the plays of William Shakespeare appeared regularly on its programme. In September 1883, Sir Henry Irvine and Miss Ellan Terry starred in *Much Ado About Nothing*. They returned in 1896 for *The Merchant of Venice*. The Lyceum did not produce pantomimes.

The Theatre Royal had a long history in Edinburgh, beginning with the Canongate Theatre in the middle of the eighteenth century. Moving north with the development of the New Town, they built their theatre in Shakespeare Square. The construction of the Post Office led them to a new site at the top of Broughton Street (standing between Leith Street and what is now the Catholic cathedral). Despite two disastrous fires, the shows went on. A variety of plays involving drama, music, comedy and dance were produce by the Theatre Royal. The famous Sarah Bernhardt performed here in July 1881 and pantomimes were also put on during the season.

Retail

Thousands of people in both Edinburgh and Leith were employed in retail. The late nineteenth century saw the growth of big shops able to offer more than one speciality range. Prices also had to be more competitive. In some cases, as with Jenners, many of the staff lived on the premises. Not all employees were treated well, but the case of one 36-year-old widow, who was caned by the manageress for removing property from the 'waste box', reflected a disturbing attitude towards staff.

The bigger stores represented a serious threat to the small private businesses which lacked the financial resources to compete. The largest of these was the Co-operative. As early as 1896 the Traders' Defence Association of Scotland Against the Co-operative Movement led resistance to the growing power of the Co-op. At a meeting in the music hall it was claimed, 'Third class work and third class wages was the cry of co-operation'. By 1905, St Cuthbert's Co-operative Association owned many shops in the city and its suburbs; stores had opened in Morningside, Corstorphine, Gorgie and Gilmerton selling a wide variety of goods.

The Tramways

'The Pilrig Muddle'

On 9 December 1893, the Edinburgh Corporation took up their right to purchase the portion of the tramway which ran through the city. This they then leased to Dick, Kerr & Co. The old Edinburgh Tramway Company continued to operate the lines in Leith and Portobello.

On the busiest route up Leith Walk it was all change at Pilrig. Treasurer Waddie of Leith blamed Edinburgh for the 'Pilrig Muddle': passengers had to change at Pilrig from the electric trams of Leith to the cable cars of Edinburgh. Despite attempts at arbitration the public were left to suffer this disruption to their commuting and travel.

Possibly to exploit this situation, the North British Railway Company opened a large station, Leith Central, at the foot of Leith Walk offering a service to Waverley and nowhere else. Thus, in 1903 Leith had five stations (Leith Central, North Leith, Junction Bridge, Leith North and South Leith – this last was closed in 1905). Yet from none of these stations could you board a train which would take you beyond the Edinburgh city boundaries.

The Cable Tramway

In June 1895, the town council decided to cable 27 miles of their tramway. Pressure from councillors led to the proposals being increased by another 10½ miles. This inevitably caused delays, so that the cabling contracts were not finally signed until 1898. Problems then arose with strikes by the engineers and the joiners, and delays in acquiring material for the cabling and paving adding to an already difficult situation.

Opposition to the 'Pilrig Muddle' was expressed at an angry meeting of shopkeepers in Earl Grey Street. The cabling at Tollcross was proving to be a considerable problem for the contractors. Shoppers were now avoiding the area. Mr David Scott, a hosier, complained, 'No businesslike council would have gone into such a scheme as cabling the tramways in such a careless and impotent way'. The first test run from Shrubhill (Leith Walk) to Tollcross ran in October 1899.

Meanwhile, the council in Leith planned to go their own way. One member of the council gave a stark assessment of the situation: 'Edinburgh will never forsake the antiquated system of cable haulage until the present Town Council of Edinburgh were in heaven'. In 1903 Leith purchased their tramway system for £60,000 and set about converting it to run electrically powered trams.

In July 1907, the town council decided by a single vote to shelve the plans to run a line along East Claremont Street. The *Evening News* commented, 'Yet another project of the sorely buffeted Tramway Committee went overboard.' In the following month, Norman Thompson, an electrical engineering consultant based in North Bridge Street, had 'come to the conclusion that despite the heavy outlay on the existing tramway it was a commercially sound proposition to convert the whole undertaking at once to electrical working'. His report highlighted the delays caused when switching lines and the general unreliability of the cable system.

In April 1909, Mr J. Walker Smith, the burgh engineer, in a report to the Tramway Committee, recommended the trolleybus system, with buses to be employed on longer routes. Finally, in February 1914, the council agreed to buy six buses for use on the south side of the city. Unfortunately, three of them were compulsorily purchased by the War Department at a loss to the Corporation of £634.

Sixteen

THE OLD TOWN

The Eighteenth Century

At this time, Edinburgh was still a walled city. Entering through the West Port brought the visitor into the Grassmarket. Here, at the eastern end, a winding road called the Bow climbed to the Lawnmarket. This wide space acted as a market, mainly for those who brought goods from their farms who then paid their dues at the Butter Tron, which stood at the top of this market place. The street contained some ancient tenements; Gladstone's Land was already over 100 years old by this time.

Leaving the Lawnmarket, the upper part of the High Street was blocked by a group of buildings known as the Luckenbooths. The Old Tolbooth, which was now used as a prison, formed their western end. Its ground floor was leased for shops. Edward Penman and Patrick Turnbull, both goldsmiths, had premises here. Turnbull even leased space out to Janet Chambers, who made grave clothes.

There were no street numbers given to the lands (tenements), so signs were placed above the shops. On the north side of this narrow way could be found the sign of the Golden Hart, followed by the Red Lion where John Thomson had a varied business. He purchased animal skins (rabbit, hare, otter and stoat) from chapmen and others up from the country. He also ran a foreign currency exchange. James Watson owned the shop next door while Alexander Peribaw could be found a little further down the street. They both sold stationery and no doubt did good business with Edinburgh's thriving legal profession.

In the main streets, the tradesmen occupied the ground floors where the public could easily access their premises. Above them lived the great variety of people who made up the Old Town. The middle storeys were occupied by the wealthier families, leaving the garrets for the labouring classes. The centre of the High Street contained the Town Cross and the Main Guard House. The latter was a dilapidated single-storey building which acted as the headquarters of the Town Guard. The Fruit Market could also be found close by. Business must have been good, for some of these stallholders were able to advertise in the *Edinburgh Evening Courant*. Such delicacies as oranges and lemons imported through Leith were extremely popular in these times. Characters like Janet Scott, Isobel Home and Lucky Law all plied their trade in the market. Lucky Law even claimed her fruit was 'as cheap as in Leith'.

On the south side, near to the Cross, James Reid sold a variety of items including cider, English ale and cutlery. Here, too, could be found the sign of the Cross Keys and presumably the tavern of that name where the Darien Riot of 1700 began. Further along the High Street you would find Niddrie's and Blackfriars Wynds.

In later years, the Old Town became overcrowded but at the beginning of the eighteenth century spacious flats were still available for sale or lease. In Niddrie's Wynd three properties were advertised, two with nine rooms, each containing a fireplace, and another with seven rooms. A fifth-storey flat in Blackfriars Wynd consisted of seven rooms, all with fireplaces, as well as a large garret.

The Old Town was not a static place and new buildings were being constructed all the time. A new stone land was raised in Niddrie's Wynd and others in Baxters Close and the Lawnmarket. In total, five new lands were advertised for lease or sale between the years 1705 and 1710.

On the north side of the High Street the line of shops and tenements continued uninterrupted, save for the narrow closes leading down to the Fleshmarket and the Nor' Loch. Charles Crocket sold tea and other goods from a shop in Timberland, opposite St Giles. Andrew Turnbull of Mary King's Close was a shipping agent, booking passages for people and cargo. George Mowbray and George Young both sold medicines from their shops near the Guard House. In Carrubber's Close there was a small manufactory producing lead shot.

The coffee houses, which sold more than coffee, were meeting places for the business people of the town. In a country where government (the Scottish Privy Council) censorship controlled the press, information could be circulated in the coffee houses. The Exchange Coffee House, run by Mr Brownlie, stood by the Cross, while John's Coffee House stood at the eastern entry to Parliament Square.

The Netherbow Port guarded the eastern end of the city and the entrance to the Canongate. This narrow gateway became a bottleneck for the growing number of wagons and carriages passing down the High Street, through the Canongate and along the Easter Road to Leith.

Joseph Taylor, who visited Edinburgh during the first years of the century, complained in his book *A Journey to Edenborough*, 'In the morning the scent was so offensive that we were forced to hold our noses and take care where we trod for fear of disobliging our shoes and to walk in the middle at night'. Hygiene does not appear to have been high on the priorities of the citizens of that time. 'The lodgings are as nasty as the streets,' continued Taylor, 'and washed so seldom that the dirt is thick enough to be par'd off with a shovel.' Things were so bad that he noted, ''Tis a common thing for a man or woman to go into a close at all times of day to ease nature'.

After the 1745 Rebellion, new fashionable houses were built on the south side. However, it was in the north that George Drummond and the town council planned a new town.

The Royal Exchange

The city, which contained many wealthy merchants, lacked a business centre. In 1753 James Ker, MP for the city, introduced a bill into Parliament giving the trustees for the new exchange the power to compulsory purchase some of the land north of the Town Cross. Much business was done, and continued to be done, in the coffee houses of Edinburgh and many an auction was carried out in John's or the Exchange, so the commissioners of the trust met in the Laigh Coffee House to select a jury to arbitrate over compensation for the property.

A large number of tenements, much of them in a poor state, were demolished. The top of Mary King's Close disappeared at this time. The first stone was laid in September 1753 with great ceremony, although much demolition work had still to be carried out. A large procession consisting of masons and the magistrates was escorted by the Town Guard to the site.

The Town Cross

On 13 March 1756, the Market Cross was taken down. This had been the scene of many public announcements and the Marquis of Montrose and Sir James Kirkcaldy of Grange had been executed at the Cross. As they began to remove the cross, a rope broke and the main pillar shattered into several pieces. The remains were later taken to Drum and placed in the care of Lord Somerville. The Netherbow Port met the same fate a few years later, as the town council sought to improve access to the Old Town.

The Bridges

A link between the Old Town and the developments to the north of the city was urgently required and a bridge was planned to cross the low ground (now occupied by Waverley Station). Building began in 1768, but before it was completed one of the arches collapsed. The delay would surely have affected the theatre which had relocated on the north side, in Shakespeare Square.

It was not until 1788 that a second bridge over the Cowgate opened up the Old Town to the suburbs in the south. The level of the High Street had to be raised, leading some residents, the owners of cellars, to object. The case went to court before an amicable settlement was eventually achieved. The new streets, North Bridge and South Bridge, or 'the Bridges', attracted considerable business, probably from the growing New Town.

Dirty and Dangerous

James Boswell recorded a walk up the High Street with Dr Johnson in 1773. The smell in the streets does not have appeared to have improved since Joseph Taylor's visit some seventy years earlier. Even St Giles Church was shamefully dirty. Johnson commented on seeing a board outside the infirmary which read 'Clean your feet'; 'There is no occasion for putting this at the doors of your churches?' he suggested.

Four years later, a correspondent of the *Caledonian Mercury* complained about the dirty streets: 'This surely might be remedied by a little attention: but that it is shameful neglected no one can entertain the smallest doubt.' A second critic later wrote, 'It would be a very difficult task to convince any stranger that Edinburgh is not, at this moment, among the dirtiest cities in Europe.' He suggested that the town council built public toilets in various parts of the Old Town.

In 1777 the town council brought in regulations to stop households throwing 'nuisances' into the street from their windows. Everything had to be laid out before 7 a.m. (8 a.m. in winter), common stairs were to be swept at least twice a week and anything found obstructing the streets could be confiscated. They even threatened their own employees with dismissal if they failed to report breaches of the Act.

The Luckenbooths

The lands which formed the Luckenbooths contained the premises of at least fifty-seven separate businesses. Many of these may also have been the homes of the principals. Thirty-six called themselves merchants so presumably they were members of the Merchant Company, from which the merchant representatives were chosen by the town council

By this time, the most easterly building, facing down the High Street, was known as Creech's Land. Here, William Creech, bookseller and publisher, carried on his business. Creech served on the town council and was later to be chosen as lord provost. He also owned a house in George Street.

Various trades operated from premises in the Luckenbooths. For the hair, there were two barbers and a combmaker. The manufacturing of clothing was represented by a haberdasher, a milliner and a shoemaker. Two engravers could be found here, as well as W & D Dowie, watchmakers and goldsmiths.

A few men of the law lived in the Luckenbooths, although James Ferguson was the only advocate. These lands did not contain a single vintner (tavern or wine seller).

In 1776 the offices of James Stirling, a banker, could be found in the Luckenbooths. He was to become master of the Merchant Company before going on to be town treasurer. During the troubled times of the 1790s, Stirling served three times as lord provost.

In 1817, this line of buildings was removed, and this opened up the top of the High Street. The old prison had been replaced by a new jail on Calton Hill. Lord Henry Cockburn (a judge of the Court of Session) described it:

A most atrocious jail it was, the very breath of which almost struck down any stranger who entered its dismal door; and as ill placed as possible, without one inch of ground beyond its black and horrid walls. And these walls were very small; the entire hole being filled with little dark cells; heavy manacles the only security; airless, waterless, drainless; a living grave.

The Grassmarket

In contrast to the Luckenbooths, the much larger Grassmarket possessed only seven men who classed themselves as merchants. In the 1770s many coaches had their Edinburgh termini in the Grassmarket. Eleven stablers, two saddlers, a wheelwright and a horse hirer were all based here. From Mrs Gibson's stables, the fast fly for Stirling departed every Monday, Wednesday and Friday at 8 a.m. John Cameron, the owner of the White Hart Inn, must have enjoyed a good trade: flying diligences to Carlisle, Dumfries, Glasgow and Stirling all departed from outside his inn, and the Carlisle coach offered a connection to London.

The Grassmarket was the home of tradesmen. No advocate or solicitor had their offices here. However, the street was best known as the site for public hangings. It was here that Captain John Porteous was lynched by a mob in 1736. In the previous century, many Covenanters had been imprisoned in the churchyard of Greyfriars and some of them were taken down to the Grassmarket for execution. A memorial to those who died there for the Covenanter cause can be seen at the east end.

The removal of the coaching services during the first decades of the nineteenth century, from the Grassmarket to the High Street and Prince's Street, led to a decline in the area. The Grassmarket became one of the most socially and economically deprived areas in the city. At the beginning of the third millennium, however, the city council set out to improve the street, with considerable success.

Passing through the Old Town gate, the road becomes the West Port. Tanners and leather merchants had their establishments here. Abraham Combe & Co. were to be found at No. 123, better known as Tanners' Close. In 1828 William Burke moved into a single room in a tenement here. This was to be the scene of many of the murders committed by the notorious bodysnatcher and his accomplice, Hare. The two streets had thirteen licensed spirit dealers between them. In 1881 Dr Robertson, minister of New Greyfriars Church, led a deputation of fifty men and women dressed in working clothes to the town council. They presented a petition signed by 1,000 residents asking for a reduction of these licensed outlets.

Liberton Wynd

Liberton Wynd was one of a number of narrow streets which were swept away during the building of George IV Bridge. The wynd contained the premises of three vintners, one of whom was John Dowie. His tavern was a favourite haunt of both Robert Ferguson and Robert Burns. This tiny inn sold Younger's Edinburgh Ale, and it appears that Dowie also served food.

The Canongate

The Canongate was a separate burgh ruled by Edinburgh Town Council. The senior bailie in the late eighteenth century was chosen from the old bailies and thus was a member of the council. He was supported by two resident bailies, also appointed by the town council. The burgh had its own tolbooth, high school and, after 1761, charity workhouse.

Many of the aristocracy, as well as others of distinction, owned property in the Canongate during the middle of the eighteenth century. *Chambers'* lists two dukes and fourteen earls.

However, the burgh had its darker side. In 1753, three residents of the Canongate, William Henry, Andrew Perrie and Elizabeth Young, were convicted for 'keeping bad and disorderly houses' and 'entertaining lewd and promiscuous company'. In the following year, the magistrates had to reinforce the guard with men from the palace after an incident of bullbaiting; a number of arrests followed.

The theatre also presented a problem for the authorities. In 1767 wilder elements, disagreeing with the decisions of the management, tore up the benches and stormed the stage. Scenery was destroyed and the performance was unable to continue. The theatre eventually moved to a site over the North Bridge.

The Canongate had its own church and burial ground where Robert Ferguson, Adam Smith and Mrs McLehose (Burns' Clarinda) are buried. In 1780, a choir of nearly 200 children from the burgh preformed in front of the minister and magistrates here.

The Canongate was the home of small tradesmen – shoemakers, grocers, tailors and baxters. Eleven brewers, many working in the North Back of the Canongate, occupied premises in the burgh, although their businesses were probably very small. The manufacturing of coaches and chaises increased rapidly between 1763 and 1783. Alexander Crichton had established his business in the Canongate, and Alexander McIntosh made starch, another item whose production was growing in Edinburgh. Only eight merchants were to be found in the Canongate at this time.

The Nineteenth Century

The Bridges in the New Century

In this time before the mass production of clothes, draperies and haberdasheries were a common sight, particularly on the South Bridge. Silk, linen and printed cottons could all be purchased here. Sinclair's Russian Warehouse at No. 43 must have had more exotic goods such as furs. Hats were an essential item of dress for the ladies of the time, and at least four shops offered them for sale. James Cooper and John White both sold jewellery from their shops on the South Bridge, while Martin and Milroy could be found on the North Bridge. The New Town had yet to become the centre of shopping, leaving much of the business in the hands of those shopkeepers on the Bridges.

In the years 1820–40 these two streets were the most prosperous shopping area in the city; North Bridge alone had nine jewellers and four goldsmiths. Successful shopping here could lead you to Mr J. Williams, who made jewel cases. Campbell & Co., P. Mackay & Son and Grieve & Phin all manufactured hats on the North Bridge, and their products could be purchased at five shops there.

No. 27 was the bookshop and publishing centre of Adam Black, who lived in Broughton Place. Black became a member of the reformed city council and went on to be lord provost and MP for the city.

South Bridge was the place to purchase material for dresses. Clothiers, milliners, drapers and even silk merchants had shops here. Seven shops specialised in hats, with Burge & Co. having their factory in the street. T. Grieve specialised in the making of straw hats while W. Johns produce that useful item, the umbrella. John Baxter at No. 4 sold Italian goods.

Irelands' bookshop and publishers produced the story of the West Port Murders from their premises on the South Bridge. This popular street also housed the Edinburgh Subscription Library, the Select Subscription Library and the Artisans' Subscription Reading Room.

The Great Fires, 1824

The south side of the High Street, between the Tron Kirk and Parliament Square, suffered from two fires in 1824. The second blaze, in November, saw the total destruction of a considerable amount of property, leaving many families homeless.

Improving Access to the Old Town

The Bridges, built in the previous century, had developed into an important retail centre. They provided a link with the suburbs to the north and south of the city. In April 1835, George IV Bridge was opened. Victoria Street removed the winding turns of the Bow, giving better access from the Grassmarket.

Another road, known then as the Western Approach, was built on the south side of the castle. This provided a wide street linking the top of the Lawnmarket with the western suburbs. Today it is called Johnston Terrace. One of the first properties to be built here was a new session school. Cockburn Street, which linked the High Street with the new railway station, was to come later.

The High Street

Apart from the many retailers, the High Street also contained the headquarters of newspapers and banks. The Royal Exchange housed the City Chambers (where the council met) and the offices of the city's officials. The offices of five banks could be found in this building, as well as the Royal Exchange Coffee House. Caddels, the paper and iron manufactures in Cramond, also had their city office at the Royal Exchange.

No. 329 belonged to Duncan McLaren, the Edinburgh draper who became the city treasurer and later lord provost and Member of Parliament. He lived for a while in Ramsey Gardens.

George Walker was a bagpipe maker, but he was not the only resident involved with music: Mr Kohler at No. 35 made violin strings.

Mr Stott, the well-known Radical councillor and former bailie, complained at a meeting of the city council about the 'indecent women continually on the streets, particularly on the High Street'. He observed that they were using public house and expressed a wish that the licensing court, due to meet on the following day, would take these facts into consideration.

The West Bow

Until the 1830s with the opening of Victoria Street, the road from the Grassmarket twisted its way up the hill to the top of the Lawnmarket by the old Butter Tron. It was very much the home and premises of tradesmen such as the metal workers (known in Edinburgh as 'hammermen'). Four coppersmiths and two tinplate workers had their businesses in this winding street. John Kellie, described as a white iron smith, and Robert Cleland, who engraved mottoes on rings, were both to be found in the West Bow. It must have been a very noisy place.

Businesses were not confined to the gentlemen. Miss Blyth, Mrs Carmichael and Mrs Cunningham were dressmakers who specialised in producing mantuas (a loose gown worn in the eighteenth century). Miss Drysdale was a milliner, while Mrs Drysdale, who may have been related to her, was a midwife. Miss Gibson ran a grocery shop in the West Bow. In the 1830s Mrs Grant at No. 82 was a leech dealer and applier – medieval medicine was still alive and sucking in Edinburgh!

Problems in the Growing City

As the population of Edinburgh grew, large numbers of poor people crowded into the Old Town in search of cheap accommodation. The Irish famine of the 1840s only increased the difficulties. Disturbances in the city in the spring of 1848 were, however, more about unemployment than the political demands of Radical politicians. In February 1849, the lord provost, Sir William Johnston, expressed his concern about the 'present distressed condition of the poor and the difficulties of finding employment'. Bread and soup, provided by the soup kitchen, was often a family's only meal of the day.

In *Oliver Twist*, Charles Dickens tells the story of the street children of London and how they became involved with criminal gangs. This problem was not confined to the British capital, for Edinburgh had its own street children. As early as 1832 *The Scotsman* was complaining that 'hundreds of children who now infest our streets have passed the ordeal of trial before 12 years'. Seventeen children, aged between 8 and 14, were found in a cellar at two o'clock in the morning. It appears that most of them had convictions for theft.

In the 1840s, various groups led by the churches began to provide education and material support for these youngsters. Reverend Dr Guthrie, with the aid of some patrons, set up the Original Ragged or Industrial School in Ramsay Lane. The congregation of New Greyfriars also opened premises for the local children. The United Industrial School in South Gray's Close was non-denominational with half the youngsters attending being Catholics; the children of Irish immigrants.

The Lawnmarket Fire, 1857

A fire broke out in the upper storey of a tenement in St James' Court. The alarm was given at one o'clock in the afternoon, leading to many acts of bravery. William Stevenson, a young bookbinder, fought his way through the smoke to rescue two very young children, one aged 3 months and the other 2 years. James Gough, a former member of the Rifle Brigade, saved five children. Both men later received medals for their bravery. Gough commented that he had already received one for killing people and now he had one for saving them.

The roof collapsed at 2 o'clock but nine engines from the city, the castle and Leith managed to bring the fire under control. The wind dropped, preventing the flames spreading to neighbouring buildings which included the Free Church College.

Fortunately, no one was hurt in the fire but thirty families were left homeless. The lord provost organised places for them in the House of Refuge and set up a fund which had raised £1,446 by the end of the month.

A Tenement Collapses

A seven-storey tenement (eight storeys at the back) collapsed at half past one on Sunday morning, 24 November 1861. It stood on the High Street between Bailie Fyfe's Close and Paisley Close. Two constables raised the alarm but the dust, and no doubt the dark, hid the full scale of the disaster. They managed to pull out seven children who had to be housed in the police cells. Neighbouring buildings were evacuated as the death toll continued to rise. In all, over thirty people lost their lives. Alexander Irvine, who was only 9, lost his father, mother, grandmother and two sisters in the disaster.

The tenement had been built in the seventeenth or eighteenth century, and had once been the business premises of Sir William Fettes, a former lord provost. An inquiry placed the blame on the installation of a boiler which had weakened a central wall.

Explosion in the Canongate

Thomas Hammond was making fireworks at the back of his shop in the Canongate. A spark led to an explosion in the premises, which were totally unsuitable for the use of gunpowder. Those in the flats above the shop were trapped and rescuers were unable to find a ladder long enough to reach them. Margaret Campbell, who was only 12, died when she jumped from one of the upper floors. The body of another 12-year-old girl, Mary Ann Edmiston, was found under the debris in the shop. Three more people also died in the explosion and nine others were injured. Anger was expressed at the failure to enforce the law against the use of explosives in crowded tenements.

'The Report on the Sanitary Condition of the City of Edinburgh'

In 1867 Dr Henry Littlejohn, Edinburgh's Medical Officer for Health, produced his 'Report on the Sanitary Condition of the City of Edinburgh'. The report examined the living conditions in some of the tenements in the Old Town. It highlighted the overcrowding and the lack of proper sanitation to be found in properties in this area:

Properties	Storeys	Inhabitants	Rooms	Sinks	Toilets
Gowanloch's Land, High Street	8	134	60	3	3
8 Cowgate	5	179	60	2	1
Scot's Land, 341 Cowgate	170	53	53	–	–
Elephinston's Land, Carrubbers Close	6	135	45	9	7

58 Blackfriars Wynd	4	130	49	3	–
Hope's Land, 268 Cowgate	6	103	36	–	–
Purve's Land, 327 Cowgate	4	119	32	2	–

'We have already seen that in Edinburgh the rule is amply borne out that the greater amount of overcrowding the larger is the mortality,' stated the report.

When infectious diseases like cholera visited the city, it was the Old Town which bore the brunt of the problem. New properties for poor working families were constructed, of which the Ashley Building in the Tron District was the first in 1854. By 1864 some sixteen new housing developments had provided accommodation for nearly 750 families.

The report went on to make four recommendations:

1   The closes needed to be properly drained and paved.
2   The owners of the tenements ought to keep them in good repair and ensure the common stairs are clean. Water and gas should be brought into these buildings.
3   Action has to be taken against the overcrowding by removing ruined tenements, lowering the heights of some of the tallest ones and placing a maximum on the number of tenants living in each building.
4   New streets should be constructed at right angles to the closes [i.e. parallel to the High Street] to give easy access for cleaning and to allow more air into these enclosed alleys.

'One of the great obstacles to the improvement of the Old Town has undoubtedly been the large pauper population it contains,' claimed the report.

The city parish council had already acted to alleviate this problem by building their new poorhouse outside the city. However, the parishes of St Cuthbert's and the Canongate were reluctant to be involved in the scheme. The report pulled no punches on this: 'The citizens should insist that it should be extended to the other two parishes of St Cuthbert's and the Canongate.'

Poverty in the Old Town in the 1860s

Investigators from the *Edinburgh Evening Courant* (January 1867) looked into the conditions of the Old Town:

In an area we saw a seamstress, an English woman, whose husband had died a week or two before our visit and who was in an impoverished state. She had 2 or 3 of a family, one of them a young woman in ill health who was assisting her sewing. The house was simply a narrow strip partitioned off a cellar and rented 1s a week. The furniture was very scanty and the cutting board formed the only bed for the family. The woman showed us 1 or 2 shirts for which she would receive 4d each, 'for,' she remarked, 'if

I asked as much as I should get people grumble so.' In order to make the barest livelihood therefore she was compelled to work during the greater part of the night.

William Anderson wrote, 'Much less is known, we venture to say of the closes of Edinburgh than parts of the interior of Africa.' He blamed 'the rapaciousness of the landlords in exacting exorbitant rents while refusing to do anything in the way of repairing the property'.

Some of the worst housing was in Stevenlaw's Close off the Cowgate. He found an unemployed labourer with a wife and five children. They possessed one bed and one cover. The family had no shoes and were all illiterate.

Mary Pyper

Mary was born in Greenock in 1795 and was brought to Edinburgh by her widowed mother. She was a very small woman who at first earned 6*s* a week making lace. Later she found employment in a trimming shop. After her mother's death she worked hard to pay off a debt of £9. Mary would wander around the Old Town selling buttons and fringes from a small basket.

In 1860, T. Constable published Mary's first collection of poems:

Here is a season of calm weather
Though inland far we be
Our souls have sight of that immortal sea
Which brought us hither
Can in a moment travel thither
And see the children sport upon the shore
And hear the mighty waters rolling evermore.

Other works were to follow. William Anderson found Mary living in Bull's Close, off the High School Yards. She was virtually blind but still rose between 4 and 5 o'clock in the morning making shirts to sell at six for 1*s* 9*d*. She told him, 'I took my porridge in the morning an' after got nae thing agin till nicht because I couldna afford it.' She would go looking for subscriptions for her poems:

I asked a lady to subscribe,
She answered – she would see.
But oh! I find she still is blind
Alas! for her and me.

Mary died in 1870 and a memorial cross was raised in Greyfriars Churchyard in 1885.

The Edinburgh Improvement Act, 1867

This Act gave the town council the power to purchase property in order to carry through improvements to the Old Town. They were permitted to borrow £350,000 for that purpose. Blackfriars and St Mary's Wynds were widened by clearing the east sides of both streets. Two new roads, Jeffrey Street and Chambers Street, were built to give better access to the Old Town. The entry to the Grassmarket at its eastern end was widened.

Not everyone was in favour of such action, although fear of the outbreak of diseases like cholera spurred many in authority to support these moves. Bailie Miller in 1870 told the council that he had visited many houses in the lower districts of Edinburgh and not found a single case of overcrowding. Councillor Gowans suggested that he should visit 18 Blackfriars Wynd, where he would find eight people living in a single room and five people in another one. Concern was expressed that the clearance of these slums would make it difficult for honest labouring families to find affordable accommodation.

Some properties, such as 66 and 68 High Street, were taken down when the Dean of Guild Court declared them to be unsafe. In 1873–74 repairs were made to seventy-one tenements which contained 838 homes, using the Public Health Act. Another forty-four tenements (365 homes) were either closed or demolished.

Greyfriars Bobby

Story One

John Grey joined the Edinburgh Police in 1853. He acquired Bobby, a Skye terrier, to use as a watchdog. Grey often did night duty in the cattle market. When Grey died in 1858 he was buried in Greyfriars Churchyard and Bobby remained by his grave in the cemetery. He received food from the proprietors of a local coffee house, which was first owned by William Ramsay and later by William Paterson.

Story Two

Bobby was a stray who frequented the grounds of Heriot's Hospital. The gardener, Peter Brown, tried to keep him out and eventually managed to push him through into the churchyard. At night he would often sleep on the common stair of a tenement at the top of Candlemakers' Row. Mrs Watson, who lived there, claimed that he would visit her husband's works before returning home with him for dinner.

Story Three

John Wilson McLaren claimed that in 1871, as a 10-year-old messenger boy, he visited Mr Traill's Coffee House at Greyfriars and saw the dog. He quoted Mr Traill as saying:

'That doggie has a bit of a history. His name is Bobby and his master a Midlothian farmer named Grey died in 1858 almost 13 years ago. He aye came here for his dinner on market days and Bobby was aye with him.'

He went on to relate how Bobby, directed by the one o'clock gun, always arrived there for his lunch. Wilson McLaren also relates the story of the children and lord provost's chambers securing the dog's freedom to roam freely in the city. Councillor McLaren criticised the members of the town council of 1889 who tried to 'rubbish the story'. John Wilson McLaren was a member of the town council from 1920 until his death in 1943. He wrote many articles about old Edinburgh and ought to be considered a reliable witness.

No doubt there will be more versions of this story so the reader must decide for themselves.

The High Street in the 1880s

There were many different small retail outlets – butchers, bakers, stationers and tobacconists. The street had a dozen spirit merchants, as well as a large number of people with businesses involved in the manufacture and sale of boots and shoes. Most of these shops were small, although McLaren's, founded by the late Duncan McLaren, was a large drapery business. Some more unusual occupations could also be found here: John Harlow was a marble and paper stainer who also made scarlet ink, while George Mackay, an ivory turner, manufactured bowls for the bowling greens.

St Giles and the Tron Kirk might dominate the western end of the High Street, but some important religious establishments could be found further down the street. St Patrick's Church and its manse were tucked in between the High Street and the Cowgate. In the years 1885–86 the congregation was served by four priests. John Knox's Free Church and the Carrubber's Close (not in the Close) Mission Hall stood on the north side. The mission supported the temperance movement and held a watch night service on New Year's Eve, in contrast to the rowdy scenes outside the Tron (1,500 people attended this service in 1889). Three years later, it was learnt that Mr Moody 'was to sing some soloes [sic], having the effect of completely filling the hall'.

Two of Britain's greatest publishers had their headquarters on the High Street. Oliver & Boyd acquired the old mansion in Tweeddale Court, while W & R Chambers could be found near the Exchange. This building housed the offices of the Chamberlain (responsible for the town's finances), the dean of guild (responsible for property), the city clerk and his depute. Here too the council held their meetings, directing the affairs of the city.

The two Heriot schools serving this area were to be found in Old Assembly and Borthwick Closes. The United Industrial School was situated near Blackfriars Street, although the emphasis had been shifted from taking children off the streets to providing accommodation and education for troubled children, most of whom had been before the courts.

Lodging Houses

By 1885, there were four lodging houses in the Grassmarket. They offered 396 beds at rates varying from 4d to 6d per night at a time when the average navvy earned around 6s (72d). Basic food – tea, bread, ham and herring – could be purchased from the management.

Around 1888 the Castle Model Lodging House opened in the Grassmarket. It was one of a number of privately run lodging houses which provided cheap accommodation for working men. This particular lodging house would only admit men and they did their own cooking. The manager, interviewed by a reporter from the *Evening News* in 1899, explained that the majority of the men had been there for two years or more. One man and his two sons had come to the house when it first opened eleven years previously. One or two of the inmates had fallen on hard times – an old schoolmaster, a 'broken down' lawyer and some bank clerks. Baths were provided for a charge of 1d, but they were not very popular, especially in winter, as many of the men had only one set of clothes. They had a piano and an organ which, surprisingly, some of the residents could play. Ladies and gentlemen from the city organised concerts for them once every fortnight. On Sundays, various missions from the churches conducted a service.

Renting even the cheapest of properties was extremely difficult for this class of men. Houses, probably only one or two rooms in a tenement, were available from £8 to £15 per annum. However, the agents insisted on an agreed tenancy of at least a year, which was not always convenient for men who had to move in search of work. New tenants, and sometimes those who had been long term, had to find a cautioner. It was not easy for a poor working man to find a member of the business community who would be willing to vouch for the prospective tenant. The market for places in lodging houses continued to grow and by the end of the nineteenth century Edinburgh had thirty-five such houses with 2,829 beds.

The Cowgate and the Drink Problems in the Old Town

The Cowgate was one of the poorest areas in the city. Five rag merchants dealing in old clothes, paper, wool, metal and glass had premises here. Eleven 'brokers' (the author believes they dealt in second-hand goods, especially clothes and furniture) advertised their businesses in this street.

The Argyle and Waverley breweries both operated from here, and the area contained a considerable number of spirit dealers and licensed grocers. Excessive drinking was a serious problem in Victorian Edinburgh. An article in *The Scotsman* on the New Year celebrations for the beginning of 1878 reported:

> The eyesore was perhaps most observable in the High Street unless indeed one dived into the Cowgate where the great bulk of men to be seen in the street, as well as a large portion of women, young and old, appeared to be in some stage of inebriety.

Excessive drinking was one of the main causes of poverty here in the early years of the twentieth century. An *Evening News* investigation into one-roomed houses discovered one occupied by a labourer, earning 22s, and his wife making 10–12s from hawking china. Their rent only amounted to 2s a week, but despite this their furniture only consisted of a broken chair, a filthy looking bed and a box which acted as a table. The journalist found the woman, aged only 25, 'motionless and insensibly drunk' minding her two children (3 years and 18 months old).

At New Year, the problem in the Cowgate, Grassmarket and West Port was increased by the practice of licensed grocers giving away bottles of whisky! It was estimated that 5,000 pints of whisky were given away in these three streets. One woman, totally unknown to the grocer, bought 4d worth of ham and received a bottle of whisky. A reporter form the *Evening News* explained, 'It was not uncommon to see women with 5–6 pint bottles in their aprons after half an hour of shopping.' The Grassmarket Undenominational Mission managed to get the trade to agree to end this practice.

Housing in the Old Town

A shortage of reasonably priced accommodation for the unskilled workers had always been a problem in the city. A survey, conducted by Mr Cooper, the burgh engineer, was completed in November 1887. It revealed that of the 8,386 homes visited, 3,269 had one room, 5,639 two rooms and 1,478 more than two rooms. The total rental value of £57,494 may seem enormous, but it works out at approximately £7 each. Here lived 29,117 people, of whom 5,726 were children.

The most shocking statistic of them all showed that 2,396 (more than a quarter) had no toilet and 2,277 were in need of some repairs, of which 629 Mr Cooper considered in need of serious action. Even more seriously, 744 of these homes had no water!

Another problem was the subdivision of even these small properties. The burgh engineer recommended greater supervision to prevent this, however ,closing houses drove more families in search of accommodation which was not always available at rents that working families could afford.

Evictions in the Canongate

In the summer of 1896 the Edinburgh Social Union bought Campbell's Close with the intention of clearing the present buildings and replacing them with tenement homes for working men. The *Evening News* claimed, 'More despicable hovels called by the name of human habitations it would be difficult to find anywhere in the city.'

However, five families comprising thirty-two people – twenty-two of them under 12 – remained in their homes until they were ejected by the officers of the union. With their men at work, the women and children lit fires and cooked their meals in the street as the rain began to fall. Mr Hendry and Mr Young, members of the parish council, arrived on the scene and advised them to return to their homes. Councillor Waterston also visited them and remained there until 10 p.m. The families explained that they were unable to find another tenancy because they needed a caution guaranteed by a businessman. They had previously paid between 1s 6d and 2s for a single room.

The next day, the head teacher of Milton House (the school opposite the close) sent them some bread and coffee for breakfast. Officials from the town council then arrived and interviewed the homeless families in an attempt to find accommodation for them.

The Bridges in the Last Years of the Nineteenth Century

The Bridges was the most prosperous area of the Old Town, forming a link between the New Town and the wealth and growing suburbs on the south side. Large stores providing clothing and household goods stood alongside the specialist shops.

J & R Allen and Scott, Low & Co. traded from the South Bridge and James Thin's bookshop was already well established here. Thin began as an apprentice at the age of 12, before opening his own shop. Seven jewellers still had shops on the Bridges, although most of this trade had moved to Prince's Street. Cranston & Elliot were situated on the North Bridge before they moved to Prince's Street in 1895.

E. Kohler & Sons owned a music shop on the North Bridge. They had problems in the autumn of 1894 when a cleaning lady began to steal their stock. A large number of items went missing, including four violins, before she was caught.

The North Bridge, which crossed the railway, had always been a source of congestion. In the years 1894–96 work was carried out to widen the bridge.

Plans were even brought forward, though not carried through, to construct a second bridge linking Jeffrey Street with Calton Hill at an estimated cost of £32,000.

The Early Twentieth Century

The High Street

In 1905, the High Street alone had twenty-two outlets for the purchase of alcohol but only five bakers and three butchers' shops. James Matthew & Son Ltd, situated at the corner of the Lawnmarket and St Giles Street, was the only large retail outlet on the Royal Mile.

A multitude of small shops and businesses still operated in the area. Publishing played an important role in Edinburgh's economy, and Oliver & Boyd now occupied the old house in Tweeddale Court while W & R Chambers had premises further up the street. The Dundee papers (including the *People's Friend*) had offices close to the City Chambers.

The area was not without its problems. The Sabbath Free Breakfast Mission and the Night Asylum could be found in Old Fishmarket Close and No. 142 housed the Children's Shelter and the offices of the Scottish League of Pity.

Constable Peter Morrison

Constable Morrison retired in April 1914 after serving thirty-four years with the Edinburgh Police. Much of his career had been spent in the Grassmarket and the Cowgate – the roughest part of Edinburgh. He claimed that during his early years of service he might have to stop a dozen fights in one evening. Apart from the usual problem characters the area attracted, it became a meeting place for navvies working on the Suburban Line and the Forth Railway Bridge. He considered that the district had improved in recent years due to a decline in drinking, the closing up of some old closes and the work of the missions. However, just prior to his retirement, Elizabeth McLaughlin of Castle Wynd in the Grassmarket was arrested for selling drink from her home. She had seven previous convictions stretching back thirty years.

The Old Town Between the Wars

The Canongate and the Cowgate were in serious decline by the end of the First World War. The former was filled with empty shops and many of the public houses had already gone. Huntly House's facade was so dirty that the writing on its front could hardly be seen. The walls of the tenements in the Cowgate

were almost black and much of the stonework in a poor condition. Many windows were either broken or covered in soot. The *Evening News* complained, 'From no part of Edinburgh has the glory departed as in the Cowgate.'

A few properties of especial historic interest did receive attention. At the beginning of 1928 proposals to turn Huntly House into a museum were rejected by the city treasurer. It took nearly two more years before the town council finally agreed to restore the property and convert it into the City Museum. The tenement known as Gladstone's Land, situated in the Lawnmarket, was condemned and scheduled for demolition, but Miss Helen Harrison bought the property in 1934 and donated it to the National Trust for Scotland, who restored it. The Marquis of Bute purchased Acheson House in 1937 and work began on repairing the building.

The problem of turning the ancient lands of the Old Town into decent housing was hindered by an Act of Parliament which only permitted subsidies to be given to *new* building projects. The situation was now bad enough to be raised in the House of Commons and not by local MPs. Mr Hannah, representing Wolverhampton, expressed his concern about the historic Taylors' Hall in the Cowgate. The council wanted to demolish it and widen the street. One other member told the House:

> Now we have seen one after another of the ancient lands torn down. I am afraid that it is no exaggeration to say that Edinburgh in the last thirty years has passed from being a first rate city from the archaeological point of view to a second rate place.

The *Evening News* showed pictures of the derelict tenements in the Canongate – Chessel's Court, Morocco Land and Achison House.

Post-War Plans for the Old Town

As the war drew to a close in 1945, the city architect, Mr E.J. MacRae, set out plans in order 'that proper use will be made of the Old Town so as to provide for the convenience of citizens as well as for the preservation of the charm of the old romantic city'. The Canongate was not to be widened, but a small triangle of buildings in front of the palace were to be removed. The report went on to state, 'The greatest concentration of old and interesting buildings in the whole of the Old Town is in the Lawnmarket, Castlehill and the West Port'.

The Grassmarket came in for considerable criticism. The north side, the report claimed, contained 'housing of bad quality', and it thus recommended the property should be demolished. This would produce the 'opportunity for a large amount of continuous housing of good quality'. No mention is made of the various taverns found here. The south side consisted of the 'obsolete Cornmarket' and 'chiefly lodging houses'. Mr MacRae wished to open up the area to reveal Heriot's School.

Much of the Royal Mile (65 per cent) consisted of housing, although only a few (estimated at 7 per cent) were up to modern standards. The area provided 1,400 homes for well over 5,000 people: 'Re-housing should be arranged as far as possible only on the north side of the streets'. Where were all the residents to go? Housing was one of the greatest problems facing post-war Edinburgh.

The city architect proposed to increase the office space of the City Chambers by acquiring the properties on the south side of High Street. This area had been rebuilt after the Great Fire of 1824 and was not considered to be of enough significant historical importance to warrant preservation. His eyes also fell on George IV Bridge in order to 'take advantage of this fine setting to make the whole north part of George IV Bridge a complete group of Public buildings'.

Housing Problems in the Canongate

The post-war housing shortage led to some homeless families squatting in empty buildings. No. 1 St John Street on the corner of the Canongate had been closed up since before the war. It was proposed to use it as an extension for Moray House College of Education. Thomas James, with his wife and four children, had spent six months in a tent near Broxburn before they moved into one of the rooms there. In August 1946 the police arrived with a sheriff's warrant and began to evict the squatters and their furniture. These included a man and his wife who were partially blind, as well as some expectant mothers. That night, two more families joined them, one of whom was James Old, his wife and 1-year-old baby, who had spent two nights on the streets. The next day sheriff's officers removed the furniture.

Councillor Rhind visited the squatters. They were given a final notice to be out by the end of November, but it was not until February 1947 that temporary accommodation was found for them at the Northern General Hospital.

No. 312 was condemned by the city engineer as unsafe due to subsidence. Thirteen families refused to leave their homes and neighbours stepped in to rescue the situation, leading to one council official commenting:

> Doors have opened all over the Lawnmarket in an amazing fashion and people have come forward throughout the week-end to take in not only homeless people but their furniture as well. The unfortunate folk seem to have been swallowed up in the homes of their neighbours and the problem of evicting them which faced us over the week-end no longer exists. Only one family was sent to Lochinvar Camp in Granton.

Rebuilding the Canongate

Demolition and restoration work began at Whitehorse Close and Whitefoord House at the foot of the Canongate in December 1946. However, the following March emergency work had to be carried out on the buildings at Morocco Close to prevent them from collapsing, although it was not until 1956 that rebuilding began here.

Finally, some five years later, the Corporation could make safe the building used by the squatters at the corner of St John Street. By 1953 it was reported that twelve schemes, providing 200 homes, were scheduled for the area. Later that year, the Canongate had to be closed because the tenement known as 'Bible Land' was in a perilous condition. Local shopkeepers complained that their trade was badly affected by the closure of the street. The following year brought the news that work would begin on Chessel's Court, where Deacon Brodie's gang had carried out their last robbery.

Advocate's Close

One of the main themes in post-war Edinburgh was the struggle between the conservationists and the developers. While the university was successfully pushing forward its expansion plans in George Square, the council were looking to increase their office space in the High Street. The city architect put forward plans to extend the City Chambers westwards, which would have led to the demolition of the old buildings in Advocate's Close. The Cockburn Association led the attack on these plans and 'the mock classical architecture' which would replace the Royal Mile frontage. Lord Provost Banks defended the decision on the grounds that the MacRae Report 1946 had allowed for this:

> That Report in a note added to the schedule of old buildings worthy of preservation states that the old tenement in Advocate's Close, High Street is in the way of obvious extensions of the City Chambers and is therefore not included in the Schedule.

However, the council did not get their own way and the buildings still stand for all to see.

Seventeen

THE NEW TOWN

The Founding of the New Town

In August 1759, a meeting of the leading landowners of the County of Edinburgh opposed the proposal to extend the city. They wanted the town council to draw up another scheme. It was reported that the lord provost, George Drummond, offered to consider their views.

Much of the initial work in the planning for the New Town was done during the provostship of Drummond. However, it was not until 1767 that the Edinburgh Extension Act was passed by Parliament and James Craig's plan adopted for this northern development. By this time, Gilbert Laurie was lord provost.

On Monday, 26 October 1767, James Craig laid the foundation stone of the first house in the New Town. Two years later, in February 1769, was constructed:

> A model of the streets and squares on the north side of this city presenting in miniature every house, church and public building with the new bridge and pleasure grounds, all proposed by the promoters of the new plan.

Progress was slow; by 1780 nothing appears to have been built west of Hanover Street. One critic placed the failure to expand rapidly at the door of the town council. The collapse of a pier on the new North Bridge also led to a delay in opening up a direct route between the New Town and the High Street.

In 1781 the town council looked at a proposal to build a circus (a square, but round in shape) at the junctions of George and Frederick Streets; this was not taken any further. More successful was the plan to construct a church for the New Town. St Andrew's Church which, by the original plan, was to be situated on the east side of St Andrew's Square, was instead built in George Street. The site in the square had been taken by Sir Lawrence Dundas, who at this time was fighting an unsuccessful case in the Court of Session against Mr Young, an architect who wished to build on the south side of Sir Lawrence's property.

Links with the Old Town

They began draining the Nor' Loch in 1763. The loch had been created as part of the defences of the town, but by the middle of the eighteenth century it had become a hindrance to development. The Old and New Towns were built on high ground on either side of the valley. The Mound was begun in 1783, using earth dug out to form the foundations of the houses in the New Town. Many of these, in true Georgian fashion, had a sunken storey but they have since been covered with shop fronts. Only one remains in Prince's Street, although you can still see some in George Street.

St Andrew's Square

This was the first part of the New Town to be completed. The eastern side of the square is dominated by the town house of Sir Lawrence Dundas, MP for the city of Edinburgh. By the late 1770s it was the home of merchants and lawyers, although Alexander Dickson, a glazier, had also established himself in the square. Sometime in the 1780s Dunn's Hotel moved here from Prince's Street before it was taken over by William Drysdale of the Turf Coffee House. Also situated in the square at this time was Bruce's Tavern.

Two streets, running north to south, pass along the sides of the square. St Andrew's and St David's Streets are named after the patron saints of Scotland and Wales. St Andrew's Street was completed by the middle of the 1770s. At that time James Morrison, the Principal Clerk of the Annexed Estates, lived there. The government was still running some of the properties confiscated after the Jacobite Rising in 1745. Here, too, lived the dowager Countess of Leven.

This street was not only the property of the wealthy. William Connochie and Malcolm Murdock, both of whom were grocers, had homes and probably businesses in St Andrew's Street. John Hume, a coachwright, had set up in the street. Many of the larger properties in the New Town had their own stables and coach houses. No doubt this provided business for the local coachwright.

One of the first people to build a house in St David's Street was the philosopher and historian David Hume, who moved here from James' Court in the Lawnmarket.

Prince's Street

By 1776 Prince's Street contained a great variety of residents. Merchants like John Balfour and Thomas Elder had moved into the street. Elder was a wine merchant and was later to serve as lord provost. Hugo Arnot, advocate and historian of Edinburgh, lived there. The trades were represented by a plumber, a tailor and a baker. Williamson's street directory lists six Mellises, all of whom were fleshers. Five of them lived in Fleshmarket Close, but the sixth, John Mellis, had acquired property in Prince's Street. Both John Baxter, an architect, and George Robertson, a garden designer, had homes and offices in the street.

The commercialisation of the street began early in its development. Mrs Miller was selling haberdashery goods by 1780 in Prince's Street. Two years later, the street had its own coffee house. Alexander Walker decided to move his hotel from Writers' Court and set up here. His hotel advertised itself as 'being [in] a pleasant and healthful situation'. The grand-sounding Royal Caledonian Hotel was established at No. 3, and John Dunn moved from the Pleasance in 1777, opening the Prince's Street Coffee House and using the upper floors as a hotel.

By 1830 most of the eastern part of the street had been taken over by shops and offices. The last commercial premises were at No. 99, occupied by Lyle's Fancy Warehouse and Hutton & Cooper, shoemakers. There were, in fact, ten shops selling boots and shoes. Seven hotels, including the Crown Hotel, the Star and McQueen's, could all be found here. Croall's, the large coach firm, had their offices at No. 2, with the General Coach Office a few doors down, and further west the White Horse Cellar Coach Office. Many of the stagecoaches now set off from the east end of Prince's Street. By this time, even the Union Canal was competing for passenger trade. They had opened an office at No. 82 for the sale of tickets.

The Miscellaneous Depot specialised in clothing and sporting equipment; you could even purchase gunpowder. Scott & Orr, the Edinburgh pharmacists, had also opened a branch in Prince's Street and there were three shops selling sheet music, as well as instruments (no recorded music at this time!). However, most of the shops specialised in cloth, to be made into clothing, and accessories.

Food was purchased in the markets which were to be found around the Old Town, although George Sanderson sold potatoes in Prince's Street. A few doors down, at No. 74, Mr Maclean was selling fruit as well as auricular seeds – a fashionable plant in the nineteenth century.

Robert Andrew at No. 43, and John Johnston, two doors down, had opened dental practices. Between them was C. Thomson, who made fishing tackle. The most unusual occupation on the street fell to John Edmonston, who was a bird stuffer.

George Street

George Street was designed as the main street of the New Town, linking St Andrew's Square with St George's Square. This was later named Charlotte Square after the wife of George III. The foundation stone of St Andrew's Church was laid on 21 March 1781. The Assembly Rooms (used for dancing) were built opposite the church. The street was wide enough to allow a horse and carriage to make a U-turn.

Three years later, Miss Lithgow moved her school from Carrubbers Close to George Street and this was the beginning of the street's link with education. By the middle of the 1830s, George Street had built up a strong educational establishment. No. 121 was occupied by the North British Academy for Young Ladies, with a wide curriculum which included writing, arithmetic, geography and history. They also offered French, Italian and German. Next door was Mr Broughton's Academy for Young Gentlemen.

At this time, at least eight residents of the street were offering tuition in various subjects, although it was foreign languages that dominated their curriculum. Mr John Christison, at No. 50, offered his students French, Italian and Spanish, while in the same building Mr Dick taught architecture and civil engineering.

George Street was the home of the partners of Forbes, Hunter & Co. This prestigious banking firm had its headquarters in Parliament Square. Sir William Forbes lived at No. 39 George Street. James Hunter, who added Blair to his name after his marriage, became MP for the city and lord provost. George Street was also the Edinburgh home of Leith MP (and later lord advocate) John Murray; he was the first member for Leith Burghs.

In the 1820s George Street contained a mixture of shops, businesses and private houses, many of which were very large. No. 53 George Street, advertised for lease in 1824, consisted of ten rooms as well as quarters for servants and cellars in the sunken area. The first case concerning building over the sunken area was raised in a town council meeting as early as 1835. The property stood at the corner of George and Hanover Streets.

In 1824, eight shops in George Street were advertising flannels, silk and cotton stockings, children's clothes and baby linens. Robert Buchanan ran a bookshop at No. 48. Further along, at No. 106 was the Bazaar Français offering fashionable goods from the French capital.

Andrew Melrose was building a grocery chain in Edinburgh which also sold tea, coffee and chocolate. He had shops on the High Street and the Bridges and in the 1830s he opened another one in George Street.

Rose and Thistle Streets

These two narrow streets ran parallel to the main streets and provided access to the stables and yards. The properties in the streets were occupied by tradespeople.

In September 1790, a small fire in Rose Street was contained by the prompt action of the City Guard. Upon investigation, a baker whose premises had been damaged had allowed his staff to put hot ashes out into a passageway. That day, a pile of timber shavings had also been dumped in the street. When the magistrate discovered that there had been previous complaints made against the baker he was fined for negligence.

In October of the following year, the City Guard raided a brothel in Rose Street. Four girls who were found there received a warning, but the 'mistress of the house of bad fame' was ordered to leave Edinburgh. In contrast to this, James Hill, who led a breakaway group from Bristo Burgher Church, opened a chapel in Rose Street in 1786.

Rose Street in the 1820s was not an important thoroughfare. Like Thistle Street to the north, Rose Street offered access to the backs of the houses on the main streets of the New Town. Wealthy residents owned their own stables and coachhouses, but horses could be bought, and probably hired, from two stables run separately by Mr Inglis and Mr Neilson.

The King's Arms stood at No. 34 Rose Street, but at this time most of the social life, which was based on the taverns, remained in the Old Town. Alex Grey and William Henderson both had veterinary practices in Rose Street and three jewellers and W. Dickson, a gold beater, had premises here. No. 180 was the Racket Court, although we cannot be sure what sports took place there.

In June 1826, after a fire in a low, damp cellar, the authorities discovered the body of Joseph MacWilliam. He had been burnt to death. There were no chairs or tables and not even a bed in the cellar. However, they found bank receipts valued at £1,499 15s 6d and deeds to property worth £1,100. Mr MacWilliam had been a very wealthy man who could have afforded a much better lifestyle.

Thistle Street had its own livery stables, owned by John Oliver. There were numerous painters to be found in both streets – no doubt the building boom and the large size of Georgian houses encouraged this trade. Edward and Madame Rosa had a chiropodist business at No. 74.

There were generally less problems among the wealthier residents of the New Town. However, in January 1830, a publican in Thistle Street was fined £5 for 'entertaining disorderly company in his house'.

At the end of February 1878, one correspondent of *The Scotsman* described Rose Street as 'a colony of loose characters'. The area gained the reputation as the 'red light' district of the New Town, although by the 1890s the police felt they had the problem under control.

While the street had its share of small businesses – grocers, bakers, butchers and confectioners – wine and spirit merchants predominated.

Charlotte Square

The square was named after Charlotte of Mecklenburg, the wife of George III. It was originally called St George's Square, but the name was eventually changed. This certainly avoided confusion with George Square, the fashionable suburb built to the south of the city.

On Friday, 19 August 1796, nine lots on the south side of the square and twelve lots on the east side were offered 'at a reduced price'. The advertisement

went on to specify that 'the whole to be built on a regular plan conforming to an elegant elevation of the late Mr Robert Adam, architect'. A year later, No. 4 on the north side was put up for sale; the initial price of £1,750 was reduced to £1,600.

St George's Church was eventually built on the west side, facing George Street, but it was not opened until 1814. In the 1960s, structural problems forced the congregation to abandon the building which they had not the funds to repair. St George's is now part of the register office.

Bellevue

By the beginning of the nineteenth century much, although not all, of the New Town had been completed. To the north the land dropped down to the Water of Leith, and some of this belonged to Heriot's Hospital. The Earl of Moray owned much of the property to the west. On the east side was the estate of Bellevue with its mature woods. Henry Cockburn considered that 'no part of the home scenery of Edinburgh was more beautiful than Bellevue, the villa of General Scott'.

In 1802 the town council bought Bellevue and began to fell the trees. 'I remember people shuddered when they heard the axes busy in the woods of Bellevue and furious when they saw the bare ground,' wrote Cockburn, in his *Memorials*. The area was divided into building plots but few of these had been built upon as late as 1817.

The New Town in the Early Years of the Nineteenth Century

The slow commercialisation of Prince's Street continued into the nineteenth century. Ann Fortune carried on the family tradition and ran the Tontine Tavern at No. 5, and by 1806 three hotels – Gordon's, Mackay's and Gregor's – were open to visitors in the street. Two years later, both W. Arnot & Co. and P.P. Shirreff, who sold drapery, haberdashery and hosiery, were trading from No. 38 Prince's Street.

Properties in central and western Prince's Street were still private houses, and ladies' hairdressers started to move nearer their clients. George Muggerland, in St Andrew's Street, and Mr Brown, in George Street, were open for business in 1800. Hairdresser Duncan Robertson could be found at No. 2 Prince's Street, where he also sold wigs and perfume.

Since horses were the only form of transport it is not surprising to find stables in the less fashionable streets. In July 1806, both Wilson and Anderson were advertising their establishments in Rose Street, and Thistle Street contained the stables of Kidd and Laurie. Donald Christie, who was over 60 years old, appeared before the magistrate 'for an attempt on a girl whom he found alone in a shop in Rose Street'. He was fined £2 with a further £5 for damages, which was the highest possible punishment the police court could impose. This is one of the few examples where the courts of these times were less severe than our courts today.

Many of the large houses on the main streets had their own stables. In 1800, No. 31 Prince's Street was advertised with a back ground and stables for two horses while No. 44 George Street, consisting of fifteen main rooms, all with fireplaces, also possessed a coachhouse and stables. No. 59 Prince's Street was advertised for sale six years later and had a fixed price of £2,000. It also had a coachhouse, as well as stabling for four horses.

George Street attracted educational establishments even in the early years of the century. No doubt the address added prestige to the school. Mrs Grieve, in collaboration with her daughter, ran a boarding school for young ladies at No. 21. They took twelve boarders but also had places for day students. The girls were offered English and French as well as writing and arithmetic. Miss Grindly and Miss Fraser also ran a school for young ladies in the street. In 1808 the partnership was dissolved when Miss Grindly married, but Miss Fraser carried on with the business. Since there was nothing for girls beyond the basic education of the session schools it is not surprising that these schools prospered. Buying property in the best parts of the New Town was a considerable investment for a small private school.

Gentlemen of the New Town

From its early years, the New Town had attracted the rich and famous. In 1802 Walter Scott moved into North Castle Street, where he lived for the next twenty-four years. Scott was clerk to the Court of Session but became famous for his work on Border ballads. In 1814 he produced *Waverley*, his first historical novel. Since he refused to acknowledge their authorship, they became known as *The Waverley Novels*.

William Creech, bookseller and publisher, had his business premises at the east end of the Luckenbooths. He made an important contribution to the *First Statistical Accounts of Scotland* by commenting on the social changes occurring during the second half of the eighteenth century in Edinburgh. Some of these were first published in the *Edinburgh Evening Courant* (1783–84) under the name of 'Theophrastus'. Creech lived at No. 3 George Street. He had served as a bailie and in 1811 was persuaded to accept the position of lord provost.

Henry Raeburn owned considerable property to the west of Stockbridge. He began leasing this land in 1813, forming Raeburn Place, Ann Street, Dean Street and St Bernard's Crescent. He also acquired a house in George Street

in 1787. Later he moved to York Place. Raeburn was knighted by George IV for his services to the world of art.

The Moray Estate

The Earl of Moray possessed a piece of land at the north-west corner of the New Town. He began leasing this property at the beginning of the 1820s, creating a very exclusive area which included Moray and Ainsley Places. John Learmonth, the last lord provost of the unreformed council, and Charles Hope, lord president of the Court of Session, both had homes in Moray Place. No. 24 became the residence of the new lord advocate in Earl Grey's Reform government, Francis Jeffrey, who was also the leader of the Scottish Whigs.

The Railways

The 1840s brought the railway boom. The Edinburgh, Leith & Granton Railway built a tunnel under the New Town from Scotland Street into their Canal Street terminal. Passengers could now travel from the centre of Edinburgh to catch the ferries sailing from Granton. The station was built at right angles to Prince's Street, east of the Scott monument.

The main station, later known as Waverley, was used by the North British Railway Company and the Edinburgh & Glasgow Company. The Caledonian Railway was excluded from this enterprise and was forced to build its own terminus in Lothian Road. In 1870 they built Prince's Street Station behind what is now the Caledonian Hotel.

George and Prince's Streets Later in the Century

In the 1850s George Street remained an important retail centre with eight jewellers and many clothing and other outlets. Photography was developing into an important business opportunity at this time and twelve photographers had premises in Prince's Street. Kennigton & Jenner (later Jenner's) were already established at Nos 47–48. Specialist shops sold French and German imports, and Robert Blair, who had moved from the Bridges, offered confectionary as well as Italian goods at his shop at No. 37. William Roughead advertised clothing suitable for those intending to travel to Australia. Most of the shops were selling clothing – everything from evening dress to baby linen.

Melrose & Co. had opened another branch of their tea shops at No. 93. Further down, James Grey & Son specialised in kitchen equipment. Their business was to survive here in George Street into the early years of the twenty-first century.

Food was still sold in the various markets in the Old Town, however, at No. 106 James Anderson had opened a butcher's shop which he appears to have shared with Mrs Carstairs, who sold fruit.

By the mid-1860s, a dozen hotels could be found here. It had also become a transport centre, with the offices of the North British Railway and Croall's Coaches at No. 4.

Robbery in George Street
Burglars, using Thistle Street Lane, broke into the back of the premises of Hamilton, Crichton & Co. of No. 41 George Street. From there they knocked a hole in the wall, gaining access to J & J Blackwood, who were silk mercers. The thieves then removed lace and other goods worth £200–300. Strangely, they completely ignored the property of Hamilton, Crichton & Co., who were jewellers. A quick search of that shop would have found goods to the value of £5,000–6,000. The safe actually contained jewellery worth £50,000–60,000.

St Andrew's Square
This was the commercial heart of the city. The Stock Exchange was based in the square and sixteen assurance (and/or insurance) companies, as well as four banks had offices in St Andrew's Square. No. 5 contained the offices of the Scottish Friendly Life Assurance and a meeting place for the 1st Midlothian Coastal Artillery Volunteers. Also found in this building were the headquarters of religious charities and missions – the National Bible Society, the Religious & Charitable Institution, Edinburgh City Mission, the Sabbath Alliance and the Scottish Coast Mission.

Douglas's, owned at this time by Thomas Slaney, was probably Edinburgh's best hotel. The guest list included Prince Amadeus of Italy (in October 1865) and the King of Denmark (in August 1874). A new dining hall and twenty bedrooms were added in 1865.

A New Arcade for Prince's Street
On Saturday, 18 March 1876, Sir James Falshaw, the lord provost, opened the new arcade in the centre of Prince's Street. The covered walkway stood at over 100ft long and 30ft wide. This new Italian-style arcade had a marble floor and heating, allowing people to shop in comfort. The upper floors formed the New Clarendon Hotel. The whole project had cost £35,000.

Prince Albert's Statue
In August 1878 Queen Victoria arrived in Edinburgh to unveil a statue of Prince Albert (made by Mr Steell's Foundry in Grove Street) displayed in Charlotte Square. The city council planned the queen's route along George

Street, which angered the owners of property on Prince's Street. After listening to a delegation from the discontented people of Prince's Street the council revised the route allowing the royal procession to return by that street.

Security on the day was tight, with 200 extra constables brought in from Glasgow. Over 800 military pensioners gave their services. The army provided 1,000 soldiers to help line the route and control the crowds. The Roxburghe Hotel in Charlotte Square leased views from their windows at costs between 5s and £1 – no wonder the proprietors of Prince's Street were up in arms when there was a chance of making so much money! The North British Railway Company alone brought 50,000 people into the city for the occasion.

On Thursday, 17 August, Queen Victoria rode in her carriage from Holyrood to Charlotte Square via George Street. The equestrian statue of the prince was unveiled by the queen and she returned to Holyrood, passing along Prince's Street.

The Chantrelle Case, 1878

The suspicious death of the wife of Eugene Chantrelle in her home at No. 81 George Street led to a police investigation. She was found in a back bedroom. Gas had leaked from a broken pipe and it appeared the lady had been overcome with the fumes. Robert Hog, a gasfitter, told the police that the break could not have been made by accident. They began to suspect poisoning, although nothing was discovered at the post-mortem. However, traces of opium were found on a sheet and on a bed gown, and an assistant at Mackay's Pharmacy in George Street remembered Chantrelle coming into the shop and buying pills containing opium.

The jury pronounced a unanimous verdict against the accused and Eugene Chantrelle was hung in a storeroom of Calton Jail on the last day of March. A fund was later set up to help the couple's children.

Prince's Street in the 1880s

Although it was still a time of specialist shops, a number of large stores were developing, providing outfitting for the family and furnishing for the home. Jenner & Co. (once Kennington & Jenner) was already well established in Prince's Street and was to be joined by Cranston & Elliott, who moved from the Bridges in 1895. Renton & Co., also at the east end, were to merge with McLaren & Son (the firm founded by Duncan McLaren, the late MP and lord provost) a year later to become McLaren & Renton. Alongside these shops, you would find a good number of clothing outlets. During this period there were a considerable number of photographers as well as jewellers and watchmakers.

Waverley Station, owned by the North British Railway Company, led other companies – Midland, East Coast and the Caledonian Railway – to take office space in this part of the street. Gone were the stagecoach offices which would have been found here earlier in the century. Railways now dominated transport, be it suburban or long distance – even the queen and her family came north by train. Those arriving at Waverley Station had the option of a dozen hotels situated in Prince's Street at this time.

Overseas travel was still controlled by the shipping companies and at No. 31, Cunard, White Star, American and the Anglo-Australian Lines all had their offices for those wishing to book a passage.

The arcade, which had been opened by Sir James Falshaw, contained several specialist shops, the largest being Richard Sprengel's Imported Fancy Goods. In December 1892, only prompt action saved the arcade when a fire broke out in the cellar of Eugene Carmouche's Swiss Warehouse.

Edinburgh's Business Centre

By the 1880s most of the elegant houses in George Street and St Andrew's Square had been subdivided to satisfy the increasing demand for office space, particularly from the professional classes. With Edinburgh's Stock Exchange in South St David's Street, it is not surprising that fourteen stockbrokers had offices in St Andrew's Square, while both George Street and Hanover Street had another six each. Accountants, architects, civil engineers and solicitors all occupied property in George Street.

Earlier in the century, George Street had been the centre of a thriving educational establishment. By the 1880s only a few private tutors remained. Mr Trotter, in his home at No. 59 George Street, prepared people for the army, civil service and other exams. He also offered classes in mathematics and bookkeeping. Next to the music hall, Mr A. Schneider gave classes in French, German and Latin. Two large educational establishments were situated in Charlotte Square – the Charlotte Square Institute for Young Ladies and the Edinburgh Collegiate School. They probably found it hard to compete with the newly established Merchant Company Schools, whose school for young ladies in Queen Street had a roll of 1,200 pupils by the autumn of 1870.

The 1890s brought electricity to the streets of the city, beginning with the principal areas of the New Town.

Eight printing businesses could be found in Thistle Street. One of these was T & A Constable, Mary Piper's publishers. James Deas & Son were lithographers and engravers. The mission hall of St Andrew's Church could be found in Thistle Street as well as the New Town Dispensary and the Edinburgh Ear Dispensary.

Fire in Jenner's

In late November 1892, a massive fire broke out at Jenner's store on the corner of Prince's and St David's Streets. The alarm was raised at 10.08 p.m. Mr Cormack, the manager, had inspected the building between 6 p.m. and 7 p.m. but found nothing amiss. The night-watchman, on his patrol through the building some hours later, smelt burning and raised the alarm.

The complex included living quarters for eighty to ninety employees. They were successfully evacuated but the building itself was severely damaged. Four firemen were hurt as they fought to contain the blaze which, at one time, threatened the neighbouring properties – The Royal, The Old Waverley and Elder's Hotels and Sinclair's stationery shop.

At this time Jenner's employed 500 staff. Huge crowds, estimated at between 50,000–60,000, watched the blaze. The next day the fire continued to smoulder and the ruined walls were pulled down. The estimated cost of the damage reached £250,000.

The new premises were finally opened on Wednesday, 8 May 1895 by Mr James Kennedy, the senior partner. The whole of the new building was lit by electricity. Staff quarters on the upper floors contained dining, recreation and reading rooms as well as a small hospital staffed by professional nurses.

Mr Hamilton Beattie, the architect of the new store, must have been a happy man. He had also designed the new store of Cranston & Elliot, who had moved after thirty years at the Bridges to 33–38 Prince's Street.

Murder in George Street, 1894

When the employees of the Royal Fire & Life Insurance Co. arrived for work at their premise in No. 13 George Street they became suspicious that all was not well. No cleaning had been done overnight and there was no sign of the caretaker, Mr Donald MacDonald. They broke into his flat and discovered the body of Joanna MacDonald, his sister, on a bed in a recess in the kitchen. She was covered with a blanket, only her feet showing. Joanna had been stunned by blows to the head and her throat cut. There was no sign of her brother.

Donald MacDonald, who had previously worked for an auctioneer in Leith, had received his notice from the insurance company after eighteen months' service. His sister earned her living as a dressmaker. MacDonald had started drinking chloral and was probably an addict. A massive search began, which included lodging houses, parks and lochs but the authorities found no sign of the man. Later in the month, the *Evening News* (July 1894) reported that a body in a 'terribly mutilated condition' was dragged out of Glasgow harbour. It was identified as that of Donald MacDonald.

The New Town after the World Wars

Leith Street

This area of Edinburgh, which linked the New Town with Leith Walk, grew in popularity in the years after the First World War. In 1920 the *Evening News* declared, 'Leith Street is undoubtedly the busiest in the town'. However, it could also be a source of problems. A mass brawl one Saturday night in 1922 led to the police rushing in with batons drawn.

It was a reputation which would continue into the second half of the century. In 1954, Joan di Marco of the Minator Restaurant sold up to a London-based Furniture Company. Her cashier had been held up at knifepoint one Saturday night. 'This street has gone from bad to worse,' was her comment to the press on the closure of the restaurant. The Rendezvous Café across the road had already closed due to vandalism – a deliberately broken water pipe had led to flooding and the loss of £300 worth of cigarettes.

Explosions in Queen Street

In August 1945, a series of five explosions ripped up stretches of the pavement in Queen Street. The BBC studios were forced off the air. After 3½ hours, the street lighting came back on. The official investigation revealed that faulty insulation had ignited a deposit of bitumen gas found below the pavement.

Queensferry Street

Parking in the centre of Edinburgh was to become a major problem for the city authorities in the post-war world. The town council began in the autumn of 1947 by restricting parking in Queensferry Street. A van driver who was caught unloading in a prohibited area was fined by the magistrate, leading to protests from local traders. Councillor George Wilson complained, 'I, along with other traders, was under the impression that we would not be inconvenienced in the conduct of our business as when the new ruling was enforced.'

Problems with the Post-War Development of the New Town

Dr Elder Dickson, who was vice principal of the Edinburgh School of Art, compared Prince's Street to Brighton Promenade. He did not mince his words: 'I think we have permitted some of the most monstrous architectural mutilations permitted in civilised communities. Some of those at the West End are almost beyond belief in their brutality and ugliness'. The street was not the only target for the critics; the Dean of the Faculty of Advocates complained, 'I never cease to wonder at the disgraceful mess that the city has made of St Andrew's Square'.

Later in 1954, the planning committee, in its report to the town council, proposed to establish guiding principles for any further developments on Prince's Street. However, you can never satisfy everybody and John Holt, a local architect, challenged the policy: 'You'll never get good architecture by control'.

Plans to Improve Parking and Shopping, 1955

A new plan was produced offering more parking space by creating three squares in Rose Street, each providing parking for 500 cars. The squares were to be linked to Prince's Street and George Street by arcades of shops. It was certainly a bold plan, but it was overtaken by events.

William Livingstone proposed that a car park and bus station be built behind the post office at the west end of Waterloo Place. To ease traffic congestion, a road would encircle the Balmoral Hotel (then the North British). A new road linking Leith Street with the High Street would pass under Waterloo Place.

Real controversy arose when the council finally came up with plans to build a car park and bus station under East Prince's Street Gardens, accessed by Waverley Bridge with the exit at the Mound. The scheme was estimated to cost £235,000. Despite opposition from the Labour group – Councillor Williamson described it as 'a hastily conceived election propaganda scheme' – in September, the Progressives forced it through the council by thirty-one to twenty-three votes. This did not end the controversy, however. Parking was a serious problem in the city centre with 11,857 vehicles driven into the area each working day. Bailie Dunbar predicted that 'the time may come when we may have to find a means of limiting parking time in the city centre'.

Criticism came from the Cockburn Association, when Dr Clark accused the leaders of the Progressives of 'bludgeoning other party members into line'. The scheme was even discussed on the BBC's *Panorama* programme. However, the government had already written to every council in the country asking them to reduce their capital spending budgets. A special meeting of Edinburgh's council was called and it was decided not to continue with the project.

Fire at C & A Modes Ltd

There were three serious fires in central Edinburgh during November 1955. The Prince's Street premises of C & A Modes Ltd, who specialised in ladies' clothes, was seriously damaged. Two policemen guarding the property stopped opportunist thief Robert Lonnie as he left the back entrance in Meuse Lane and an examination found he was wearing nine blouses and four woollen jackets, as well as carrying a dress. He was fined £10.

The fire had been caused by an electric iron which had not been switched off. The resulting fire sale proved more exciting than the fire. Two women arrived eleven hours before the opening of the shop and by 9 a.m. a queue had formed in the street. The police, who were there in force, only allowed fifty shoppers in at a time. There were certainly bargains to be had with 79 guinea coats reduced to £10 and, in some cases, even less.

Conservation Versus Development

The conflict between conservation and development became a major issue for the New Town. George Street wanted the height of the Georgian buildings to be raised to create more office space. Eglinton Hotels, owners of the George Hotel, proposed to build a new block rising to 178ft with another 11ft for a lift tower. Planning permission was denied, despite the architect claiming the building would enhance the skyline!

Traffic was another problem facing Edinburgh's city centre. The rise in the number of cars led to clogged-up streets making it impossible for buses to run to time, especially in the rush hour. Parking, or the lack of it, was also a serious problem. Proposals to build underground car parks beneath Queen Street Gardens came to nothing. The new Castle Terrace car park came in at a massive £400,000 – thus, each parking space cost over £500.

The three statues in the centre of George Street were again threatened with removal as the city looked to speed up traffic travelling through and across the street. Councillor Maurice Heggie, to prove that this was not necessary, drove a 35ft lorry round all three statues. Eventually the city council restricted access to Prince's Street to buses, taxis and bicycles. Today, the new trams run along the street before terminating in St Andrew's Square. Prince's Street is closed for festival parades and the Hogmanay event.

Prince's Street also faced changes as some of the old buildings were removed to be replaced by the modern architecture of the 1960s. The New Club at No. 85 and its neighbours were redeveloped during the decade. This produced a striking contrast to the Georgian and Victorian buildings that formed Edinburgh's main street.

Eighteen

EDWARDIAN EDINBURGH AND THE FIRST WORLD WAR

Edwardian Edinburgh

Prince's Street

Three large stores – Renton Ltd, Jenner's and Cranston & Elliot – were now situated near the east end of Prince's Street. John Wright & Co. occupied Nos 104, 105 and 106, where they sold millinery and ladies' clothing. Forsyth's opened their new store in 1907; this shop also specialised in tartans and handknitted Shetland goods. A large store at the western end of the street was owned by Robert Maule & Co.

The demand for personal photographs continued with eight studios, mainly in the centre of Prince's Street – at this time, few people owned their own cameras. Many jewellers, goldsmiths and watchmakers had gravitated towards the street, attracting the custom of wealthy clients. Some of the leading political groups of the time had clubs and offices here and the Scottish Liberal Association's offices could be found at No. 95 while their rivals, the Liberal Unionists, who opposed Irish Home Rule, were at No. 80. The Scottish Liberals and the Conservatives had clubs for their members close by. (Prior to the First World War, Scotland was dominated by the Liberal Party and even the Unionist split failed to weaken their hold.)

In March 1907 two horses pulling a carriage bolted in Prince's Street. The police tried to stop the animals but this only led to a constable being injured. Finally, it fell to a cabman to bring them to a stop. Its occupant, Lady Steele, the wife of the lord provost, was shaken but uninjured.

Later in that same month, Thomas Renton, a coachman, dropped Mr MacDonald of Portobello in Castle Street before directing the carriage back to Prince's Street. The horse slipped and Renton was thrown onto the road. It then wove its way through the traffic on this busy street and down Waterloo Place before a carter stopped it at the Abbeymount. He kindly brought the horse and carriage back to Prince's Street. The highway was shared by the many horse-drawn vehicles and cable cars; the new motor cars were just making their appearance.

One of the biggest cultural influences in the twentieth century began during its first decade. The new 'picture palaces' brought early moving pictures to the public. The Prince's Cinema opened at No. 131 Prince's Street a few years before the war broke out.

Following the drop in tourist numbers in 1909, the state of West Prince's Street Gardens was brought up. It was claimed that it had become 'a loafer's paradise'. Parents would no longer permit their children to use the gardens and 'visitors making their way forward through such a squalid mob must consider what sort of citizens the Scottish capital rears', reported the *Evening News* in August 1909.

A Shooting in Elm Row

In March 1901 John Hume, a 30-year-old joiner, entered the baker's shop of John Smith & Son in Elm Row. He pulled out a revolver and fired at Catherine Grant, one of the young shop assistants. Fortunately, she ducked, but more shots followed. However, 'Hume's aim was as bad as his intentions and none of the shots took effect' (*Evening News*, March 1901). Colonel Alan Colquhoun, who was in the shop at the time, tried to disarm Hume but received a flesh wound for his trouble. Hume then shot himself and was taken to the infirmary. Later he was charged with assault using a lethal weapon.

John Hume had previously lodged with Catherine Grant's father and had developed a 'liking' for the 17-year-old girl. A plea of insanity was rejected as Sir Henry Littlejohn had found him quite sober and rational. Hume was sentenced to twelve years in prison.

Robert and Walter Pattison

The firm of Pattison Ltd, spirit merchants, were declared bankrupt in 1898, but questions began to be asked about the business methods of the two brothers. It took another three years before the evidence collected led to prosecutions. The *Evening News* commented, 'Great surprise is expressed in commercial circles at the long delay that took place before the Crown Authorities took steps to affect the arrests.' The brothers were charged with false accounting – overstating the company's profits.

They had also borrowed over £39,000 from the Clydesdale Bank. This was a loan taken by the company which was then appropriated by the brothers for their own use. One of the scams they had set up in a warehouse (probably in Constitution Street, Leith) involved the purchase of cheap Irish whisky at 11½d a gallon. Some Scotch was added and the barrels were labelled 'fine Old

Glenlivet' – worth 8s 6d a gallon! It was never put on the market. Robert Pattison was found guilty on all four charges and sentenced to eighteen months, while his brother, found guilty on only two charges, received nine months. Quite a few observers (and no doubt creditors) were astonished at the leniency of the sentences given by Lord McLaren.

The Stockbridge Explosion

In 1860 the Tod Brothers, flour millers in Leith, acquired the Stockbridge Mill. During the middle of the 1890s they purchased a gas engine to run the machinery of the mill and in 1901 the company decided to replace this with a new electric one. Messrs Stewarts of Bonnington bought the old machine and sent five of their men to Stockbridge to remove this old gas engine.

The mill complex included a building on the street which contained three shops on the ground floor. Above these were the mill offices and storerooms. The gas engine was in the yard behind this building. It is believed that the men failed to turn the gas completely off, and the explosion which followed killed all five men, as well as James Thomson, the mill manager. Others were injured and the mill itself damaged in the resulting fire. Mr Bowie, a grocer and wine merchant, had practically the whole contents of his shop blown into the street, and 'A tin of meat made a very clean looking hole in a shop window opposite'.

One tenement literally had a window blown in. The two ladies occupying a flat discovered a 'heavy window frame blown right into the middle of the room'. They had escaped without injury, not being in that room at the time.

The Great Storm, November 1901

The revenue cutter *Active* lay 1½ miles off Granton. In the high winds the ship dragged her anchors, leaving her to be driven onto the East Breakwater of the harbour. She then broke up and sank. Only three of the twenty-three crew on board at the time survived the disaster. The Swedish ship *Bele* pulled two men out of the water and the third man was found by one of the porters wandering round the harbour.

Four yachts in Granton were also sunk by the storm, leaving only their masts to peer above the water. Signal and telegraph lines collapsed in the high winds, disrupting railway traffic.

Hardship for the Poor

The first months of 1905 brought considerable distress to the poor of the city. The lord provost, Sir Robert Cranston, and some of the leading citizens set out to help those suffering hardship with the aid of the *Evening News'* Shilling Fund. The Corn Exchange in the Grassmarket became the main feeding station. Other soup kitchens were set up in Causewayside, Greenside, Stockbridge,

Gorgie and the Canongate. The army provided cooks and even town councillors lent a hand, as reported in the *Evening News* in January 1905:

> There was something of humour and pathos in seeing a town councillor unbending to a tiny youngster while he handed over a bowl of soup with the gentle admonition, 'mind your fingers, my dear, it's rather hot'.

Another supporter of this work was Mr H.E. Moss of the Empire Theatre who donated £50 to the Shilling Fund. At the first opening of these soup kitchens on Monday, 9 January, food was prepared for 800–900 people, but even that was not enough. Sir Robert Cranston personally handed out the soup and bread. An observer commented in the *Evening News* of January 1905, 'Destitution was written hard on almost every face and there was ample evidence of the great need there is for such a scheme as was inaugurated today.'

Reverend Aitken Clark of the Cairns Memorial Church in Gorgie led the effort in that district. This soup kitchen fed sixty-three families comprising 200 individuals. 'There is more genuine distress among the artisan class than during my nine years work in the city,' he told a reporter.

The town council set up a job creation scheme employing an extra 1,182 men in various departments. This was later estimated to have cost £5,000–6,000. The Shilling Fund gave Provost Mackie in Leith £25 to aid his relief work in the port.

Flora Clift Stevenson

Flora Stevenson was born in 1839, the youngest of eleven children. Her father, James Stevenson, was a partner in the Jarrow Chemical Company. On his retirement James set up home in Edinburgh with some of his children. The 1872 Act setting up school boards gave an opportunity for women to take an active role in public service and Henry Kingsley persuaded Flora to stand as a candidate. In 1873 she was duly elected as a member of the Edinburgh School Board, a position which she held until her death in 1905.

Flora, like her sister Louisa, wished to improve the educational opportunities for women. Louisa Stevenson, who served on St Cuthbert's Parish Council, worked tirelessly to improve access for women into higher education. In 1894 she opened a residency for women students in George Square. The University of Edinburgh awarded her an honorary LLD in recognition of her work in this field. Sir Ludovic Grant commented, 'It was fitting that one who was so instrumental in bringing university degrees within the reach of women should herself receive our highest degree.' Louisa died in 1908.

Flora Stevenson became convenor (chairman) of the attendance committee, responsible for prosecuting parents who refused to send their children to school. She proposed the idea of setting up a day industrial school to deal with this problem. However, it took some fifteen years before Parliament passed an Act allowing the school boards to carry this through.

Many children from poor families lacked proper clothing and food and Flora joined the Committee to Aid Destitute Children, set up in 1883. With the support of the Courant Fund, they raised money and took in clothing for the children of the poor. Flora acted as joint treasurer with William Skene.

She became convener of the School Work Committee, where 'Miss Stevenson's mastery of the detail and grasp of the whole facts of the subjects connected with the Board made her admirably suited to fill that very important position'.

In 1900 she was elected chairman of the school board. Three years later, the university made her an honorary Doctor of Law. She was granted the Freedom of the City of Edinburgh, becoming only the second woman, after Baroness Burdett-Coutts, to receive the recognition.

Flora Stevenson fell ill during the summer of 1905 and passed away in St Andrew's on 28 September. In their obituary, the *Evening News* summed up her contribution to the education of girls: 'Much of the changed attitude of the public towards that question was due to her untiring labour.' At the time of her death the board controlled thirty-four schools in the city.

The United Free Church

The year 1900 brought the union of the Free Church of Scotland with the United Presbyterian Church. However, some members of the Free Church wished to remain outside the union and a battle began for control of Free Church property. Although small in numbers (they were known as the 'Wee Frees'), they had a few supporters in the city. The ministers of Buccleuch and Greyfriars Free churches refused to join the United Free.

The matter drifted into the courts and in 1905 a decision forced the United Free members of St Columba's to hand over their building to the Free Church. As one elder put it, 'They were going out 900 strong to make way for 22 persons, none of whom had a very lengthy connection with the congregation.' However, they had to leave and a touching report by the *Evening News* summed up the effect on its individual members:

> The evening service was particularly touching and occasionally there were outward manifestations of feeling on the part of the congregation. Many of the older people who presumably had a long period and probably hereditary interest in the church felt their eyes fill as the crisis in the congregation's history was spoken of.

The government set up the Elgin Commission in an attempt to solve the dispute and ensure a fair distribution of property. Its report, issued in 1907, gave St John's (formerly Dr Guthrie's church) and Elder Memorial Church in Leith to the Free Church in Edinburgh. St Columba's was given to the United Free Church, who also received the Assembly Rooms on the Mound.

The Poorhouse

Those entering the poorhouse were placed in the charge of an inmate. Their clothes were removed and fumigated while the resident doctor gave them a medical examination before they were dressed 'in the distinctive clothes of the institution'. One man, reporting on his stay in the poorhouse, told the *Evening News*, 'There I was then, in a short space of a day, transferred from a liberty loving subject into a pauper'.

The labour master put them to work bunching sticks for firewood and those who possessed a trade received suitable tasks while others were employed in the garden. The rations of food were the bare minimum. Our new inmate complained, 'I specifically say, and that without contradiction, that the quantity sanctioned by the Local Government Board is more often under than over the authorised amount'. Meals consisted of meal and milk (porridge) with soup (pea or vegetable) and bread at lunchtime. Twice a week they received 2–3oz of suet pudding. Since the inmates were only given thirty minutes for lunch, food had to be consumed quickly.

Life in 1908 at the Craigleith Poorhouse was described 'by one who has experienced it':

7.00 a.m.	Rise.
7.45 a.m.	Work begins.
9.00 a.m.	Breakfast of porridge and buttermilk – 'It is called butter milk, I suppose, because it does not bear the slightest trace of having any connection with butter.'
	Short service for Protestants.
9.45 a.m.	Work begins again.
2.00 p.m.	Dinner of soup and 8oz bread – paupers on extra jobs got 4oz beef.
2.45 p.m.	Return to work until 5.00 p.m.
6.00 p.m.	Supper of porridge and milk – aged and frail received tea and bread. This was followed by a short service. [Inmates were then free to use the 'day room' – overcrowded and smelly – until 8.30 p.m.]
9.00 p.m.	Lights out – the gas lighting was turned off at the mains raising safety issues.

Some inmates were rewarded with supplies of tobacco, but it was against the rules to possess matches. Once a fortnight they were allowed a bath, but since the water was not changed the benefits of this were dubious.

The Suffragettes and the Movement for the Franchise

This movement was led by a number of groups, some of which were more militant than others. In the years leading up to the First World War, the Women's Social and Political Union, with its Edinburgh headquarters in Frederick Street, disrupted public meetings and even set about causing criminal damage in their attempts to persuade Parliament to give the vote to women.

On Saturday, 5 October 1907, the women's suffrage movement held a rally in Holyrood Park and 2–3,000 women marched from the park through Regent Road and Prince's Street to the Synod Hall. Banners proclaimed:

> Scots wha hae votes men.
> Scots wha haena votes women.

Miss Mair, President of the Edinburgh National Society for Women's Suffrage, took the chair.

Some progress had been made, and women were now eligible for seats on the town council. In 1907 women were allowed to stand in the elections for local councils and Lady Steele put her name forward for St Stephen's Ward. Although there were two seats available, she was defeated by John Murray and William Findley. However, she still polled over 1,100 votes.

The following year, Clarice McNab was elected to Leith Burgh council. She later married Ben Shaw, secretary of the Scottish Labour Party. Clarice went on to become MP for Kilmarnock. She died in October 1946.

As the years drew on towards the war, the militant group became more aggressive. In June 1913, Emily Davidson was killed when she carried her protest to the Epsom Derby. Hunger strikes by the imprisoned suffragettes were followed by forced feeding. When this failed, the government released them and, after a suitable time consuming food, they were rearrested. In April 1914, Miss Arabella Scott was released from prison in Edinburgh only to be picked up on the promenade in Brighton. She was detained and returned to Edinburgh.

In Edinburgh the militant group appears to have followed the national movement by attacking property. A bomb at Blackford Observatory and fires at a house in the Grange and at Fettes College were blamed on the suffragettes.

The churches became the next target. An evening service at South Leith United Presbyterian Church was interrupted. Soon they turned their attention to more prominent churches. In the words of an *Evening News* reporter in Monday, 20 October's edition, 'Yesterday a voluntary choir introduced variations in St Giles Cathedral in the form of chanted petitions for the ring leaders of the militant movement.' A few weeks later, they carried their protest to St Mary's Cathedral.

When war broke out, the suffragettes turned their energies to helping those disadvantaged by the conflict. At their Christmas sale, Miss Mair told the patrons that they would turn their efforts to helping the Soldiers' and Families' Association. They organised working parties to produce clothing for the Red Cross, Belgium refugees and soldiers' families. Their permanent staff were allocated to assist alleviating women's unemployment and helping the Soldiers' & Sailors' Families' Association.

The Distress Committee

At the beginning of the twentieth century, local government services were provided by various elected boards. Schools were governed by the school boards while poor relief and the workhouses came under the control of the parish councils. Town councils provided much of the funding through their assessments, but they had no say in the decisions of these bodies.

The general economic downturn in the middle of the first decade led the government to set up distress committees. By the end of February 1909, the Edinburgh Distress Committee had provided relief to nearly 5,000 people. At this time they had 1,452 people in their employment. However, this came at a cost – a cost to the city council that had no say in the use of these funds. The controversy increased when the committee purchased Muireston Farm for £5,500 in the autumn of 1907 with the permission of the local government board. When asked about this at a town council meeting, Treasurer Harrison explained that he had no details either, as members of the distress committee had taken good care that nobody should have any details. The dispute eventually came before the Court of Session, who ruled that the town council had no powers in the matter.

Sectarianism, 1909

Jacob Primmer raised the spectre of an Irish Catholic takeover of the Edinburgh Infirmary. In a letter to Miss Gibb, the superintendent of nurses, Primmer based such claims on a statement in the *Catholic Herald*. The managers replied, denying that any such move was being attempted by the Catholic Church. They had recently, in their application procedure, dropped any inquiries into candidates' religious persuasions.

The Edinburgh School Board had agreed to provide books, free of charge, for pupils from deserving families who attended 'voluntary schools' – these were Roman Catholic and Episcopal schools outwith their control. The election of the new board in March became a single-issue matter. Councillor Leishman, a member of the board, complained that 'he regretted the appearance of anything like the sectarian bitterness in education'. Even the *Evening News* joined in, publishing a list of candidates in two columns – one for the free issue of books and one against. Four of those candidates who favoured the free issue of books to voluntary school pupils failed to get elected.

At a lecture held in May at the Central Hall in Nicolson Street, the guest lecturer was a Mr Ruthven, who was a former priest. His talk was advertised as 'showing how the Church of Rome deliberately trains its members in the practice of systematic thieving'. This was a challenge to the employment prospects of young Catholic girls in domestic service. It appears a good number of them turned up for Mr Ruthven had hardly started before Catholic hymn books were produced and the girls began singing 'The Faith of Our Fathers'. After several attempts to continue the lecture had failed, the police were summoned, but the presence of a dozen constables made no difference. Stewards managed to eject two of the objectors before the meeting was abandoned.

In November, members of the Council of the Protestant Daughters and Sons of Freedom Society placed questions before those seeking election to the town council:

Do you pledge yourself not to make concessions to the Roman Catholic Party?
Will you oppose the appointment of and the giving of money to Popish or Prelatic Chaplins to the City Hospital?
Will you refuse to vote a Papist into the Magisterial Chair? [Councillor Cullen was to become the first Catholic Bailie since the Reformation in 1560.]

Councillor Moscrip counter-attacked:

One question he [the member of this society] said really covered the lot. It was simply intolerance setting up one religion against another and is not the purpose and duty of their representatives to breed antagonism because the community comprised all religious factions and creeds.

The Budget, 1909

Lloyd George's budget proposed increases in death duties as well as rises in taxes on tobacco and alcohol. Income tax rose by 2d and the chancellor introduced a supertax to be paid by the rich. Fear of the expanding German Navy led to demands for the increase in the number of new battleships, but the cost would have been prohibitive without extra taxation. The huge Liberal majority in the House of Commons secured the passage of the Budget. However, on the last day of November it was rejected by the House of Lords. Parliament was dissolved and an election was held in January 1910.

In Edinburgh, Leith and Midlothian, the Liberals held on to their seats. Sir Robert Cranston, a Unionist and a former lord provost, failed to take Leith from its long-serving MP, Mr Munro Ferguson.

At Westminster, the government led by Herbert Asquith had a mandate to carry the Budget and limit the power of the Upper House. The death of Edward VII in May only delayed matters. In 1911, the Lords accepted the Parliament Act which restricted their power of veto over legislation, particularly in financial affairs.

The Marine Gardens

The Marine Gardens in Portobello opened at the end of May 1909. The bandstand and a concert hall with enough room to accommodate 2,500 people had been brought from the exhibition grounds at Saughton. A skating rink and a promenade hall were added. For those looking to the more exotic, the management built a Palestine Village as it would have been in biblical times and a menagerie with painted scenery.

From the start the gardens were in financial trouble, with attendances dropping well below expectations. Blame was placed on the poor summer weather and the high cost of tramway fares. Mr Maxton told the shareholders, 'The only thing satisfactory about the report was that the Board were going to retire'. Two years later, in 1913, the new board recommended that the company should be wound up as the debenture shareholders demanded their money. However, an agreement was reached and the 'gardens' continued to function.

During the first year of the war, the Marine Gardens were taken over by the War Office. At a meeting in March 1915, the chairman refused to divulge the amount of money the company was receiving for the lease of the gardens. Mr Swan demanded that this be placed before the shareholders but his motion was defeated.

The Usher Hall

In June 1896, Andrew Usher of Blackford Park had called on Lord Provost MacDonald to offer him £100,000. This was to be spent on a new hall for the city. Mr Usher left the details, especially the choice of the site, to the town council. The first site to be recommended lay between Fountainbridge and Morrison Street but this was rejected. Other proposals for the Canal Basin, Chambers Street, Castle Terrace and even St Andrew's Square were turned down. It was not until March 1911 that tenders were issued and work began on the chosen site in Lothian Road. In July of that year, the new king (George V) laid the foundation stone – it had taken fifteen years!

The City Finances, 1911

The battle over 'economy' began early in 1911. The lord provost, a former city treasurer, considered that a rise in the rates would not be necessary. Treasurer Leishman disagreed, claiming that they might need to raise the rates by 2*d* in the pound. Edinburgh had the advantage of a high rate of collection – 94.58 per cent in 1910 – but the treasurer was determined to keep control over expenditure, which did not endear him to those on the council spending the money.

Proposals to give special payments (honoraria) to certain senior council officials met with opposition from both within and without the council. The superintendent of works, on a salary of £550, was to be given a bonus of £500. Although this failed to pass, they did agree to raise his salary. The road surveyor received £100 and Dr Kerr of the Colinton Fever Hospital was given £150. In contrast to these lavish bonuses, the limewashers on 18s a week were refused a rise of 2s. The *Evening News*, in an editorial, was concerned at the growing personal element being introduced into these matters – it appears they had a point.

The Great Lafayette

Sigmund Neuberger, an American with Jewish ancestry, was performing one of his illusion acts when a fire broke out on the stage of the Empire Theatre in Nicolson Street. Prompt action by the management, who lowered the safety curtain and organised the evacuation of the theatre (around 3,000 people), prevented a major disaster. However, those on the stage were not so fortunate. The thick smoke led to ten deaths, including that of the 'Great Lafayette'. Alice Roberts, a small girl and only 17 years old, suffocated as she worked the mechanical teddy bear. Some animals, including Lafayette's dog, Beauty, also died in the fire. Sir Edward Moss summed up the whole tragedy with the words, 'You can soon put a theatre all right but you can't repair loss of life'. Lafayette and his dog were buried in Piershill cemetery.

Brewing, Distilling and Bonded Warehouses

Brewing remained one of the most important industries in the city until the late twentieth century. By 1845 Edinburgh had twenty-six breweries, most of which were situated in the Canongate and neighbouring streets. The Pleasance was the home of two large businesses – Bell's Brewery (originally Bell & Keir) and the Pleasance Brewery. Seven breweries alone were based in either the North or South Back of the Canongate.

In the first half of the nineteenth century two distilleries (Sudbury and Canonmills) had developed by the Water of Leith. The Lochrin Distillery stood close to the basin of the Union Canal, although it appears to have closed before 1850.

In the 1880s Lorimer & Clark established their brewery in Slateford Road, while William McEwan's business was expanding in Fountainbridge. By the close of the century, however, new breweries were being constructed around Craigmillar – Deuchar Ltd had built their Duddingston Brewery here, and Dryborough & Co. already owned a brewery at Duddingston Station. In 1905, five large companies carried out brewing in Craigmillar.

By 1896 the north side of Commercial Street in Leith was lined with bonded warehouses storing whisky and other spirits prior to them paying duty. Some of these warehouses remained until the 1970s. In June 1955, a massive fire in Leith led to the destruction of Hill Thomson & Co. Ltd's warehouse. The combustible nature of the whisky and rum added to the dangers faced by the fire brigade. Fire spread to the roof of McDonald & Muir's, and even the Caledonian Bonding Co. Ltd was threatened by the flames. Local people evacuated their homes but the fire was soon under control. Hill & Thomson had employed 150 men and women in their warehouse. However, by the end of the twentieth century Edinburgh's breweries had been taken over by multi-national businesses and the smaller breweries had been closed. Only the brewery on Slateford Road now remains of this once thriving industry.

Retail

The early part of the nineteenth century saw the rise of Duncan McLaren. From a small drapery business in the High Street, his reputation grew, allowing him to be elected as a member of the town's first reformed council. He became treasurer, helping a bankrupt Edinburgh come to terms with its creditors. Later he served as lord provost and a Member of Parliament.

The bigger stores represented a serious threat to the small private businesses which lacked the financial resources to compete. The largest of these was the Co-operative. By 1905, St Cuthbert's Co-operative Association owned many shops in the city and its suburbs. Stores had opened in Morningside, Corstorphine and Gilmerton. In Gorgie Road, groceries were sold at Nos 10 and 264. The Co-operative butchers sold their meat at Nos 14 and 264 and operated a bakery at No. 266. They also had shops which sold furniture, boots and shoes, clothes, drapery and drugs. In total, St Cuthbert's Co-operative had thirty-nine grocery departments, twenty-eight butchers and twenty-three bakeries spread across the city.

Feelings ran high at the beginning of 1907, when 'G.W.' wrote to the *Evening News* making this suggestion, 'I don't say every employer should, or would, not employ a co-operator but hold that he has a perfect right to do or not to do so'. The matter did not rest, with 'Defiance' replying, 'I am a working man and have derived great benefit from the store, as many hundreds of my kind have done in the past, and will assuredly do in the future'.

The Cinema

The early years of the twentieth century saw the arrival of moving pictures. These were in black and white and contained no sound, but nevertheless they proved to be exceedingly popular. Cinemas, or 'picture houses' as they were then called, were built to provide for this new entertainment craze. By the beginning of 1914, Nicolson Street and the adjoining square had three such houses. Fountainbridge became the home of the Coliseum and the Palladium. Even Prince's Street was not immune, with the New Picture House and the Prince's Cinema. The High Street boasted the Tron, while down Leith Walk were Pringle's New Picture Palace and the Salon.

Leith itself had the Leith Picture House and the Palace. Along the coast in Portobello High Street could be found the Cinema Theatre, while in nearby Bath Street stood the strangely named Bungalow Electric Theatre. Morningside, Gorgie and the Haymarket (Dalry Road) now each possessed a picture house of their own – a sure sign of the popularity of the new silent, black and white, moving pictures in the city.

The Health of the City Before the First World War

From 1861 the death rate in Edinburgh began to fall. In 1912, the city had a population of around 320,000. The 6,700 births, a rate of 2.08 per cent, was the lowest since records began:

	DEATH RATE	BIRTH RATE
1861	2.3 per cent	3.3 per cent
1871	2.78 per cent	3.4 per cent
1881	1.8 per cent	3.2 per cent
1891	2.0 per cent	2.8 per cent
1901	1.78 per cent	2.4 per cent
1911	1.4 per cent	2.1 per cent

The major concern of the Medical Officer for Health (Dr A. Maxwell Williamson) was the infant mortality rate. He concluded in his report, 'Where these highest rates prevail the worst housing conditions and the densest and most closely packed together series of tenements largely consistent of houses of one or two rooms.' Voluntary lady visitors (numbering around 300 by 1912) had helped to reduce the problem.

The highest death rates for children under 5 could be found in:

St Giles Ward	15.5 per cent
St Andrew's Ward	14.7 per cent
St Leonard's Ward	13.9 per cent
Portobello	13.7 per cent

Merchiston, with a rate of only 4.6 per cent, was the lowest in the city. During 1912 a total of 702 children under a year old had died.

Slum Property

The major areas of concern during the nineteenth century had been the closes leading from the High Street and the Canongate, as well as the homes in the Cowgate and the Grassmarket. Here, the once large flats had been divided up to provide cheap single-room dwellings. At the beginning of the new century, much of the property in the district to the south – the Pleasance, Arthur Street, Prospect Street, Richmond Street and Carnegie Street – had fallen into disrepair. 'A Social Student' writing in the *Evening News* told the readers, 'The houses are dark, dismal and uncomfortable'. Here, the once five or six-roomed houses had been converted into single-room homes.

Children at Work

As late as 1913, Alexander Fairgrieve, who manufactured cardboard at Spylaw Mill in Colinton, appeared in court charged with employing children without a certificate of fitness. They were under 14 years of age and did not possess an exemption from the school issued by the school board. At the time of his visit, Mr Thomas Brow, the factories inspector, told the court that the children had been hidden. Mr Fairgrieve pleaded guilty, claiming that he was on holiday when the arrangements had been made.

Two years later, the owners of Wood's Bottle Factory in Portobello were charged with employing boys at 11.30 p.m. and not keeping a register of employees. The boys, Samuel Moore and James Gibson, were both under 14 and attended school from 9 a.m. until 3 p.m. before commencing work in the factory at 6 p.m. The shift did not finish until 5 a.m. Not surprisingly, both boys had eventually collapsed with exhaustion. The sheriff asked, 'Are they still alive?' and fined Wood £10.

Chip Shops

During the 1890s and the opening years of the twentieth century, ice cream shops with their poor hygiene and late opening hours had presented problems to the authorities. However, the town council had moved to license such premises. Then the chip shops became the new attraction. Many of the Italians who had settled in Edinburgh moved from the ice cream shops into this new trade. According to the *Evening News*, 'A wet Saturday or Sunday evening means a veritable gold mine to the chip merchant.' Although the chip shops offered takeaways, they also provided table service. It was claimed that 'plain wood and sawdust made up a chip shop's furniture', together with a large number of mirrors which enabled the owners to keep an eye on their patrons. By 1914 they had introduced gambling machines into these cafes.

The First World War

The First Casualties

Shortly after the outbreak of war, HMS *Amphion* was struck by a mine and sank. Only 131 of her 283 officers and crew were saved. Among the casualties was Alfred James Luxton from Juniper Green, who had worked for Fairgrieve's and Kinleith Mills before signing up as a stoker. Another victim was John Maxwell, a signal boy, whose father was the church officer of St Giles.

The Early Effects of the War

Germans, Austrians and Hungarians living in Edinburgh and Leith were arrested by the authorities and imprisoned in Redford Barracks. Leith, with its important European trade, was the home of about 600 (figures vary in different accounts) aliens of whom 100 were classed as enemy citizens.

Problems arose over Germans who had adopted British citizenship. Three university staff were forced to resign and an assistant librarian ended up in Redford Barracks. The chocolate factory of William Schultze on the Portobello Road was requisitioned by the army. Standing 60ft high, its flat roof offered a fine view of the shipping passing through the Firth. Later in the war his son, also William, a private in the Cameronian Highlanders, was killed on the Western Front. The sheriff refused William's request to act as executor, despite the fact that he had lived in Scotland for fifty-four years. A second son was fighting in East Africa. The case was passed to the Lords of Session, who reversed the decision in favour of William Schultze.

Flag and Flower Days helped to raise money for charitable causes such as Belgian refugees, whose country had been overrun by the Germans in the first months of the war.

The Royal Scots

The eighteen battalions which made up the Royal Scots in 1915 were recruited from south-east Scotland. Recruiting offices sprang up all over the city as various notables sought to raise soldiers for local regiments. Sir Robert Cranston, now a colonel, led the work to create an Edinburgh Battalion for the Royal Scots. Sir George McCrae also set out to raise another battalion (16th Royal Scots), opening recruiting offices in Castle Street and Henderson Terrace. His volunteers were housed in Heriot's Hospital. They did not reach the front until the beginning of 1916. A year later, Lloyd George chose Sir George to be chief whip in his coalition government, leading him to resign his post.

Lord Rosebery, once prime minister, raised a smaller battalion of men which became known as the Bantam Battalion. They trained at the drill hall in

Annandale Street. Some, like the 2nd and 12th, were serving in France (during 1915) while others had been sent to the Dardanelles. George Wilson, from the Lawnmarket, captured an enemy gun position and turned the weapon on the Germans. His fire was so effective that it was believed he killed nearly 300 men. Then he rescued his wounded comrade, bringing him back to the line. For this action Wilson was awarded the Victoria Cross.

In September 1916, an *Evening News* reporter found Wilson selling newspapers on the corner of George IV Bridge and the Lawnmarket in order to supplement his pension of 16s a week. He was living with his sister in Bank Street. Wilson explained, 'Since I got ... last knock about at Loos, I was gassed and wounded, I am not fit for work as I use to be.' His case was taken up by Major Robertson VC, who was in charge of recruiting in Edinburgh. After consultation with the lord provost, Wilson was sent to a farm colony at Polton for six months, after which the council promised to find him suitable work.

May 1915 brought the death of the first serving town councillor when Lieutenant Colonel James Clark was killed by a shell in France. On Saturday, 22 May, three trains ran into each other at Gretna Junction. One of the trains contained members of the 4th Royal Scots, many of whom came from Leith and the surrounding area. A public funeral was held in Leith with all shops closed in the town. Provost Malcolm Smith and the whole council attended. Many of the victims were buried in Rosebank cemetery where a memorial was erected in memory of those killed in the disaster.

During the First World War, the Forth contained important elements of the British fleet. Ships approaching the Firth had to take on a pilot at the Isle of May. However, on Sunday, 2 April 1916, the port was attacked by a Zeppelin which destroyed a warehouse and killed two people.

Lord Provost Sir Robert Kirk Inches

Robert Inches was born in 1840. His father owned a printing business in Old Assembly Close. With his uncle James Hamilton, they formed Hamilton & Inches, gold and silversmiths. He became a member of the council in 1900 and, at the age of 72, succeeded Sir William Brown in the office in 1912. The new lord provost was therefore not a young man and it was hoped that this would bring about a quieter time in Edinburgh's history. This, of course, was not to be and Robert Inches found himself in the centre of the war work.

During the summer of 1915, the *Evening News* published a series of articles criticising the lord provost. Lack of action and lack of leadership were the main complaints levied at him: 'He was asked to do little and he did it quite well'. The most damning pieces were attributed to an unnamed member of the town council who complained:

The tendency in official circles to drift along as if all was well and everything possible was being done has been very marked and will continue to be so until the council as a council is shamed out of its complacency.

The council always referred controversial matters back to committees when they were unwilling to make a decision. At a time of national crisis, this was not appropriate. Matters went deeper when 'Town Councillor' claimed, 'The reports of the council Meetings indicate lack of control over debate and lack of guidance in moulding opinion'. 'Town Councillor' remained anonymous, but Treasurer Hugh McMichael complained that 'recruiting for the Royal Scots has been scandalously neglected'.

Eventually, Robert Inches turned on the *Evening News* and its contributor: 'He never for a moment associated any member of the council with such a scandalous statement, and it was only a scandalous rag of a paper that could possibly put it in'. The attacks stopped.

The government, through a Provisional Order, decided that local elections (held in November) would not take place in 1915. However, internal matters which included the selection of the lord provost and the bailies could be carried through. Robert Inches agreed to continue in the office.

In the 1916 New Year's Honours List, the lord provost received a knighthood accompanied by a very supportive article in the *Evening News*. The lord provost was praised for his work with recruitment and his leadership in setting up the manufacture of munitions in the city. His daughter, Mrs T. Miller, was taking an active interest in assisting the families of soldiers and sailors.

By the summer, discussions had begun about the election (by the town council) of a new lord provost. Sir Robert remained active and some favoured retaining him rather than creating conflict in a battle for the provostship. Eventually Sir Robert told the council that he did not wish to continue and John Lorne McLeod became the new lord provost. Sadly, he did not survive to see the end of the war.

Edinburgh, 1915

An observer in the *Evening News* claimed, 'The matter of soldiers' dependants is one of the most interesting social problems cast up by the war.' Men from Edinburgh and Leith joined the forces in large numbers, leaving their families behind. Allowances were given to soldiers' and sailors' dependants each week:

Wife	12/6 (twelve shillings and six pence)
Wife and child	17/6
Wife and two children	21/–
Wife and three or more children	23/–

The loss of so many men threatened the smooth running of businesses and local government. The Tramway Company in Edinburgh lost around 460 men to the colours. In June, despite opposition from some of the men, thirty-four women were taken on as conductors and one lady was chosen as an inspector.

The war brought a rapid rise in the prices of most household goods. Food was particularly affected by wartime inflation and so war bonuses were paid to assist workers on low incomes.

The army was not the only group seeking men. The manufacture of munitions and the naval dockyard at Rosyth offered good wages to labourers.

One of the first groups to suffer in the changing conditions was the city's landladies. Some were even forced to sell their furniture in order to keep going. At this time, both the War Office and the Red Cross refused to billet convalescing service personnel with these women.

Fortunately, only Private James Crichton of the Royal Field Artillery took his work home. He visited a pub in the Cowgate and showed one of the employees a shell. This exploded, killing the man and injuring Crichton so badly that he died later in the Royal Infirmary.

James Thin

James Thin was born in 1824 and began work at the age of 12 as an apprentice bookseller. Eventually he opened his own business and became established in premises on South Bridge. Robert Louis Stevenson was one of many to patronise his shop. James was baptised in Bristo Place United Presbyterian chapel and remained a member all his life. He served as an elder in the church for over sixty years. Hymns were his main interest: he owned 2,500 volumes of them and was considered an expert on the subject. James Thin died in April 1915 at the age of 91. His business continued into the twenty-first century, before being taken over by Blackwell's.

Elsie Maud Inglis

Elsie was born in Naini Tal, India, on 16 August 1864. When her father, John Inglis, retired he brought his family to Edinburgh. She became one of the second generation of women seeking to become doctors. Sophia Jex-Blake had already established her Edinburgh School of Medicine, despite opposition from the Medical School at the university which refused to accept women. Clinical instruction was given at Leith Hospital as the Royal Infirmary was controlled by the University Medical School. However, Sophia Jex-Blake's autocratic rule led to a split and Elsie, with the help of her father and his friends, established a rival medical college for women in 1889. She studied in Glasgow before taking a post in London.

In the 1890s she set up a medical practice in Walker Street with Jessie MacGregor. Difficulties still remained for women seeking to enter the profession and Elsie helped to found a Women's Hall of Residence in George Square. In 1904 Dr Inglis set up the Hospice at 219 High Street. This provided medical help for the poor women of the Old Town. Four years later, an infant milk depot was added. In 1905 Elsie Inglis was appointed as a consultant to the Bruntsfield Hospital, despite the opposition of Dr Jex-Blake who had retired to Sussex. The two hospitals were amalgamated in 1911.

Women did not have the parliamentary franchise so Elsie joined the Edinburgh Society for Women's Suffrage which was led by Mrs Priscilla Bright McLaren, the widow of Duncan McLaren. She was one of a number of women who tried to get the vote for women graduates in university constituencies. This was blocked by the Court of Session. Elsie Inglis continued to support the cause and resigned from the Central Edinburgh Women's Liberal Association (she was vice president) when the party, despite its large parliamentary majority, refused to give the vote to women. She disapproved of the more violent tactics being advocated by some women's groups.

When war broke out in 1914, Elsie Inglis played a major role in the setting up of the Scottish Women's Hospital. Active service units provided medical attention for the wounded, while others worked tirelessly at home to raise the funds for the work. A hospital was set up in the old Cistercian Abbey of St Louis de Royaumont in France, while another hospital opened at Kragujevatz in Serbia, where an outbreak of typhus added to the problems of the war. Dr Inglis arrived there on 5 May 1915.

Towards the end of October, the Serbs and the Scottish Women's Hospital abandoned Kragujevatz in the face of the Austro-Hungarian advance. A new hospital was set up in Krushevatz, but soon the town was occupied by German soldiers as the Serbs continued to retire southwards. Dr Inglis and some of her team were captured and sent to Vienna. The American Ambassador from Berlin secured their release and the women were taken to Switzerland. She returned to Britain where she heard that the Serbian government had awarded her their highest honour, the Order of the White Eagle.

Dr Inglis soon returned to the front, helping to support the Serbs who were now fighting with their Russian allies in Rumania. The women arrived in Archangel in northern Russia on 10 September 1915. It took them nine days to reach Odessa on the Black Sea coast. The party joined the Serbs and their allies, the Russians and Rumanians, who were trying to stop the German advance through Rumania. Eventually Dr Inglis set up a hospital unit in the Rumanian town of Braila, just west of the Danube delta, before retiring first to Galatz and then to Reni.

The unit of the Scottish Women's Hospital was forced to return to Archangel, travelling across Russia which was now disintegrating into revolution. The journey took four weeks. Sadly, Elsie Inglis was already seriously ill. The party sailed from Russia on the SS *Porto* and landed on the Tyne. Elsie Inglis died a few days later (27 November 1917) in the Station Hotel at Newcastle. She was only 53 years old.

After a service in St Giles, Elsie Maud Inglis was laid to rest in the Dean cemetery. In 1925, the Elsie Inglis Memorial Hospital was opened as a tribute to her service.

Edinburgh, 1916

One of the major social problems to come out of the war was the increase in alcohol consumption among many of the wives of the volunteers. By February, the magistrates' court had dealt with 300 cases. Nurse Sibbald, who worked with these women, was appointed as a probation officer by the court. She had responsibility for seventy cases given to her by the Soldiers' and Sailors' Association and another 300 from the police court. The nurse had to stop some wives sending money to their husbands when it was needed at home to support the family.

The authorities began to demand a 'blackout' of the city. Evening classes came to an end, and the council closed the public baths an hour after sunset. In mid-March twenty-three shopkeepers were prosecuted for not having adequate screening to prevent the light escaping. The precautions proved to be well timed, for on Sunday night, 2 April, two Zeppelins approached Edinburgh.

L14 and L22 dropped twenty-seven high-explosive and seventeen incendiary bombs. Alois Bocker, in L22, had visited Leith before the war as a merchant navy officer. He dropped his bombs on the port, damaging a whisky bonded warehouse and killing two people. The next place to receive direct hits was the Grassmarket, where eleven people died and twenty-four civilians were injured.

Attacks on merchant shipping by German submarines threatened the food supplies of the country. To ease the pressure placed on limited stocks people were encouraged to grow their own vegetables. The town council led the way and by the summer of 1916 had laid out eight sites for use as allotments. Rents varied from 10s 6d to 23s. Greenhouses and buildings over 3ft tall were not permitted. The Merchant Company and the Heriot Trust also put aside land for allotments. By the beginning of 1917 over 41 acres at twenty different sites had been allocated for the allotments. The scheme continued to expand with Mr J.S. Chisholm of the Edinburgh College of Agriculture giving advice every Thursday in his column in the *Evening News*. By the summer of 1917 there were 1,716 allotments covering 96 acres. Potatoes were the main crop, but cabbages, peas, beans, turnips, onions and leeks provided extra nutrition.

Edinburgh's citizens continued to raise money for the war effort. In 1915, Flag Days had produced over £30,000 for such causes as the Red Cross and the Soldiers' & Sailors' Help Society. They began collecting bottles and jars in a big recycling effort; the Boy Scouts did much of the door-to-door work. Two shops in George Street were used in the evenings by the sorters. The following year, everyone had a paper collection. Scrap white paper sold for £4 10s a ton.

Edinburgh, 1917

Inflation

Rising prices affected everyone. Edinburgh Town Council was paying 'war bonuses' to enable their employees to keep up with the rising cost of living:

	Pre-war (1914)	May 1917
Dozen eggs	9d	18–33d
Potatoes, 14lb	10–11d	23½d
Peas, 1lb	3d	9–11d
Sugar, 1lb	2d	5½–6d
Flour, 1lb	14d	24d
Bacon	14d	21d

The depredations of U-boats led to shortages and thus to rising prices. However, suspicion was rife that some people were profiteering. The government appointed a food controller and local committees were set up to ensure the regulations were enforced. By the end of the year, some success had been achieved in an attempt to halt the rise in prices:

	Pre-war (1913)	Early 1917	Control (Dec. 1917)
Sausages 1lb	9d	20d	18d
Steak mince 1lb	14d	28d	23d
Stewing beef 1lb	11d	26d	20d

The 4lb loaf of bread which had been 6½d before the war cost 12d at the beginning of 1917. Food Control had reduced the price to 9d.

The cost of clothing had also risen dramatically. Ladies boots, which had stood at 13s 6d before the war, at the end of 1917 cost 34s a pair. Shoes were little better. Once only 8s 11d, ladies' shoes now cost 29s.

Moneylenders

Some women were exploiting their neighbours, who were often the wives or dependants of soldiers. A correspondent of the *Evening News* wrote, 'Some of the money lending harpies mask their unscrupulousness by being kindly and neighbourly and poor women are being caught in the net'.

One lady whose husband was fighting in France borrowed 10s. Interest for the first week was 1s, for the next week 2s and 3s for the third week. Soon she had paid out 25s without reducing the original loan. Fortunately, her brother found out and threatened to go to the police and much of the money was then paid back.

The Mound Huts

The Mound Huts were opened in early 1916 to provide cheap accommodation and board for soldiers and sailors passing through Edinburgh. The initial funds to set up this service were given by Mrs Corsar of Murrayfield and her brother. The Boys' Brigade helped to equip them. Demand was so high that the 150 beds were inadequate and 100 more were added. Bathing facilities were also provided. Eighteen to twenty volunteers staffed the huts each night.

Edinburgh, 1918

In January 'Julian' visited the city as part of the War Savings Effort. Julian was one of the new weapons of war – a tank. It was placed on the Mound and raised well over £4 million in a week. Later in the year it visited Leith as part of a tour around Britain.

The successful continuation of the war depended on the production of munitions. This was dangerous work and unfortunately accidents did happen. Miss Euphemia Cunningham, originally from Dunbar Close in the Canongate, was awarded an OBE for gallantry after an explosion in a munitions factory. The presentation was made in the City Chambers.

Firstly, as chancellor and then as prime minister, David Lloyd George had led the country through the difficult years of the war. In May 1918, in recognition of this service, Edinburgh Town Council awarded him the Freedom of the City.

One of the casualties of the war was Portobello Pier. Purchased by Mr Galloway for £1,500, it provided a port of call for his steamers travelling from Leith to the Fife coast. The war put an end to these pleasure trips and the pier became redundant. It was eventually demolished in June 1918.

The large number of unattached servicemen, some from foreign parts, brought many single girls out onto the streets of Edinburgh. One correspondent of the *Evening News* demanded that these 'giddy battalions of "flappers" would be cleared off the streets'. However, there was also some sympathy for the women who had nowhere to go. Marriage was one route open to women whose employment and wages had been restricted. Only the war had allowed them to take jobs with the tramway companies and considerable resistance to the entry of women had been put up by the professional world.

The Influenza Epidemic

Influenza reached the city in June and at the beginning of July, the school board closed their schools in order to prevent it spreading; Heriot's Trust and the Merchant Company soon followed. Two deaths had already occurred, but more were to follow. The last three weeks of October saw 145 deaths in Edinburgh alone. During the first week of November (the last of the war), 160 people in Edinburgh and twenty-three in Leith died from influenza. Worldwide, this epidemic killed more people than the war.

The End of the War

The tremendous effort to continue the war put a great strain not only on the economies but also on the political systems of Europe. Russia collapsed in 1917 and later that year power fell into the hands of the Soviets under the control of the Bolsheviks. Austria–Hungary was on the verge of disintegration by the summer of 1918. At the same time, the French and British on the Western Front were being reinforced by fresh troops from the United States.

The Armistice came on 11 November 1918. That evening, Prince's Street was so packed with people out to celebrate the end of the war that the traffic had to be stopped.

Nineteen

THE INTER-WAR YEARS, 1918–39

The 1918 Election

Lloyd George and the Conservatives continued the wartime coalition into the December election on a platform of improving housing and working conditions. The cost of living had risen by 74 per cent during the four years of the war. The parties now had to appeal to a new group of electors because, for the first time, women had the vote.

The Liberals were divided between those loyal to Lloyd George, who supported the coalition, and the Independent Liberals led by Asquith. Despite this division, the Independent Liberals won East Edinburgh and Leith. William Graham took Central Edinburgh for the Labour Party. The other three seats were taken by the coalition candidates, leaving the city divided equally between the coalition and the opposition parties. This was not reflected in the country as a whole, where Lloyd George's coalition won an overall majority of 327.

Local Politics

Edinburgh's local politics began the inter-war years dominated by an independent grouping that became known as the Moderates and later, the Progressives. They tried to balance the needs for improvement, especially with slum clearance, and keeping rises in the rates as low as possible. Only the Labour Party offered any opposition and they were slow to build up a powerbase on the council. The Communists put forward candidates for a few wards but failed to obtain any seats.

In the 1919 local elections (all local elections were still held at the beginning of November), Labour made gains on councils throughout Britain. However, in Edinburgh all six of its candidates failed to gain a seat on the town council. In Leith the party won three seats.

The Problems Facing Edinburgh

Housing

The challenge was to build a large number of houses to replace overcrowded and insanitary homes. In 1924, Councillor Harvey, the convener of the Public Health Committee, said, 'The problem of dealing with the slums was the most urgent problem of the day'. Sadly, his attitude changed when he became treasurer. The Labour leader, Councillor Gilzean, proposed a rise in the rates to fund an increase in the number of houses being built by the council.

North Leith had four times the density of population of Edinburgh before 1920. As a consequence, infant mortality was a third higher than the rest of the city. Various emergency measures were tried in order to ease the problem. The council took over the army camp at Duddingston; they planned to convert the forty or fifty huts into three-roomed houses. Building homes out of steel was another 'quick fix' proposal, although it did lead to opposition in some cases. In 1926 the Dean of Guild Court, responsible for planning permission, opposed plans for 250 steel homes in Lochend.

The area of St Leonard's had some of the worst slums in the city and a housing scheme to provide new homes was begun in Niddrie. This new development was a long way from the centre of the city and created its own problems. Families who had grown up in St Leonard's and Leith were separated from their local community. During the years of the Depression, 75 per cent of the population of Niddrie was unemployed and most of the rest had only low-paid work.

The new housing was very basic, leading Councillor Gibson in 1934 to describe their appearance as 'like pies coming out of an oven'. The following year, a group of residents set up a Tenants' Defence League to press the council to hold down the rates.

The lack of public medical facilities also led to growing discontent in the area. Prior to the 1936 council elections, a distressing case was raised at a meeting in Craigmillar School. The police were accused of failing to send an ambulance immediately, leading to the death of a child. That night the child's grandfather, who lived in the same house, also died. The father, whose wife was in poor health, then received an eviction notice.

At the Amalgamation, Leith had been promised new housing but nine years later there were many single-end apartments, housing eight to eleven people, and one three-roomed flat was actually the home of nineteen people! Not only were these buildings overcrowded and lacking proper sanitation, but some of them were in a dangerous state of repair. The wall of one tenement collapsed leaving a 15ft gap from top to bottom. Fortunately all thirty-two persons living in the building escaped without serious injury.

In the middle of the decade, houses were built in Lochend for those displaced by the clearance of slum housing. This was hardly enough to tackle the problem. Another 1,500 houses were built in Granton and further building took place to the west of the city in Saughton and Stenhouse.

By 1936, a total of 33,896 people had found new homes in Edinburgh. Over 20,000 of these were in houses which had been built either by the Corporation or with grants from them. Private builders were also putting up homes. In 1936, Ford & Torrie Builders, of Queen Street, were advertising villas in Milton Road and Marionville. The city expanded west along the Queensferry Road. North of this area, Blackhall and Davidson's Mains grew rapidly. New homes were also built for private sale in Colinton and Corstorphine. By the late 1930s the private companies were building more homes than the council.

Some (probably many) of the buildings in the historic heart of the city had deteriorated to such an extent that action had to be taken. Guthrie Street, formerly College Wynd, was demolished. Sir Walter Scott had been born in a tenement in this street. The council saved Huntly House, turning it into a museum for the city. In 1934 a Miss Harrison bought the condemned property in the Lawnmarket known as Gladstone's Land. She gave it to the newly formed National Trust for Scotland, who set about restoring the tenement. Today the visitor can see a shop and rooms as they would have been in the seventeenth and eighteenth centuries.

Poverty and Unemployment

The second major problem facing Edinburgh in the years between the wars was unemployment. After the Great Crash of 1929, the figure rose rapidly. In September of that year 11,673 people were unemployed in the city (this includes Leith). Twelve months later, the figure had reached 18,256. It continued to rise, before reaching a peak of 23,466 in February 1932. Although numbers began to fall, there were still over 20,000 people without work in 1935.

Unemployment meant poverty and homelessness. Even before the slump there was real poverty in the heart of the city. During the three months of winter 1926–27 the Simon Square Soup Kitchen gave out 33,960 portions of soup and 24,580 rolls. At the same time, the Police Aid Clothing Scheme gave shoes and clothes to nearly 5,000 children.

Hostels and missions for the homeless were based in the Grassmarket and the Cowgate where the poorest members of society tended to congregate. The Castle in the Grassmarket and The Britannia in the Cowgate offered beds for the homeless. The churches, who came in for considerable criticism during the inter-war years, had organisations working tirelessly in these poor streets.

The Amalgamation

Soon after the First World War, the government decided to increase the size of Edinburgh by giving it control of the new suburbs – Cramond, Colinton, Gilmerton, Corstorphine and Liberton. However, the most controversial part of the bill was to bring Leith back under Edinburgh's control. Prior to the local elections in 1919 the council had received two anonymous letters warning them, 'In the event of the Corporation taking the untimely step of forcing a Bill at this juncture, it is intended to form a committee of prominent citizens who will take steps to oppose the proceedings in Parliament'. At the end of January 1920, Leith Town Council organised a plebiscite (referendum). Only 5,357 voted for amalgamation; the vote against the proposals was 29,891. It was a decisive result which the government ignored.

The Edinburgh Music Festival

In the second half of the century, Edinburgh became famous for its cultural festivals. Some of the events which later made up the Edinburgh Festival had their roots in the inter-war years. In May 1920 the first Edinburgh Music Festival opened. It took the form of a series of competitions in singing and dance. Included in the programme were songs in English, Gaelic and Scots. There was even a section for action songs to encourage young children to take part. Competitions for piano and elocution were also offered. Although the festival grew slowly, May was a busy month in the city with the Church General Assemblies and the Infirmary Pageant.

Shipbuilding

The nineteenth century had seen dramatic changes in shipbuilding. Steam-powered vessels driven by paddle wheels challenged the fast sailing boats on the coastal trade. The invention of the screw propeller soon made the paddle wheel redundant. Wood was replaced by steel and new skills took over in the yards.

In the eighteenth century the shipyards were to be found in North Leith. They were sufficient for the building of small vessels up to 100ft in length. In 1810 Robert Dryborough's dry dock measured 117ft by 49ft and the building yard was little larger. The expansion of the docks led the yards to move into the deeper water of the new harbour. S & H Morton's in the Victoria Dock launched the *Bolingbroke* in 1863. She was a clipper of 1,200 tons and 205ft in length. Eighteen years later, the *Scotia*, produced in the same yard, was even bigger at 325ft.

Leith could not compete with the massive shipbuilding developments along the Clyde and had to concentrate on smaller vessels. Nevertheless, in 1890 Ferguson & Ramage launched four steel-built screw-driven steam ships as well as a steam yacht and a sailing barque. Scott, Morton & Co. also built four steel-hulled screw-driven ships that year. The third yard, owned by Hawthorne & Co., launched six vessels that year, two of which were steam powered.

By the end of the First World War, Leith was left with one yard owned by Henry Robb Ltd. The years that followed the Second World War brought a marked decline in British shipbuilding as large and modern shipyards in the Far East took a stranglehold of the trade. The company merged with Caledon of Dundee and became part of British Shipbuilders in 1977. Work became scarce and the shipyard was closed seven years later.

Granton

The main businesses in Granton during the inter-war years were centred round the harbour and the gasworks. Waste, in the form of ash, was dumped into the Forth only to be swept back onto local beaches. Eventually, when pressure was placed to clean up the area, the council turned to an old quarry as a site to hold the ash.

In January 1922, Corporation buses opened a route linking Granton with the city. The trams were to follow. In the same month, three masked men held up the Royal Bank in Granton Square before escaping on a motorcycle down Boswell Road. Five men were later arrested in Glasgow and a motorcycle recovered.

A less daring robbery was carried out on a shop in Lower Granton Road by two men. The assistant escaped and sought help from the neighbouring butcher. The robbers fled with only two packets of cigarettes.

Granton was still a small suburb linked to the town with developments along the shore. The land to the south was not developed until the 1930s, when the town council built the estate of Granton Mains as part of their plans to clear the slums in Leith.

Transport and Accidents in 1924

On the last Monday in July, a passenger train heading for the ferry at Port Edgar ran into the rear of a suburban train in Haymarket Station. Four people were killed and another thirty injured. The signalman claimed that the signal was set

to 'danger' and thus the Port Edgar train should have stopped. The driver told the inquiry set up to discover the cause of the accident that the signal showed the line was clear. The accident was put down to a signalling fault.

In 1922 the council had decided to replace the old cable car system with electric trams. This brought Edinburgh into line with Leith which already had an electric tramway. Gone was the 'Pilrig Muddle', where passengers had to change from electric trams to the cable cars. In June, the lord provost opened the electric tram route in Edinburgh; he drove the first car up Leith Walk, although not as far as its terminus in Liberton.

Confusion over transport policy are not a new problem. The council passed a provisional order to establish a tram route through George Street which would have led to the removal of the statues. The Tramways Committee assumed that the council decision was final and proceeded to have the street dug up for the rails. Bailie Deas motioned for a delay in the proposals without seemingly realising the work was in progress. Lord Provost Sleigh expressed his concern about the statues, 'These are national statues although Edinburgh had the custody of them'. The council then voted to delay any plans to remove the statues by forty-three votes to nineteen. The line was eventually opened in 1925 with the statues remaining in place. The route did not prove to be fully utilised.

The Shores of the Forth

Considerable concern was expressed in some quarters at the lack of investment in Edinburgh's coastal resorts. A large electric power station was built in the middle of Portobello – a popular beach resort in the 1920s – and the gasworks at Granton was dumping its ash into the Forth, much of which was then washed back onto the shore at Silverknowes.

Portobello had its Marine Gardens and the stadium was used for football (Leith Athletic), speedway and greyhound racing. There was also a popular dance hall. The town (and particularly the promenade) lacked shops, flowerbeds and seats. Unfortunately, proposals to build a pier remained just that.

Some unemployed men were used to remove boulders from the beach.

In 1928, one exasperated correspondent of the *Evening News* wrote:

It is not too much to say that if Portobello, with its very favourable site, had been the property of any municipality but our own we should long ago have been reaping the harvest that follows on the making of a popular holiday resort.

In the autumn of 1935, the old mill buildings were demolished to make way for a large outdoor swimming pool.

Cramond and the western shore fared even worse, despite the efforts of Bailie Poole to keep the issue alive. The shore suffered from litter and had no seats. One writer to the *Evening News* complained:

> The lord provost, magistrates and councillors of our city have performed a work, not accomplished by any other organisation I know of, in transforming one of the most beautiful, attractive and historical waterfronts of our country into a seaside slum.

Strong words, but they reflect a feeling that the council had little interest in the outer suburbs and explain the opposition in Leith to the amalgamation with Edinburgh in 1920. By the end of the century, Cramond became one of the most prosperous and popular areas in the city, with the council even commissioning a report on 'The Preservation of Historic Sites by the Mouth of the Almond'.

The Infirmary Pageant, 1925

One Saturday in May was set aside each year for the raising of money for the Royal Infirmary. This took the form of a parade through the streets, with collectors encouraging donations from the crowds of spectators. Schools and other organisations built floats and prizes were awarded for the best displays. Even students from the university took part. It was a day to be enjoyed and to raise money for a worthy cause.

It was usually a day without controversy, however, in 1925 some 'good citizens' objected to one of the floats. A letter to the *Evening News* read, 'I refer to the unseemly and scanty dress of some of those taking part and the effort apparently to appear before the public gaze in an almost nude condition'. Some other people objected to the prominent position given to the city's fire brigade. All this was a little harsh when the volunteers had to brave a wet weekend to raise over £4,500. Hopes were high that the final count might pass £6,000. The students alone added £1,200 to this.

Leith Infirmary held its own pageant later in the month. It was conducted on much the same lines as the larger Edinburgh pageant, although it may have gained from the better weather later in the month.

The Visit of Ramsay McDonald

In 1925, Ramsay McDonald, the first Labour prime minister, was awarded the Freedom of the City. The Usher Hall was used for the ceremony. The

prime minister sent the lord provost £200, a considerable sum in those days, to be used to entertain people from some of the poorer districts in the city, so 600 elderly folk and 2,000 schoolchildren came to the Waverley Market. The Queen's Own Hussars and the Police Pipe Band provided the music. A magician and a group of dancers entertained this audience. Even the prime minister and the lord provost made an appearance at the festivities.

Sport and Popular Entertainment in the 1920s

The decade following the First World War was not a memorable time for Edinburgh's two most senior football teams – Heart of Midlothian and Hibernian. Hearts had lost many players in the war and in 1922 they unveiled their war memorial at the Haymarket.

The professional game in Scotland was divided into two leagues, and in the Second Division, St Bernard's played at the Gymnasium, situated between Royal Crescent and Eyre Place.

Edinburgh's fourth side was Leith Athletic. They began their post-war campaigns playing in the Powderhall Stadium but eventually moved to the Marine Stadium in Portobello. The season 1929/30 began sensationally when their first match at Armadale was abandoned just before full time, owing to a pitch invasion. The team played well and it was not until the last Saturday of 1929 that they suffered their first league defeat.

The Scottish rugby team played their last international match at Inverleith against France before moving to their new stadium at Murrayfield. At this time, Rugby Union was an amateur game and most of the top Edinburgh teams were made up of former pupils of the private schools.

The most charismatic character to achieve sporting prominence was an Edinburgh University student called Eric Liddell. He was a tremendous sprinter who won a place in the British team for the 1924 Olympic Games, held in Paris. Liddell refused to run in the heats of the 100 yards because they were held on a Sunday. He won a bronze medal in the 200 yards. He was then entered for the 400 yards and won the gold medal in a world-record time. Liddell, who was born in China, returned to that country doing missionary work until his death a few years after the end of the war. He is remembered in Edinburgh through the work of the Eric Liddell Centre at Holy Corner.

In the 1920s, dance halls were popular places for entertainment. Many a married couple first met in a dance hall. The Marine Gardens (Portobello), Maxines (Tollcross) and the Victoria Halls (Leith) only charged a shilling for an evening's dancing. The Dunedin in Picardy Place was more expensive at 2s 6d, while the Palais de Dance in Fountainbridge charged the highest price at 3s 6d.

There were also private dancing clubs. The Savoy in Cockburn Street was raided at 2.30 a.m. one Sunday morning in April 1929. The management were charged with 'shebeening and public dancing without a licence'. Two years earlier, controversy had struck these dance halls when it appeared that some of them were operating a colour bar.

The city was filled with cinemas showing black and white silent films. The city had nearly thirty cinemas and Prince's Street alone had four cinemas – the Palace, the New Picture House, the Picture House and the Prince's Cinema. Further out from the city, Stockbridge and Fountainbridge had two cinemas each. Leith had the Capitol and Gorgie had the Tivoli. The Ritz opened in Rodney Street in 1929.

The biggest change came in 1929 with the introduction of the 'talkies'. On 10 June the New Picture House showed Al Jolson in *The Singing Fool*. Others followed, installing the equipment needed to broadcast sound. By November the Playhouse was advertising itself proudly as the 'Home of the Talkies'. *The Jazz Singer* soon followed at the Salisbury and the Regent.

Edinburgh had five theatres, of which the Royal Lyceum and the King's remain to this day. The Theatre Royal, the Empire Palace Theatre and the Alhambra in Leith Walk put on live shows.

Radio, or wireless as it was then known, was in its infancy. During the 1920s the BBC broadcast from 3 p.m. until 10 p.m., but by 1930 the hours had been stretched to 10 a.m. to midnight. Much of the time was filled by musical programmes.

The Edinburgh Tattoo

The Edinburgh Tattoo, which was to become a popular part of the post-war festivals, began in 1926. It was not held on the Castle Esplanade but out in Dreghorn above Colinton. The Tattoo appears to have been an immediate success, with an estimated crowd of 60,000 attending the close of the first Tattoo on 2 October 1926. By 1929 the programme had become very ambitious with mock-ups of a Q-ship and a submarine. They even went as far as constructing a model of a Border tower house. Two hundred performers formed the mass pipe band that year.

The General Strike of 1926

When the clocks struck midnight at the end of 3 May 1926 the General Strike began. Many workers, particularly those in the mines and docks and those providing transport services, came out on strike. So too did the printers, preventing the publication of daily news reports. Volunteers were called upon to act as special constables and to man the trams.

On Tuesday, 4 May, a deputation warned the lord provost that if the trams were not stopped the electricity workers would join the strike. At 1 p.m. the deputation was informed that the trams would continue to run. Two hours later, the electricity workers in Edinburgh joined the strike and volunteers took over. The trams kept going with the council providing free food, drink and cigarettes for the volunteers. The cost, nearly £2,000, was added to the Tramway Account. After the strike, one of its supporters claimed, 'The whole administration of the city during the strike period was scandalous in the extreme and worthy of condemnation'. On Thursday, 13 May, the drivers returned to work.

It was a time of tension and confusion. An accident occurred on the railway east of Waverley Station, when a passenger train, due to temporary signalmen, struck some goods wagons. The LNER (London & North Eastern Railway) management claimed that the pickets refused to help, although the railway workers manning the picket line claimed their offer of first aid assistance was refused. They were, however, unwilling to take part in the attempt to clear the line.

Mr Henderson, who arrived in Edinburgh on the third day of the strike, claimed that he walked 'into the thick of a general riot'. He informed the *Evening News*, 'The conduct of the police in the streets of Edinburgh was absolutely brutal'. Old men and women were being assaulted by the police. The Secretary of State for Scotland agreed that a crowd of several thousand people had formed, containing 'disorderly elements of which there was a large nucleus in the crowd'. Of course, it is difficult to know the truth of the incident but it seems likely that untrained volunteers may have overreacted to what appeared to be a dangerous situation. It is probably a credit to both sides that order was maintained in the city.

The strike came to an end within a fortnight but the miners did not return to work. In the 1920s coal was the fuel used to produce gas and electricity, but fortunately it was summer so demand for heating and lighting would have been low. However, the council was certainly concerned about the diminishing stock of coal at Granton Gasworks.

The Highland Show, 1927

At the beginning of 1926 plans were afoot for the holding of the 1927 Highland Show in Edinburgh (the event at that time had no permanent showground). The lord provost and the council favoured the Meadows as the best site for the show, however, an Act of Parliament dating back nearly a century prohibited building on this land. Two Highland shows had been held on the Meadows in the middle of the previous century, so they began to seek a way round this, but opposition started to grow from groups who used the Meadows for recreation.

The cricketers got in first, but the Edinburgh Education Authority (a body independent from the council) also weighed in. Local schools with a combined roll of 11,901 pupils used the Meadows as playing fields. The Highland Society claimed that they would be clear by the middle of August (when schools returned after the summer break). The real problem was that they required four to four and a half months to complete all the preparations and clear away after the show. If this had been agreed, the Meadows would have been closed to the public for much of the summer.

A new proposal then appeared, offering the prospect of holding the show in Saughton Park. The Highland Society were reluctant at first to accept the move but finally had to agree to the inevitable. The show opened in Saughton Park in the last week of July. A massive crowd of 39,477 attended on Thursday, 28 July. At the end of the fourth day, 86,793 people had visited the showground.

May 1929

May proved to be a busy month for the city. At the beginning of the month Lloyd George came to Edinburgh. He visited the offices of the *Evening News*; the paper had always been a strong supporter of the Liberal Party. On a sadder note, Walter Brown, who had survived the war winning a Military Medal and a Croix de Guerre, was killed at the Marine Gardens Speedway. He fell off his bike and was hit by the rider following him.

Six hundred years before, King Robert the Bruce had given Edinburgh a charter confirming its rights and privileges. A huge pageant, performed by local children, was held in Prince's Street Gardens. The Duke (later King George VI) and Duchess of York attended the event. They also unveiled the statues of Bruce and Wallace which stand at the gateway to the castle. The duke was in the city as Commissioner to the General Assembly. At the same time, the Free Church Assembly was meeting in Edinburgh. Both assemblies were putting together an agreement that would lead to reunion of the churches. Celebrations to mark this event were held later in the year at the Industrial Halls in Annandale Street.

The general election held in May gave Labour three of the six seats; Earnest Brown held Leith for the Liberals; and the Conservatives held on to North and South Edinburgh. In the country as a whole, Labour won 288 seats, the Conservatives 260 and the Liberals, led by Lloyd George, had the balance of power with fifty-nine seats. However, not all Liberals supported Lloyd George; the wartime prime minister still divided his party. Ramsay McDonald, as leader of the largest party, became prime minister. Margaret Bonfield, Minister of Labour, became the first woman Cabinet minister – women had served on Edinburgh Town Council, but none had represented the city in Parliament.

The Local Government Act (Scotland), 1929

This gave greater powers to the county and city councils. In Edinburgh, education was until 1930 run by an independently elected board. Now this was abolished and power transferred to the city council. Other functions, like the control of health and the police, were now placed under the authority of the city. Much of these powers were already enjoyed by Edinburgh Council. The new large county authorities took over the work of the more local parish councils.

Traffic and the Streets

Monday, 27 January 1930 should go down in history as one of the great days for the City of Edinburgh. On that day, the police made no arrests at all!

However, crime and disorder will, and always will be, part of life in every large city. The numbers of those appearing in the courts after the New Year celebrations show a steady decline in the years following the First World War. After Hogmanay in 1913, 177 arrests were made. Twenty years later this had fallen to only thirty-three. Money was always limited, and with this in mind the police introduced the 'police box'. Miscreants could be taken to a box and assistance summoned immediately. This enabled the police to reduce the number of police stations and free up officers for front-line duty.

The 1920s saw an ever-increasing use of the city's roads. The twentieth century love affair between man and the motor car had begun. Despite introducing a 'Safety First' campaign, accidents and resulting fatalities remained high:

	DEATHS	ACCIDENTS
1928	53	1,089
1929	47	1,038
1930	62	996
1931	56	937
1932	78	892

Uniformed inspectors were sent to schools to remind children of the dangers of roads and measures were taken to improve traffic control. Traffic lights were introduced into Edinburgh in 1930 and fines had to be imposed to convince motorists of the importance of obeying the signals. The Minister of Transport, Leslie Hore-Belisha, introduced pedestrian crossings marked by an orange globe on a pole. Like many new inventions, they were not popular with the (motoring) public. March 1935 brought the speed limit of 30mph to all built-up areas. The result of these measures was a remarkable drop in the number of accidents and fatalities on the streets of the city:

	DEATHS	ACCIDENTS
1934	30	360
1935	13	300

Communism and Unemployment

Communism had burst into the spotlight with the revolution in Russia in November 1917 (it was known as the October Revolution because Russia had remained on the old calendar). Left-wing views took hold in the west of Scotland but they made little impression in Edinburgh. Communist candidates, even in the poorest areas like St Giles, St Leonard's and Leith, failed to secure more than a handful of votes.

The Depression produced a huge rise in unemployment in the city. It rose from 11,673 in 1929 to nearly 20,000 by the end of 1930. The Unemployed Workers Movement was led by Communists like Fred Douglas. In 1930, they disrupted a meeting of the Trades and Labour Council. One of the leaders of the unwanted deputation complained:

> Unemployment is getting worse every day under the Labour Government and we are asking you people who are responsible for the Labour Government to do something to assert your power in order that the conditions of the unemployed may get ... [drowned out by shouting] ... We are asking you to join us in the struggle to improve the lot of the unemployed.

Coiners in the 1930s

Police raided a workshop in Muireston Lane Crescent. There they found what was described as a 'miniature mint'. In total, 128 counterfeit half-crowns (there were 8 to the pound) were recovered. A further search led to the discovery of dyes, chemicals, a hydraulic press and a rolling mill. A powerful gas engine had been used to run this machinery. John McFarlane received a three-year sentence and Mary McAllister, one year. The judge warned them that it was a serious crime which at one time had been punishable by death. At this, Mary McAllister fainted.

John and Dorothy Coutts were arrested in 1936. They were producing one shilling coins (20 to the pound) and appear to have been driven to crime by unemployment. John Coutts was a shoemaker who had only worked for fifteen weeks in the previous four years and had four children to support. Bailie Gilzean sentenced John to six months; his wife received three months.

Scottish Nationalism

Scottish Nationalism consisted of diverse groups who found it hard to form a united platform. Lewis Spence founded a Scottish National Party in Edinburgh during the mid-1920s. He went on unsuccessfully to fight a by-election for North Midlothian. At this time, the Nationalists were so divided that when they did come together it resulted in further splits. Eventually even Lewis Spence resigned because he was unable to agree with the 1932 manifesto.

The Nationalist movement was still finding its feet and looking for causes to support. Republican ideals and 'Pan-Celtic' views found expression among some of its leaders at this time. Three Scottish Self-Government and two Scottish Patriot candidates stood in the council elections for 1932. None of them won a seat.

Mrs Mary Riddle

The heroine of 1932 was undoubtedly Mary Riddle of Portobello. A small boy fell into the mill pond by the power station. Mary Riddle, a neighbour, rushed to save the child but she herself was drowned. She left a husband and a young family. Money was raised to help her family and a concert in the town hall was given for 'the local woman who lost her life in a brave attempt to save a neighbour's child from drowning'.

The Navy in the Forth

The Forth had its own naval base at Rosyth. In October 1934 we know that HMS *Barham* was in the Forth, as two of her crew were arrested in Leith Street for causing a disturbance. HMS *Nelson* was also at anchor close to the Railway Bridge. They were joined in the Firth by the new German pocket battleship *Deutschland*, which was anchored off the Port of Leith. She had arrived on a goodwill visit. Later she was to be renamed *Lutzow* and took part in the Battle of the Barents Sea. The first visitor to the ship was Andrew Ducker, the German Consul. Crowds came down to Leith to see the ship, but bad weather prevented people from visiting her. Officers from the *Deutschland* were entertained in the wardroom of HMS *Nelson*.

Armistice Day, 1934

It was now twenty years since the first soldiers had left for the war and, in 1934, 11 November fell on a Sunday. A special service was held in the Assembly Halls in George Street. Admission was by ticket only, but not everyone realised this and some veterans of the war were turned away at the door. To add to the discontent, the old soldiers who had fought in the battlefields of Europe found themselves at the back of the parade. One angry veteran, Robert Armour MC, wrote to the *Evening News* complaining, 'In 1914 we were at the front ... in 1934 we are at the rear'.

Fascists in Edinburgh, 1934

A meeting of local Fascists, who were known as 'Blackshirts', was held in the Usher Hall. This was addressed by the man who led the British Fascists, Sir Oswald Mosley. Plans to hold a march through the centre of Edinburgh had been blocked by the council and a hostile crowd greeted some of the Blackshirts, but the event led to no serious trouble. The Fascists had few followers in the city and although they did put up candidates for some of the wards, they gathered small support.

The Protestant Action Society

The council also refused to allow a meeting of the Protestant Action Society to take place on Calton Hill. Another group, the Protestant Vigilance Society, sent members to seek signatures to support their views. They stood outside the two general assemblies in May. Part of their campaign document read, 'Certain innovations and evils which have no warrant in the Word of God do manifestly tend to the re-establishment of the Popish religion and tyranny to the subversion of the True Reformed Religion'.

Sectarian groups were beginning to gain support in the city and in November 1934 they contested some seats at the local elections. John Cormack, leader of the Protestant Action Society, won North Leith. The next year they won two more seats – both in Leith – giving them three members on the town council. Only four votes prevented them from taking Dalry from Labour. They thrived in areas of poverty where the voters felt that the established parties had failed them. Housing and unemployment were the central planks of their platform. They were openly anti-Catholic.

A meeting of the Catholic Society held in the music hall was picketed by a large crowd of their supporters. The police estimated that this crowd had grown to 2,000–3,000 by 7.30 p.m. The archbishop's car was surrounded when protestors broke through police lines. Even mounted police had to be used to control the crowd and escort them down Hanover Street to the Mound. Three people were charged with breach of the peace; two of these were Protestant Action Society councillors – John Cormack and James Marr.

Internal divisions began to appear in 1937. During March of that year, the executive of the Protestant Action Society resigned and Cormack took complete control of their affairs. The election in November led to the loss of two seats on the council – one of those was John Cormack in North Leith. However, this proved to be only a temporary setback for the party. The following year he was returned, giving the Protestant Party six members on the council. That year 11,000 people voted for them in the local elections.

St Andrew's House

The old prison which had been built at the beginning of the previous century was pulled down, leaving a gap on the south side of Calton Hill. The Governor's House, with its tower and battlements, still remains. A considerable discussion took place over a new building for such a prominent site. The government had set up the Scottish Office in 1887, but the department had its offices in London. It was decided to remove them to Edinburgh and construct a new building on the site of the old prison. The result of this was St Andrew's House.

An Incident at the Empire Theatre in 1936

A group of students on a Rag Week stunt broke into the backstage area of the Empire Theatre during a performance. They tied up the doorman and broke into the dressing room of Miss Renee Houston, who was changing between acts. The actress was tied up and bundled into a car and a ransom of £25 was demanded. Mr Henshall, the proprietor of the show, refused to pay the money.

Four students were arrested but only three were charged, and the incident gave the student body as a whole a bad name. Mr Henshall, who had previously given the cast permission to attend a charity ball held by the university students, withdrew his offer. Student leaders disassociated themselves with the kidnapping. In the end, two students were fined for the offence.

St Trinnean's School for Girls

Notice was given on Wednesday, 14 October 1936 that St Trinnean's School, run by Miss C. Frazer Lee, was to move from its home on Dalkeith Road to Woodburn House in Canaan Lane. It was the stories given by the former pupils of this school which enabled the cartoonist, Robert Searle, to create the *Girls of St Trinian's*, the unruliest mob of schoolgirls in fictional history. Later, three films were made about their adventures and further films were produced in the 1960s and in 2007.

The First Months of 1937

Divisions had appeared in the Labour group on the council when Councillor Cathcart accepted the chair of a committee against the wishes of the party. He was supported by Councillors Muter and Hogg. The Edinburgh Labour Party removed the whip (suspended them). Their action was confirmed by the party's Scottish executive. Eventually Councillor Muter, after twenty-five years as a member of the Labour Party, joined the National Liberals.

Things became so heated on the Education Committee that Councillor Ballantine said that he would 'take Bailie Coltart outside'. The prospect of two councillors who were responsible for the education of the city's children fighting was only ended when another member offered to take the bailie's place.

A man who, in his day, would have had no trouble in dealing with such a matter, returned to Edinburgh. He was Ensign Ewart. His remains had been found in a cemetery in Salford and brought to Edinburgh to be laid to rest on the Esplanade. Ewart served in the Royal Scots Greys and had captured an Eagle at Waterloo. Today there is also a public house in the Lawnmarket bearing his name.

March proved to be a difficult month for the travelling public. A snowstorm at the beginning of the month blocked many roads leading into the city. Another blizzard disrupted Edinburgh on the night of 11/12 March. Only early morning snowploughs kept the trams going. To add to their misery, SMT bus drivers came out on unofficial strike. This took time to settle and the dispute was not over until 19 March; the drivers returned the next day.

The Hermitage of Braid

The first owner of these lands was a Flemish knight, Sir Henry de Breda. He lived during the reign of William the Lion. In 1631 the estate came into the possession of the immensely rich Sir William Dick. He was a strong supporter

of the Covenant and became Provost of Edinburgh in 1638, but the Civil War brought bankruptcy for the former provost and he died in poverty. His family eventually recovered from this disaster and his grandson, Sir James Dick of Prestonfield, was elected lord provost in 1679. However, the family no longer had interest in the estate of Braid.

In 1772 it was bought by Charles Gordon, an Edinburgh solicitor, who had inherited a large fortune from his father. He built the mansion and laid out the gardens. The Hermitage was finally bought by John McDougal in 1937. He informed the lord provost that he had made provision in his will to leave the estate to the city of Edinburgh. The lord provost suggested that if he gave the estate to the city immediately, everyone would benefit.

Towards the War

By 1937 the Civil War in Spain had alerted everybody to the dangers of mass bombing raids on towns and civilians were potentially now in the front line. It was realised that the bombs would not only destroy property and kill people caught on the streets but they could start serious fires. In February, Firemaster Peter Methuen presented proposals to the city council to protect the public from fires that might be started by bombing. He wanted 500 auxiliary firemen and fifty auxiliary fire stations.

Fire coverage had not kept pace with the growth of the city and there was not a single fire station in the southern suburbs of the city. As the war drew nearer it was felt that five new stations were needed to give proper fire cover.

In November 1938, volunteers were recruited for the Air Raid Warning organisation and 3,723 wardens who would be responsible for the blackout came forward. Another 2,607 had first aid qualifications and would be able to help with casualties should bombs strike the city. Finally, 724 men offered their services as auxiliary firemen – more than had been originally planned for.

Plans for more Housing

Despite the extensive building programme carried out by the city council during the years between the wars, there was still a desperate need to build more homes at rents which the ordinary working folk of the city could afford. One councillor complained that it was no longer 'Sunny Leith' but 'Slummy Leith'. The Protestant Action Society was well represented in the port. John Cormack demanded a programme which would produce 3,000 homes per year; other parties claimed that this target was impossible to achieve.

The next year, 1938, the council proposed to build 4,080 homes in West Pilton. The original plan had been to construct only eight houses per acre, but a shortage of land led this to be raised to twenty-four per acre. Such a dramatic change suggests that more than just land was in short supply.

Plans were also ongoing at Sighthill. The council were looking not only to build new homes but also a racecourse by the Calder Road. Treasurer Will Darling kept a close eye on rising expenditure and he opposed plans to build a city airport on the grounds that most of those which had been built so far were running at a loss.

Poverty in Edinburgh

Unemployment remained high. There were still over 17,000 people out of work in Edinburgh, Leith and Portobello. One correspondent of the *Evening News* wrote about his shock at seeing three schoolgirls aged between 9 and 13:

> All three were pitifully thin and pitifully clothed and their shoes as I had not imagined even the poorest children wore nowadays. Their coats, miserable inadequate rags, hung on their meagre bodies and they all had that look of semi-starvation which none can mistake.

Conditions in the slums, particularly in Leith, were very poor. Washing and toilet facilities were completely inadequate and many people struggled to buy food and fuel, but much of this poverty was hidden away from the more prosperous citizens. The Grassmarket remained the home of the poorest people in the city and Alexander Barrie and his Grassmarket Mission appealed for clothes, coal and fuel for them.

The Highland Show

The first Highland Show had been held on an acre of land at the back of Queensferry House in 1822; it had been purely a show for fat stock. The show was then taken to various towns in Scotland, returning occasionally to Edinburgh. After a considerable dispute, the 1927 show was held in Saughton Park and the 100th show was also held in the park in 1931. The final show before the outbreak of war opened in Saughton on Tuesday, 20 June 1939. Crowds were good, but the hoped-for record numbers were not achieved.

Twenty

THE SECOND WORLD WAR

Evacuation

The evacuation of children and their mothers from the city began as early as 1 September 1939. Schools remained open all through the night registering the children to be evacuated from the capital. The first evacuees' train departed at 8 a.m. By 4 September, over 30,000 women and children had left Edinburgh for safer locations in the Lothians and Borders, as well as Fife. However, after a week, with no sign of an aerial attack, they began to return. A second attempt to evacuate Edinburgh's children began a week later. By Monday, 11 September another 2,000 had registered.

Unfortunately, all was not well in the reception areas. Sir Robert Spencer-Nairn complained that a large proportion of the children from Edinburgh were in a filthy condition. According to the provost, 'The children sent from Edinburgh to Lochgelly were a positive disgrace'.

Food and eating habits also led to friction. The Board of Education complained, 'Some of the children are unaccustomed to regular meals of any kind and ordinary table manners are unknown to them. They are not familiar with the kind of food that is being given to them.' They discovered that children liked fish and chips, sausages, suet puddings, fruit, gravy and fried bread. On the other hand, they disliked green vegetables, soups, fat, rhubarb, salads and cooked cheese. Here is a menu drawn up for evacuated children from a restaurant set up in East Lothian:

Monday	Lentil soup	Apple dumpling/tart
Tuesday	Mince, mashed potato & turnip	Rhubarb dumpling/tart
Wednesday	Scotch broth	Stewed apple & custard/milk pudding
Thursday	Shepherd's pie	Jellied fruit
Friday	Scotch broth	Ground rice & apples
Saturday	Potato soup	Blancmange/stewed apples

By the end of November over 15,000 children, mostly from the primary schools, and 500 teachers had been evacuated. Schools in the city had insufficient shelters (and sometimes none) to protect their pupils in the event of an air raid. Yet, by the beginning of 1942 this had been reduced to 3,700 children and 100 teachers.

The Blackout

The blackout, while designed to hide the city from night attacks by aircraft, produced its own problems. Whether travelling by tram, with their newly painted white buffers, bus and car, or on foot, the hours of darkness brought its own dangers. A man was killed by a bus near Hillend and another by a car in Dalry Road. In January 1940, the speed limit in the city was reduced to 20mph. At the same time, the RAF expressed dissatisfaction with the blackout.

The dark, unlit nights of a Scottish winter led to the revision of shop closing hours to 6 p.m. in November. Evening services in the churches, where the large windows made blackouts nearly impossible, and evening classes held in schools were curtailed.

The blackout may have contributed to the quietest Hogmanay known in Edinburgh as no arrests were made by the police for disorder in the twelve hours after 10 p.m. on 31 December!

Air-Raid Shelters

Work on the building of air-raid shelters was underway by the beginning of 1939. Water from the Christmas storms had increased the weight of the soil placed on the roofs and this led to one shelter in the Meadows collapsing. A young girl was killed and two other children injured when they fell through the roof of a shelter dug in Roseburn Park.

January 1940 proved to be the coldest month in Edinburgh since 1881. The heavy winter rains forced the authorities (mainly the fire brigade and the auxiliary fire brigade) to pump out the shelters which were below ground.

By the beginning of October 1941, the Corporation had sufficient shelters to protect 350,000 people. Throughout the year, work had been carried on 7,500 Anderson shelters to prevent them from flooding. Improvements had been made to some shelters in back greens and basements, but a shortage of manpower and materials hampered progress. A city official advised shelter owners to leave the doors open to allow the air to circulate and thus discourage damp.

Portobello Pavilion

A headline in one of the August 1939 editions of the *Evening News* read, 'Hope for the New Brighton of the North'. After over thirteen years of planning, proposals were put forward to build a huge pavilion on the Promenade. Here the visitors would find a restaurant, a concert hall and a variety of shops. In front of this, a pier would run out into the sea. The estimated cost was £45,000.

Sadly, the project was abandoned, making Portobello Edinburgh's first victim of the war.

Edinburgh's First Air Raid

On the afternoon of Monday, 16 October 1939, the Germans launched an aerial attack on the Forth: the naval base and dockyard at Rosyth was their target. Anti-aircraft batteries in the city opened fire but the sirens failed to warn the citizens and four people were injured from the falling fragments of the shells. The attack, carried out by Junker's 88 bombers, was the first air raid launched against the British mainland.

At sea, some weeks later, HMS *Belfast* struck a mine close to the Isle of May. Fortunately, no one was killed but the cruiser had to be towed back to Rosyth. Mines presented a constant danger to coastal shipping including the fishermen based in the local ports like Leith and Newhaven. (HMS *Belfast* is now moored on the Thames close to Tower Bridge.)

HMS *Cossack*

In December 1939, the Germans scuttled their pocket battleship, *Admiral Graf Spee*, after a battle with British cruisers off the River Plate. Her supply ship, *Altmark*, escaped from the South Atlantic carrying prisoners taken from British merchant ships sunk by the *Graf Spee*.

HMS *Cossack*, a tribal-class destroyer, was based in Leith during the early months of the war. Her crew gave some musical entertainments to the people of the port. While patrolling off the Norwegian coast, she cornered the *Altmark* in Josing Fiord. Despite being in neutral waters the crew of the *Cossack* boarded the *Altmark* and released the prisoners. These men were then brought back to Leith.

HMS *Cossack* was sunk in November 1941 and Seaman Green, a 20-year-old Edinburgh lad, was killed and another man from the city suffered severe burning.

Italians in Edinburgh, 1940

The spring and summer of 1940 proved to be a disastrous time for Britain and her allies. First Norway and Denmark fell to the Germans, and then the Netherlands, Belgium, and finally France, succumbed to the German advance. With the fall of France in sight, the Italians declared war on Britain and France.

There was, and still is, a large Italian population in Scotland. Many of them had arrived in the early years of the century seeking a better life. They became prominent in the catering trade, owning firstly ice cream shops and later restaurants. A number of these were situated in Leith Walk. The entry of Italy into the war in June 1940 led to demonstrations, and not a few broken windows, against people of Italian descent. In Edinburgh, about 160 men from the Italian community were arrested and interned.

Juvenile Crime in 1941

With so many of their parents committed to war work (including fathers away with the forces), juvenile crime rose rapidly. On Saturday, 26 July 1941, twenty-six juveniles with an average age of only 11 appeared before the sheriff. The majority of them were charged with housebreaking.

Not until March 1942 was Chief Constable Morren able to report a fall in juvenile crime. He blamed the rise in the early years of the war on the initial excitement and nervous tension. However, that did not see the end of the problem. In 1944, underage boys were visiting billiard saloons and gambling considerable amounts of money which they had previously stolen. On 4 March, two Leith boys faced twenty charges of theft while, five days later, seven boys from Gorgie appeared in court to answer fifteen similar charges. In all these cases the money had been spent in billiard saloons.

Scrap Metal and Waste Collections

By the end of 1940, the city had collected 319 tons of scrap metal, much of this from railings. The lord provost began a campaign called 'Railings for Scrap' to encourage home owners to donate their railings to the war effort. Edinburgh, with its many sunken Georgian basements, had a large quantity of railings. A big effort was made so that by May 1941 the Cleansing Department could claim that they had now collected sufficient scrap to build 600 tanks and the equivalent amount of paper to that imported by three ships. Yet before the end of the year it was claimed that the citizens still wasted 10 tons of paper per week, either burnt or thrown away.

The Lady Provost's Comfort Fund

Lady Steele managed this fund until her husband's retirement in November 1941. By that time, the ladies of Edinburgh had produced the following for British servicemen:

Pairs of socks	23,606
Scarves	9,481
Pairs of gloves	12,100
Helmets	8,314
Pullovers	2,280
Pairs of sea boot stockings	900

They had also provided meals for the soldiers travelling north to take part in the attack on the Norwegian port of Narvik in June 1940.

In November 1941, William Darling became lord provost and the responsibility for the running of the Comfort Fund fell to his wife. After the cruiser HMS *Edinburgh* was sunk in the Barents Sea escorting a convoy to Russia, the Comfort Fund gave aid to the survivors. With no new *Edinburgh*, the city went on to adopt the recently commissioned battleship HMS *Howe*. The lord provost and his wife travelled to the Clyde where they presented a plaque displaying the city's coat of arms to Captain Woodhouse. He had previously commanded HMS *Ajax* at the Battle of the River Plate. In 1943, HMS *Howe* received £100 and HMS *Leith* was given £25 from the Comfort Fund.

Lady Darling also arranged to send Christmas parcels to all the Edinburgh men and women serving overseas. Writing materials were particularly valued by the troops and General Montgomery wrote (on captured Italian notepaper) to thank Lady Darling for the gift from the Comfort Fund. When he made his first visit to the city in February 1944, he was able to express his appreciation in person.

Allotments and Food Production

Following the example set in the First World War, a big effort was focused on allotments and the production of food at home. Each Friday, A.C. Swanston published his column in the *Evening News* giving advice on the production and storage of food grown at home. By 1941 German submarine actions were seriously interrupting supplies carried across the Atlantic.

At the end of the first year at war, Edinburgh had turned 51 acres over to food production. The effort continued so that by June 1941 the city had 3,200 allotments. Even schools became involved and golf courses were turned over to grazing (golf continued even so). Some handed over large areas to the plough and Duddingston lost its first fairway.

The Ministry of Agriculture introduced the 'Dig for Victory' campaign. Leaflets were produced giving vital information and encouragement. Potatoes (they even recommended the varieties to grow) and seasonal vegetables became the staple food for the allotment owners. Other advice included methods to eradicate pests and Leaflet No. 7 was called 'How to make compost'. At the beginning of 1942 the new lord provost announced that the city had set aside land for 5,000 allotments.

In 1943 the Scottish Education Department began to put pressure on local authorities to arrange an autumn holiday to free the children to help harvest potatoes. They claimed that 3 per cent of the 1942 crop (60,000 tons) had been lost through a shortage of labour. Edinburgh Education Committee refused to comply with this request.

Potatoes played a large role in the diet of wartime Britain. Here is a recipe from the *Evening News* in January 1944 for mince floddies:

Required 1½lb grated raw potatoes, ½lb mince beef, 1 onion (grated), 1 tablespoon chopped parsley, salt & pepper, fat for frying.

Mix together potato, beef, onion, seasoning and parsley. Heat fat. Drop the mixture in spoonfuls into it and cook slowly until golden brown on both sides.

Rationing

Britain depended on imported food and rationing was introduced in January 1940, although the plans had been developed in the preceding years. Sugar, butter, bacon and ham were all subject to the new regulations, then tea and meat followed. Cheese was finally rationed in early 1941. By June of that year, everyone had to register with a supplier to obtain eggs.

Clothing, first rationed in 1941, had further restrictions placed on it in the next year. Buttons were in short supply so there were no more double-breasted coats and none could be put on sleeves. Turn-ups too disappeared from the new 'utility' clothes. For women, pleats could no longer be produced and skirts had to have their lengths reduced. One representative of the Edinburgh tailoring trade commented, 'I don't think they can make women's skirts any shorter than they are already'.

Utility clothing was followed by utility furniture. The government also placed a maximum price on many goods, in order to prevent the inflation which had

occurred in the First World War. This helped to check demands for increases in wages and thus eased industrial relations problems. However, with the growing number of regulations, the authorities had to ensure that these were carried through in the shops.

Air Raids

The second air attack came on 26 June 1940, after the Germans had occupied France. Five 250lb bombs and a number of incendiaries were dropped on open ground close to Craigmillar. Three more raids, targeted at the docks, followed in July – eight people were killed and a further thirty-eight injured in these attacks.

September brought two raids on the 29th. In the early morning, a 500lb bomb was dropped on Duff Street but fortunately no one was hurt. The evening raid led to the deaths of three people in Crewe Place.

Two small attacks occurred in October and November, and after a lull of four months, on the night of 14/15 March 1941 seventy incendiary bombs were dropped on Abbeyhill.

On the night of 7 April 1941 two landmines were dropped on Leith, causing three deaths and 131 injuries. Part of David Kilpatrick's School was damaged; they may have been targeting the railway, since a second landmine struck the embankment close to Largo Place. At the same time, some incendiaries were dropped on the north-west of the city.

Niddrie was hit in the following month, after which there were no raids until July 1942. Casualties in these raids were light (eighteen killed, 212 injured) compared to many of the cities that were attacked by the Luftwaffe.

The Town Council

Parliament had decreed that no council elections should take place during the hostilities. In Edinburgh, where the Moderates held a majority over their Labour and Protestant rivals, the parties were forced to choose a new lord provost and five new bailies. The Moderates met and selected their nominees for all the posts without consulting the other parties on the council.

The next meeting of the town council was chaired by Bailie Margaret Geddes, the first woman to do this. The Labour Party boycotted the meeting and the Moderates' nominee, former treasurer William Darling, was chosen as lord provost.

Auxiliary Policewomen

About 100 women volunteers gave their services to the Edinburgh Police, staffing canteens, driving police vehicles and carrying out various clerical duties. It was proposed to provide them with uniforms at a total cost of £891. Councillor Darling (soon to be lord provost) believed that since they had been set up by the government that they should bear 50 per cent of the cost. Councillor Hardie was more forthright in his opposition: 'Are there any young women sheltering behind a police uniform when they should be in munitions or something really useful?' he asked. A correspondent of the *Evening News*, who must have had some inside information, came to their defence, arguing that the women were unpaid volunteers; work in the canteens had to be covered from 7 a.m. to 11 p.m.; the uniform would offer them some protection when returning home so late at night. Drivers, on average, worked twenty-one hours a week while clerical volunteers provided around 37½ hours each week and all this work would have had to be done by an overstretched police force.

Edinburgh, 1942

The year began with a large crowd (estimated at over 1,000) welcoming in the New Year at the Tron. The police explained that there were less people carrying the large quart bottles.

Some 3,700 children and 100 teachers still remained exiled from the city. Many of those who had returned, or had not been evacuated, were back in full-time education.

Winston Churchill

Winston Churchill, the prime minister, arrived in the city on 12 October to be met by the lord provost and his wife at the station. He was taken to the Esplanade to inspect members of the Civil Defence Force; the Police Pipe Band provided the music. Afterwards, at a rally in the Usher Hall, Churchill was presented with the Freedom of the City. In characteristic style, he told his audience, 'To show weakness to such a man as Hitler is only to encourage further atrocities and you may be sure no weakness will be shown'.

By the autumn of 1942 the war was reaching a decisive stage. The Eighth Army had defeated the Germans and Italians at El Alamein and was driving them back into Libya. In the west, the Americans had landed an army in Oran, threatening the German Africa Corps in the rear. They were also driving the Japanese out of Guadalcanal, in the Solomons. Years of Japanese advance in the Pacific had come to an end.

Meanwhile, with winter approaching, the German armies had failed to break the Russians, who were clinging on in Leningrad, Moscow and Stalingrad.

Salvaging Books for the War Effort

As part of a nationwide scheme, Edinburgh, a large publishing and printing centre, set about collecting all the 'unwanted' books in the city. The firms of Douglas & Foulis (Castle Street) and Robert Grant & Son (Prince's Street) each provided 2,000 volumes. The lord provost challenged the city to hand over 1 million books, but the campaign struggled in the first week with only 250,000 handed in. However, they eventually received 1,297,800 books, weighing 300 tons. Some of them were sent to the troops as reading material, while the rest was recycled due to the paper shortage.

Nursing Sister Josephine Connolly

Sister Connolly received her call-up papers on the day before the war broke out. She served in France and only just escaped from the advancing Germans, leaving the port of St Nazaire on the day before France surrendered. Sister Connolly, who lived in Edinburgh, was then posted to the Mediterranean where she served on a hospital ship.

Her first trip was to Piraeus to aid the wounded being evacuated from Greece. With the imminent fall of Crete, Sister Connolly's ship made two voyages to the island. During the second of these, the ship was bombed, resulting in one death and eight injuries. Sister Connolly commented, 'We don't have much time to think what might happen to ourselves.'

They returned to North Africa and the sister found herself trapped with the British troops in Tobruk. She managed to escape and was then posted to a hospital in Suez. It was not until the summer of 1943 that Josephine Connolly was able to return to her home in Edinburgh.

Edinburgh, 1943

The Housing Problem and Plans for the Post-War City

Despite the large building projects carried out by the town council and private companies during the 1930s, housing still remained the largest challenge facing the city. The war had led to the drafting of many men into the armed forces or the manufacture of munitions (everything from ships to shells). The Corporation owned about 16,000 houses but they lacked the labour to maintain them properly. They were also struggling to complete the 300 new homes in Pilton.

As early as May 1943, Lord Provost Darling persuaded the council to set up a committee consisting of only three men to advise on the future development of Edinburgh. The proposal met with some resistance. A motion to add three councillors to this committee was defeated and an attempt to have the matter reviewed (a common delaying tactic) also met with failure. Sir Thomas Whitson, a former lord provost, Sir Donald Pollock, Rector of Edinburgh University, and Mr J.L. Clyde KC were the 'three wise men'. It took them only a few months to produce 'The Clyde Report'.

No Turkeys for Christmas!

The war had led to a cut in Scotland's turkey production but the birds could still be obtained from Northern Ireland. Edinburgh normally took about 10,000 turkeys, but in 1943 the Ministry of Food allocated all those birds to six cities. The only Scottish city to receive any birds from Northern Ireland was Glasgow. The Edinburgh West MP raised the matter with the ministry but to no avail.

The Death of John Wilson McLaren

John Wilson McLaren was born in the Grassmarket during the year 1861. The early death of his father left his mother a widow with four young children – John was the only one to survive into adulthood. He left school early to help his mother. His first job was to act as a messenger, firstly for a bookseller and then a newsagent.

In 1871 he visited Traill's Coffee House at Greyfriars where he met the dog, Bobby, and learnt something of his history from Mr Traill himself. Wilson McLaren developed an interest in the Old Town, writing for newspapers and magazines. One of his last articles retold the story of Greyfriars' Bobby as related to him by Mr Traill.

Despite having little formal education he began writing poetry. 'Rhymes Frae the Chimia-Lug' came out around 1881. In that year, he spent a pleasant afternoon exploring the wynds and closes off the High Street in the company of Robert Louis Stevenson. Other books of poetry followed. By this time he had qualified as a compositor working for Ballantyne, Hanson & Co.

In 1920, Wilson McLaren entered the town council as a member for George Square Ward. He served as a bailie, convenor of the Works & Furnishing Committee, and Captain of the Orange Colours. By the beginning of the war he was the longest-serving councillor – a man whose mother had witnessed the hanging of William Burke. John Wilson McLaren died in December 1943.

The Health of the City

Dr Clark, Edinburgh's Medical Officer of Health, was concerned about the high infant mortality rate that prevailed in some parts of the city. It had fallen from 14 per cent to 5.3 per cent at the end of 1943, yet for some areas which contained a large amount of slum property, the figures remained stubbornly

high. In North Leith, the infant mortality rate was 11.2 per cent. However, other factors were involved, for the rate had risen even in the new housing schemes such as Niddrie.

Tuberculosis presented a problem for the city's health, leading to Dr Clark recommending a screening programme, 'Theoretically if every person in the community had his chest X-rayed regularly and those few people who were found to have some abnormality receive treatment the problem of chest disease would slowly disappear from the medical map.' The first radiography unit was opened in Warriston Close for an initial outlay of £4,100. This unit could X-ray 120 people per hour at an annual running cost of £3,900.

Edinburgh, 1944

D-Day
On 6 June 1944, the Allies launched a massive attack on the beaches of Normandy. Some of the seriously wounded soldiers were brought to Edinburgh where they were transferred to the Royal Infirmary.

Edinburgh suffered air raids during the war, but these did comparatively little damage to the city and the docks and Henry Robb's shipyard with its nine berths was put into wartime production. The workforce increased from 900 to 2,000 men. During the war they built fifty-four vessels, of which forty-two were for the Admiralty. Robb's produced smaller ships – frigates, corvettes, armed trawlers and tugs. Such vessels provided protection to convoys of merchant ships carrying goods essential to the war effort and the survival of the country. To supply the D-Day invasion forces the Allies created their own harbours using Mulberry pier heads – thirteen of these were built in Leith.

Evacuees
In the summer of 1944, London and the south-east of England came under attack from the German V rockets. Over 3,000 women and children came to Edinburgh to escape these attacks. Volunteers provided homes, but the rising demand led the authorities to threaten compulsory billeting. An unhappy 'D' wrote a letter of protest to the *Evening News*: 'How many of these people gave a moment's thought to Scotland or her troubles in peace time?' He replied to his own question, 'No one disputes that English evacuees must be provided for, but why not in their own country?'

Meanwhile, the British and American forces were driving the Germans back towards the Rhine. V2 bases in France fell into the hands of the Allies, ending the danger to those living in the south-east.

The Bevin Boys

A shortage of both miners and coal led the government, under the leadership of Ernest Bevin, to recruit (or force) young men to take jobs in the pits from December 1943. According to the Home Secretary Herbert Morrison, some 16,000 youths had been selected by ballot to serve in the mines. Robert Laidlaw of Broughton Street refused to work in Dunfermline Colliery. His mother complained to the sheriff, 'I had a son killed in the mines and another entombed. Robert will not go down the pit.' He suffered from claustrophobia and Sheriff Jamieson took an aggressive stance towards the boy asking, 'What about claustrophobia in Saughton?' Having refused to pay a £4 fine, he was sent to prison for thirty days. The sentence and the sheriff's comments brought letters of protest. 'I think it is generally agreed that this boy and his mother are deserving of every sympathy,' wrote one reader.

The Changing of the Guard

In November 1941, the Progressive group on the town council had used their large majority to ensure the election of Treasurer William Darling to the position of lord provost. The new lord provost had been born in Carlisle. He had served an apprenticeship as a draper in London, even selling hat pins on the street and sleeping in a hostel at 1 shilling a night. He later worked in Sri Lanka and Australia before coming to Scotland. In 1914 Darling joined the Black Watch as a private soldier, but soon rose through the ranks to be commissioned in 1915. William Darling was later awarded the Military Cross.

After the war he transferred to administration in Ireland. At an official function in the City Chambers, Bailie Duncan described the lord provost as 'the man who with equal facility and nonchalance met Michael Collins in the back room of a Dublin pub with their revolvers on the table between them'. In 1922 he returned to Edinburgh to join his uncle's firm in Prince's Street.

William Darling joined the council in 1933, serving as treasurer from 1937 to 1940 and lord provost from 1941 until 1944, receiving a knighthood in 1943. He was frequently photographed wearing uniform while carrying out his official duties. After the war he stood as a Conservative candidate for South Edinburgh and, despite the Labour landslide, held the seat for the party.

John Falconer, who had also served as city treasurer, succeeded William Darling. He was a solicitor and had represented Colinton ward since 1932. The problem of the position of lady provost immediately arose as John Falconer was a widower. However, his daughter, Diana, was serving with the WRNS and she was released from the navy to carry out her new duties as lady provost – probably one of the youngest women to hold that position. At the end of the year she appeared at a reception in the City Chambers wearing her chain of office over her uniform.

Portobello

Effie Payne, who originally lived in Edinburgh but now resided in Lancashire, was shocked when she took a short trip to the resort. She wrote to the *Evening News* in July 1928:

> I cannot imagine the Council of any English town or city being so short sighted as to let a place with such possibilities as Portobello turn into what is almost a slum – dirty houses, dirty shops, dirty sand. Everywhere there is a broken down forlorn air that is both sad and depressing.

It was left to Councillor Mrs Esta Henry, a representative from the Canongate ward, to press for the redevelopment of the front. She wanted to see a large concert hall with facilities for outside broadcasts spreading Portobello's name throughout the land. A large hotel on a floodlit boulevard would enhance the seafront.

She blamed the power station chimney for the polluting soot found in the open-air pool and suggested that a new pool should be built at Joppa. However, the councillor lost her seat as an independent for the Canongate ward in the municipal election of November 1945.

Twenty-one

POST-WAR EDINBURGH, 1945–59

The General Election

Most of the country registered their votes on 5 July 1945, but Edinburgh, due to the holidays, did not vote until 12 July. Other parts of the country also delayed their polls. Thus, the results were not announced for another fourteen days. To the surprise of many who thought it might prove a close contest, Labour were returned with an overall majority of 146 and Clement Attlee became prime minister.

Edinburgh reflected the national trend and Sir William Darling, despite being operated upon for appendicitis, retained the safe seat of South Edinburgh for the Conservatives. Councillor Gilzean, leader of the Labour group on the town council, took Edinburgh Central. A rougher fight took place in Leith, where Mr J. Hoy (Labour) accused Ernest Brown (National Liberal and former minister) of neglecting the port. With a 9,000 majority, it would appear that the people of Leith agreed with him. Labour now held four of the six seats in Edinburgh and Leith.

Mr Pethwick-Lawrence, MP (Labour) for East Edinburgh, was raised to the peerage leading to a by-election. George Thomson, the lord advocate, retained the seat for Labour with a comfortable majority of 5,817.

The New Government

Clement Attlee's Labour government were faced with massive debts which had built up during the war. Assets had been sold, thus aggravating the balance of payments difficulties. Industries were worked hard during the conflict, leaving little opportunity to proceed with maintenance programmes. On top of this, the new government had plans to create a national health service as well as to bring essential industries, such as the coal mines and the railways, into public ownership.

Nationalisation plans were opposed by the Progressive majority on the town council. These proposals might lead to the city losing ownership of the gas supplies (acquired in 1888), the trams (acquired in 1894) and the power station (built in 1895). Treasurer Andrew Murray asked, 'What then can nationalisation give to Edinburgh that we, as the present owners, are unable to give?' He estimated that the market value of these businesses was £38 million. Edinburgh gas prices were well below the national average, and might be subject to a substantial rise if they were acquired by the government.

The Housing Problem

Housing was the major priority for all local authorities in the post-war period. Edinburgh was fortunate that bomb damage had been slight compared with many other large cities. The city had expanded rapidly after the First World War with the number of homes increasing from 90,000 to 131,000. Various types of prefabricated temporary houses were allocated to the city. West Pilton, Muirhouse and Sighthill were chosen as the main sites for such building schemes. In May 1946, the council promised to build 5,000 permanent and 4,000 temporary houses.

However, all did not go well with the plans for these new homes. Shortages of materials and skilled labour soon led to the 'blame game'. Builders were using skilled men to convert large houses into private flats while council work was held up. In Muirhouse fifty houses required painting before they could be let to the public; unfortunately there were only four men for the job. Opposition groups criticised the council for its lack of method and organisation of contracts.

Squatting was a growing problem for the authorities, with homeless people moving into any vacant property. Former military camps often made up of Nissen huts were targets for families seeking a home. By the end of 1945, fourteen families had occupied some empty huts on the Crewe Toll Military Camp. They were eventually moved to Granton House.

Nearby, in Granton Road, the old camp of Lochinvar was used to house homeless families. A communal kitchen provided facilities for the residents but this was to prove disastrous for Mrs Watson. While she was preparing a meal a fire broke out in her hut, killing her children, John (aged 3) and Anne (aged 1).

At Craigentinny Camp a gang broke into two storage huts, destroying the buildings and removing the contents. Squatters living in nearby huts heard nothing.

The Municipal Elections, 1945 and 1946

After the massive victory in the general election, the Edinburgh Labour Party had high hopes for the first municipal elections since 1938. Although they managed to win seven more seats, this was not enough to prevent the Progressives retaining control of the town council:

Progressives	39
Labour	26
Independents	2
Protestants	2

The following year produced little change, with Labour only gaining a single seat (Calton ward) from the Progressives. Councillor Horne, one of the Protestant group, lost his seat in Leith. These municipal elections established the town council as a body controlled by two parties.

Rationing Continues

Shortly after the general election, the new Minister of Food, Sir Ben Smith, told a press conference:

> There is no prospect of any improvement in rations. The restoration of recent cuts is something for the future. It is too early to say what benefits we shall derive from the end of the Pacific War. Ultimately if shipping is available, the position should improve.

In fact, things got worse.

In March 1946 the Edinburgh butchers were complaining about the quality of meat – too much fat. Problems within the Cabinet led to the resignation of the Food Minister. The summer of 1946 brought a threat of bread being rationed. The *Evening News* received an 'avalanche of letters on bread rationing', and a protest meeting was held in the Usher Hall. Edinburgh bakers joined in the opposition but, despite the complaints, rationing began on Monday, 22 July. This was followed in August by a milk shortage in the city, 'Some Edinburgh housewives [are] with less milk this week than during the war'. The local food officer blamed the wet weather and the start of the new school year (children received milk in school).

The awful winter of 1947 led to restrictions on potatoes. Paper for the press and meat rations for the public was reduced. However, it was announced that petrol would come off the ration at the beginning of October. Much disappointment must have been felt when the government informed motorists that rationing would not only continue but the amount of fuel was to be cut by a third.

The Problems Facing Leith

Edinburgh had been excluded from Development Area status so that there would be no government support for the introduction of new business. The

city's coastal strip, Leith, Newhaven and Granton, depended on industry for employment.

Business in Leith Docks was at a low ebb. Coal exports had fallen dramatically – once 3 million tons per annum had left the port but in the first six month of 1946 only 80,000 tons were exported. The loss of a large number of ships during the war had also damaged the coastal trade. Leith's other markets in the Baltic had suffered badly in the conflict and the Soviet Union occupied Poland, Lithuania and Latvia. Timber imports had fallen by 50 per cent and Denmark's exports to Leith were a quarter of their pre-war level.

The Currie Line operated fifteen ships from the port before the war. In 1946 this was reduced to two. The one bright spot in the docks was Robb's Shipyard. At the end of the year they had four cargo ships and a tug on the stocks. However, the prospects for repair work were not good.

Winter, 1947

This proved to be one of the worst winters in the twentieth century. Storms struck after New Year forcing the fishing fleet (some thirty vessels) to remain in harbour. One official of a Granton trawler company with twenty-five years' experience complained, 'In my recollection this is the first time the boats have been unable to sail after the New Year holiday. We have been unlucky in getting this bad spell of weather when the boats were due to put to sea.'

Edinburgh fared better than many parts of England until, at the end of January, the temperature fell to 12.4°F. The cold weather and light falls of snow continued into February. An icicle over 20ft long hung from the aqueduct which carried the canal over the Water of Leith at Slateford.

On 26 February, a huge blizzard swept across Scotland and northern England. The *Flying Scotsman* arrived in Waverley five hours late and the *Night Scot* was delayed for nine hours by the weather. Another storm on 12 March led to the city being cut off. Snow prevented travel to Bo'ness, Lauder, Berwick, North Berwick and Peebles and drifts 5ft deep blocked Cramond Road, despite its proximity to the sea.

To add to these difficulties, coal was in short supply. All the country's electricity and gas were produced using coal and the railways depended on coal for their locomotives. Most people had coal fires to heat their houses. Homes and businesses had their power cut from 8.30 a.m. to 11.30 a.m. and at 1.30 p.m. to 3.30 p.m. Street lights were switched off, except at important junctions. The first night of this new blackout brought four cases of bag snatching.

The building of new homes was badly affected with over 11,000 man hours lost daily, even before the March storms struck.

The First International Festival of Music and Drama

Planning had begun as early as the autumn of 1946 for the Festival of Music and Drama. Rudolf Bing became its first director, with Basil Spence (who was later to design Coventry Cathedral) appointed architect for the festival. However, not everyone supported the festival. The poet, Hugh MacDonald, in a radio broadcast called it 'snob-art, a cultural pretext covering hard commercialism and desire for money'. He went on to claim that the cultural life of Scotland was centred in Glasgow and that the Edinburgh Festival was only for the rich. Ticket prices were indeed high. The lord provost retaliated, 'What we need is the enthusiastic support of everyone to help us in this new idea and not to discourage it at the outset'. They were trying to set the festival up on a sound financial basis.

The festival opened on 24 August with a service in St Giles. Every one of the 1,600 seats was allocated. The Glyndebourne Opera Company performed at the King's Theatre and their artistic director, Professor Carl Ebart, having seen the floodlit castle, said in the *Evening News* of September 1947, 'Already we foreigners have come to love your castle, but now it's more impressive than ever'. Tickets for the last concert of the Vienna Philharmonic Orchestra produced a 300-yard queue around the Usher Hall.

The festival was not without its critics. The Scottish TUC rejected the motion at a meeting in April 1952 that 'the festival will present the best in British, and in particular Scottish, music and drama and only infrequently include foreign performers'. This was proposed by a representative of the Musicians' Union.

The festival committee continued with its policy of presenting an international event with orchestras and companies from far afield. This cost money and often led to a deficit in their accounts. In 1951, the New York Philharmonic Symphony Orchestra and a ballet company from Yugoslavia cost over £50,000 and would explain that year's deficit of £38,834. Three years later, the losses had been reduced to just over £30,000, despite the Glyndebourne Opera, Sadler's Wells Ballet and the Old Vic Theatre Company leaving them with a deficit of over £40,000. That year, the Edinburgh Tattoo contributed £11,000 towards the festival's finances.

Festival funding was always a delicate matter, so in 1959, Eric Linklater suggested that 2*d* should be added to the rates in order to pay for the return of the Glyndebourne Opera Company. No action was taken on this, but criticism was directed at some of the events in that year's festival. Michael Benthall of the Old Vic Company complained, 'There is, I think, a curious feeling of lethargy about the whole of the festival.'

Despite all the political tensions in Europe, the festival had avoided controversy until 1959, when the Czech Philharmonic Orchestra refused to play with Hungarian violinist, Johanna Martz. She had escaped from Nazi-occupied Hungary in 1944 and now lived in Switzerland. The orchestra failed to explain their position and Johanna went on to play with the Royal Philharmonic at the Usher Hall.

The National Health Service

The Labour Minister of Health, Aneurin Bevan, set up the National Health Service by an Act of Parliament in 1946. This came into effect in July 1948. The Edinburgh Executive Council of the National Health Service was formed to place authority in local hands. Meetings commenced at 8.15 p.m. in order to suit the members of the board who were doctors and dentists. However, town council members were unhappy with this. At the October meeting, Councillor Allan became the second member to hand in his resignation. Councillor Cormack went on to inform them, 'You are getting my resignation next month'.

The Edinburgh Floods, August 1948

The floods at the beginning of the month hit the prefab houses in Craigmillar. The swollen Niddrie Burn washed away a 6-year-old girl and her body was later found on the beach.

Later in the month, a wet weekend was followed by a further downpour in midweek, causing floods in the city and also in the Lothians, the Borders and Northumberland. During the night of 12/13 August, Lord Provost Andrew Murray visited Niddrie, Craigmillar and the Inch to witness the problems facing flooded households. Later that night, the Water of Leith breached a wall at Warriston and water rushed into the Powderhall Stadium. The lord provost called for a boat and set about rescuing the greyhounds whose kennels had been flooded. Twenty of the 189 dogs were drowned. The Greyhound Racing Association sued the council for the sum of £14,980, but the court found the council was not liable.

Electricity and Rising Prices

The electricity industry had been nationalised at the end of April 1948. The supply, once controlled by Edinburgh Corporation, was now placed in the hands of the Electricity Board. Edinburgh handed over a £35,000 surplus, but soon prices began to rise. Treasurer Miller, leader of the Progressives and thus an opponent of the Labour government, complained that the only notification was 'a small advertisement ... in the local press without explanation or information'. For him, 'Secrecy appears to be one of the characteristics of the new boards.' He feared that increasing electricity prices would lead to a rise in tram fares. Councillor Airlie (Labour) replied to this criticism of nationalisation.Councillor Grieg Dunbar joined in the debate. His normal summer bill was £5 17s 11d; now it had risen to £8 – an increase of 35.7 per cent.

Public Health in Post-War Edinburgh

In 1946, City Treasurer Andrew Murray (later to become lord provost) wanted to end the charges for patients using the city's hospitals. He argued, 'This city – in the interests of public health – can afford that sum [patients only contributed £14,902 out of £206,910 cost of the hospitals]. No one would object to facing up to that expense.' It would mean an extra halfpence on the rates.

Dr W. Clark, the Medical Officer for Health, reported on the improving conditions in the city: the infant mortality rate had dropped to 3.2 per cent.

The Chief Sanitary Inspector, Mr Ritchie, brought forward plans to tackle the nuisance of smoke. Coal burnt by household fires and by the railways polluted the centre of the city. 'The Castle Area' received 293.61 tons of soot per square mile every year. The 'Abercrombie and Plumbstead Report' (of which, more later in this chapter) had recommended the removal of the railway from Prince's Gardens and restricting Waverley Station to local traffic.

Tuberculosis

The biggest challenge now facing the authorities was TB. A mobile X-ray unit allowed the health department to make checks on factory workers who were unable to attend the unit at Warriston Close. It was believed that early diagnoses would save lives.

In 1954 Dr Seiler, the new medical officer, targeted Pilton where a community-led project set out to contact all 20,000 inhabitants of the suburb. Pupils from Ainslie Park School delivered letters in support of mass X-rays and 300 members of the local community set out to visit every person in Pilton. Dr Seiler claimed that this was the first community project of its kind. Altogether, 11,239 people were X-rayed in four weeks.

Following this successful campaign, in 1955 the Public Health Department targeted Central Leith. X-ray units were placed at Leith Library and in Cable's Wynd. Businesses in the port contributed towards the advertising campaign to persuade residents to go and get checked for TB. John Berry Ltd donated a washing machine for a prize draw. With a target of 10,000, the campaign began slowly and only 633 were seen in the first two days. However, the momentum picked up and by the end of the first fortnight they had taken over 8,000 X-rays and went on to exceed their target in the third week.

In 1956 the TB X-ray campaign turned to the south side of the city. In Holyrood, Newington, Craigentinny and Craigmillar, 11,154 residents attended the mobile clinic. This was achieved without any community input. In Liberton and Portobello this work was supported by local initiatives. Nearly 30,000 people passed through the X-ray machines, leading Dr Seiler to say, 'This has been the most successful campaign we have run in Edinburgh' (*Evening News*, October 1956).

The Health Department then planned an ambitious programme to X-ray 300,000 people during March 1958. To encourage attendance, 10,000 volunteers were sought to visit and leaflet all twenty-three wards of the city. Twenty-seven X-ray units from different parts of the country were brought to Edinburgh. A circus tent, courtesy of Bertram Mills, was erected in West Prince's Street Gardens. Prize draws for those who came to be X-rayed offered a house in Corstorphine, a pension for life and a car. Smaller prizes were also donated by various businesses. Over 87,000 people were X-rayed in the first week, with Vivian Leigh drawing the prize for a bedroom suite donated by the Scottish Co-operative. The lowest take-up was in George Square ward, achieving 89 per cent of those targeted, while in Murray-Cramond 121 per cent was reached. Revised figures showed that from December 1957 to the end of March 1958 a total of 308,747, or 84.4 per cent, of the city's population was X-rayed and 342 new cases of TB were discovered.

A Civic Survey and Plan for the City and Royal Burgh of Edinburgh

Patrick Abercrombie and Derek Plumbstead published plans for the future of the city. They claimed, 'The rebuilding of Prince's Street … is inevitable in the next 50 years.' They had no time for the buildings that had been developed during Georgian, Victorian and Edwardian times, 'Though the result was only to be expected and Prince's Street may justly claim to have variety, it cannot in any sense be considered to have the attractive picturesque character of medieval architecture'. An illustration in the report showed a uniform line of five and six-storey flat-roofed buildings along the whole length of the street. Traffic crossing the town from east to west (always a problem in Edinburgh – it averaged 1,800 vehicles an hour in 1946) would be carried on a three-decked roadway formed beneath Prince's Street with an open arcade facing the gardens.

Having produced a roadway to take the busy east–west traffic, they turned to creating a bypass for the Bridges. A tunnel at the top of Leith Walk would carry the new road under Calton Hill; it then travelled beneath the High Street before crossing the Cowgate. The road continued, passing between the Pleasance and Nicolson Street and heading south to Burdiehouse and Straiton.

Prior to the building of the city bypass in the early 1980s, traffic coming from the south on the A1 had no direct route to take it through the city. The report proposed a major road cutting its way from Portobello, westward to Granton. In Leith it would pass along the north side of the Links, with a sliproad taking traffic onto Leith Walk.

Waverley Station was to be reduced to a terminus for suburban and local Scottish services. 'The new combined terminal station at Morrison Street, which entirely supersedes the Caledonian Station at the West End and Waverley Station only so far as long-distance traffic is concerned' would force the two railway companies (Caledonian and North British) to share passenger facilities. A tunnel passing under the Meadows linked this new station with the east coast mainline. They hoped that 'with the covering in of the railway and the station the Valley Gardens may be greatly improved and extended to restore the original shape of the valley'.

They considered the problems facing Portobello, which the report recognised as a seaside resort. To prevent the sand from being eroded by the sea they suggested a pier be constructed to form a barrier against the tides sweeping away the sand.

Crime in 1949

The crime figures for 1949 (issued in April 1950) showed a slight decrease, but drunkenness continued to be a problem with 993 cases. Of these, 125 had been committed by non-residents. More shocking was the fact that only thirteen people accounted for 136 convictions.

A pre-Christmas crimewave struck the city at the end of the year. During the last week of January 1950, a total of nineteen children appeared in court, facing various charges including the smashing of shop windows and the subsequent theft of toys and sweets. The next week, twenty-one boys were brought before the magistrates – most accused of housebreaking and theft. Four days later, four more boys made their appearance, facing charges of stealing from the new prefab houses in West Pilton.

Electricity Cuts

The South-East Scotland Electricity Board began a series of power cuts in November 1950. Areas as far apart as Corstorphine, Comely Bank and

Willowbrae were without power for a whole afternoon. On 22 November, the 'normal load shedding' combined with a breakdown at Portobello Power Station led to the trams coming to a halt between 8.30 and 11 a.m. In Prince's Street, staff arrived late for work, lighting in the shops dimmed and the lifts moved at a crawl. A week later, Leith faced the cuts but the trams continued to run. Even the Sick Children's Hospital did not escape.

On Monday, 18 December, power cuts struck Leith, some lasting up to five hours. Shops in the Kirkgate and even the bonded warehouses (whisky stores) had their supplies cut from 10.30 a.m. until 5 p.m. The fall in power led to a reduction in the reception of the shortwave radios used by the emergency services.

George Square

The university required room for expansion and the demolition of property in George Square would enable them to achieve their aim, as well as providing an open area within the campus. The historic square had been developed before the New Town. Here, the Dundas family of Arniston (MPs for the city in the years before the Reform Act in 1832) had their town house. The parents of Sir Walter Scott had lived in the square and the novelist spent his early years here.

With its historic connections and Georgian architecture, it is not surprising that opposition to the demolition of these houses gathered pace. In a letter to *The Scotsman*, the Cockburn Association, the Saltire Society, and even the Old Edinburgh Club put forward their views against the plans of the university. The town council held discussions with the vice chancellor, Sir Edward Appleton, in order to reach a compromise. They approved the university's plans.

The university revealed its final plans for the square: the property on three sides was to be demolished and replaced with new blocks, which included one rising to fourteen storeys. By this time in 1959, opposition to the proposals could even be found on the general council of the university, however, the Secretary of State refused to intervene. The town council accepted the need for the university to expand and voted by forty-six votes to thirteen in favour of the vice chancellor's plans.

'Fowl Play'

As late as 1951 a considerable number of citizens still kept hens. A spate of thefts came to an end when a constable stopped two men who were carrying large sacks. When asked to explain themselves, the young men (aged 17 and 20) claimed the sacks contained coke (a type of coal). The constable refused to accept their answer and the youths took to their heels. Robert Scott was soon caught and his sack found to contain fifteen hens. His companion, James Young, was picked up later by the police. In court the two young men faced fourteen charges of stealing 113 hens.

The Progressive Party and Local Elections

The Progressive group which dominated the town council had no links with other political parties. They were a centre-right alliance whose wartime leader, Sir William Darling, became Conservative MP for South Edinburgh. Despite the national trend towards greater Labour representation in local government, the party was unable to seize control in Edinburgh.

The municipal election in November 1946 brought twenty-seven Labour members onto the council. This still left the Progressives with a comfortable majority of eleven. The average turnout that year was still only 39.4 per cent.

The results of the 1949 local elections were a disaster for Labour, with the party losing eleven seats. Two years later, Labour won majorities in Glasgow and Aberdeen but in the capital they held only fifteen seats compared to their Progressive rivals, who had fifty-two councillors. The turnout, on a wet day, averaged 30.5 per cent. (This was nearly equalled in 1957 when overall turnout reached only 30.9 per cent.) Polls in Pilton and St Giles fell short of 19 per cent.

In 1955, electioneering began badly. Meetings at Fernieside and Central Leith only brought out five electors each, and one less turned up at Portobello. Although the visiting speaker brought four friends and the meeting attracted two reporters, only one elector turned up at Bonnington. At South House in Liberton no one turned up. However, interest eventually picked up and this ward had the highest turnout of 49.8 per cent. The general election held later that month brought 70 per cent of electors to the polls, although it produced no change in the representation for the city.

Hustings in the Canongate Tolbooth proved a lively affair with 400 electors having to listen to the candidates in the street. So heated did the audience become that the Unionist (Conservative) candidate, Ralph Harris, complained of mass intimidation. A steward had to separate two women in what Tom Oswald, the sitting Labour MP, claimed was the 'biggest sensation in the Royal Mile since the entry of Bonnie Prince Charlie to the Capital'.

John Dunbar, the city's treasurer, claimed in 1958, 'It is a fact that no member of the Progressive group is compelled to vote in the town council contrary to their own conscience. It is a fundamental part of the Progressive Constitution that this should be so.' Bailie Magnus Williamson replied on behalf of the Labour group: 'If what the Treasurer says is true there must be some very elastic consciences on the Progressive side of the house.' In May of that year, Labour took seats in the Liberton and South Leith Wards, narrowing the gap in the town council.

The Greenside Murders

The bodies of Lesley Sinclair (4½ years old) and Margaret Johnston (3 years old) were found in a toilet after a six-hour search. John Lynch, an unemployed labourer living nearby, was arrested. At his trial, Annie Hall, who shared an apartment with him, told the court that she had left a pair of stockings hanging up. On her return, she found only a single stocking. Was the missing stocking used to strangle the girls? Hall also claimed that she had heard Lynch shouting to a policeman, 'Take me. I did it.' After a three-day trial the jury returned a unanimous verdict in less than an hour.

Lynch's counsel launched an appeal claiming that the bulk of the evidence against him was circumstantial. The house where the prosecution believed the murders had been committed was unlocked and open to any passer-by. The appeal was dismissed and John Lynch was hung in Saughton Prison on 23 April 1954.

Floods in the City

At the end of 1953, heavy rain led to the Murray Burn overflowing in Sighthill. Firemen had to pump water out of gardens in Parkhead Crescent and Parkhead Drive and children were evacuated. Some children also had to be carried over the flood water in order to reach school. Pilton, Fairmilehead, Peffermill and Craigmillar also suffered in a downpour which produced nearly 4cm of rain in twenty-four hours.

The following October, a month's rain fell in three days. Parkhead Crescent suffered again as the Murray Burn overflowed. Water poured down Melville Drive by the Meadows. Before the end of October, another downpour brought the waters of the Murray Burn into Parkhead Crescent again, as well as causing a landslide off Castle Rock, blocking Johnston Terrace.

'Drape' Boys

The latest fashion for young lads consisted of pipe trousers, drape jackets and crepe soles. Dance halls provided meeting places for young people in the 1950s and the large numbers attending these at the weekends made it difficult for the management to supervise all the activity. On just one Saturday night, 1,900 teenagers attended the Palais de Dance.

A few groups of boys dressed in drape suits were known to cause trouble, raising the wrath of Councillor Cormack who demanded more controls over these places of entertainment. There was little for these teenagers to do, particularly on a Sunday. Many of them would descend on Portobello. Arriving at around 7 p.m., they wandered along the promenade and the adjacent streets for two or three hours. Although they do not appear to have caused trouble, such large numbers of lively young people obviously disturbed the local residents.

One Friday night in October 1954, at the other end of the city, a group of thirty visiting 'drape-suited youths' attacked some local men outside a dance hall in Sighthill. The police arrived and drew their batons to disperse the crowd, but did not make any arrests.

In May of the following year, Councillor Cormack was finally appointed a bailie by the town council. Two youths who appeared before him for a breach of the peace outside a dance hall in Leith Street received sixty days in prison. The councillor made it clear that he was determined to 'wipe out rowdyism in Edinburgh dance halls'.

The Craigleith Quarries

The two quarries at Craigleith in north Edinburgh had produced the stone which built the New Town. By 1955, the high cost of extracting the rock led to a collapse in the market. Messrs James Miller & Partners had taken a twenty-five-year lease on the smaller quarry which no longer had a market for its stone. Fortunately for them, the town council had 100,000 tons of rubbish and required a landfill site. However, the quarry now contained 3 million gallons of water. The Gas Board, who owned the other quarry, gave their consent for this water to be pumped into the larger quarry.

Fires in Leith, 1955 and 1956

Post-war Leith contained a number of bonded warehouses which stored whisky and other spirits. In June 1955, a fire broke out at Hill, Thomson & Co. Ltd, in Quality Lane. The staff, consisting of 150 men and women, made their escape safely but the firemen were hampered in their attempts to control the fire when the roof, and later, parts of the walls collapsed. At the same time vats of whisky burst into flames, adding to the dangers faced by the brigade.

Despite damping down the roof of the neighbouring Macdonald & Muir warehouse, the fire took hold there, forcing residents in Quality Lane and Water Street to abandon their homes. At one time, a third warehouse owned by the Caledonian Bonding Co. Ltd stood in danger of being caught up in the blaze. However, disaster was averted and by the afternoon the firemen had taken control of the situation, allowing the residents to return.

The following year, a fire broke out on the 6,500-ton cargo ship *Cairnavon* in the Imperial Dock. At 2.15 a.m., smoke began to fill the accommodation area, trapping some of the crew who had remained on board. Led by the second officer, the crew began to tackle the fire. Soon the brigade arrived and within half an hour had the situation under control. Sadly, three men died from inhaling the smoke and a man and a woman were taken to Leith Hospital. At the inquest, the cause of the fire was put down to a cigarette, but there was insufficient evidence for the jury to confirm this.

Chaos in Gorgie

In October 1955, a bullock escaped from the Gorgie Auction Market. Children had to remain in their schools and traffic stopped. The animal attacked a van and then a bus before chasing two women, who managed to take refuge in Gorgie Memorial Hall. 'It just came at us. I was paralysed for a moment with fright and then I ran as hard as I could,' Isabelle Shaw told reporters. The police brought in William Todd, the manager of a local gunsmiths, who shot the bullock.

Water Shortages

The year 1955 proved to be a dry one, and in September George Baxter, the burgh water engineer, appealed for everyone to save water. Reserves which had stood at 5,000 million gallons in the previous September had now fallen to 2,000 million. Repairs at the Talla Reservoir, the lack of rain and the increased demand from industry were blamed for this problem (industrial consumption had increased by over 50 per cent in ten years). By the end of October, the city had only forty days' supply left. Luckily, heavy rain on 9–10 December eased the problem, leading to a rise in levels at Glencourse and Gladhouse reservoirs.

Then 1959 proved to be the driest summer in the Edinburgh area since records began in 1785. Cuts to the supply were introduced in October, with each district having its water turned off from 7 p.m. to 7 a.m. twice a week. Despite these measures, by the end of the month the city had only enough water for fifty-seven days. The Water Department were looking to increase this to eighty days before they eased up on the rationing. Fortunately, the second weekend of November brought heavy rain which continued in spells for the rest of the month. Reserves rose to 125 days' supply, enabling the Water Department to end the rationing of water.

Rising Costs

The City of Edinburgh, like every other corporation in the country, faced rising costs. In the ten years following the end of the war the cost of providing services to the city had doubled:

1946–47	over £2.5 million
1957–58	over £6.6 million

Treasurer Dunbar was clearly worried about the 1956–57 estimates as pay increased for the police, teachers and council staff, and the Transport Department continued to run at a loss despite increases to the fares. Eventually, in 1957 a large rise in the rates was agreed by the town council.

The End of the Trams

At the beginning of the 1950s the Civic Amenities Committee decided to reduce the tram service by 25 per cent and introduce buses to replace them. It was a controversial decision, which led to protests from concerned citizens. However, the war and the post-war austerity programme had prevented necessary maintenance. Lord Provost James Miller feared that the track foundations were collapsing and it was decided to lift the redundant rails.

The services continued to be withdrawn until, on Friday, 16 November 1956, the last tram driven by James Kay led a procession of vehicles through the streets before it reached the Shrubhill Depot. One of the passengers was Stuart Pilcher, who had been head of the Transport Department in 1923 when the trams had finally replaced the old cable cars. Bailie Cormack commented, 'This is the cheeriest funeral I have ever seen.'

Petrol Rationing

The major knock-on effect from the Suez Crisis was a shortage of petrol (tankers from the Middle East took the long route round the Cape instead

of using the canal), which led the government to introduce rationing on 17 December. Motorists were allocated 6–10½ gallons per month, dependent on the size of their engines. Fewer drivers took to the roads on Sundays and bus services had to be drastically reduced in the evenings and on Sundays to produce a 10 per cent saving on fuel consumption by the city's bus fleet. At that time, top-grade petrol cost about 32p a gallon.

Britain's ally, France, also suffered shortages, leading to the decision to cancel the Monte Carlo Rally. A motion requesting that the government reconsider rationing was defeated in the town council by thirty-six votes to twenty-six. Rationing lasted until 15 May 1957, by which time British tankers were again using the Suez Canal to bring oil from the Middle East.

The Ice Rink

The Murrayfield Ice Rink and Sports Stadium Ltd was formed in 1938, with the building complete by September 1939. The War Department immediately requisitioned it and the company had to wait until 1951 before they took control of the premises. The ice rink was reopened the following year, offering 4,000–5,000 seats for ice shows. These and the public skating paid their way, but this was insufficient to compensate for losses elsewhere. In 1956 the liquidator was called in. Shareholders and creditors lost out as the contents and premises were sold to the only bidders, a group of Edinburgh businessmen. The council had refused to allow the building to be converted to accommodate light industry so the new owners continued the business.

The Bruntsfield and Elsie Inglis Hospitals

The South-Eastern Regional Hospital Board refused to set up a women-only shortlist for the post of consultant at Bruntsfield Hospital for Women and the Elsie Inglis Maternity Hospital. The Bruntsfield (linked with Dr Sophia Jex-Blake, Edinburgh's first woman doctor) and the Elsie Inglis (one of the early leaders of women's medicine in the city) had always had a woman consultant. The issue became very heated, with a petition signed by 26,000 people, including the lord and lady provost, and questions in Parliament. Ten Edinburgh women took the matter to court. For the hospital board, it appears to have been a matter of principle rather than a determination to secure the appointment of a male consultant. Sheriff Harald Leslie QC complained about the 'arrogance' and 'aloof and dictatorial attitude' of the board.

The matter came before Lord Walker in the Court of Session, who tried to persuade both sides to reach an agreement. When this failed, he ruled that the hospital board must first advertise for a woman consultant, and only failing finding a suitable candidate should it be opened to a man. In May 1958, after over a year of arguments, the board announced the appointment of Dr Marjory A. Keith as consultant physician to the two hospitals.

The Highland Show

After suffering heavy losses in their previous shows (Inverness £25,000 in 1956, Dundee £8,900 in 1957) the Royal Highland and Agricultural Society decided to purchase an 86-acre site at Ingliston to use as a permanent showground. This would reduce the costs incurred in the erecting, dismantling and transporting of equipment required for the show.

The property included Ingliston House (built in 1946), West Mains Farm and land tenanted by the local golf club. It was hoped that the proximity to developing transport links – Turnhouse Airport, the new Forth Road Bridge (opened 1966) and the city bypass (opened 1985) – would encourage more people to visit the show.

Slum Properties

By the late 1950s, Edinburgh possessed three major areas of slum property – Leith, St Leonard's and Greenside. Situated on the edge of Calton Hill, Greenside was the smallest of these. Plans for the purchase of 256 homes, housing 571 people, were brought before a public inquiry in September 1959. Some theology students had set up a mission in the district and a report published in *Life and Work* listed the many problems faced by the inhabitants – poverty, unemployment, poor housing, alcoholism and isolation.

In November of that year, three GPs in Leith complained about the state of many of the houses in the port – overcrowded, infested with rats and still dependent on outside toilets. Another problem facing the inhabitants was a reduction in transport services. The Town Hall, which could have offered space for community projects, remained closed. Some 7,000 people needed to be rehoused.

The centre of the town – Dock Street, Coburg Street, the Shore, Bridge Street, Sandport Street, Tolbooth Wynd and the Kirkgate – contained much of this slum property. James Hoy, the local MP, raised the matter, only to receive an official reply stating that the Secretary of State 'is satisfied that Edinburgh

Corporation are fully alive to the responsibility invested in them by Parliament for dealing with dangerous buildings and sees no reason to intervene'.

Accusations of 'differing and delay' were directed at the Corporation over its failure to deal with the 700 slum houses in the St Leonard's area of the city during an October meeting of the council. When Bailie Brechin said that he had looked into other areas which also needed help, Councillor Patrick Rogan replied, 'Rubbish, you have explored nothing deeper than a plum pudding'. When Bailie Jamieson reminded him that there were others on the waiting list, Rogan replied, 'These people have been waiting for 50 years.'

The whole issue became headline news in the following month when 6 Beaumont Place, the 'Penny Tenement' (so called because the owners, Bangor Tenement Co. Ltd, had tried to sell it for a penny), collapsed during the night. Two people were injured – a mother and child – and nineteen families had to be evacuated. Patrick Rogan, who was one of the local councillors, told reporters, 'I think people have had a miraculous escape. Surely at last this should wake up the Rip Van Winkles in the Corporation.' Matters grew worse when a crack appeared in a gable end in neighbouring Dalrymple Place, forcing twenty people to evacuate the building. One woman resident of the district told reporters, 'This has now become the most popular street in Edinburgh. We've never seen so many councillors or Corporation officials here before.'

Engineering

Edinburgh was not a city dominated by heavy industry but it still possessed important companies leading the way in engineering. Brown Brothers, founded in 1711, produced hydraulic steering gears and stabilisers for ocean liners like the *Queen Mary* and the *Queen Elizabeth*. In 1959 they were taken over by a large consortium of shipbuilders which included John Brown of Clydebank, Harland & Wolff Ltd, Swan Hunter and Vickers Ltd.

Bruce Peebles & Co. built electrical transformers and other large components for power stations. The Scottish Hydroelectrical Board, the Kincardine Power Station and some generators in Wales purchased equipment from the company. In September 1959 three large transformers were taken to the Imperial Dock in Leith to be shipped out to Australia. A further eleven were ordered by the State of Victoria and another three for substations in South Australia. They later merged to become Parsons Peebles. The recession at the end of the 1970s hit the company hard; 445 jobs were lost in 1980 and a further 210 became redundant in the following February.

Ferranti developed radar and fire control systems for the new English Electric supersonic fighter and in September they had to extend their premises on Ferry Road. The company also produced the Mercury Computer. By the end of 1959, it had sold twenty of these at a cost of £250,000 each. Two new computers, the Orion and the Atlas, were being developed, but these were to cost more. These machines were still the exclusive preserve of big business. Contracts for electronic equipment to be installed in military aircraft for the Dutch and Belgium governments added £20 million to their order book.

The Ecurie Ecosse Racing Team

Ecurie Ecosse was founded by David Murray, an Edinburgh chartered accountant and racing driver whose career came to an end after crashing his Maserati at the Nürburgring in 1951. With the help of W.E. 'Wilkie' Wilkinson and Jaguar, the team, based in Merchiston Mews, won eight races in the following year.

In 1956, Flockhart and Sanderson won Le Mans. The next year proved even better, with Ecurie Ecosse taking first and second places at Le Mans. During the late 1950s both Innes Ireland and Jack Brabham drove for the team. Even Jim Clark was behind the wheel in the 1959 Tourist Trophy race, although he failed to finish.

Speaking to the Ecurie Ecosse Association early in 1962, David Murray told the members that he would no longer be able to provide the £20,000 a year required to support the team. They had competed in 126 races, winning sixty-eight as well as gaining forty-three second and thirty-nine third places. Problems finding a new car were partly solved for that summer with the arrival of two new Tojeiroes. However, only one was available for Le Mans and its gears seized up after eight hours.

Competing in continental races was proving very expensive and during the 1960s Ecurie Ecosse cars only appeared on British tracks. The team eventually folded, only to be reformed for a short time in the 1980s.

Changes in Retail During the Twentieth Century

The development of cheaper factory-produced goods in the twentieth century undercut the smaller businesses. In 1870, Edinburgh had over 300 dressmaking establishments, but as more and more clothes could be bought inexpensively 'off the shelf', the demand for handmade items disappeared. By 1955 only six outlets offered the services of a dressmaker. The number of boot and shoe makers in the city crashed from 189 in 1914 to just thirty-seven by 1955. Cabinetmakers and upholsterers, once thriving trades even well into the twentieth century, saw their numbers drop from over 200 establishments in 1920 to only sixty-two by the middle of the 1950s.

Conversely, some more specialised shops, like pharmacists and butchers, actually had more outlets in the city in 1955 than in 1870.

The small retailers had already seen the threat of the Co-operative movement before the First World War. The growth of large shops which could buy in bulk offered a challenge to these businesses. The late twentieth century brought the arrival of the supermarkets and the large out-of-town shopping centres which could offer cheaper goods and parking for their clients. Edinburgh now has a considerable number of these centres – the Gyle, Cameron Toll, Hermiston Gait, Straiton and Craigleith. Many towns have seen their high streets suffer, as more and more people choose to shop in the suburbs. However, tourism has proved a valuable asset to shops in the centre of the city and most of the retail establishments on the Royal Mile cater for visitors. The International Festival, the Fringe, Hogmanay and other festivals attract people into the city centre where they spend their money in shops and restaurants.

Golden Wonder Crisps

William Alexander owned a small bakery business in the Dean Village. The bakery was busy in the morning but there was little work for them in the afternoon. So, in 1947 he decided to use the vacant time for the production of potato crisps using 'hard pans' of boiling oil. Five years later, the business was so successful that he had to move into larger premises in Leith. Another six years saw Golden Wonder Crisps and their advertising slogan 'pop a crisp in' appearing in shops throughout Scotland. Further expansion bought Golden Wonder to a new factory in Sighthill when William Alexander purchased three of the most advanced crisp-making machines from America. The new factory, which employed 250 people, was completely automated; it took only fifteen minutes to turn the raw potatoes into packets of crisps.

Twenty-two

THE LAST DECADES OF THE TWENTIETH CENTURY AND BEYOND

Education and the Baby Boom

Fifteen years after the cessation of hostilities the post-war baby boom was creating a demand for more places in secondary schools as well as presenting a future challenge to further education. The council had already opened Liberton in 1958 and Gracemount and Forrester in 1959. The next year brought Craigroyston and Firrhill to take the education bulge.

With Heriot Watt College no longer offering classes for trade skills, the Corporation set out plans for a new further education college based around the old tower at Merchiston, the former home of the Napier family (John Napier was a famous mathematician who invented logarithms). The development plans required the purchase of properties in both Blantyre and Mardale Crescents – a move unpopular with local residents. Ambitious proposals to build three or even four more technical colleges were floated at the end of May 1961. Work finally began on the Merchiston campus in January 1962, with the aim of opening the college for students in summer 1964.

Lorne Street Primary School (off Leith Walk) was being converted to take the electrical engineering classes for Napier College, but a fire led to the collapse of the roof and the bell tower. Fortunately, all the workmen were safely evacuated from the building. The authorities were confident that the damage could be repaired and the work completed on time.

Municipal Politics, 1960–74

The Progressive Party still dominated the council, but by 1960 the Labour Party had formed a substantial block numbering twenty-eight members. The Liberal

Party began to mount a challenge, winning Corstorphine in 1961 and taking seats in Newington and Merchiston the following year. With the Progressives having thirty-three seats and Labour thirty, the five Liberal members held the balance of power. The choice of Duncan Weatherstone, the Progressive nominee, for lord provost, depended on the votes of the Liberal member.

In 1967, the Conservative Party put forward candidates for the first time, taking two seats. Eventually the Progressives' hold over the city council became dependent on the Conservative group, who held the balance of power. Another group gaining prominence on the council were the Scottish National Party who, by 1970, held seven seats making them the third largest party, although still well behind the Progressive and Labour parties. However, in 1971 they lost all their seats to a resurgent Labour Party. The following year saw the election of the Labour leader, Jack Kane, to the position of Lord Provost of Edinburgh.

Local government reorganisation led to the setting up of a two-tier system to run the affairs of the city. Lothian Region, which also included East Lothian, Midlothian and West Lothian, were to become responsible for transport and education. The Edinburgh-based Progressives could not compete in this new environment and amalgamated with the Conservative and Unionist Party.

Community Councils

As part of local government reorganisation, community councils were to be set up to represent local areas that might be remote from the large authorities. Edinburgh District decided that these were not required in the city and refused to implement the proposals. Some opponents of these new bodies felt they would just become pressure groups dominated by the same political activists. However, Councillor Brian Rutherford pointed out, 'Edinburgh District are attempting to become the only area in Scotland without Community Councils'. The matter even reached the Edinburgh Presbytery where the Reverend R. Rae told the members, 'The District Council's evasion is simply a piece of political cynicism'.

Fun and Games

The New Swimming Pool and Meadowbank Stadium

Amid Edinburgh's hopes to host the Commonwealth and Empire Games, a bleak picture had emerged of the city's swimming pools. Out of a total of seven, six pools had been built during the reign of Queen Victoria. The Civic and Amenities Committee rejected sites at the East Meadows, Hope Crescent and Meadowbank in favour of Roseburn Park. Local residents opposed the plan, concerned by a potential reduction of the size of their only local park and fearing that the pool would bring more traffic to the area; 900 residents signed a petition against the committee's plan. The Roseburn residents' representatives met with members of the town council to press their case. The plan was dropped and by the beginning of 1962 the committee was looking to include a pool in the rebuilding plans for the Meadowbank Stadium.

The city had hoped to host the Games in 1966 but their bid was rejected in favour of the West Indies. However, hopes for the 1970 Games remained high. This would require an athletic stadium, an Olympic-size swimming pool and an arena for indoor sports. The committee proposed to build all these facilities at the site at Meadowbank, which was being used as a speedway stadium. However, when the estimated costs for the scheme reached £2 million, the council pulled out of the plan.

The Meadowbank Affair

An examination of the accounts of the Edinburgh Highland Games of 1978, sponsored by Glenlivet Distillers, revealed some irregularities in the payments to athletes. It appeared that some 'amateur athletes' had received more than their legitimate expenses. The extra money had not been sanctioned by the district council who ran the games. An investigation discovered that the receipts from the previous year's games had been lost. The inquiry was closed, but the problem of payment to amateur athletes was an international one.

The 1980 Highland Games were expected to make a loss of £200, but the actual figure reached a staggering £11,773! Glenlivet decided not to renew their sponsorship and denied a claim by Councillor George Monies that *they* had invited some of the athletes to the games, thus incurring extra expense.

The Commonwealth Games, 1970 and 1986

In the summer of 1966, Edinburgh was confirmed as the host city for the 1970 Commonwealth Games. The new swimming pool (Commonwealth Pool) had already received council approval and plans for the sports' stadium at Meadowbank were well advanced. Some members of the council were concerned at yet another large-budget project to be placed onto Edinburgh's finances. The expenses relating to the festival subsidy and the possible purchase of a civic theatre worried councillor Donald Swanson, while councillor Pat Rogan called it 'a waste of time and money'. The depute chamberlain (responsible for the city's finances) assured the public that 'any financial losses suffered in the running of the Games will not be met by Edinburgh Corporation' (carefully worded to exclude the initial costs of the pool and stadium!).

Opponents of the heavy cost of the new Games facilities came up with rival proposals. Easter Road Football Stadium, home of Hibernian FC, and the open-air pool at Portobello, suitably covered, offered much cheaper alternatives. However, after many heated debates both schemes were defeated.

The final threat to the 1970 Games was a boycott from some African nations who had been angered by Marylebone Cricket Club (England's international touring team) supporting a tour of South Africa. The boycott on this occasion came to nothing and on 16 July 1970 the Duke of Edinburgh opened the Games. In total 1,700 competitors from forty-two countries marched out at Meadowbank in the opening ceremony. The Scottish team comprised 153 members, and the ten-day event culminated with Ian Stewart winning the 5,000 metres for the home nation.

The Commonwealth Games Council for Scotland approached the district council with the suggestion that Edinburgh apply to host the 1986 Games. Central government made it clear that the cost must be borne by Edinburgh and not the nation. Rupert Murdoch, the owner of several British newspapers, helped to raise the £15 million needed to run the event. Another boycott caused by the refusal of the British government to apply sanctions against South Africa reduced the number of nations competing to the lowest since 1954.

Challenges of the Twentieth Century

The Problems Facing Leith

William Kerr, a Liberal candidate for the council, complained, 'Leith has always been forced to accept the role of Cinderella', but he had his doubts about Edinburgh in the part of the fairy godmother. The population had declined and was likely to continue to do so with slum clearances.

The case of Leith Town Hall reflects the delays faced by the port. Damaged by a German landmine in 1941, the hall was not reopened until 1960. It took nearly twenty years to carry out the necessary repairs!

The docks remained the central focus of business in Leith, but the facilities were inadequate to handle the new larger ships. Bigger cargo vessels and the new cruise liners were unable to dock in the port. Proposals were put forward to build a large lock at the entrance to the Western Harbour, as well as widening and deepening the approach to the Imperial Dock. This would create thirteen deep-water berths. Unfortunately, the cost of £4 million required a government grant. The Minister of Transport, Ernest Marples, rejected the scheme as the estimates continued to rise.

The Potato Shortage

In April 1962, Dominic Terry of the Edinburgh & District Fish Fryers' Association complained of the threat to their businesses brought about by the rising cost of potatoes. He feared that by June, prior to the harvesting of British potatoes, the whole country would be faced with shortages. He blamed the Minister of Agriculture and the Potato Marketing Board for restricting the number of acres available for growing potatoes. Farmers who exceeded their quota had to pay £10 for each extra acre they gave to potatoes.

Mr Stodart, an MP for Edinburgh and a potato grower, pointed out in an article in the *Evening News* that the weather affected the yield per acre. Thus, while demand remained steady (the UK population ate an average of 200lb per year), the quantity produced varied remarkably. The cold wet winter of 1961–62 had led to lower yields.

Fortunately, in early June a cargo containing 17,000 sacks of potatoes arrived in Leith from Cyprus. Problems arose when the Egyptian moth was discovered in a few of these, but fumigation saved the importers from having to return the whole cargo. Prices dropped by 3*d* per lb but this did not satisfy the Fish Fryers, who claimed that twenty-three shops had been forced to close temporarily due to high prices. However, by the end of the month Cyprus potatoes were supplemented by the new crops from southern England and the Irish Republic. Soon, East Lothian and Ayrshire potatoes were entering the market, ending any fear of shortages.

Vandalism

William McLeod, head of a large building company working in Gracemount and Craigroyston, told the *Evening News*, 'There is absolutely no doubt about it, vandalism is worst in Edinburgh by a long, long way. And there is no question about the fact it is getting worse.' Eastern Electrical Services had lost over £350 at Gracemount through vandalism. They placed the blame on the town council for their failure to protect their building sites. The cost of damage caused by vandalism in the new housing scheme at South Clermiston reached £1,000. This did not include the cost of £400 worth of copper wire stolen from the site.

The Corporation had decided to replace the prefabs at Muirhouse. As the residents moved out the vandals struck, breaking windows and doors, and damaging fittings and fences as well as starting fires. Stations marked for closure also became targets. Fires were started at Newhaven and East Pilton. Two brothers, aged 19 and 16, later pleaded guilty, as well as admitting setting fire to Slateford, Merchiston, Murrayfield and Craigleith stations.

Two years later in 1964, Pat Rogan, chairman of the Housing Committee, admitted that vandalism in Leith was 'the worst I have ever seen'. Night-watchman John McDonald had to face the problem: 'I'm frightened to death at night of the young hooligans. I actually fear for my life.' Much of the trouble was caused by boys aged 12–15 egged on by the girls. Vandalism was to remain a problem on building sites in the city for some time.

Rents for Council Houses

Rising costs forced Treasurer Herbert Brechin (later to be lord provost) to raise both rates and rents. Rising costs of both wages and materials had to be covered by increases in the city's income. Brechin proposed to add a rent supplement

for those households that had higher incomes – tenants earning over £600 a year would face a £12 supplement and every working son and daughter would add an extra 5 shillings a week. Wives earning over £4 per week added another 4 shillings to the weekly rent. The prospect of rents being based on earnings rather than the size of the property brought protests from the Labour side of the council. Councillor Kerr complained that more staff would be needed for 'tracing and ferreting out working-class women who are earning a few coppers extra on a part-time job to tax them a few shillings a week'.

In 1963, no party held an overall majority. The Progressives, with thirty-three councillors, were the largest party, but Labour held thirty-one seats and the Liberals three. There were also two unelected members. However, twelve Labour councillors were barred from voting on the rents scheme as either they or their wives were council tenants. The Secretary of State at first refused to lift this ban, but finally agreed to allow the twelve Labour councillors to take part and vote on the new proposals. In the end it did not matter, as the three Liberal members sided with the Progressives giving them a comfortable majority.

Problems in the Suburbs

New houses in the outer suburbs offered homes for young families but provided few facilities for their needs. Ratho, in 1976, had just a bowling club and one football pitch and plans for a community centre with a games hall, a squash court, play facilities for children and a meeting room for pensioners were dropped by the regional council. The estimated cost had doubled and so the region proposed to provide for some of these needs in the new local primary school. Unfortunately, building was not due to start until 1983!

Currie and Balerno, once dominated by their papermills, faced similar problems. Currie had its high school, but Balerno had only a large primary. The old school, known as the Annex, had had to be reopened to accommodate the growing number of pupils. This displaced three playgroups, an art club and the library. Lothian Region eventually agreed to building Balerno High School, which also provided halls, evening classes and rooms for local clubs.

'The Steamies'

The 1970s was a time of high inflation and other economic difficulties. In order to save £30,000, the district council decided to close the public washhouses known as 'the steamies'. Those people who lived in the closely packed tenement flats of Edinburgh therefore had no place to dry their clothes. Pressure came particularly from the ladies using the washhouse in Henderson Row, and it was proposed to take the matter to the Local Government Ombudsman. At the beginning of April, the washhouses in Henderson Row and Portobello were closed. However, the Labour group on the council came forward with a proposal of opening the washhouses for part of each week. The compromise was accepted and the facilities continued to be used for a little longer.

'Holes in the Ground'

Gap sites in the city centre, known locally as 'holes in the ground', not only put the city in a bad light but also cost the council money. In 1976, Councillor James Kerr, leader of the Labour group on the district council, complained that the Castle Terrace site alone cost the city £45,000 a year in lost rent and rates. The plans to build an opera house in Castle Terrace had been abandoned, but no prospective developer had expressed an interest in the site.

A little further west stood the former Lothian Road Goods Yard, which the city had purchased from British Rail for £1 million. The loan charges for this amounted to £70,000 a year. The large site at Morrison Street, near the Haymarket Station, spent many years as a car park before approval was granted for building work (a previous plan had been rejected on the grounds that the main block was too high). Work only began here in 2016.

The site of the Scottish Bus Depot in New Street became known as Caltongate. Early in the new millennium, plans were drawn up to fill this gap site, however, owing to its proximity to the Old Town, any development faced the scrutiny of conservationists fearing that high-rise buildings might overshadow the historic Royal Mile. Challenges to the plans put forward for the site came to nothing when the 2008 banking crisis ended funding for this project.

The Castle Terrace site attracted interest from several hotel groups. After a stormy meeting in November 1978, in which Councillor David Brown was ordered to leave after his refusal to withdraw a claim that 'he [the lord provost] has picked the developer already!' The developer in question was the Hilton Hotel Group. A critical report of the plans alleging a breach of building regulations by Mr Ron Cooper was withdrawn on the grounds that he had not seen all the plans. Even this project ran into financial difficulties.

'The Winter of Discontent'

Faced with economic difficulties and high inflation, Prime Minister Jim Callaghan set a 5 per cent limit on all pay rises. Not all the trade unions whose members suffered from increasing prices were content with this. At the beginning of 1979 there was a national stoppage by lorry drivers and by the end of January it was estimated that 6,000 workers in the Edinburgh area had been laid off because supplies were not reaching the factories. By 13 January, supplies at Bellevue Cash & Carry had nearly been depleted.

Edinburgh had its own particular difficulties brought on by a combination of bad weather, heavy snow and low temperatures, and disputes with the gritters. Gritting lorries only left the depots at 8 a.m. (well into the morning rush hour)

and completed their shifts by 4 p.m. There was no night work. All vehicles, and especially buses, struggled in the terrible conditions and on 13 January, temperatures at Turnhouse Airport dropped to -17°C.

Public service workers, from manual workers to civil servants, were involved in disputes over pay. Schools were closed when janitors came out, hospitals faced shortages of clean bed linen and a strike at water filtration plants led to an appeal to the public to boil all water.

The Lothian Region and Government Cuts

The new Conservative government elected in 1979 set about controlling public spending in the hope of reducing inflation and improving the economy. All areas of government, including local councils, were expected to play their part and grants allocated by central government were reduced. Lothian Regional Council refused to accept this, and Councillor Eric Milligan put their position clearly: 'The Labour Party were not elected to administer cuts and we have no intention of carrying them out.' To compensate for the smaller grant from the government they proposed to raise the rates by 50 per cent.

Labour Councillor Peter Wilson suggested a compromise, pegging the rise to 37 per cent. In a heated six-hour debate, in which one councillor spoke for the compromise and voted *against* it, the ruling Labour group scraped home. Despite the crisis, they continued to take on more staff. Liberal Councillor Donald Gorrie put it bluntly: 'Taking on nearly seventy new staff now in the Education Department is akin to the *Titanic* hiring a new barman after it struck the iceberg.' A new Act passed through Parliament giving the Scottish Secretary George Younger powers to compel local authorities to fall into line with government policy. The Region finally agreed to make £30 million of cuts to its budget.

The two-tier system of local government was never a satisfactory scheme and in 1994 the large regions were abolished and all powers given to the district councils.

Traffic Problems

The number of private cars and commercial vehicles on the roads began to increase rapidly in the post-war era. Travelling up the A1, traffic had to navigate its way through Leith to reach the Forth Crossing (the ferry, and later the bridge) and Central Scotland. This problem was not finally addressed until the 1980s with the construction of an outer ring road (the A720), which swept round the south and west sides of the city.

The city centre presented a major obstacle to traffic. To solve this problem, the council decided at the end of 1966 to build an inner ring road. This would sweep round Edinburgh, cutting across the Meadows and ploughing through the densely packed areas to the north of the city. However, growing opposition led to the dropping of the scheme.

Various measures were designed to encourage commuters to use the buses and greenways, with bus-only lanes introduced during the rush hours in 1997. New car parks were built on the approaches to the city, forming a Park and Ride system. In the centre, Prince's Street was restricted to buses, taxis and bicycles.

Pollution in Edinburgh

Once known as 'Auld Reekie' because of its layer of smog, measures had been taken to improve the air quality of Edinburgh. The first smokeless zones had been introduced in the 1960s and the conversion of the railways from steam to cleaner diesel and electric had a big impact on a city whose main station was in the centre. However, with the rapid increase in traffic, the fumes from exhausts caused a deterioration in air quality, particularly on major routes leading to the city centre. A report in 1991 picked out West Maitland Street at the west end, Hillhouse Road, part of the route leading to the Forth Bridge, and St John's Road in Corstorphine. Despite proposals to control the flow of traffic, twenty-five years later St John's Road remains the most polluted road in Scotland.

The Congestion Charge

Edinburgh Corporation decided to reduce the quantity of traffic entering the city by introducing a congestion charge. In fact, they proposed not one but two charges. The first would cover the busy city centre and the second was to be taken on the boundary of the city. In February 2005, a referendum was held in Edinburgh and the idea was thrown out by an overwhelming majority.

The Edinburgh Trams Project

In modern times nothing has been more controversial than the Edinburgh Trams Project. The original plan linked Edinburgh Airport with the city centre and the ports of Leith and Granton.

Construction began in July 2007 with services such as gas, water and sewage having to be removed from beneath the path of the new tram lines. Roads in the central area were dug up and traffic, including buses, was diverted. Costs also began to rise and in 2010 members of the council began to question the whole project as costs reached £600 million. The following year plans to terminate the line at the Haymarket were blocked by the Scottish Government who threatened to withdraw funding. Eventually cuts had to be made in the face of rising costs. A third of the line – down Leith Walk and along the coast through Newhaven to Granton – was never completed, although plans to complete the Leith Walk extension are at the time of writing under consideration. In 2014 the tramway was opened and passengers can now travel from Edinburgh Airport to St Andrew's Square. An inquiry into the Edinburgh Trams Project has been set up in the hope of explaining the massive overspend.

Dutch Elm Disease

Dutch elm disease was discovered in southern Britain in the 1960s and within a decade it had reached epidemic proportions in the South. It was first discovered in Edinburgh in 1976 and over the next twenty years the city lost some 12,000 trees. Prince's Street Gardens once had nearly 140 elms, but by 1995 the number was halved. Now there are just a few elm trees remaining in the gardens.

The Anna Kesselaar Case

John Calder organised a Conference for Drama at the McEwan Hall. It opened on 7 September 1963, at the end of the Edinburgh Festival. In order to liven up the event he hired Anna Kesselaar, a photographer's model, 'to be wheeled across the organ gallery in a state of nudity on a trolley' (the *Evening News*, 9 December 1963). However, both Calder and Kesselaar were charged with indecent behaviour and appeared before Bailie McGregor. Miss Kesselaar told the court, 'The organisers told me I would be employed in the capacity of a professional model and that it would be law-abiding.' The bailie found them not guilty.

The Edinburgh Festivals

At the very first festival in 1947, eight companies had performed in Edinburgh outside the official festival – 'on the fringe of the festival'. This led to many other groups coming to take advantage of the large number of visitors seeking to enjoy music and drama, and in 1958 the Festival Fringe Society was set up to assist these companies, but not to interfere with their programmes. The Edinburgh Festival Fringe has now grown into the world's largest arts festival. Every August they bring colour to a crowded city with many impromptu cameos on the streets of the Old Town.

The Edinburgh Festival soon attracted other events to the city. The Film Festival opened in the early 1950s, bringing many famous names to Edinburgh. Then 1978 saw the first Jazz Festival, followed five years later by the Book Festival. All these events continue to prosper despite criticisms, financial problems and the rise of competitors hoping to attract the visitors who fill Edinburgh each August.

The latest of these festivals is the Hogmanay Party held each New Year. After the first Hogmanay, concern was expressed that the huge crowds who attended made it impossible to handle any emergency which might occur. Restrictions had to be placed on numbers and Prince's Street was closed to all but ticket holders. Despite the traditions of New Year revelry and the enormous crowds, the event has not attracted any trouble. Only high winds, not uncommon in Edinburgh, have led to the cancellation of Hogmanay so far.

By the 1960s the Edinburgh Festival had become an important international event. However, despite its success, it was still a target for critics as it tried to balance the demands for an exciting programme against the limitations of its funds. The actor Duncan Macrae attacked the festival committee (always chaired by the lord provost): 'The aim promoted by this ridiculous and ignorant bunch who do the Festival is doing the opposite to anything that would give them the legitimate claim to culture.'

Providing grants to subsidise the events brought the festival into the political sphere and many councillors worried about yet another demand on the city's budget. Accusations of elitism and complaints that the money would be better spent on slum clearance were often produced when the council's grant was discussed. Finally, in 1987 the festival committee appointed their own fundraiser and finances improved.

The stage of the King's Theatre proved too small for the performance of large operatic productions and in 1969 Professor Liebermann of the Hamburg State Opera led the complaints, thus beginning the Edinburgh Opera House saga. Howard & Wyndham, owners of the King's Theatre, were hoping to sell it to the city and were unimpressed by such criticism. It was not until 1991 that Edinburgh Corporation purchased the old Moss Empire Theatre in Nicolson Street from the Rank Organisation for £2.6 million. Another £11 million was spent converting the building into the Festival Theatre. Opened in 1994, the venue was large enough for grand opera but versatile enough to be used for other functions.

In 1992, W. Januszuzak wrote in the *Guardian*, 'I am simply not interested in witnessing one more stage of its horrible and relentless and, yes, tragic transformation into a minor local event.' The fact that this particular year's festival had fewer international companies may have influenced his judgement, but it failed to absorb the realities of the situation. Twenty years later, the festival was still attracting large audiences for its events.

By the second decade of the twenty-first century, the shops and restaurants of the New Town, who paid some of the highest rates in the city, felt that they were missing out on the lucrative business provided by the large crowds seeking to explore the festival. It was becoming largely based on the south side of the city, George Street was closed to traffic, and even marquees appeared on the street.

Whisky Galore?

When Benjamin Duffield worked for the Cleansing Department, he noticed that sometimes the filter pads used in the whisky blending and bottling processes were

thrown away. Some years later he had changed careers, running a garage in West Bowling Green Street, Leith. A friend from the Cleansing Department supplied him with some of these discarded pads. Putting them in a spin dryer, Duffield was able to recover a considerable volume of whisky. Since he was a teetotaller, his mechanics and other helpers received the benefit of free whisky. Unfortunately, however, this spirit had not paid the excise duty and in 1967 the Inland Revenue prosecuted him, so ending his little private enterprise.

Devolution for Scotland

The government proposed to set up assemblies for Scotland and Wales, devolving some decision making from Westminster to the regions. The Act of Parliament not only required a majority in favour of an assembly but at least 40 per cent of the electorate must support the move. The Conservative Party and some Labour MPs had their doubts. Tam Dalyell, Labour member for West Lothian, asked whether it was right that Scottish MPs should therefore be allowed to vote on matters which only concerned England. The 'West Lothian Question', as it came to be known, has never been answered. The referendum, held on 1 March 1979, brought a small majority in favour of the assembly – 77,435. Only 32.8 per cent of the electorate voted 'yes', and thus the target was not achieved. Any further thoughts of devolution at that time were swallowed up by the forthcoming general election.

The Scottish Parliament Building

The referendum of 1997 produced a 74 per cent vote in favour of devolution. The building of the old Royal High School in Waterloo Place had been proposed as the new home of the devolved Parliament. However, Donald Dewar wanted a new building for a new age. The public were given a totally unrealistic figure of £40 million, and unsurprisingly costs rose and the scheduled opening date of 2001 fell behind. It opened three years later at a cost of £414 million.

Edinburgh Airport

On 1 April 1971, Turnhouse was handed over to the British Airports Authority (BAA) who immediately applied to build a second runway. This would ease the problem of crosswinds which had led to much traffic being diverted. Objections, particularly from residents under the proposed new flight path, led to a public inquiry. This decided in favour of the residents and the BAA application for a new runway was rejected. However, the Secretary of State reversed the decision and the BAA was allowed to proceed.

The Suburban Railways

Many of the suburbs of Edinburgh had rail links with the city centre. During the war (November 1943), passenger traffic on the Balerno branch was discontinued, closing stations at Balerno, Currie, Juniper Green and Colinton. In 1947 the line from North Leith through Junction Bridge, Bonnington and Easter Road to Waverley followed. Four years later, services to Davidson's Mains and Barnton were axed.

British Railways were losing money. Investment was placed on diesel and electric traction while unprofitable branch lines were to be closed. This policy was set out in 1963 by Dr Beeching. The year before the Beeching Report was published, two suburban lines, one in the north (Leith North, Newhaven, Granton Road, East Pilton, Craigleith, Murrayfield and Dalry Road) and one in the south (Duddingston, Newington, Blackford Hill, Morningside, Craiglockhart and East Gorgie), were shut. Finally, on 6 September 1965 the old Caledonian station at the end of Prince's Street closed. Closure of the line, which brought in commuters from Corstorphine, met with resistance, with Mr J.A. Stoddart, a local MP, asking the question – 'Can the buses cope?'

Powderhall Stadium

In 1995 the Scottish Greyhound Racing Company, which owned the stadium, was in deep financial trouble. It was home to the Edinburgh Monarchs speedway team who had been forced out of their Meadowbank home by the 1970 Commonwealth Games. The Powderhall Sprint, held every New Year, eventually moved to Musselburgh. They owed Bass Leisure £1.8 million for the purchase of the property and had to be placed in receivership. Fortunately, a consortium came up with £3 million and took control of Powderhall. Edinburgh Monarchs Speedway team eventually moved to Livingston. However, the racing had proved unprofitable and large blocks of flats now fill the whole site.

The Changing Face of Politics

The two-tier authorities (Lothian Region and Edinburgh District) were abolished and in April 1995 the citizens of Edinburgh went to the polls to elect their new council. A total of 252 candidates contested the fifty-eight seats. The Labour Party won a stunning victory, taking thirty-four seats and leaving the

Conservatives with only fourteen and the Liberal Democrats with ten. The Scottish Nationalists failed to take a seat.

The general election which brought Tony Blair to power in 1997 brought disaster on the Conservative Party in Scotland. They lost every seat, with the *Evening News* commenting, 'The upset made the Texas Chainsaw Massacre look like a tea party in Morningside'. Once, the right of centre Progressive Party had ruled Edinburgh, but from 1970 the Labour group held a majority of seats. Labour held thirty-one seats with their rivals the Liberal Democrats and the Conservatives holding just thirteen each. The Scottish Nationalists only managed to win a single place on the council.

The position changed remarkably in May 2007, when the Nationalists became the largest party in the Scottish Parliament. The city council was then dominated by the four parties:

Liberal Democrats	17
Labour	15
Scottish Nationalists	12
Conservatives	11

The new politics led to a coalition and an end to the era of one party dominating the council.

The Banking Crisis, 2008

The Bank of Scotland was founded in 1695 with the Royal Bank receiving its charter in 1727. The growing industrialisation led to a demand for capital and Edinburgh, with the headquarters of these two big banks, became the banking centre of Scotland. Sir James Hunter Blair, Sir James Stirling and Sir William Fettes were bankers as well as lord provosts of the city. In the years 1772 to 1810 Edinburgh had twenty-one private banks but these were soon reduced by amalgamations and closures. The Bank Charter Act forced banks to hold gold reserves and restricted the issue of notes; only in Scotland were banks able to continue issuing their own notes.

By 1880 the big banks had opened branches in Edinburgh and Leith. The Royal Bank now had ten branches in the city. Edinburgh's financial sector, based on banks, insurance and other institutions, continued to grow and prosper. However, in 2008 over-expansion and unwise investments threatened the very existence of the Halifax Bank of Scotland and the Royal Bank. Only government intervention prevented a collapse of the two banks.

REFERENCES

Space does not permit a detailed list of individual references.

Much of the first chapter is based on archaeological discoveries printed in the *Proceedings of the Society of the Antiquarians of Scotland*. The early historic period, once known as the Dark Ages, did produce some contemporary writings – Bede's *History of the English Church and People*, as well as histories by Nennius and Gildas. Aneiran's poem, 'The Gododdin', gives an account of the late British rulers, while the 'Anglo-Saxon Chronicle' tells the story of English and Danish settlement. All these works have to be treated with care as they were produced long after the events. Bede certainly disliked the British and their church.

The medieval era offers more documents – 'Callendar of Documents', relating to Scotland, the Exchequer Rolls and various charters. The chronicles of John of Fordun and Abbot Bower offer accounts of people who lived during the period. The fifteenth century also saw the first recording of the activities of the town council. These 'Burgh Records' provide the basis for the story of the city during the sixteenth and seventeenth centuries. John Knox's *History of the Reformation in Scotland* and the diaries of John Nicoll (relating to the Commonwealth) and Lord Fountainhall (the Restoration) offer contemporary, if not unbiased, accounts of the times.

The eighteenth century saw the arrival of newspapers like the *Edinburgh Evening Courant* (whose advertisements give an interesting view of the city) and the *Caledonian Mercury*. Everyday life in the city is first described by Joseph Taylor who visited Edinburgh in the first years of the century. Later, James Boswell, in his *Edinburgh Journals*, and Lord Henry Cockburn, in his *Memorials*, give personal insights into life in the city. Peter Williamson produced the first *Edinburgh Directory* in 1776–77. This was followed by the Post Office directories, both of which list the commercial premises as well as the products made and sold along the various city streets.

The nineteenth and twentieth centuries brought a regular supply of newspapers. *The Scotsman* was set up to oppose the Tory-dominated city council in the years before the Great Reform Bill. The *Edinburgh Evening Courant* and, later, the *Evening News* provide reports of life in the city. The *Dictionary of National Biography* and its Scottish equivalent give accounts of important figures in Edinburgh, while reports by Littlejohn, Plumbstead and Abercromby, and others, offer insight into the affairs of the city.

A lot of good work has been produced on local history within Edinburgh, including Baird's *Annals of Duddingston and Portobello* in 1898, Tweedie and Jones' work on Currie and Ratho parishes, and Charles Smith's *Historic South Side*. More specialist works include Ireland's *West Port Murders* and Stanfield's *Lost Railways of Lothians*.

The quotes from the poet Aneirin are reproduced from Steve Short's 1994 translation, published by Llanerch Publishers, Felinfach.

ABOUT THE AUTHOR

JOHN PEACOCK was born in Newcastle-upon-Tyne but brought up with his younger brother in the centre of Darlington, where his father was a copper smith at North Road Railway Works until it was closed in the Beeching cuts, and where his mother's family, the Atkinsons, owned property in the town. He attended Ashville College in Harrogate before going on to read History at Durham University. After a year at Dundee College of Education he taught in East Dunbarton and Essex and then came to Edinburgh, where his first post was in Leith at the Links Primary School. He went on to teach in Broughton and Colinton before finishing his career in Balerno at Dean Park Primary School.

Chronological
map of Edinburgh,
John Bartholomew,
1919

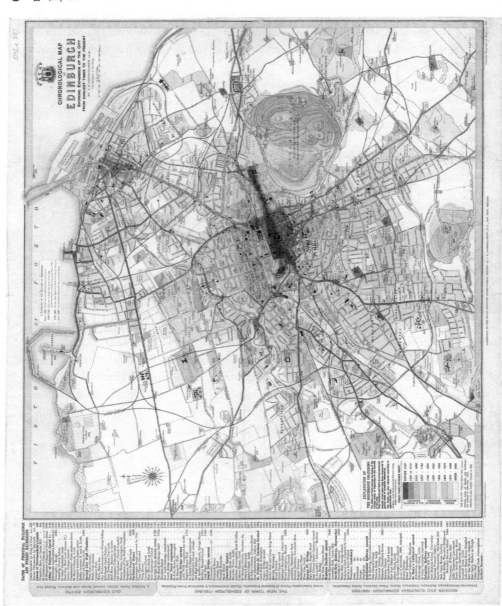

INDEX